THE FUNERAL ELEGY AND THE RISE OF
ENGLISH ROMANTICISM

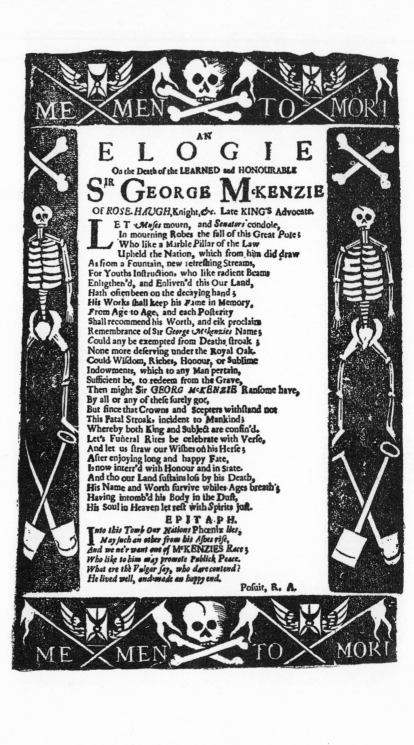

THE FUNERAL ELEGY

AND THE RISE OF
ENGLISH ROMANTICISM

By

JOHN W. DRAPER

1967

OCTAGON BOOKS, INC.

New York

TO
CHESTER NOYES GREENOUGH

PREFACE

What bulky Heaps of doleful Rhymes I see!
Sure all the world runs mad with Elegy;
Lords, Ladies, Knights, Priests, Souldiers, Squires, Physicians,
Beaux, Lawyers, Merchants, Prentices, Musicians,
Play'rs, Footmen, Pedants, Scribes of all Conditions.

SO wrote the merry elegist in 1695; and, to these items, he might well have added the dissenting clergy who lamented their pious colleagues with lingering ecstasy over death-bed scenes and charnel-house decay. However, his catalogue is wide, if incomplete, and at least does justice to the scribblers of courtly eulogy and paid-for panegyric. Of the elegiac pieces of the age, some are bald statements of the physical facts of mortality; some, expressions of Christian hope; and some, the quips and cranks of poetic display, the *tours de force* of the virtuoso rather than the sorrowings of the bereaved. To the modern reader, their Attic salt has somewhat lost its savor, though sometimes a country newspaper —in remoter parts, at least—still prints commemorative rhymes; and, indeed, if half the elegists who unhappily found a printer had only been content to waste their sorrows on the desert air, the present study had been much mitigated, and the general average of English poetry much advanced.

But still, even to the finical modern eye, the elegy has a legend to display: he who would study our Anglo-Saxon ancestors may well peruse such pieces, though it be a hard penance; for life and death and the life to come are too basic in the minds of men to be neglected in the study of their past; and the elegy, because it was written by all sorts and conditions—and therefore generally ill-written—expresses their conventional ideas in their conventional cant language. Indeed, the elegist is the Atropos of the Muses: he slits the thin-spun life, and ushers his subject into the hereafter with the assurances of such immortality, literary or divine, as he would crave, and consoles the mourners with such a eulogy of his virtues as they most desire. Readers must not complain when such eulogies bear scant relation to the subject's life and character, but should rather look in them, not for what he was, but for what his age and social class wished itself to be, righteous, or witty, or decorously refined. Examined in this light, the elegies are an admirable medium for the study of social ideals; for surely no one supposed that they spoke the immediate truth (the elegists themselves said so, though not about their own!): the practitioner of elegies falsified the actual for the sake of the ideal; and, even when lying with a glorious and patent candor about the royal personage or reverend gentleman in question, expressed his generation's concept of royalty and of reverence. These ideals vary and fluctuate, and reflect in their evolution those subtle changes that compose the history of culture; and the study of these subtle shiftings during some five generations of English life is the business of the present volume.

Indeed, all sorts and conditions of men wrote elegies, read elegies, and had elegies written upon them. Elegies have come down to us in volumes, in pamphlets, in manuscripts, and in broadsides; many are anonymous; and some are the single work of an unknown author. In this vast Cimmerian desert, the present writer has made many false steps and blind excursions; and, for such lapses as may still appear, he craves that the critical reader will consider his difficulties when he appraises his mistakes; but such errors must indeed be numerous and weighty to alter the general meaning and results.

Most elegies of the period, one reads only for one's sins; and the present historian, as far as possible, has spared his readers this improving exercise: a few passages are quoted at length; many are referred to but briefly; and a multitude that hardly concern Romanticism are cursorily dismissed. The author, moreover, has tried to write in a packed and pithy manner that might assuage somewhat the reader's elegiac pains as he surveys the flat pastures of prolixity and skirts the tear-drenched bogs of mortuary bathos. Those that hunger and thirst after such righteousness as a further perusal might impart may seek in the footnotes for guidance where they may fulfil their desire. The references to sources and authorities are complete within each chapter; and such scholars as regret the lack of appended bibliographies have only to use the index in connection with the notes. In the case of manuscripts, broadsides, and the rarer pamphlets, some effort has been made to note the library in which they can be found. The illustrations, considerably reduced in size

from the originals, are intended not only to lend an appealing touch
but also to exemplify sundry pertinent matters of broadside typography. The book aims to combine pleasure and profit: to be useful
to the learned and not quite displeasing to the *amateur* of letters.

It has been usual to look at the eighteenth century from the point
of view of the nineteenth, or sometimes of the twentieth, which
has developed notions quite of its own. The present writer has
attempted rather to take his stand, if such a translation be possible,
in the seventeenth century, and instead of looking for "Romanticism" in the age of Pope and Johnson, to examine this period for
such things as it shared with the generations of Dryden and Donne.
The eighteenth century was an age of results as well as causes; and
a study of the traditions that lay behind it may well throw light on
the new phenomena that arose. This evolution, moreover, must be
examined in the light of political, economic, and social history, of
philosophy, folk-lore, liturgics, and any other field of contemporary
thought that can possibly illuminate it; for he who ventures upon
a study of culture, though it be but a single phase, is unfortunately
required to profess all knowledge as his province. Thus chronologically, reign by reign, and socially, class by class, the subtle
shadings of the relationships of men and of their current attitudes
and habits of thought must be observed, recorded, illustrated, and
explained; and the funeral elegy in this wise interpreted as the
outward symbol of deeper things.

The present study took its start six years ago when the author
read in Ashton's *Social Life in the Reign of Queen Anne* a brief
notice of the broadside elegies of the period; and it occurred to
him that here lay the origin of the graveyard poetry that ushered
in Romanticism. Since then, he has pursued the matter intermit-
tently, as opportunity allowed. In the course of the investigation,
so much material came to light that was not generally available to
scholars—especially broadside elegies of the seventeenth century
surviving in unique copies—that it seemed appropriate to edit a
selection of such pieces. Thus came into being a companion volume, *A Century of Broadside Elegies*,[1] in which one hundred of
such broadsides are photographically reproduced and edited with an
introduction and notes.

[1] *A Century of Broadside Elegies*, Ingpen and Grant, London, 1928.

For the present volume, thanks are due to the University of Maine, and especially to the John Simon Guggenheim Memorial Foundation, for greatly increasing the time and the facilities available. The Foundation not only made possible the necessary residence in England but also out of its largesse, assisted in the publication of the ensuing study. In collecting materials, the following libraries have chiefly been drawn upon: Harvard University Library, the Library of the Boston Athenæum, the Library of the Massachusetts Historical Society, the Boston Public Library, and the Library of the University of Maine, in America; in England, the British Museum, Lambeth Palace Library, the London Guildhall Library, the Library of the Society of Antiquaries, the Bodleian, the Library of Worcester College, Oxford, and the Pepysian Collection at Magdalen College, Cambridge; in Scotland, the Signet Library, the National Library of Scotland (formerly the Advocates' Library), and the Library of the University of Edinburgh. Thanks are due to the curators of these institutions; and to the librarians of the Free Library and of Chetham's Library, Manchester, the Library of the University of Glasgow, the New York Public Library, the Library of the University of Pennsylvania, and the Library of Congress, for courteous and helpful replies to letters of inquiry.

To certain friends and colleagues also, and to the New York University Press, I take pleasure in giving grateful acknowledgement: to Professor C. N. Greenough of Harvard and to Dean G. D. Chase of the University of Maine for the reading and criticism of the manuscript; for occasional references and suggestions, to Professor G. L. Kittridge of Harvard University, to Sir W. A. Craigie of the University of Chicago, and to Professor I. T. Richards of the University of Maine. Thanks are also due to Professor A. H. Nason for much assistance and encouragement in this as in many other scholarly ventures, and for many hours spent over the manuscript and proofs; and to the author's wife who relieved him of much reading in seventeenth century diaries and records. To this community of scholarship and whole-hearted coöperation, much of the good in the present volume is due.   J. W. D.

London,
May 1, 1928.

CONTENTS

CHAPTER I. THE PROBLEM.
The great quantity and significance of graveyard poetry, 3.—Scholarly neglect of the subject, 5.—Definitions of the elegy, 6,—And its species, 7.—The funeral elegy, 9.—Its imputed origins, 10;—Its untoward appearance in the midst of Neo-classicism a challenge to scholars, 11.—Attempts at explanation: mere reaction insufficient as a cause for the rise of Romantic melancholy, 12;—Milton's influence as an explanation, 13, —The exploding of this theory, 14;—Other literary influences also insufficient, 17;—Biographical explanations satisfactory only in isolated cases, 19;—Philosophy insufficient to explain the generality of the vogue, 20;—Sociological explanation hinted at by several authors, 21.—Possibilities of this approach, 22.

CHAPTER II. THE FUNERAL ELEGY AND THE CAVALIERS.
The ubiquity of elegiac verse, 24.—Classical traditions in the Renaissance elegy, 25,—The Christian tradition of mortuary poetry, 26,—In the reign of James I, 27.—Caroline mortuary poetry: the School of Spenser, 29;—Jonson and his School, 31;—Donne, 33;—his School, 35,—including among others, Vaughan, 36,—Cleveland, 38,—King, 39,—Cowley, 40,—Minor figures, 42.—Summary of the three Schools, 45.—Reading of the lower classes, 46.—Elizabethan broadside balladry, 47.—Early broadside elegies in general, 48,—In the Library of the Society of Antiquaries, 49.—Possible origins of the broadside elegy, 51.—Broadside balladry and Puritanism among the bourgeoisie, 52.—Cavalier broadside elegies in the reign of Charles I, 52,—During the Civil War, 53.—Broadsides on the execution of Charles I, 55.—Decline of Cavalier elegies in the 1650's, 56.—Cavalier satire of the elegy as the Puritans take over the form in the 1650's, 57.—Summary, 59.

CHAPTER III. THE FUNERAL ELEGY AND THE PURITANS.
Difficulty of dividing types of literature according to the social class of the readers, 61.—Increasing social cleavage of the reigns of Elizabeth, James, and Charles I, and the effect on literature, 62.—The social, religious, and political contrast between Cavalier and Puritan, 63.—The psychology of Puritanism and of Neo-classicism, 64.—The melancholy of Puritanism, 65,—Apparent in their prose, 66.—Paucity of Puritan poets, 69.—Milton's earlier poetry neither melancholy nor Puritan, 70. —The Royalist Quarles as the Puritan ideal of poetry, 71.—Quarles' elegies, 73.—The *Emblems* as a contribution to mortuary literature, 75. —The popularity of Quarles during the hundred years after his death, 76.—Minor Puritan poets, 77.—Gradual acceptance of the funeral elegy by the Puritan clergy, 78.—Elegies on the death of Barnardiston in 1653,

79,—Especially the elegy by Burrell, 80.—Elegies on the death of Whitaker, 82.—General Puritan opposition to broadside balladry, 83.—Puritans' gradual acceptance of the broadside elegy, 84.—Puritan elegies on the Earl of Essex in 1646, 85.—Miscellaneous Puritan elegies in the 1650's, 86:—On women and children, 87;—On military heroes, 88;—Reluctance of the Puritan clergy to accept the broadside elegy, 90.—Summary of Cavalier and Puritan elegiac literature during the 1640's and '50's, 90.—Religious *versus* æsthetic sincerity among the Puritans, 91.

CHAPTER IV. THE FUNERAL ELEGY IN LITURGIC USE.
Social utility and the fine arts, 93,—And the elegy, 94.—Contemporary comment on the use of the elegy at funerals, 95.—Origins of the funerary use of elegies, 96.—The Elizabethan "lament," 97.—Heraldic records silent on the use of elegies at funerals, 98.—The use of elegies at Anglican funerals, 99.—Decline of this use after the Restoration, 101.—Sporadic continuance in the eighteenth century, 104.—The Calvinistic dissenters opposed to funeral rites: the Presbyterians, 107,—Scotch Presbyterian funerals, 108,—And funerals of the Scotch Episcopalian gentry, 110;—The Independents, likewise opposed to funeral rites, 111;—but more favorable for political reasons during the Commonwealth, 112,—especially for military heroes, 113.—Non-conformity still continuing the custom after the Restoration, 115.—Proof of the custom in Puritan New England, 117.—Summary, 118.

CHAPTER V. THE FUNERAL ELEGY IN THE REIGN OF CHARLES II.
The political and cultural decline of the middle classes during the Tudor and Stuart dynasties, 121.—The reign of Charles II as a reaction from the Commonwealth, 122.—Elegiac literature in relation to social movements in the 1640's and '50's, 123.—Melancholy out of fashion after the Restoration, 124;—The corresponding change in the courtly elegiac poets, e.g., Dryden, 125,—Stevenson, 126,—And minor elegists of the age who wrote in Classical style, 127.—Many satiric elegies and parodies of the elegy, 128.—The continuance of the Puritan tradition in Flatman, 129.—The broadside elegy, 131,—Occasionally Classical, 132;—Types used for women, 133,—For the military and the learned, 134,—For the Anglican clergy, 135,—For satire, chiefly political, 136.—Mortuary tone of elegies on dissenters, 139,—Of non-conformist devotional pieces, 140, —Of Puritan attempts at satire, 141.—Pieces on Puritan ministers especially mortuary, 143.—Melancholy cultivated by the non-conformists as good in itself, 145.—Other mortuary themes, 146.—The elegies on Charles II as a summary of the age, 147.—Psycho-social explanation of these varying reactions toward death in different classes, 150.—The rise of Sentimentalism among the bourgeoisie and its psychological genesis, 152.—The funeral elegy and rising Sentimentalism, 153.

CHAPTER VI. THE FUNERAL ELEGY IN THE AMERICAN COLONIES.
The southern colonies dominated by aristocratic settlers; the middle colo-
nies cosmopolitan; New England, bourgeois, 155;—The funeral elegy
unknown in the South, rare in the middle colonies, common in New
England, 156.—The earliest pieces similar to and contemporary with the
Puritan Commonwealth pieces, 157.—The funeral elegy accepted by the
severest New England Puritans, 159.—Minor Caroline elegists, 160.—
Cotton Mather's elegies, on Collins, 163,—On Wilson, 164,—On Clark,
164.—New England elegies in the reign of William and Mary, 165.—
Versification and style, 166.—Queen Anne elegy more generally applied
and less mortuary, 167.—Growth of the elegy in rural districts, 168.—
The didactic elegy, 169.—Later continuance of the mortuary elegy, 170.
—Its slow decline, 172.—Summary, 175.—Delayed rise of Sentimentalism in New England, 176.

CHAPTER VII. THE FUNERAL ELEGY AND THE NEO-CLASSICAL COM-
                 PROMISE.
Incipient compromise between Royalist and Non-conformist in the reign
of Charles II, 178.—Social effects of the reign of James II, 179.—Rise
of the bourgeoisie under William and Mary, 180.—Locke as the apologist
of the social and political compromise, 182.—Its chilling effect on religion, 183.—Cultural effect of the compromise, the ideal of the Christian gentleman, 185.—Continuance of the aristocratic tradition in the
elegy, 187.—Continuance of the Puritan elegiac tradition, 189.—Especially elegies on Mead, 190.—Many elegies that combine Cavalier and
Puritan traditions, 192.—This tendency exemplified in paraphrases of
David's lament over Jonathan, 194,—In the elegies on Queen Mary in
contrast to those on Charles II, 195,—In the lack of satiric elegies, 196.
—The mortuary elegy not characteristic of the Non-Jurors, 197.—Influence of social compromise on the style of the elegy, 200,—Classical and
Cavalier influences combined with Biblical and Puritan, 201.—Exclusion
of Puritan emotionalism from the Neo-classical compromise, and its survival and development into Sentimentalism, 203.—Pomfret as an incon-
sistent summary of Cavalier, Puritan, Neo-classical, and Sentimental poetic
styles, 205.

CHAPTER VIII. THE FUNERAL ELEGY IN SCOTLAND.
Intolerance of Presbyterianism in Scotland and slow growth of the funeral
elegy, 207.—Crude format of Scotch broadsides, 208.—Spenserian elegies
of the reign of James VI, 208.—Sporadic elegies of the mid-seventeenth
century, 209.—English reprints and the rise of Episcopalian elegies in
the 1680's, 210.—The elegies of Paterson, 212.—The 1690's and the
acceptance of the elegy by Scotch Presbyterianism, 214.—The elegy after
1700: eulogies of peers and notables, 215,—Elegies on ladies, 217,—On
royalty, 219.—Appearance of Romantic elements, 219.—Military eulo-

gies, 221.—The satiric elegy, 221,—The funeral elegy and Thomson's *Seasons*, 223.—The mortuary Sentimentalism of the elegies on the elder Blair, 224.—Life and early writings of the younger Blair, 225;—The elegiac tradition and the content of *The Grave*, 226;—The elegiac tradition and the style and detail of *The Grave*, 227.—The decline of the funeral elegy in Scotland, 230.—Summary of its contribution to Romanticism, 232.

CHAPTER IX. THE FUNERAL ELEGY IN THE REIGN OF QUEEN ANNE. The Augustan age of social compromise, 233.—The established order supported by the givers of literary patronage, the Church, the Court, and the nobility, 234.—Gradual rise of the bourgeoisie; their taste, and their increasing patronage, 236.—Decline of religious emotionalism among this class, and their increasing use of art as an emotional outlet, 236.—Effect on art, especially its loss of ethos, 238.—Addison as an expression of Neo-classicism; Steele, of Sentimentalism, 241.—Influence of Sentimentalism upon Neo-classical æsthetics and on drama and gardening, 242.—Increase of elegies that unite Cavalier and Puritan traditions and that show Sentimentalism, 244.—The broadside elegies, 246.—The mortuary manner an established decorum in the reign of Queen Anne, 247.—Elegies in the purely Neo-classical tradition, 249.—Survivals of the Puritan tradition in Watts, 250,—Sentimentalized in Mrs. Rowe, 253.—Minor elegists in the Puritan tradition, 254.—Growth of Nature-description in the elegy: its sources, 255,—Its development in the Commonwealth, in New England, and in Scotland, 257.—The Sentimentalizing of Nature-description in the Augustan period, 259.—The Puritan mortuary tradition as the source of the Romantic treatment of rural Nature, 261.

CHAPTER X. THE FUNERAL ELEGY IN THE REIGN OF GEORGE I. Growing power of the bourgeoisie under the Whigs and Hanoverians, 263.—Intemperate tastes of the newly rich, 266.—Sentimental trend in religion, 266,—Accelerated by reaction from the philosophy of Mandeville, 267.—The Anglican Church, faced with Sentimentalism, Deism, and antinomianism, expends its efforts against the last two, and so tolerates the first, 269.—Few broadside elegies in the reign of George I, 269. —Increased publication of books by minor poets, 271.—Elegies on the death of Addison, 273.—Few satiric elegies, 273.—Rise of the generalized elegy, 274.—General poems of contemplative melancholy, 276.— Cultivation of melancholy for its own sake, 278.—Early appearance of Gothic elements in the elegy, 279.—Parnell and the Gothic elegy, 281. —Continuity of Spenserian influence in the elegy, 282.—The rise of the bourgeoisie and the increasing vogue of the Gothic, of Spenser, and of other Romantic influences, 283.

CHAPTER XI. THE FUNERAL ELEGY IN THE REIGN OF GEORGE II. The power of Walpole and the Whigs confirmed, 285.—The Wesleyan

Movement and its appeal to the lower classes, 286.—Its emotional exaltation closer to Laud and to Donne than to Puritanism, 287.—The illiteracy of the lower classes makes Methodism a very minor literary influence, 289.—Immediate social effect of Methodism, the weakening of aristocratic Neo-classicism, 289.—Hervey and Methodism, 290.—Continuance of mortuary literature among older bodies of dissent, 291.—The broadside elegies of Guttridge, 293.—Great volume of elegiac writing, 295.—Hill, West, and Smart, 297.—Elegiac types in periodical literature, 298.—Lingering of the elegy in the provinces, 303.—Its decline in strictly literary circles, 304.—Elegiac influences in Young's *Night Thoughts*, 306.—Verbal and tropic borrowings, 307.—Gray's peculiar qualifications to make a summation of the elegy, 309.—The plan and purpose of Gray's *Elegy* in the light of mortuary tradition, 310.—Detailed borrowings, 311.—The seventeenth and eighteenth centuries compared in elegiac evolution, 312.

CHAPTER XII. THE FUNERAL ELEGY AND THE RISE OF ENGLISH ROMANTICISM.
The evolution of the bourgeoisie in modern times, 314.—The funeral elegy as an index of this evolution during the reign of Charles I, 315,—During the Commonwealth, 315,—During the reign of Charles II, 317,—During the reign of James II and that of William and Mary, 318.—Sentimentalism and Puritanism, 320.—Sentimental and Romantic characteristics of the seventeenth century funeral elegy, 320.—The rise of the Neo-classical compromise, and its inability to assimilate elegiac melancholy, 322.—Satiric use of the funeral elegy, 323.—Increasing power of the merchant class in the reign of George I threatens the Neo-classical compromise, 324.—Evolution of the new emotional taste during the eighteenth century, 325.—Relation of the funeral elegy to the rise of Romanticism, 326.—Definitions of Romanticism, 327.—All definitions unsatisfactory that limit Romanticism to purely æsthetic phenomena, 328.—Broader definitions as a social and cultural entity, 330.—The funeral elegy as related to Romanticism thus defined, 331.

APPENDIX A. NOTES ON THE SYMBOLIC USE OF THE WILLOW.
The Elizabethan use of the willow for distressed love, 335.—The change to a mortuary use in the latter seventeenth century, 336.—Eighteenth century use of the willow, 337.

APPENDIX B. NOTES ON THE FUNERAL ELEGY AND THE POETRY OF ROBERT BURNS.
Burns' acquaintance with the funeral elegy indubitable, 338.—His imitation of a wide variety of styles, 338.—His serious pieces and the elegiac tradition, 339.—His satiric pieces and the elegiac tradition, 340.

INDEX. 343.

LIST OF ILLUSTRATIONS

An Elogie On Sir George Mc Kenzie (Library of the University of Edinburgh)..................................*Frontispiece*

An Elegie, on the Death of Collonell John Luttrell (British Museum broadside) 84

An Elegiack Memoriall of the Right Honourable Generall Deane, &c. (British Museum broadside)......................... 112

An Elegy Upon the Unfortunate Death of Captain William Bedloe (Luttrell Collection, British Museum)..................... 148

Great Britains Lamentation: Or, the Funeral Obsequies of Mary, Queen of England (British Museum broadside)............. 196

An Elegy on The Much Lamented Death of Sir Roger L'Estrange (British Museum broadside) 246

Title-page of the first edition of Gray's Elegy (from the copy in the British Museum)................................. 310

THE FUNERAL ELEGY AND THE RISE OF
ENGLISH ROMANTICISM

CHAPTER I

THE PROBLEM

IN the year 1731, the two most significant English periodicals of the day united in declaring that "every churchyard" resounded with elegies;[1] and, indeed, the first half of the eighteenth century witnessed the culmination of an elegiac wave that had long been accumulating scope and power. Of these elegies, a few have survived in manuscript, some in the collected volumes of accredited poets, some in thin folios, such as were commonly used for the publication of short pieces, some on broadsides adorned with wide black margins and mortuary symbols, and a constantly increasing proportion in the pages of current periodicals. Some were written by sorrowing friends, some by the myrmidons of Grub Street, and some by reverend ministers in praise of deceased colleagues, pious implorators, we hope, of holy suits. In its first five volumes, the *Gentleman's Magazine*, although printing rather little original verse, found space for some fifteen such lucubrations,[2] together with a smart parody *On the Death of a Favorite Cow*;[3] it advertised a prize of fifty pounds for the best poem on the allied subject of Life, Death, Judgment, Heaven, and Hell, and filled an entire number with the competing verses.[4] During the following five-year period, it gave its readers twenty-three elegiac pieces[5] and three satires of the *genre*;[6] and, during the 1740's, elegies continued to flourish with profusion, if not with vital luxuriance.[7] In the heyday of its success, the elegiac urge produced not only such wretched stuff as regularly graced the broadsides and the periodicals but also some lines of permanent

---

[1] *Gent. Mag.*, I, 11, quoting from the *Grub Street Journal*.

[2] *Gent. Mag.*, I, 261; II, 971, 1025; III, 542; IV, 267, 286; V, 101, 103, 103-104, 155, 323, 327, 381, 549, 674-675.

[3] *Ibid.*, III, 604.

[4] *Ibid.*, V, July, 1735.

[5] *Ibid.*, VI, 158 (misnumbered 156), 221, 417, 616, 680, 740; VII, 178, 183, 247, 374-375, 693, 762; VIII, 102, 214, 317, 482; IX, 41, 152, 379, 434-435; X, 30, 89, 518.

[6] *Ibid.*, VIII, 99-100; IX, 42; X, 461.

[7] The amount of verse in the *Gentleman's Magazine* almost doubles about 1740; and the elegies, therefore, although almost as numerous, are relatively fewer. From 1741-1746, there are twenty-three such poems, a more sprightly tone predominating; from 1746 to 1751, there are seventeen examples together with three Latin elegies, some translations, and several pieces of generally elegiac atmosphere.

merit, including perhaps Parnell's *Night-Piece on Death* and certainly Gray's *Elegy in a Country Church-Yard*.[8] Poems of a kindred type, furthermore, such as Blair's *Grave* and Young's *Night Thoughts*, have a recognized significance in the course of English and Continental literature: for over a century, they were universally esteemed by the middle class, such a literary eruption as the Spasmodist School attesting to their influence even in the reign of Victoria;[9] and, in France and Germany, they were much admired. This historical significance is no matter of accident; for the graveyard poets, by generalizing the subject-matter of the elegy and freeing it from the confines of merely occasional verse, bridged the transition between the elegy proper, which flourished so rank in the seventeenth and early in the eighteenth century, and the melancholy of nascent Romanticism both in England[10] and on the Continent.[11] Indeed, Thomas credits Young with being the origin of "le pessimisme voilé de Goldsmith" and of a similar trend in Cowper, Crabbe, Blake, and later poets;[12] and Saintsbury

[8] The latter stanzas on the "Youth to fortune and to fame unknown" show that the *Elegy* was intended to lament a specific person, perhaps West, perhaps Gray himself. *Night Thoughts* was supposed to be inspired by several synchronous deaths in Young's family; the *Night-Piece* seems to lament Parnell's wife; and the *Grave*, Blair's father.

[9] See a MS. thesis by A. D. McKillop in Harvard University Library, in part published in the *Pub. Mod. Lang. Assoc. Am.*, XL, 743 *et seq.*

[10] Many writers, from Beers (*History of English Romanticism in the Eighteenth Century*, New York, 1898, 186) to Miss Reed (*Background of Gray's Elegy*, New York, 1924, *Preface*), although admitting marked differences from contemporary Neo-classicism and noting strong influences on Romantic poetry, prefer not to call these poems Romantic. Scholars, however, who define Romanticism as an emotional urge can hardly avoid admitting such pieces into the category. (*Cf.* E. Gosse, *History of Eighteenth Century Literature*, London, 1896, 208 and 212; I. Babbitt, *Rousseau and Romanticism*, Boston, 1919, 323 *et passim*; H. H. Clark, *Mod. Lang. Notes*, XXXIX, 129; and K. Müller, *Robert*

Blair's Grave und die Grabes- und Nachtdichtung, Weimar, 1909, 99 *et passim.*)

[11] French Romanticism seems to have developed at least in part from English, transmitted by Diderot, Prevost, and others (See J. Texte, *J-J. Rousseau et les Origines du Cosmopolitanisme Littéraire*, Paris, 1904) and in part perhaps as an independent development in the person of Rousseau, whose background of Genevan Calvinism helped to produce a similar effect (P. M. Masson, *La Religion de J-J. Rousseau*, Paris, 1917). In Germany, also, there was a strong English influence (M. L. Price, *Univ. of Cal. Studies*, Berkeley, 1919, Chap. VIII). In both countries, Blair, Young, and Gray were especially important. (See W. A. Nitze and E. P. Dargan, *History of French Literature*, New York, 1922, 371-372; M. B. Finch and E. A. Peers, *The Origins of French Romanticism*, London, 1920, Chaps. I-V; and J. Barnstorff, *Youngs Nachtgedanken und ihr Einfluss auf die deutsche Litteratur*, Bamberg, 1895.) In Spain, also, Young and Gray were particularly influential. (E. A. Peers, *Mod. Lang. Rev.*, XXI, 404 *et seq.*)

[12] W. Thomas, *Le Poète Edward Young*, Paris, 1901, 494-495.

notes that Young and Blair provided "by a rather strange way, a return to Enthusiasm."[13] Not only on the poetry but on the prose also of the century, this school of writers was a determinant force; for their influence, passing into fiction, colored the Gothic romance;[14] and, indeed, to Continental eyes, it bulked so large that Goethe in his *Autobiography* credited English authors in general with a predeliction for the funereal in setting and atmosphere. A literary movement, therefore, that was possessed in its day of so great a vogue, that treated of so perennial a subject, that has left so plain a mark upon subsequent writings, and that bore fruit in a poem that is perhaps the most popular lyric in the English language—such a movement asks of its chronicler no apology for his essay.

Despite its promised fertility, however, scholars have cultivated but slightly the elegiac field: its confines have been but casually explored, and even its limits are only vaguely defined. Bailey[15] declares that the elegy, although difficult of definition, is chiefly concerned with "Love, Grief, and Death"; and he subdivides it into the long narrative elegy, the short lament, and the poem of general elegiac reflection. In a hasty survey, he sketches its progress through English literature, and says something of its relation to the epitaph and to other allied poetic forms; but he neither outlines its evolution nor even consistently records the development of any single phase. Miss Lloyd's treatment,[16] likewise, comprises a mere series of appreciative comments on individual poems arranged in more or less chronological order. She seems to make the most inclusive application of the term *elegy* in the pieces she edits; but

[13] G. Saintsbury, *The Peace of the Augustans,* London, 1916, 64.

[14] W. L. Cross (*The Development of the English Novel,* New York, 1905, 99 et seq.) suggests, without actually stating, that Smollett's *Humphrey Clinker* brought this motif into fiction. *Cf.* Saintsbury (*The English Novel,* London, 1913, 155 et seq.), who seems uncertain as to the origins of the Gothic romance. More recently J. R. Foster (*Publ. Mod. Lang. Assoc. Am.,* XLII, 443 et seq.) has urged that the Gothic romance goes back to Prevost and other French authors of his generation. Prevost, however, as Texte pointed out, wrote largely under English inspiration; and so Foster's theory can hardly be taken as necessarily disagreeing with the present suggestion that the Gothic romance borrowed heavily of the mortuary poetry of the earlier eighteenth century.

[15] J. C. Bailey, *English Elegies,* London, n. d., *Introduction.* See also W. F. M. Phellipps (*Book of English Elegies,* London, 1879), who apparently, like most of the others, takes the term in its loosest sense, if one may judge from the poems he includes under that title.

[16] Mary Lloyd, *Elegies Ancient and Modern,* Trenton [N. J.], 1903, *Introduction.*

her "history" takes account only of such poems as seem to her to possess artistic value.   The volume by Box,[17] which attempts in ten pages to give the definition, origin, and evolution of elegiac literature, would seem to draw its conclusions with more finality than circumspection.   Hunt's *Meditative Lyrics*[18] is hardly more helpful; and Canon Beeching's promised study[19] was apparently prevented by his death.   Indeed, a late reviewer was not unjustified in stating that a full survey of the growth and efflorescence of the English elegy "is still wanting."[20]   The present investigation must, therefore, first describe the limits of the elegiac field, and especially of the funeral elegy, and then determine the significance and the influence of the type by a rather extensive survey of mortuary and commemorative poetry from the reign of James I to the period of Gray's *Elegy*.

A nice definition of the elegy in general and of the funeral elegy in particular is not easy of formulation.[21]   The Greek word is primarily metrical in meaning, and refers to a type of iambic couplet.[22]   The earlier Greek elegies were usually martial or amatory in subject-matter; the later, political or moral.   Thus the Roman Tibullus and his imitator James Hammond wrote love-elegies; a jubilant Puritan wrote a *Congratulatory Elegie* on the victories of the Earl of Essex;[23] and many English "elegies," although ordinarily possessed of some basic element of the querulous, bear no direct relation to death.   Shenstone composed *Elegies* upon any subject that pleased his fancy, defended this catholicity by citing precedents in an introductory *Essay*, and apparently felt that any short poem done in Hammond's characteristic quatrain

[17] Charles Box, *Elegies and Epitaphs: a Comprehensive Review*, Gloucester, 1892, 1-10.
[18] T. W. Hunt, *English Meditative Lyrics*, New York, 1899.
[19] H. C. Beeching, *English Elegiac, Didactic and Religious Poetry*, was listed some years ago by E. P. Dutton and Co. in their series, Channels of English Literature.
[20] B. C. Clough, reviewing Saintsbury's *Minor Caroline Poets* and Grierson's *Metaphysical Lyrics*, Mod. Lang. Notes, XXXVIII, 52.
[21] *N. E. D.* gives three senses: (1) a song of lamentation, especially a funeral song or lament for the dead; (2) vaguely used in a wider sense; (3) poetry or a poem written in Classical elegiac meter. All the quotations under the first heading down to that from Gray's *Elegy*, seem to refer merely to songs of lamentation in general, although the editors could have found early examples in the restricted sense of a funeral lamentation over an individual.
[22] The root-meaning of ἔλεγος is obscured by the fact that it seems to be a loan-word of Oriental origin, possibly Hittite.
[23] *A Congratulatory Elegie Offered up to the Earle of Essex*, London, 1641. A copy is to be found in the library of Worcester College, Oxford.

might properly be termed elegiac.[24] The Greeks and the Romans, however, in more popular usage, commonly employed the elegiac meter for epitaphs, a plaintive subject-matter to which its syncopated rhythm gave it special adaptation; and, thus, since Classical meters hardly apply in English poetic nomenclature, the word *elegy* in our language has usually been associated with poetic substance rather than form—especially with death, and most especially the death of some particular individual. When thus confined to the death of a single person, the elegy, if it be short, shades into the brief epitaph; or, if long, into the extended versified eulogy. When it is more general, it shades into the epigram, as in Prior's translation of Pseudo-Hadrian's "Animula, vagula, blandula"; or, as in Young's *Night Thoughts,* into the versified treatise. Sometimes it snatches a grace from satire, both in parodies of the elegiac form and in the more strictly satiric vein of Swift's *Pastoral Elegy* on the death of the notorious "Lady Hilaretta." Its true elegiac nature, moreover, is often disguised, as in *Lycidas,* under a mass of pastoral machinery descended from Theocritus' *Lament for Daphnis,* and augmented by irrelevant episodes, compliments to a patron, satire on Church or State, or other conventions derived through Renaissance imitators from Vergil;[25] and in Christian writings, it may have affinities with the hymn, the sermon, or the funeral oration. Thus there is a wide penumbra to the term; but the substance generally immanent in its modern uses is the idea of death and the sorrow of death. It is neither so long as the didactic poem, nor so short as the epitaph; and, unlike both of these, it usually expresses the sorrow of immediate loss rather than the permanent aspects of grief.[26]

If the elegy be hard to disengage from allied poetic genera, it is equally difficult to subdivide into species. Goldsmith, writing with the most significant elegiac output of the century before him, mentions at random some four subvisions; but the headings over-

[24] William Shenstone, *Works,* London, 1764, 4-5.

[25] The development of the pastoral elegy has received considerable attention in connection with the history of the pastoral in general. A bibliography of the subject as appended to Marion K. Bragg's *Formal Eclogue in Eighteenth Century England, Univ. of Maine Studies,* Orono, 1926, Bibliography III.

[26] Wordsworth states this categorically in his essay *Upon Epitaphs;* but such a definition seems of dubious application either to Gray's *Elegy* or to Tennyson's *In Memoriam.* The elegy and the epitaph seem to be particularly liable to confusion.

lap, and seem to have no common basis of differentiation.[27] Else-where, however, in his *Life of Parnell,* he clearly distinguishes from other contemporary tendencies "all those night-pieces and church-yard scenes" that began, he says, with Parnell's *Night-Piece on Death* (1722): the elegiac poetry of an obviously funereal tone was evidently a distinct category in his mind. The presence of such a tone, inherent in the recurrent images of death and bodily decay, is perhaps the clearest characteristic of the funeral elegy. One might also describe the type as individual rather than general in its subject; and, in its literary tradition, as Christian rather than Classical: it is usually inspired by the death of a single person; and its images and ideas are borrowed from the Christian sepulchre and from Christian theology rather than from the stock of Roman mythology or of pastoral convention. Although many pieces only distantly approximate the form, and although few if any examples contain all the possible funeral elements, yet a more detailed sum-mary of these elements may perhaps be attempted. The funeral elegy may start with a touch of nature-description, a thick grove of cypresses or churchyard yews, perhaps a cavern, owls, and a death-knell tolling through the night; something may well be said of the disease and death-bed scene of the subject, and an antici-patory suggestion of the charnel-house, of worms, and of the decay of the body; this naturally leads to the matter of tombs, perhaps a mortuary church, or an ancient lichened vault, or an overgrown country graveyard. Then, if not before, description and narra-tive give place to pensive moralizing on the uncertainty of life and on death, the great leveller of all. In extreme cases, there may be a vivid reference to hell; but the latter part of the poem is almost sure to be taken up with a panegyric of the dead and a declaration of his heavenly reward, analogous to the apotheosis that furnishes the climax to similar pastoral pieces.[28] In short, the char-

---

[27] Goldsmith, in *On Eulogies for the Great Dead* in *The Citizen of the World,* refers to (1) the graveyard type, the "bard" being "some pensive youth of science who sits deploring among tombs," (2) the pastoral type, which he describes as "most usual," (3) the patriotic elegy, referring presumably to such poems as Collins' *Ode Written in the Beginning of the Year 1746,* and (4) the pathetic fallacy, which is not so much a type of poem as a figure of speech current in all elegies and derived through pastoral tradition from Vergil and Theocritus (Miss Bragg, *op. cit.,* 7-8 and 14). Gold-smith's division, moreover, does not seem to allow for the large number of elegies that are not pastoral and were written upon the deaths of clergymen, men of letters, and other private persons.

[28] Cf. the recipe for a pastoral elegy in *The Guardian,* No. XXX, April 15, 1713.

acteristic funeral elegy not only sings the praises of the deceased but also with a pious gusto details the most dismal memoranda of death.

The term *funeral elegy*, which the present writer has chosen to designate the type, seems first to have appeared as the title to one part of an extended poem called *An Anatomy of the World*, written by Donne on the death of Elizabeth Drury in 1611;[29] and its first use for a distinct composition seems to have been in a *Funeral Elegy, Consecrated to the Memory of his ever honored Lord, John King, Late Bishop of London* (1621).[30] The term is fairly common throughout the seventeenth century,[31] and was regularly employed by two of the most confirmed practitioners of the elegiac art, John Taylor, the Water-Poet, and the Scotch broadside-writer Ninian Paterson. The poets, however, have small regard for nominal consistency, and are quite as likely, if they attach any defining title, to refer to such verses simply as "elegies," or as "odes," "pastorals," or the like.[32] But the term "funeral elegy" was not chosen merely because of its use by poets of the seventeenth and eighteenth centuries, or merely because of the mournful character of the contents: these pieces seem commonly to have been composed either for the funeral rites, at which they were sometimes recited or sung, or for the subsequent procession when they were affixed to the hearse on its way to the grave; sometimes they seem to have been thrown into the grave along with appropriate symbolic flowers; and, in both New England and Old, they were printed on broadsides and presumably distributed among the mourners. The funeral elegy, in short, had, at least on occasion, some sort of liturgic use, when the body of the deceased was "funerated."[33]

---

[29] Chettle's *Mourning Garment* (*Harl. Misc.*, III, London, 1744, 514) contains a pastoral "Funeral Song" on the death of Queen Elizabeth. Elizabethan elegies were commonly termed "laments." See also [Robert Allyne], *Funeral Elegies*, London, 1613. A copy is to be found in the Huntington Collection.

[30] The title-page credits this piece to one Richard Argall. Anthony à Wood could find nothing about any such person; and *D. N. B.* suggests that it is a pen-name.

[31] E.g., G. Lauder, *Aretophel or a Funeral Elegy On the Death of the Earle of Buccleuche* [1634]; S. F., *Sportive*

Funeral Elegies, 1656; and William Walsh, *Funeral Elegy upon the Death of the Queen Mary*, London, 1695.

[32] Sometimes authors chose hybrid designations, such as Robert Gould's *Mourning Swain, a Funeral Eclogue*, London, 1700, D'Urfey's "funeral poem" on Queen Anne, Mallett's *Funeral Hymn* (*Poems*, ed. Cooke, 117), the anonymous *Funeral Poem to the Memory of Sir John Cook*, 1710, Payne Fisher's *Elogia Sepulchralia*, London, 1675, and similar Latin terms in *Suffolk's Tears*, London, 1653, 13 and 64.

[33] As it is impossible to know just how many and just what elegies were so used,

Goldsmith seems to have imputed the origin of mortuary poetry to Parnell (1722);[34] and modern scholarship has done little to define more exactly the date of its inception. Gosse apparently dates the new tendency "toward the close of Pope's career."[35] Thomas seemingly puts it somewhat earlier, and ascribes it to the influence of Pope's *Eloisa* and his *Elegy on an Unfortunate Lady*.[36] Miss Reynolds points out that "the spirit of sentimental poetry . . . found early expression in the night-piece of Parnell and Lady Winchelsea."[37] Clark states that Parnell "restored melancholy to literature."[38] Van Tieghem seems to be of the opinion that the Romantic elements in *Night Thoughts* were essentially an innovation;[39] and De Maar declares the *Night-Piece* to be the "first 'churchyard' poem of the eighteenth century."[40] In short, the poetic beginnings of mortuary melancholy have usually been set well down in the first half of the eighteenth century. A study, however, of the more obscure writings of the period reveals a considerable body of material, reaching back into preceding decades; and Miss Reed, who more recently began to work this vein, pointedly remarks in her *Preface*: "I found to my surprise that the more closely I inspected 'romantic beginnings' such as, for instance, Parnell's *Night Piece on Death*, the more readily they resolved themselves into elements thoroughly familiar to readers of the preceding century. . . ." Unfortunately, she deliberately omits what is perhaps the most fruitful field of research, the elegiac poetry of the period;[41] and it remains for the present writer to traverse this area. As subsequent pages cannot but show, neither Pope, nor Parnell, nor Lady Winchelsea, can properly be taken as originating the

the present author employs as differentia matters of plan, subject-matter, and apparent purpose.

[34] Chateaubriand called Gray the founder of "cette école mèlancholique" (Finch and Peers, *op. cit.*, 51)—an inaccurate statement, even if he limited his remarks to the French imitations of his own period; for Young and Blair, whose work preceded Gray's, were both influential in France.

[35] E. Gosse, *op. cit.*, 207 *et seq.*

[36] Thomas, *op. cit.*, 102. He adds that the type was continued in Parnell's *Night-Piece* and in Croxall's *Vision*.

[37] Myra Reynolds, *The Treatment of Nature in English Poetry*, Chicago, 1909,

271. Lady Winchelsea's melancholy seems very slight, hardly enough to associate her with this group; and, in her edition of this poetess, Miss Reynolds does not claim for her any great influence upon early Romanticism.

[38] H. H. Clark, *Melancholy in Edward Young*, Mod. Lang. Notes, XXXIX, 129.

[39] M. van Tieghem, *La Poésie de la Nuit et des Tombeaux en Europe au XVIIIe Siècle*, Brussels, 1921, Preface.

[40] H. G. De Maar, *History of Modern English Romanticism*, Oxford, 1924, 1, 183.

[41] Amy L. Reed, *op. cit.*, 25-26. Cf. C. A. Moore's review in *Mod. Lang. Notes*, XL, 431.

poetry of melancholy, or indeed, as even reviving it: the funeral elegy achieved literary importance at least at early as the Commonwealth period, and, great in quantity, if not in excellence, continued in an unbroken stream during the hundred years that followed.

The existence of this corpus of "lamentable" elegies—as the authors with unconscious wit occasionally called them—in the midst of restrained British Neo-classicism, must perforce be a matter of scholarly concern. More than a generation ago, Lecky, in his monumental history, complained that the emotional poetry of the eighteenth century, the poetic counterpart of Methodism, had "scarcely obtained an adequate recognition in literary history"; [42] and the untimely appearance of this body of writings, incongruous in its age as the fabliaux among the Mediæval romances, has proved, especially of recent years, a challenge to historical critics, and has called from them at least passing explanations of its existence. Of these explanations, some have been simple; some, complicated; some, based on *a priori* philosophic conceptions; some, on general literary history; some, on the biography of an individual author; and some, on the social conditions in which his talents developed: they have been strangely diverse; and the theory that formerly received the majority of suffrages has of late been severely attacked, if not quite exploded. The present study can hardly omit a summary of the history of this problem; and it is therefore necessary to set forth, one by one, the different opinions that scholars have advanced.

Various conceptions of Romanticism, its essence and its evolution, have played a considerable part in diversifying the approach of critics toward the mortuary poetry of the early eighteenth century; for, whether or not one calls this material Romantic, [43] one can not call it Neo-classical; and it must somehow be accounted

[42] W. E. H. Lecky, *History of England in the Eighteenth Century*, New York, 1893, III, 120.

[43] Scholars differ as to the point where Romanticism begins. De Maar, for instance, considers it a perennial phenomenon (*op. cit.*, Chap I), as must also such writers as associate it with Sentimentalism; Beers would seem to place its beginnings in the early eighteenth century with the "Spenserian revival" (*op. cit.*, Chap. III); Miss Reed can find no Romantic melancholy before the mid-century (*op. cit., Preface*); and Helene Richter starts "die Angänge" with Goldsmith, and apparently recognizes no Romantic development before his time (*Geschischte der Englischen Romantik*, Halle a. S., 1911-1916),

for in the welter of contemporary tendencies. Those historians
of literature whose theory of change is largely summed up in the
single concept of *reaction*, and who see in each new movement
merely an equal and presumably opposite rebound from the previous
literary mode, are inclined to explain the rise of Romanticism on
this basis; and, if they take the Graveyard School as Romantic,
they are sure to follow a reasoning substantially like that of
Doughty: "Reason, sorely tried, gives way; a natural reaction
from an age of common sense. Through gloom, sorrow, insanity,
lay a way of escape, and men took it.[44] . . . In this lay the foundations of 'romantic melancholy.' . . . Time had wrought its
revenge."[45] The passage of years and the human-all-too-human
desire for novelty are indeed not without influence in shaping
the course of history; and Courthope, who refines upon this attitude, has expressed an indubitable, if secondary, truth when he
describes Romanticism as an outcome of Whig dilettantism, typified
by the person Horace Walpole—a dilettantism that started during
the early Hanoverian ascendancy, and that, craving superficial novelty, turned to Gothic architecture, to Sentimental gardening, and
to romances and tales of terror.[46] He elsewhere suggests that the
elegiac poetry of the mid-century was another phase of the same
tendency.[47] More recently, Korff has also taken up this opinion.
He finds Humanism "eine Gegenbewegung gegen die im Christen-
tume verkörperte metaphysische Zielsessung des Lebens aufgefasst,"
and adds that, with Romanticism, we are "zu einer metaphysischen
Lebensauffassung zurückgekehrt."[48] Romanticism, according to
this view, is a reaction to the Middle Ages, with the retention of
some characteristics of Renaissance Humanism. For at least two
reasons, the reaction-theory seems inadequate: mere reaction toward

[44] This author would seem to look upon
reason as a disease as compared to which
insanity is health; and, even more strangely, he would seem to impute such a view
to the generality of mankind.

[45] O. Doughty, *The English Lyric in
the Age of Reason*, London, 1922, 25
et passim. Doughty seems to regard the
literature of the early eighteenth century
as quite homogeneous.

[46] W. J. Courthope, *History of English
Poetry*, London, 1895-1905, V, 360 *et
seq.* Courthope elsewhere supplements

this theory with a sociological explanation that will be treated later. P. van
Tieghem (*Le Préromanticisme*, Paris,
1924, 21 *et seq.*) also seems to think
that Romanticism had its rise in mere
reaction.

[47] Courthope, *op. cit.*, V, 378.

[48] H. A. Korff, *Humanismus und Romantik*, Leipsig, 139. The Preface is
dated 1924. De Maar uses this theory
to account for the literature of melancholy (*op. cit.*, Chap. XIII).

novelty, although it may account for the decline of a literary type, cannot of itself explain the rise of a new type to replace it: the reaction from Neo-classicism might have been toward a true Classicism—and, indeed, Collins and Gray exhibit such a tendency, and the increasing accuracy of Latin and Greek translations would confirm it[40]—or toward Realism, a literary bent apparent alike in the *Trivia* of Gay and the nature-descriptions of Warton; or the interest in literature might have passed over into another art, or to political struggles, as it did during the fifteenth century, or to religious struggles, as in the Commonwealth Period. Indeed, unless one enlarges upon Schiller's idea of the *piquant* and *frappant* as the essence of Romantic art, and defines Romanticism as change *per se*, a sort of æsthetic expression of the Will-to-Novelty, one has difficulty in answering the question why, in this particular case, the desire for change happened to produce Romantic art rather than any other type: to say that a thing is caused by reaction, does not explain why the reaction took that especial form. In the particular instance under consideration, moreover, the reaction described by Doughty could hardly have operated as more than a secondary cause; for, as the history of the funeral elegy makes clear, graveyard poetry arose, not after, but along with, the rise and triumph of Neo-classicism. Both the urge for reaction and the dilettante craving for novelty may at times have exhilarated the movement; but the basic reason for the rise of funeral poetry must be sought elsewhere; and, indeed, most scholars have endeavored to find grounds more relative than this to explain a literary phenomenon that attained to such wide dimensions and yet so utterly failed to conform to the established literary formulæ of its age.

During the last century or more, perhaps the chief concern of exact scholarship has been the tracing of influences of one literary work upon another. Such activities are a natural outcome of the evolutionary thought of the age; and, although this school of research may at times point out literary sources where they are either non-existent or quite secondary to some deeper explanation, yet learning is greatly indebted to this group of *savants*. The mortuary poetry of the eighteenth century, viewed from this angle,

[40] See the present author, *The Theory of Translation in Eighteeneth Century England, Neophilologus*, VI, 241 *et seq.*

used regularly to be set down to the influence of Milton, a point
of view perhaps best illustrated in the studies of early Romanticism
by Professors Beers and Phelps.[50]   Beers treated of the movement
as the "*Il Penseroso* School,"[51] and ascribed its "atrabilious humor"
to the "reaction against gayety" that, he says, set in after the deaths
of Pope and Swift in 1744 and 1745.[52]   Unfortunately for the
chronology of this theory, the printing of several of the poems he
cites—Blair's *Grave* (1743), for example, and the first part of
Young's *Night Thoughts* (1742)—antedated the two deaths that
are described as occasioning such poetry.   Gray's *Elegy,* moreover,
was certainly well under way before 1744;[53] and Parnell's *Night-
Piece on Death* (1722), which constitutes one of the best examples
of the "atrabilious humor"—not to mention Pope's *Eloisa* and the
writings of a host of obscure poetasters—was printed over twenty
years before.   In spite of all this, the pronouncement of Beers has
passed until recently as vulgate doctrine.[54]   It is indeed true that
in this, as in much other poetry of the century, Milton's influence
at times appears, and, here as elsewhere, grows with the growing
of the century; but to refer the School essentially to the influence
of *Il Penseroso* is an attitude for which neither the recent student
of Milton nor the historian of Romanticism can find convincing
evidence.

   The attack upon this theory proceeds from several different
quarters.   As early as 1915, Good pointed out that *L'Allegro* and
Il Penseroso were but little read before 1740 and that they seemed
to owe their popularity to the settings in that year by Handel;[55]
and he significantly remarked that, even around the mid-century,

[50] W. L. Phelps, *The Beginning of the
Romantic Movement,* Boston, 1893. See
especially 87 *et seq.* The basis of this
thesis was derived from Beers' lectures
at Yale, which he later published as *A
History of English Romanticism in the
Eighteenth Century,* New York, 1898.
   [51] Beers, *op. cit.,* 175.
   [52] Beers' general definition of Romanticism as a revival of the Middle Ages
is hardly consistent with his theory of
the provenience of mortuary poetry.
   [53] T. Gray, *Selections from the Poetry
and Prose,* ed. Phelps, Boston, 1894,
Preface.
   [54] He seems to be followed in the main
not only by Phelps (*Romantic Move-*

ment, 87) but also by Dixon (*Romantic
Revival,* New York, 1898), Dowden
(*Proc. Brit. Acad.,* 1917-1918, 275 etc.),
Babbitt, (*op. cit.,* 323), and Sherburn
(*Early Popularity of Milton's Minor
Poems,* Mod. Phil., XVII, 522 *et seq.*):
the misfortune of eighteenth century
study has been a tendency of scholars,
starting with a pre-conception of dislike,
to search for the exceptional, and so to
pass over the commonplace, which often
has greater historical significance.
   [55] This had already been mentioned by
Beers (*op. cit.,* 149), and seems first to
have been suggested by J. Warton in his
Essay on Pope.

they were used only "somewhat seriously at times as a model or form of expression for the outlet of certain poetic feelings generated in the earlier stages of Romanticism." [56] Later Havens, in his monumental work on Milton's influence, showed that although some interest in the minor poems is to be found in the earlier part of the century, their "vogue appears to have begun about 1742." [57] He did not find even a single brief parallel between *Il Penseroso* and *Night Thoughts*.[58] He did not list Parnell's *Night-Piece*, or Blair's *Grave*, or Hervey's *Meditations*, or Gray's *Elegy*, as showing any influence of Milton's octosyllabic poems.[59] Thus Milton scholars categorically deny that their author is the only begetter of these ensuing pieces. The influence of one or another of Milton's works may sporadically appear in the borrowing of an odd phrase or in a similar choice of meter; but *Il Penseroso* is in the main quite distinct in its characteristic images, in its atmosphere, and in its theme; and De Maar, the most recent historian of English Romanticism, finds no influence of *Il Penseroso* on either Young or Blair, whom he takes as the "chief exponents" of the School.[60]

The reasons for this *volte face* of scholarship are to be found partly in the facts of chronology, partly in the lack of verbal borrowings, and, most recently, in the rather wide difference in atmosphere and point of view. The "divinest melancholy" of Milton and Parnell's "melancholy state" have quite distinct mental colorings. Miss Reed has traced the history of "melancholy," its chief definitions, uses, and connotations, from its early appearance as a medical term in Burton and elsewhere[61] to its more general

[56] J. W. Good, *Studies in the Milton Tradition, Univ. of Ill. Studies*, Urbana, Ill., 1915, I, 169 and 250.
[57] R. D. Havens, *Influence of Milton on English Poetry*, Cambridge, Mass., 1922, 441. See also Havens, *Mod. Lang. Notes*, XXIV, 226-227.
[58] *Ibid., Appendix A*, 590 *et seq.*
[59] *Ibid., Bibliography II*, 669 *et seq.* In the case of Parnell's *Night-Piece*, Havens is perhaps extreme. Miltonic influence on it has been noted by Seccombe (*Camb. Hist.*, IX, 187), by Cruickshank (quoting Gosse in *Thomas Parnell*, in *Essays and Studies by the English Association*, Oxford, 1921, VII, 57) and by Sherburn (*Early Popularity of Milton's*

Minor Poems, Mod. Phil., XVII, 522). De Maar, writing more recently than Havens, re-asserts with parallel quotations, this influence. He also points out, however, that Parnell's melancholy was morbid, whereas Milton's was not (*op. cit.*, I, 182).
[60] De Maar, *op. cit.*, I, 183.
[61] See also Dr. Timothy Bright, *A Treatise of Melancholie, Containing the causes thereof, & reasons of the strange effects it worketh in our minds and bodies: with the physicke cure, and spiritual consolation of such as have thereto adjoined an afflicted conscience*, London, 1586. Miss Reed does not refer to this work.

application, in the mid-eighteenth century, to pleasing and pensive reverie. As regards Milton's use, she finds:

In *Il Penseroso* Milton seems to react against Burton's conception altogether, and while keeping the word melancholy to describe the thoughtful mood of the man who loves to be alone by night, indoors or out, reading or simply musing by himself, or who by day courts the brown shadows in the close coverts of a wood by the brook, he deliberately rejects all the associations of the word with disease, madness, suicide and fear. Deliberately, also, he sets up a new set of connotations, with saintliness, with wisdom, with beauty, with leisure, with poetry, philosophy, and music, with lovely outdoor scenes, and with a widening experience maturing with age.[62]

In the seventeenth century, the term was regularly "derogatory": it meant "a disease recognizable by its effect on the mind and temper," symptomized by chronic depression and apparently causeless fear, a disorder such as afflicted the poet Collins, popularly termed melancholia, and among modern alienists known as manic-depressive insanity. Milton's "divinest melancholy" has nothing of this;[63] but it is to this tradition that the graveyard poets chiefly belong. Their definition of melancholy, except possibly in the case of Gray, who had more of restraint, was quite of this sort; and, from their seventeenth century predecessors, they depart only in their attitude toward the thing thus defined.[64] In the seventeenth century, melancholy, as in Burton, usually appears as a disease to be assuaged; but, among the dissenters, it seems to have been cultivated especially in the elegy as a state profitable to the soul. The eighteenth century seems to have derived its attitude from this

[62] Miss Reed, *op. cit.*, 19 *et passim*.

[63] Milton was apparently not quite alone among the great poets of the period in this interpretation of melancholy. Henry Vaughan's lines beginning "Fair and young light [Christ]! My guide to holy Grief and soul-curing melancholy . . ." seem to have a similar conception, though with a more religious coloring. This attitude toward melancholy, the meter of the poem, and the two-line summary at the end, suggest that it was written under the inspiration of *Il Penseroso*. The comparative jerkiness of the meter may be due to the influence of Donne, or to Vaughan's lack of success in imitating the airy rhythms of Milton. The reference to "night ravens," the rhyme of "melancholy" and "Holy," and the reference to the will o' the wisp in the fifth line suggest *L'Allegro;* and one feels that the stanza set off at the end is an expansion of the final couplet of Milton's octosyllabic poems. If this be Miltonic, it is almost the only case of influence of the octosyllabics during the period (Havens, *op. cit.*, Chapter XVIII).

[64] Reed, *op. cit.*, 23-24, 188 *et seq.* Gray's concept of melancholy approximates most closely to that of Milton, and, perhaps because of his Greek studies, is more balanced and less emotional.

view; and it favored melancholy, sometimes for religious reasons, sometimes as a proof of exquisite "sensibility," and often for the mere pleasure of its agreeable titillation to the sense: the imp of the perverse possessed the poets of a morbid yearning, or at least tempted them to assume such a yearning as a literary pose attractive to a large class of readers. Burton felt that melancholy should be cured by prayer and edifying study; Blair and Young accepted it as the norm of religious experience and a proof of superior refinement, and so keyed their whole mental life to a higher emotional pitch.[65] Graveyard horrifics, therefore, would seem to have their root in the seventeenth century England, but not in the *Il Penseroso* of John Milton.

Milton, however, is not the only author on whom has been fathered the mortuary poetry of the early eighteenth century. Writing in 1895, Barnstorff found the content of *Night Thoughts* to be in the moralistic vein of the *Spectator* and its form mainly under the influence of Pope. He also gave incidental mention to Milton and to Shakespeare.[66] Perhaps, however, the most detailed statement of literary influences appears in Müller's monograph on Blair and the Graveyard School. He finds that Blair "bildet sich vornehmlich an Shakespeare's starker Gefühlsdichtung und an Norris' geistlicher Poesie." He refers especially to *Hamlet, Henry IV Part II, Romeo and Juliet*, and *Julius Caesar*; the parallels he gives hardly prove more than that Shakespeare was a source for an occasional phrase or comparison. The great Shakespearean vogue of the time of Garrick, moreover, was distinctly subsequent to the rise of graveyard poetry. John Norris of Bemerton, the follower of the Cambridge Platonists, who is remembered as writing a reply to the Deist Toland and composing several lugubrious lyrics, is an early exponent of the common graveyard theme of the worthlessness of life; but he is hardly to be associated with any other aspect of the School.[67] Of the other influences, Müller notes the *Book of Job*, Milton, especially the passage on Sin and Death in *Paradise*

---

[65] This Sentimental attitude seems to have been anticipated in Fletcher's stanzas on melancholy in *The Nice Valor* (?1613). This poem may have inspired Milton's octosyllabics; but Milton did not borrow its Sentimentalism.

[66] J. Barnstorff, *Youngs Nachtgedanken*

und ihr Einfluss auf die deutsche Litteratur, Bamberg, 1895, 9 *et seq.* Pope's *Eloisa* and his *Elegy* may also have influenced the content of Blair and the others. See Thomas, *op. cit.*, 102.

[67] Grosart had already suggested this influence in his edition of Norris, 45.

Lost, Fletcher, Webster, Massinger, Quarles, Addison (the very
Aristotelian passage in which he recommends pity and fear!),[68]
and a number of eighteenth century poems most of which might
well be included within the Graveyard School itself.[69] This list
is very miscellaneous and not altogether convincing. Müller's
monograph,[70] although a useful assemblage of possible influences,
does nothing to explain how or why this multiplicity of influences,
even granted that they all actually operated, happened to be set
going in this particular way at this moment in literary history.

To this miscellany of Biblical, dramatic, seventeenth century
and eighteenth century sources, Miss Reed[71] adds the following
items: Ecclesiastes and the Psalms from the Bible, and Lucretius,
Vergil, Horace, Seneca, and Martial, from the Latin Classics:
these, she declares, were the influences on the literature of melancholy in the reign of Queen Anne and the generations before and
after. Such a list recalls to mind the ubiquitousness of literary
influence and the uncertainty of assigning works to specific sources.
Perhaps all of the items in Miss Reed's list left traces upon the
development of the funeral elegy; but the prominence of Biblical
and also of Classical origins implies a certain contradiction; for,
at the time of the early development of the funeral elegy during
the mid-seventeenth century, but few authors show extensive borrowings from both these sources in the same literary performance.
The Commonwealth and the Restoration periods saw much religious writing under the influence of the *Bible*[72] and much poetry
under the influence of the Classics; but the combinations of both
traditions, each extensively drawn upon as in *Paradise Lost,* was
of rare occurrence; and, in the elegy indeed, the Classical-pastoral
type and the Christian-funeral type are sufficiently disparate to
form two distinct lines of development. The question, moreover,
still remains as to just why these various authors cited by Müller
and Miss Reed should have exerted so much influence in the direction of morbid melancholy about the time of the reign of Queen
Anne. Literary research, in short, along lines Miltonic, Biblical,

---

[68] *The Spectator,* No. 418.

[69] Young's *Last Day* (1713), Parnell's
Night-Piece, Tickell's *Elegy on Addison,*
Mallett's *Excursion,* and Pope's *Elegy to
the Memory of an Unfortunate Lady.*

[70] K. Müller, *Robert Blair's "Grave"
und die Grabes- und Nachtdichtung,* Weimar, 1909.

[71] Miss Reed, *op. cit.,* 126.

[72] See the *Term Catalogues,* ed. Arber,
London, 1903, *Preface,* xiv.

or Classical, although it probes deep, can hardly be said to pluck the heart out of the mystery.

Carried to its *summa* of excellence by the great Sainte-Beuve, biographical criticism has claimed many votaries among succeeding scholars; and some have tried to apply it to the present problem. Thomas says that Young's Oxford training helped to make him the poet of reaction against Neo-classicism;[73] Clark seeks causes for Young's melancholy in his psychology;[74] and Saintsbury suggests that "discontent with the non-appearance of canonries, deaneries, bishoprics, had as much as the deaths of Lucia, and Narcissa and Philander to do with dictating *The Complaint,* and that a late but sane conclusion that they were not coming at all was at the bottom of *Resignation.*"[75] De Maar, moreover, accounted for the "funereal tone" of Parnell's *Night-Piece* "by Parnell's own mood," and referred to Gilfillan's biography to support his contention;[76] and it is obvious that Blair's early efforts at elegy and Biblical paraphrase helped to form his graveyard style. Rash, indeed, would be the denial that authors of any particular group were influenced by their individual lives; but the mere accident of a given *penchant* in a given person clearly cannot explain the simultaneous rise among a multitude of authors, great and small, of a given type of poetry; and, if it were a common element in all their lives that brought about this sudden release of melancholy upon the literary world, then surely the cause is not to be described as individual, but as social, economic, philosophic, or what not: it belongs not merely to the single author but to his climature and countrymen.

The cross-currents between the various arts in the eighteenth century have been somewhat studied;[77] and a good deal has been done to trace the mutual reactions of literature and philosophy;[78] but, although the Sentimental trend of Shaftesbury and the early

---

[73] Thomas, *op. cit.,* 55.

[74] H. H. Clark in *Mod. Lang. Notes,* XXXIX, 129 *et seq.* Was this melancholy real or merely a sort of Byronic pose?

[75] G. Saintsbury, *The Peace of the Augustans,* London, 1916, 62-63.

[76] De Maar, *op. cit.,* I, 182.

[77] E.g., I. Babbitt, *The New Laokoön,* Boston, 1910; Myra Reynolds, *Nature in*

English Poetry, Chicago, 1909; and *William Mason, A Study in Eighteenth Century Culture,* New York, 1924, by the present author.

[78] E.g., Sir Leslie Stephen, *History of English Thought in the Eighteenth Century,* New York, 1902; and I. Babbitt, *Rousseau and Romanticism,* New York, 1919. Cf. A. O. Lovejoy, *Publ. Mod. Lang. Assoc. Am.,* XXXIX, 229 *et seq.*

appearance of "natural" gardening, and of Sentimental-bourgeois drama[79] and fiction[80] have by no means been ignored, yet the ethical and æsthetic study of these phenomena has helped but little to disentangle the Gordian knot, and would seem to have proved among scholars the apple of discord rather than the sword of Alexander. Philosophy, be it for better or worse, is too abstract to play any great rôle in the lives of the profane vulgar, who are ruled rather by habit and immediate interest; and the main current of early eighteenth century æsthetics, when the tide of the Sentimental was rising, certainly was favorable rather to Neo-classical restraint. The investigation of these subjects has proved illuminating and useful, but for the most part has done little to explain how the movements that they chronicle came into being. The study of literary criticism also has thrown some light upon the authorities, English,[81] French, and Italian,[82] to whom Romantic theorists turned for justification of their opinions; but English Romanticism, unlike German, would seem to have developed more by the *faits accomplis* of practice than by the reasoned inquiry of theory: even when Addison wrote his famous essays on the imagination, an expansive emotionalism had already become apparent in Sentimental comedy, in gardening, and in some types of poetry. To prove, moreover, that an opinion or point of view was extensively borrowed from a given source at a given period, does not show *why* it was so borrowed, or why it happened to achieve so great a vogue.

For the study of the social and economic background of eighteenth century literature, there exists a multitude of books, popular and learned, on the manners, on the social structure, and on the industrial development of the period; nevertheless but little, since the publication of Lecky's *History*, has been done to associate this material with literary movements.[83] Rather recently, however,

[79] E.g., E. Bernbaum, *The Drama of Sensibility*, Boston, 1915; and A. Nicoll, *A History of Early Eighteenth Century Drama*, Cambridge, 1925.

[80] Helen Sard Hughes, *The Middle-Class Reader and the English Novel*, Jour. Eng. and Ger. Phil., XXV, 362 et seq.

[81] J. W. Krutch, *Comedy and Conscience after the Restoration*, New York, 1924. Cf. a review by the present author, *Mod. Lang. Notes*, XLI, 332 et seq.

[82] J. G. Robertson, *Studies in the Genesis of Romantic Theory in the Eighteenth Century*, Cambridge, 1923.

[83] E.g., G. F. Richardson, *A Neglected Aspect of the English Romantic Movement*, Univ. of Cal. Publ., III, Berkeley, Cal., 1915.

several scholars have suggested that such a study promises to bear fruit. In treating of the religious lyric, Courthope attributes its rise to the Non-conformists and the Non-jurors, to whom religion appealed "through the heart rather than through the head."[84] If the religious lyric, why not the analogous graveyard elegy, which, among the dissenters at least, was of much older growth? If the graveyard elegy, why not other phases of incipient Romanticism? The hypothesis is not unattractive; and, indeed, several writers in recent years have held some such opinion. Masson suggested that Rousseau's Sentimental belief in his innate excellence was derived from the Calvinistic doctrine of Election;[85] and indeed it is hard to distinguish between a Sentimentalist and a Calvinist who believes himself saved. Schöffler showed that graveyard poetry previous to 1750 sprang chiefly from Protestant parsonages,[86] although he did not study the broadside elegy, which would greatly have strengthened his thesis. Van Tieghem, on the other hand, like Korff, seems to associate the movement rather with the Renaissance than with the Reformation;[87] and Professors Legouis and Cazamian seem to combine both theories in their recent history:

Les meditations de minuit, la hautise de la tombe, les effusions du deuil intime et le plaisir de pleurer, se rattachent directement par leurs racines à la renaissance de l'esprit puritain que favorise l'ascension de la classe moyenne.[88]

They give due weight, moreover, to the rise of the bourgeoisie as an ever-increasing influence after 1688,[89] and associate with it the synchronous rise of Sentimentalism in the arts;[90] but, like van Tieghem, they do not seem to find any artistic expression of these Puritan literary tendencies much before the middle of the eigh-

[84] W. J. Courthope, op. cit., V, 327 et seq.

[85] P. M. Masson, La Religion de J-J. Rousseau, Paris, 1916, I, 37.

[86] H. Schöffler, Protestantismus und Literatur, Leipsig, 1922. Cf. the present writer in Mod. Lang. Rev., XXII, 18n. The earliest intimation of such a theory as applied to English literature would seem to have been made by Gilfillan (Life of Quarles, prefixed to the Emblems, Edinburgh, 1857, 194).

[87] P. van Tieghem, La Poésie de la Nuit et des Tombeaux en Europe au XVIIIe Siècle, Brussels, 1921, 4 et passim. He dates the rise of the School about the middle of the eighteenth century in all the major literatures of Europe, an attitude that hardly applies to England.

[88] E. Legouis and L. Cazamian, Histoire de la Littérature Anglaise, Paris, 1924, 800. Miss Reed suggests a like attitude (op. cit., 111-112).

[89] Legouis and Cazamian, op. cit., 748.

[90] Ibid., 765.

teenth century, when they had already suffered a sea-change into incipient Romanticism.

Upon this entire problem, the vogue of the funeral elegy has a very direct and significant bearing. It forms a considerable body of literature throughout the Neo-classical period; it is the parent stem of graveyard poetry; and its growth can be traced far back into the seventeenth century. Its appearance is not to be explained on the basis of mere reaction; the influence of Milton is but an incident in its history; and other literary influences merely show on what tradition these poets of melancholy formed their style, and not why they assumed a sombre, not to say horrific, tone. In a few writers, such as Lady Winchelsea, the facts of biography may be all-sufficient to explain this yearning for "a new shudder"; and something of it may have come over into literature from philosophy and from the other arts; but these could not have given it the first incentive, for it appears rather earlier in poetry than in the ethics of Shaftesbury or the gardening of Kent or the comedies of Cibber and Steele. The explanation would seem to inhere in a great social movement rather than in the realms of art or thought; and this great social movement seems to consist mainly of the rise of the trading-classes to wealth, their consequent return to artistic patronage and their re-interpretation of Protestantism on a Sentimental, instead of a Calvinistic, basis. Such a change would especially affect clergymen and the sons of clergymen, who, as Schöffler has pointed out, wrote most of the graveyard poems. It should particularly affect the Presbyterian, Independent, and Baptist dissenters, who were, in the seventeenth century the most zealous guardians of Calvinism; and, indeed, the poetry of this class should especially illustrate the evolution of Sentimentalism from Calvinistic origins—if such an evolution took place. Most historians seem to suppose that the dissenters—or Puritans, as they were called in an earlier day—had no special and distinctive literature of their own, except perhaps Milton, who was far from being an orthodox Calvinist; and, indeed, their theology was opposed to artistic expression; but the fact remains that there exists a distinctive elegiac literature that can in large part be definitely associated with this socio-religious group, and that presents a strange and interesting contrast to the poetry, even the elegiac poetry, that was produced for aristocratic consumption. These Puritan funeral elegies seem rather to have escaped the attention of scholars, partly perhaps because they are such wretched stuff as poetry, but more especially because they exist for the most part only on rare broadsides that have never been collected or reprinted,[91] and assume a dignified position in volumes of poetry only during the first half of the eighteenth century: thus most writers give this late date for the inception of the melancholic school. The present volume is written to chronicle the rise, evolution, and influence of this body of poetry, to show something of its economic, social, and philosophic relations, its similarities and differences with the contemporary evolution of the courtly elegiac style, and to throw what light it can upon the beginnings of English, and so of all European, Romanticism.

[91] See *A Century of Broadside Elegies, being ninety English and ten Scotch broadsides, Illustrating the Biography and Manners of the Seventeenth Century,* edited by the present writer, London, 1928.

CHAPTER II

THE FUNERAL ELEGY AND THE CAVALIERS

CHRISTIAN custom, and also the sentiments proper to mankind, have indeed, to quote Sir Thomas Browne, "handsomely glossed the deformity of death"—glossed it with the arts of sculpture and painting, with a dramatic and arresting ritual, and with the repeated consolations of elegiac poetry. This poetry of lamentation, springing from so universal an experience, seems to be, in both locality and time, almost coëxtensive with literature itself. The mood of the Chinese lyric is predominantly elegiac;[1] the tenth book of the *Rig Veda* contains several funeral hymns; the lament of David over Saul and Jonathan,[2] referred to by a seventeenth century writer as a "funeral elegy,"[3] is one of the oldest parts of the Bible, being probably an extract of the lost *Book of Jashar*; and, in Homer, Briseis delivered a lamentation over the body of Patroclus, and Andromache over the corpse of Hector. Beowulf was buried with a *sorh-leoð*; and Attila with a "cantus funereus," if we may trust the forty-ninth chapter of Jordanes' *Getica*;[4] Saint Dunstan in his vain and unsaintly youth loved "trifling legends" and "funeral chants"; in popular balladry appears the coronoch of *Johnny Campbell*; and such pieces as *The Pearl* and *The Boke of the Duchesse*, not to mention minor examples,[5] indicate that in Mediæval England the poetry of death was not uncultivated. During the Renaissance, Skelton's *Phyllyppe Sparrowe*, Sir Thomas More's rhyme-royal stanzas on the death of Elizabeth of York,[6] and Sir John Cheek's "learned elegie" on Edward VI,[7] show that this tradition was by no means

[1] One of the first elegies still preserved would seem to be the lines by Liu Hêng on his father, "cut off in his pride," dating from the second century before Christ.
[2] *II Samuel*, i, 18-27. This was many times rendered into verse during the seventeenth century; and the lament for Jephthah's daughter served as an inspiration to Herrick.
[3] Robert Fleming, *Mirror of Divine Love*, London, 1691, 195.
[4] F. Klaeber, *Publ. Mod. Lang. Assoc. Am.*, XLII, 255 *et seq.*

[5] E.g., the elegy in Percy's *Reliques* on the death of Edward I, and such poems as *Against my Will I Take my Leave* (*Religious Lyrics of the Fourteenth Century*, ed. Brown, Oxford, 1924, 134), and a number that treat generally of death.
[6] The best text would seem to be that in Halliwell's *Yorkshire Anthology*, London, 1851, 332 *et seq.*
[7] See Thomas Hearne, *Collection of Curious Discourses*, London, 1773, I, 340.

allowed to subside; but with the borrowing of the term *elegy* arose
an increasing tendency, especially on the part of the more aristocratic makers, to imitate Classical archetypes, and to compose either
pastoral eclogues or eulogistic threnodies that, consonant with the
Renaissance love of fame, are Pagan panegyrics rather than Christian laments.   In general, this Classical tone can readily be distinguished from that of the more native funeral elegy: Ovid, for
instance, in his dirge over Tibullus, seems to doubt the existence
of an after-life, and, if there be such, to picture it as a sort of
Elysian symposium; Propertius, in his lines beginning "Desine,
Paule, meum lacrimis urgere sepulchrum,"[8] touches upon the inev-
itability of death and the uselessness of lament rather than upon
bodily decay or the horrors of the grave; and Catullus sings of
death with a gaiety like that of Herrick, skeptical yet resigned.[9]
The printing of the Latin elegiac poets took its start even among
the incunabula;[10] and imitators soon appeared on the Continent,
both in the original and in the vulgar tongues.[11]   The English
Renaissance borrowed immediately of the Latin Classics, and indirectly through Italy; and from France, the classicized poetry of
Jodelle, Desportes, and Garnier was carried across the Channel
into Elizabethan England.[12]   Thus Spenser's *Astrophel* and the
scores of other elegies on Sidney's death were generally composed
in a style that was Pagan and Classical; and furthermore, Shakespeare's references to "dire-lamenting elegies" and "odes on haw-
thorns and elegies upon brambles" are clearly calculated to the
meridian of the love-elegy.[13]   During the early seventeenth century, this Renaissance tradition continued, especially in the courtly
circles of the Cavaliers: of the pieces called elegies, many were
Classical love-poems; and even in those that were occasioned by
death, the arch-purpose is commonly ignored to give place either to
a eulogy of the subject's good deeds or to a casuistical discussion
of life, death, and the life hereafter.   In the non-elegiac litera-

---

[8] Propertius, *Lib.* IV, *El. XI.*
[9] E.g., Catullus, No. XCVI.
[10] There were at least six separate editions of Propertius before 1500, not to
mention two of Tibullus, ten of Catullus,
and eight of the three poets together.
[11] E.g., The Latin elegies of Publius
Faustus (1496), and *Elegiarum Libri
Tres* of Elesius Calentius (1503).

[12] Sidney Lee, *The French Renaissance
in England*, New York, 1910, 202 and
210 *et seq.*
[13] *Two Gentlemen*, III, ii, 82, and *As
You Like It*, III, ii, 380. With the elegies on Sidney, compare *Greene's Funerals* (1594) by the adulatory "R. B."

ture, oddly enough, of the Elizabethan and Jacobean periods, the note of melancholy is more common. Dr. Bright's *Treatise*,[14] Donne's sermons, Burton's *Anatomy* and other prose pieces, religious and medical, treat lengthily of the subject; the drama portrays melancholy not merely in the "malcontent type,"[15] but also in such occasional lyrics as Shakespeare's dirge "Come away, death"[16] and John Fletcher's lines in *The Nice Valor* beginning "Hence, all you vain delights"; and lyric poetry, outside the drama, is more and more commonly given over to a pensive coloring as in *Death's Summons* by Nashe and in Southwell's *Image of Death*; later in Beaumont's octosyllabics *On the Tombs in Westminster Abbey* and in Davison's *Poetical Rhapsody*,[17] and later still and even more markedly in Phineas Fletcher's *Religious Musings* and in Quarles' *Emblems*. The existence of this rather extensive body of literature makes the rarity of the funereal note in the elegy especially striking. This rarity is probably to be explained in part by the Anglican emphasis on immortality and in part by the tendency of the Puritans to avoid poetic composition; so that Anglican elegies are not likely to be mortuary and Puritan elegies are not very common. Burton professionally testifies that the Puritans were "far gone with melancholy";[18] and, had they been more inclined to kindle incense at the Muse's flame, mortuary elegies would doubtless be more numerous. The present chapter, leaving the funeral and bourgeois tradition for later treatment will sift through first the Cavalier lyrists and later the broadside balladists, who, though catering to the public at large, generally espoused the cause of the House of Stuart. Thus, such elegies as are pertinent to the present study may be examined and their proportion and relationship to the great body of elegiac writing noted and explained.

[14] Dr. Timothy Bright, *A Treatise of Melancholy*, 1586 (2 eds.) and 1613. See Miss M. I. O'Sullivan, *Hamlet and Dr. Timothy Bright*, Publ. Mod. Lang. Assoc. Am., XLI, 667 *et seq.*

[15] See Amy Louise Reed, *The Background of Gray's Elegy*, New York, 1924, 12 *et seq.*; E. E. Stoll, *Mod. Phil.*, III, 281 *et seq.*, etc. Such examples have been cited as Antonio, Don John, Jaques, and perhaps Hamlet, in Shakespeare; Vendice in Tourneur's *Revenger's Tragedy*; and Malevole in Marston's *Malcontent*.

[16] For a selection of such poems, see Mary Lloyd, *Elegies Ancient and Modern*, Trenton, [N. J.], 1903, I, 61 *et seq.*

[17] See *Rare Poems of the Sixteenth and Seventeenth Centuries*, ed. W. J. Linton, London, 1883, 214.

[18] Burton, *Anatomy of Melancholy*, London, 1898, 700. Elsewhere, he refers to them in like manner, 669 *et passim*. See also such a poem as *The Great Assize*, described by its editor as written in "true cobler-puritan style" (*Roxburghe Ballads*, ed. Chappell, London, 1871, *Publ. Ball. Soc.*, I, 394).

To discuss the writings of every sub-minor elegist who meditated an all-too-thankless Muse during these merely introductory
decades seems a needless refinement of assiduity. Suffice it to say
that in the early seventeenth century the elegiac *genre* was widely
if not always wisely, cultivated by those who had a debt of gratitude or an old score of enmity to pay, or who, with ulterior motives of a merely pecuniary cast, hoped to beguile from some opu-
lent mourner the niggardly rewards of patronage: in 1613, the
death of Prince Henry produced a whole volume of Scotch elegies[19]
and innumerable English lamentations,[20] including at least one
that described his death and funeral and the woe of the survivors.[21] The 1616 edition of Sir Thomas Overbury's poem, *The
Wife*, advertised "many newe Elegies upon his untimely and much
lamented Death";[22] the passing of Ben Jonson was sung in at
least twenty-six more or less elegiac pieces;[23] and the outburst of
sardonic exultation at the murder of Buckingham in 1628 expressed itself in a whole sheaf of manuscript poems, for the most
part satiric funeral elegies.[24] In these early seventeenth century
pieces, the death of the individual is usually glossed over, and
made the mere occasion for a panegyric or diatribe in the characteristic Renaissance fashion, or perhaps for an ecstatic contem-

[19] *The Mausoleum or the Choisest Flowers of the Epitaphs written on the Death
of Prince Henrie*, Edinburgh, 1613. None
of these poems has a particularly graveyard tone.
[20] The *Three Elegies* on Prince Henry
by Tourneur, Webster, and Heywood
were published with alternate pages in
solid black. Such sable garnitures occasionally appear in seventeenth century
elegiac volumes (e.g., P. Fisher, *Threnodia Triumphalis*, London, 1659, which
appeared with black margins, a type of
ornament that had shortly before been
introduced into elegiac broadsides). Crashaw would seem to refer to this custom
(*Poems*, ed. Tutin, 155) in the lines:
Dear relics of a dislodged soul, whose lack
Makes many a mourning paper put on
    black!
[21] *An Epicede or Funeral Song: On
the most disasterous Death, of the High-
borne Henry Prince of Wales*, London,
1612. The comparatively few elegies on
Queen Elizabeth suggest that patronage
was, usually, the elegist's chief motive.

[22] Overbury's death by poison in the
Tower gave to these elegies a journalistic
motive that, despite their melodramatic
cast, removes them somewhat from the
present category.
[23] Ben Jonson, *Works*, ed. Cunningham, London, 1903, III, 496 *et seq*. This
collection does not include Herrick's several poems on Jonson, some of them
elegiac. There are also at least five
Latin elegies.
[24] *Poems and Songs Relating to George
Villiers, Duke of Buckingham and his
Assassination by John Felton*, ed. Fair-
holt, printed by the Percy Soc. from
Sloane MSS. No. 603. This must have
been an occasion of much Puritan rejoicing; and some of the poems (e.g., *Upon
the Duke's Death*, 52) suggest their point
of view. The satirical elegy was not
new: in 1569 had appeared a bitter *Epitaph upon the Life and Death of Dr.
Bonner, sometime unworthy Bishop of
London* (*Harl. Misc.*, London, 1744, I,
595 *et seq.*).

plation of immortality; and funerary touches—the pains of illness, death-bed scenes, the terrors of hell, corporeal mortification, worms, damp charnels, and graveyards deep in the shade of cypress and melancholy yews—such as concern the present study, are very rare. The poems, furthermore, that enjoyed the cognomen of *elegy* are often those most remote from the mortuary type.[25] Thus, although "elegies" abound, and even elegies written on the occasion of death are not uncommon, yet funeral elegies are only of sporadic occurrence when the extravagant and erring Muse of the author forsook the marked and walled Elysian fields to wander in the glimpses of the moon.

Of Caroline poetry, a narrower inspection is necessary: most of these writers lived on into the Commonwealth period and some even after the Restoration; and no investigation of the poetry of the reign of Charles II is complete without some consideration of the courtly schools that flourished previous to the Civil War. These poets, moreover, are the immediate antecedents of the Commonwealth, when the funeral elegy seems first to have attained prominence; and they have a special importance as showing, yet in solution, those elements that were to be crystalized in the new literary species. The true poetry of this period, as distinct from the efforts of tombstone masons and bereaved relatives, has been divided into three fairly distinct schools:[26] that of Spenser, which was strictly Elizabethan, ornate in imagery, melodious in numbers, emotional in appeal, and idealistic in theme; the School of Donne, in which melody of the verse was sacrificed to intellectual curiosity of image and theme, and in which cynicism toward this world stood sharply in contrast to a devout longing for the next; and lastly the School of Jonson, which seems to have retained something of Spenser's music, but reacted to simplicity of image and conventionality of idea—what oft was thought but ne'er so well expressed. If Spenser and his disciples are essentially Elizabethan, Donne and his followers mark a recrudescence of Mediæval religious belief[27]

---

[25] Possibly this is because the English Renaissance hesitated to call by a name with Pagan associations a type of poetry that they used to celebrate the death of a Christian friend or patron. Such a prejudice, if it ever existed, died out during the seventeenth century.

[26] See F. E. Schelling, *A Book of Elizabethan Lyrics*, Boston, 1895, xxxiii.

[27] See Mary P. Ramsay, *Les Doctrines Médiévales chez Donne*, London, 1917. Of course, Donne was not without Renaissance religious influences also. See L. I. Bredvold, *Religious Thought of Donne, Studies in Shakespeare, Milton and Donne, Univ. of Mich. Publ.*, New York, 1925.

combined with the intellectual casuistry of the Renaissance; and Ben Jonson and the "sons of Ben" express a kind of Roman purism of the latter Renaissance that looks forward to the rise of Neoclassicism. Not all the poets of the age adhere entirely to any one of these three schools;[28] but, on the whole, the classification is convenient and adaptable to the present purpose.

The School of Spenser, the earliest of these lyric tendencies, has little to offer the historian of the funeral elegy. Spenser himself, although politically and religiously a Puritan,[29] was, in his literary antecedents, a child of the Middle Ages and of the Italian Renaissance;[30] and his elegies contribute to the mortuary tradition nothing of significance. His immediate follower, Drayton, approaches nearest to the funeral elegy in his poems *Upon the Death of Sir Henry Raynsford* and *Upon the Death of Mistris Elianor Fallowfield:* in the former, the sad event is a "heavy crosse" to the poet, who beats his breast "that there should be a woe So high, that words cannot attaine thereto," but who nevertheless pens a hundred and twenty-eight lines, for the most part a poetical essay *de amicitia*; and, in the latter, he contents himself with animadversions on the injustice and uncertainty of "accursed Death." William Browne's more important work is entirely pastoral; and, although he occasionally sits "weeping on a senseless tomb," he is given over to Spenserian aureate terms and Elizabethan hyperboles rather than to concrete graveyard details. The most apposite of his elegies to the present study is that on Prince Henry, which was probably composed very much *ad hoc,* and which he happily describes as "A text of woe for grief to comment on" with "tears, sighs and sobs." The last stanza illustrates at once its ingenuity of exaggeration and such funeral quality as it possesses:

---

[28] Cowley's couplets, for instance, pertain to the Jonsonian tradition, but many of his metaphors to that of Donne; and the two Fletchers, although obvious and avowed Spenserians, borrow tropes from Donne and occasional suggestions from Mediæval sources such as *King Hart.*

[29] See T. W. Hunt, *Spenser and the English Reformation, Bibliotheca Sacra,* LVII, 39; Lilian Winstanley, *Spenser and Puritanism, Mod. Lang. Quart.,* III, 6 and 13; F. M. Padelford, *Spenser and the Puritan Propaganda, Mod. Phil.,* XI,

85; and A. H. Tolman, *The Relation of Spenser and Harvey to Puritanism, Mod. Phil.,* XV, 549. After some debate, it would seem evident that Spenser was a Low Church Anglican, a Puritan only in a rather mild sense.

[30] He shows the influence of Tasso, Ariosto, and the Italian pastoralists and sonneteers, of Malory and the writers of metrical romance, and of Chaucer and his imitators English and Scotch. See F. I. Carpenter, *A Reference Guide to Spenser,* Chicago, 1923, 134 *et seq.*

When last he sicken'd then we first began
To tread the Labyrinth of Woe about,
And by degrees we further inward ran,
Having his thread of life to guide us out.
But Destiny no sooner saw us enter
Sad Sorrow's maze, immured up in night,
    Where nothing dwells
    But cries and yells
Thrown from the hearts of men deprived of light
When we were almost come into the centre;
    Fate, cruelly to bar our joys returning,
    Cut off our thread and left us all in mourning.

The poet deliberately omits all description of the Prince's illness, death, and funeral, and does not even end with assurance of his immortality. The only realistic touches are the "cries and yells" of the mourners. The poems by Giles and by Phineas Fletcher on the deaths of Queen Elizabeth and of Prince Henry are done in the combined styles of the *Shepheardes Calender* and the *Faerie Queene*, eked out with odd conceits and lengthy but unsustained pathetic fallacies; and the elegy *Eliza* on Sir Antony Irby consists of two allegorical cantos that serve to illustrate only the perverse adaptation of a great poet's style to an inappropriate purpose. Patrick Hannay's two elegies (1619) on Queen Anne further exemplify the *summa* of hyperbolic sadness, without even suggesting the earth earthy of an actual graveyard;[31] Thomas Heywood's *Funerall Elegie* on Sir George Saint Poole is a *seriatim* panegyric, virtue by virtue, and his *Funeral Elegie upon a vertuous Maide* suggests the Elizabethan madrigal style;[32] and the royal historiographer, Thomas Stanley, although he did not avoid elegiac themes, always pursued them in the mannered style of the Petrarchists or of Guarini and Marini.[33] The ornate figures of the Spenserian poets left scanty room for the homely details of fact; and sadness is only sadness when it may speak its own simple language.

Quite as far removed was the School of Jonson from the poetry

[31] See *Caroline Poets*, ed. Saintsbury, Oxford, 1905-1921, I, 695 *et seq.* One attempts to scale the apogee of the lachrymose by suggesting the possibility of a new Deluge; the other, by noting the effect of the tearful countryside upon the volume of the Thames.

[32] Thomas Heywood, *Pleasant Dialogues and Drammas*, London, 1637, 252 and 254.

[33] In 1651, he brought together in one volume poems on *The Night, The Tomb,* and like subjects, without a single graveyard touch. See *Caroline Poets, ed. cit.,* III, 112, 123, 139 etc.

of Christian death and burial. Æglamour's lament in *The Sad Shepherd* represents the normal Jonsonian variation of the elegiac theme; for most of it is sung in either pastoral or Pindaric strain; but two of Jonson's latter elegies at least occasionally harmonize with the funereal motif. The poem *On the Lady Jane Pawlet*[34] opens in a style that, in an inferior metempsychosis, might, in the 1650's, have celebrated the death of a dissenting minister:

> What gentle ghost, besprent with April dew,
> Hails me so solemnly to yonder yew,
> And beckoning woos me, from the fatal tree
> To pluck a garland for herself or me?
> I do obey you, Beauty! for in death
> You seem a fair one. O that you had breath
> To give your shade a name! Stay, stay, I feel
> A horror in me, all my blood is steel;
> Stiff! stark! my joints 'gainst one another knock!
> Whose daughter?—Ha! great Savage of the Rock!
> He's good as great. I am almost a stone!
> And ere I can ask more of her, she's gone!—
> Alas, I am all marble!

The "torturers, her doctors" occupy with their ministrations the latter part of the poem. The *Elegy to my Muse the Lady Venetia Digby*, although it mentions the "vulture Death," is, on the whole, a less pointed example. Jonson's poetic offspring add little to the matter of the present study. Some sing the passing of pet animals, and bridge the gap between Lesbia's sparrow in Catullus and Burns' "Lament in rhyme" for "poor Mailie";[35] some, like the elegist of Suckling,[36] knell, not so much the passing of a Christian soul, as the literary apotheosis of an inspired seer. Herrick associates death either with the "Carpe diem" of Horace or with a joyous assurance of immortality; Lovelace, although usually restrained in style and merely laudatory in theme, is now and then led, probably by the

[34] This elegy is dated 1631 (*Works, ed cit.*, III, 354n). The poem struck the taste of the eighteenth century; for Pope borrowed its first two lines for the opening couplet of his *Elegy* on the unfortunate lady; and Warton called it a "pathetic Elegy." It still has its admirers; for Herford and Simpson (*Ben Jonson*, Oxford, 1925, II, 381) find the passage quoted above to be possessed of a "mysterious beauty." Possibly Jonson's lapses into futile rhetoric are due to his habit of writing his poems first in prose.

[35] For a considerable collection of the elegies of the period on birds and other pets, see Mary Lloyd, *op. cit.*, 47 *et passim*.

[36] See *Upon the Death of Sir John Sutlin* [Suckling], 1642.

influence of Donne, which appears elsewhere in his poetry, to such a mortuary fragment as the following:

> Enter the dismal Chancell of this roome
> Where each pale guest stands fixt a living tomb. . . .[37]

The elegies of Katherine Philips, "the matchless Orinda," are, for the most part, a restrained commingling of the consolatory and the panegyric, as her position as a link between the School of Jonson and the Restoration poets would imply; but, in her *Reverie,* she emotionalizes and idealizes the Sabine farm of Horatian convention, and takes the first step toward converting it into the Romantic tower of ivory. Hers is the gentle Epicurean theme of Pomfret's *Choice*; but she treats it as if writing after, rather than a generation before, his time, and sentimentally refers to "a brook that sob'd aloud and ran away" and to the "Death, dust and darkness" that await us in the unrespective tomb.[38] Denham's verses on Cowley are not so much an elegy as a survey of English poetry with an extensive appreciation of Cowley; and Waller's heroic couplets *Upon the Death of Lady Rich* are in no sense a funeral elegy. It is significant, however, that during the Commonwealth period, he elegized *Upon the Death of the Lord Protector* in a somewhat forced emotional strain that seems to reflect his effort to adapt himself to another style:

> We must resign! Heaven his great soul does claim
> In storms, as loved as his immortal fame;
> His dying groans, his last breath shakes our isle,
> And trees uncut fall for his funeral pile. . . .[39]

In general the "sons of Ben" were too busy with living and too Classical in their literary models to give poetic utterance to the

[37] Richard Lovelace, *Poems,* ed. Wilkinson, Oxford, 1925, II, 79, *Elegie on the Death of Mrs. Cassandra Cotton.* A similar passage occurs in Shirley's elegy *Upon the Death of King James,* a description of the bed-chamber "Where the pale body of the king was laid."

[38] See *Caroline Poets,* ed. cit., I, 556. Her elegiac grief is quite decorous; she is given to moralizing; and, as in the lines on Mrs. Owen, she will occasionally turn her elegy into a panegyric *de senec-*
tute. Divine Meditations and Elegies by John Hagthorpe (1622) contains a poem *To Death* which has a slight mortuary note in its last stanza.

[39] This hyperbole has some basis in fact: there was a severe storm a few days before Cromwell's death; and the "dying groans" furnish at least one realistic death-bed touch. The poem as a whole, however, is given over to military eulogy.

terrors of death.   The Jonsonian elegy, indeed, seems to make every effort to look the thing it is not, smiles rather than weeps over its dead, and at the occasional risk of impropriety almost makes merry in the room they left.

The poems of John Donne, although but few of them were printed before the posthumous volume of 1633, were written, for the most part, early in his long life, and seem to have circulated widely in manuscript.[40]   Two themes, both characteristic of the adolescent Muse, particularly recur in his pages: love and death. By a characteristic irony, which one is tempted to attribute to the author's intention, his *Elegies*, but for a single mention of "pale and wan Death's terrors," are upon the former subject.   His funeral pieces are collectively entitled *Epicedes and Obsequies*, but some of the individual poems he calls "elegies."[41]   To this melancholy Dean, variety was the very spice of art; and the urge for the unusual displayed itself not only in the preciousness of his style but in the paradox of his themes; and to produce this piquancy of the unexpected, his poetry becomes a sort of chameleon's dish, an *olla* of attitudes toward his two favorite subjects.   Marini and other Continental poets, moreover, who cultivated in a hot-house profusion the melliferous but sterile felicities of the Latin elegy, set before him an example of metaphoric luxuriance that he did not ignore.[42]   In *The Dissolution*, he treats of death in the matter-of-fact strain of the philosophic realist:

> She's dead; and all which die
> To their first elements resolve. . . .

Then follows a sort of chemical consolation for the loss of the departed—the same general theme as Shakespeare's lines on "imperial Cæsar"—from which the poet professes to extract comfort![43]   Sometimes Donne's approach is through not natural but metaphysical philosophy.   There is something of this, commingled with much panegyric, in the *Elegy upon the Untimely Death of*

[40] See Donne, *Poems*, ed. E. K. Chambers, I, xviii *et seq.*

[41] Donne's poems are difficult to classify, for he seems to delight in hybrids and in breaking in sunder the bonds of poetic definition.

[42] See M. Praz, *Secentismo e Marinismo in Inghilterra—John Donne, Richard Crashaw*, Florence, 1925.

[43] In subject and idea, though not in title or plan, *The Dissolution* is a strange sort of funeral elegy, and so may be included here.

the Incomparable Prince Henry, a succession of asymmetrical heroic
couplets ornamented with figures in the poet's most "conceited"
style, and opening with the line: "Look to me, faith, and look to
my faith, God." There is a reference to the Prince's "putrifaction," but the poem as a whole is lacking in the mortuary.
Sometimes Donne's eulogizing is not of the mind but of the body,
as in his *Funeral Elegy on Mrs. Elizabeth Drury*, whom he com-
mits to posterity in the sonnet style of the 1590's. Sometimes, as
in *The Relic, The Damp, The Will, The Funeral*, death appears
as a good fellow, a new and lively acquaintance some day to be
encountered upon this *via dolorosa*; sometimes, as in the tenth of
his *Holy Sonnets*, death is swallowed up in victory. Like other
poets of the mournful Muse, Donne turned to the Old Testament;
and, in his translation of the Book of Lamentations, which, in
common with his age, he ascribed to the prophet "Jeremy," he has
some funeral touches, for the most part borrowed from the original. The poem that seems most nearly to approach the type of
the funeral elegy, would seem to be his *Obsequies of the Lord
Harrington;*[44] but, even here, eulogy of the departed and a consequent certainty of future Salvation form the dominant theme.
The poet imagines himself at Lord Harrington's grave, and writes
in a style that cannot but remind the reader of Gray's famous
stanzas:

> Thou seest me here at midnight; now all rest;
> Time's dead-low water; when all minds divest
> Tomorrow's business; when the laborers have
> Such rest in bed, that their last churchyard grave,
> Subject to change, will scarce be a type of this;
> Now, when the client, whose last hearing is
> Tomorrow, sleeps; when the condemned man
> Who when he opes his eyes must shut them then
> Again by death, although sad watch he keep,
> Doth practice dying by a little sleep. . . .

Donne's lapses into the funeral elegy are hardly more than occasional variations in his already eccentric orbit; to him and to his
poetic followers of the religious school of Laud, bodily decay was
insignificant as compared to the ecstatic liberation of the soul that

<hr>

[44] He died in 1614.

accompanied it.[45] The mortuary elements are doubtless owing in part to Donne's urge for novelty, and in part also to the fine Alexandrian artifice popularized at the time by the authors of Italy and Spain.

Of the poets that continued his tradition, the chief names are Herbert, Carew, Vaughan, Cleveland, King, and Cowley.[46] Herbert was an enthusiast in the original sense of that much-abused word; his soul was so utterly imbued with the Catholic tradition of the early seventeenth century English Church that his concept of the grave, like Donne's, is associated, not with bodily dissolution, but with the glory of the beatific vision; and such strange religious symbolism as *The Pulley* is clearly the effect of the pious allegorizing of the *Bible* that had gone on since the time of the Maccabees and that gave authority, *mutatis mutandis*, to a poetry of homely, sometimes perhaps incongruous, symbolism.[47] The Muse of Carew is more secular: his is not the flaming screed of the *vates* but the fine Italian hand of the *doctus poeta*. His *Obsequies to the Lady Anne Hay* and his epistle *To the Countess of Anglesey* on the death of her husband trick out the tears of the author in the bravest trappings of rhetoric; and his *Elegy upon the Death of Dr. Donne*, written perhaps as a subtle posthumous compliment, very much in the style that Donne himself affected, is indeed an odd poetic obituary, combining literary criticism with the refinements of "metaphysical" eulogy.[48] The several elegies of Crashaw furnish but little mortuary material. His translation of the *Dies Iræ*, although not strictly elegiac, could hardly omit some such details; but his elegy on Dr. Porter is a mere extension

---

[45] Perhaps because of the strictures of the Puritans, or perhaps because of religious optimism, Donne feels called upon to give special theological justification for mourning and lamentation, and cites the weeping of Jesus at the death of Lazarus (*Sermons, Selected Passages*, ed. L. P. Smith, Oxford, 1920, 205).

[46] Nethercot includes Quarles in this group (*Stud. in Phil.*, XXII, 81; and *Jour. of Eng. and Ger. Phil.*, XXIII, 173); but, in the present study, it is more convenient to treat him in a later chapter. The Rev. F. E. Hutchinson takes Quarles as belonging to the School of Spenser, and especially as a satellite

of Phineas Fletcher (*Camb. Hist. of Eng. Lit.*, New York, 1907-1916, VII, 53).

[47] The homely and the religious seemed more congruous to the Middle Ages and the early Renaissance than to us, who for the most part limit our religion to Sunday mornings. The religious painters of the time of Botticelli illustrate this by combining miracle and everyday events on the same canvas or fresco.

[48] The other elegies on Donne, written by Walton, Chudleigh, and others, and printed in his *Poems* of 1635, generally adopt a similar tone.

through forty-four lines of the pathetic fallacy; his *Elegy on Mr. Stanninow* is similar; his three poems *Upon the Death of Mr. Herrys* are given over to devout contemplation occasionally pointed by *outré* metaphors; and the three "elegies" of his *Alexias* combine religious edification with an occasional Classical allusion. He does, to be sure, elegize *Upon the Death of a Gentleman* somewhat in the tone of Hamlet's graveyard musings; but his usual attitude toward death is epitomized rather in a few exquisite lines from his *Epitaph upon a Young Married Couple*:

> Peace, good Reader, do not weep.
> Peace, the lovers are asleep! . . .
> Let them sleep: let them sleep on,
> Till this stormy night be gone,
> Till the eternal morrow dawn. . . .

Henry Vaughan, the Welshman, presents a field full of folk for the contemplation of the elegist. He was a Royalist, like most of the Welsh, but hardly a Cavalier; for he seems to have been attached neither to the Court like Suckling, nor in all probability to the army like Lovelace. Some early years in London, however, brought Classical influences to bear upon him; and, among his works, one finds the elegy *Daphnis* an amœbean pastoral. Even in the *Elegy on Mr. R. W.*, killed at Routon Heath in 1645, in which he breaks away from the Vergilian tradition, the lines seem restrained, almost cold, coming from the lips of a fiery bard of Wales. The author states his grief—rather than letting one infer it from his manner—compares the subject of his poem to a mighty tree blown to the ground, delivers a long eulogy with figures in the style of Donne, wonders what funeral "exequies" were performed over the body, and in the most Pagan spirit of the Renaissance, promises his subject immortality—in his own verses! Is this a fitting Christian funeral elegy? Of the same tenor is the poem *On the Death of Mr. R. Hall*; but here Vaughan, instead of promising a mere literary fame, more appropriately leaves him "to be read more high, more quaint, In thy own blood a soldier and a saint." Vaughan's unnamed elegies beginning "Thou know'st for Whom I mourn" and "Silence and stealth of days!" are quite in Donne's manner, ingenious casuistry glinting with the brightest colors of rhetoric. He most nearly approaches the funereal in the lines, composed not earlier than 1653, *To the Pious Memory of C[harles] W[albeoffe] Esquire.*[49] Whether this difference in tone is due to his conversion, about 1650, to the pietistic mysticism of Herbert,[50] or to matured poetic evolution, or to changing poetical fashions of the Commonwealth, is a matter difficult to determine:

> Now that the public sorrow doth subside,
> And those slight tears which custom springs are dried;
> While all the rich and outside mourners pass
> Home from thy dust, to empty their own glass,[51]
> I—who the throng affect not nor their state—
> Steal to thy grave undress'd[52] to meditate
> On our sad loss, accompanied by none,
> An obscure mourner that would weep alone.
> So when the world's great luminary sets,
> Some scarce known star into the zenith gets,
> Twinkels and curls, a weak but willing spark,
> As glow-worms here do glitter in the dark. . . .

And the poem continues with references to a "hermit's cell," "rich shrines and altars," "ascending incense," and "sad retirement." Then comes a long eulogy; and, toward the end, Death's "wrath" and "thick, black night" are overcome by Christ's redeeming power. Some of Vaughan's poems on more general religious subjects help to make up for the paucity of funereal details in his elegies. He evidently appreciates the beauty of "Dear Night," and seems almost to enjoy its "Horror";[53] but the horror of death, for him, is quite submerged in religious consolation.[54] His *Day of Judgment,* however, has three stanzas on the awfulness of eternal damnation, though very restrained in concrete details; and his *Relapse,* when his soul "slipt Almost to Hell," says of the devils merely that he "heard them howl." His *Charnel House* is perhaps best illustrated by its opening couplet:

> Bless me! what damps are here! how stiff the air!

[49] See Vaughan, *Poems,* ed. Chambers, II, 189 *et seq.*

[50] This conversion seems to have taken place on the occasion of a severe illness.

[51] Possibly a reference to a feast after the burial, as in Scotland, but more probably the line means that the mourners go home from the dust of "C. W." to empty the dust in the hour-glass of their own lives.

[52] I.e., not in formal street attire.

[53] E.g., *The Night,* and *The Lamp.*

[54] E.g., *Death a Dialogue, Resurrection and Immortality, Death, The Obsequies,* and the poem beginning "O day of Life, of light, of love!"

Kelder [cauldron] of mists, a second fiat's[55] care. . . .

It has been described, perhaps unjustly, as "morbid":[56] at all events, the similarity of the subject to Blair's *Grave* serves happily to illustrate the difference in treatment of the same theme in the two centuries. Vaughan's style is metaphysical, distended with learned tropes and periphrastic felicities; Blair revels in downright, gruesome realism. Vaughan's appeal is theological, and effective upon the intellect; Blair's titillates the emotions and assaults the nerves. Such are the *gradus ad libidinem sentiendi* that the present study designs to illuminate; and one is tempted to believe that Wordsworth, when he turned for inspiration to the poetry of Henry Vaughan, was merely illustrating literary atavism, and reverting to one of the originals of his own poetic school.

John Cleveland, whose wide popularity makes him an index of mid-century Cavalier taste,[57] presents, in his earlier poetry, despite much tropic extravagance, but little funereal matter. His *Elegy on Ben Jonson* is a free imitation of Jonson's own style; his *Elegy on Dr. Chad[d]erton*, written about 1640, suggests the facile charm of Prior; and the elegy on His Grace of York is, not quite justly, satiric, as appears in the brief appended epitaph:

> Here York's great Metropolitan is laid,
> Who God's Anointed, and His Church betrayed.

His lament on Edward King, with its "Muse's rosary" of "pious beads" that his eyes "weep down";[58] and his lines on the execution of Archbishop Laud, while trying to outdo the commonality of poet's grief, constitute an unintentional travesty of sorrow. Later in his *Elegy upon King Charles the First*, he introduces some realistic touches: the "bloody wood" of the block, and the "bloodless cheeks and bloodshot eyes" of the Cavalier mourners.[59] The cli-

---

[55] A reference to *Genesis*, i, 3, and doubtless also to Donne's *Storm*.

[56] The Rev. F. E. Hutchinson so describes it (*Camb. Hist. of Eng. Lit.*, VII, 44).

[57] *Caroline Poets, ed. cit.*, III, 4.

[58] With a fine, though unconscious, felicity, the poet remarks:

I am no poet here; my pen's the spout

Where the rain-water of mine eyes runs out. . . .

Cf. some of the hyperbolic expressions of grief on the part of Puritans in Old and New England later in the century.

[59] Cleveland never gave up the Royalist cause: witness his manly letter to Cromwell when some officious Roundheads imprisoned him at Yarmouth. He died in 1658, probably from jail-fever.

max of disasters to the Royalist cause during the 1640's seems to have obliged the poetic chronicler to adopt an ascending scale of lamentation, until all sense of Jonsonian poise and symmetry was lost. Bishop Henry King, also an unflinching follower of the unhappy Charles, shows likewise a tendency to vary his manner between the styles of Jonson and of Donne.[60] In general, he represents the "*via media* of metaphysicality";[61] but, in a few of his later pieces, one notices at least some tendency, as in Cleveland, to linger over the lamentable. His elegy on Gustavus Adolphus, written presumably shortly after the death of the Swedish king in 1632, starts with a concrete, if somewhat hyperbolic realism:

> Like a cold fatal sweat which ushers death,
> My thoughts hang on me, and my lab'ring breath
> Stopp'd up with sighs, my fancy, big with woes,
> Feels two twinn'd mountains struggle in her throes. . . .

The lines on the beheading of Charles I—if they be really his—illustrate this tendency even more fully; and the *Elegy on Lady Stanhope* opens with a lightly drawn, but none the less effective description of her "exequies," as the seventeenth century termed the procession after the funeral to the grave. The elegies of both these poets, staunch and unconciliatory Royalists, seem, during the Puritan period, to depend most directly upon the influence of Donne, and, perhaps on this account, to approximate, more closely than before, to the funereal type as defined in the present study. This increasing realism may have sprung in part from a Puritan literary impulse unconsciously absorbed; but it seems safer to assume that the style of these Royalist poets about 1640 was deepened and diverted toward melancholy themes and toward the great seventeenth century master of disillusionment, by the disillusion and bitterness of an age when horror on horror's head seemed to accumulate.[62]

[60] In his *Elegy to Donne* (line 46), he calls himself a follower of Donne's Muse; but perhaps he exaggerated for purposes of posthumous compliment.

[61] *Caroline Poets, ed. cit.*, III, 164.

[62] One seeming difficulty with this theory is the publication, during this period, by such Royalist poets as Sir Francis Wortley (*Characters and Elegies*, London, 1646), William Strode (1600-1645, *ed. princ.* of his poems, 1907), and Robert Heath (*Clarestella*, London, 1650), of "divers Elegies" and "Elegiack tears" that are not mortuary in tone. Most of these poems, however, were doubtless written earlier; and the light tone of the elegies on William Lawes, which were certainly composed during the 1640's,

The elegiac work of Abraham Cowley falls into three significant chronological groups, the first ending in 1656 when he returned to England from abroad, made his peace with the Commonwealth, and for the nonce took on the outward semblance of a convinced, or at least a resigned, Puritan. The second period naturally closed with the *astræa redux* of Charles II in 1660. Cowley, therefore, illustrates the evolution of poetry, and especially of funeral poetry, during the resign of Charles I, the Commonwealth, and the reign of Charles II,[63] and in the person of a single poet shows the effect on literature of the alternate predominance of two conflicting social strata. The elegiac product of the early period consists chiefly of high encomium heralded with all the circumstance of metaphysical device. The lines *On the Death of Mr. Jordan, Second Master of Westminster School,* are indeed so finely inept that they had pleased us more, had they but pleased us less. The elegy on Crashaw is a much superior performance, with some Christian and some Classical allusion, but nothing strictly mortuary. During this period, Cowley, like others of the School of Donne, was too much concerned with the immortality of the spirit to let his mind linger upon the decay of the flesh. His second, or pseudo-Puritan, manner shows a change that is reflected in the apologetic preface to the volume of 1656: the poet implies that his earlier labors are but vanity of vanities; and he refers, perhaps a bit unctuously, to the "Clouds of Melancholy and Sorrow" that are upon him. How far this is the mere affectation of the Puritan demeanor, and how far it is repentance, real or assumed, for his Royalist errors, one cannot easily determine: perhaps he found it conveniently consonant to both regards. In 1657, upon the death of the famous anatomist, William Hervey, Cowley committed to writing a lament, quite of a different sort. The first stanza will suffice:

It was a dismal and a fearful night.

can perhaps be explained by the fact that they were written to be set to music (*Choice Psalmes . . . With divers Elegies,* London, 1648).

[63] The exact dating of many of Cowley's poems seems impossible; but the elegies on Wotton (c1639), Van Dyke (c1641) and Crashaw (c1649) are at least approximately dated by the deaths that occasioned them; and those on Jordan and Anacreon also appeared in the volume of 1656, and so must have been written before that date. This *Miscellanie,* as the *Preface* announces, was for the most part written when Cowley was "very, very young." The apologetic tone of this *Preface* was perhaps occasioned by fear of Puritan opposition.

Scarce could the Morn drive on th' unknowing Light,
When Sleep, *Deaths Image*, left my troubled brest,
  By something *liker Death* possesst.
My eyes with tears did uncommanded flow,
  And on my soul hung the dull weight
  Of some *Intolerable Fate*.
What Bell was that?   Ah me!   Too much I know.[64]

The poet—or perhaps only the printer—fearful that the reader
might miss the most affecting touches, lends them the emphasis of
italics.   Later, we have *"Death's Agonie"*; and, in the midst of
the eulogy of Hervey's intellectual qualities, appear scattered fune-
brious details such as the reference to the darkness of the grave in
the sixth stanza, and the cypress tree "which Tombs does beautify."
There are some Classical touches, such as the reference to the
"Ledæan Stars," and an occasional lapse into the pathetic fallacy;
but the poem as a whole is of a very different tenor from Cowley's
earlier elegies.   Is the historian justified in the inference that it
represents Cowley's poetic conversion to Puritanism, and that he
adopted this mortuary tone to accord with his new political principles?   At all events, the elegies of the third period, after the
Restoration, are more nearly a return to his first manner than a
continuation of his second.   At one time, he seems to have been
disgusted with the entire *genre*:

  Tis folly all that can be said
    By living Mortals of th' immortal dead,
  And I'm afraid they laugh at the vain tears we shed.[65]

The poem continues in cynical vein, and suggests that it seems
"ridiculous to grieve."   Perhaps because of the advent of happier
times, the religious note, even that of the first period, is largely
given over; and his two elegies on the Earl of Balcares and on
Mrs. Katherine Philips consist chiefly of eulogy.   The latter has
one mortuary touch in which "prophane Disease" is compared to
a "wild Zealot"—a glance at Cowley's former Puritan friends

---

[64] *Ode on the Death of William Her-vey.*   E. Rhys (*Lyric Poetry*, London, 1913, 236) says that 'Gray's *Elegy* "would never have been written" but for this poem.   He could hardly have realized the quantity of such material during the intervening century.

[65] Cowley, *Poems*, ed. Waller, Cambridge, 1905, 413.   Cowley's verses are echoed in a broadside on the "eminent" non-conformist divines Pledger and Wells (1676).   See the Luttrell Collection in the British Museum, I, No. 118.

that suggests that he associated them with the funereal in poetry. Two non-elegiac pieces, moreover, of this period deserve mention: the *Resurrection* for its gruesome reference to *"tortur'd Men, Their Joynts* new *set*, to be new *rackt* agen"; and *The Complaint*, in which he describes himself, rather complacently, as "The Melancholy Cowley"—melancholy, it would appear, chiefly because the largesse of Charles II was less abundant than might be desired: thus *The Complaint* may be taken as addressed chiefly to his purse; and it expressed with a refreshing disingenuousness the motive that actuated most of his fellow-elegists. It cannot, however, be omitted from the present survey; for, as late as 1772, Richard Hurd praised it for possessing "sensible [Sentimental] reflecting melancholy,"[66] which he found presumably in the rather conventional elegiac description with which the poem begins:

> In a deep vision's intellectual scene,
>   Beneath a Bow'r for sorrow made,
>   Th' uncomfortable shade,
>   Of the black Yew's unlucky green,
> Mixt with the mourning Willow's careful [sorrowful] gray,
>   The Melancholy *Cowley* lay.

"Great Cowley" then, in most of his elegiac writing, was indeed "O'er-run with wit," but can hardly be described, in the words of the youthful Addison, as "lavish of his thought," or of concrete descriptive details. The single elegy of the short second period is his one truly mortuary piece; and otherwise, aside from an occasional phrase or line, his work is clearly in the Classical traditions of the Renaissance.

A group of minor poets, more or less under the ægis of Donne's exalted name, display, during the two mid-century decades, the same tendency toward the funereal already pointed out in Waller, King, Cleveland, and Cowley. Lord Herbert of Cherbury, celebrating the virtues of "Dr. Dunn,"[67] hesitated to use "Those common words, which men may even rake From Dung-hil wits," and which he finds "so defil'd, Slubber'd and false, as if they had

---

[66] Cowley, *Poems,* ed. Hurd, London, 1777, II, 111n. For the reference to the "mourning Willow," see Appendix A. The immediate popularity of the poem is attested by its imitation by John Cave in *Daphnis, A Pastoral on the Death of Mr. Francis Wollaston*, Oxford, 1685. A copy is to be found in the Bodleian Library (Wood Coll. No. 429).

[67] Lord Herbert of Cherbury, *Works*, ed. G. C. Moore Smith, Oxford, 1923, 59.

exil'd Truth and propriety. . . . " Even in the early 1630's, apparently, the more fastidious felt that the multiplicity of elegies had so spoiled the vocabulary of grief that tropic extremes were inevitable; and the psychological law of limen forced the seeker of fresh, and supposedly authentic, expressions of grief further and further afield to the periphery of elegiac metaphor. Lord Herbert's *Elegy over a Tomb* contains several stanzas of meteorological pathetic fallacy that were perhaps intended to console the relics of the departed; but it is scarcely a funeral elegy. "J. T., Mr. of Arts" gave a vivid description of the plague in *Worcester's Elegie;*[68] Edward Browne in his elegies on the Royalist Lord Mayor Campbell (1642) and on Alderman Abdie (1640)[69] compared death to a Sergeant, a figure borrowed probably from *Hamlet*[70] and destined to become a staple of elegiac fancy for a hundred years; and an anonymous *Elegie* on Sir Arthur Chichester,[71] though mainly panegyric biography, falls toward the end into the mortuary attitudinizing of the decade:

> Yea, the whole Realme will make a dolefull cry,
> To make an Earthquake for his *Elegie.*
> The swift wind shall be reasty, as afraid
> To waft the noise, lest all the land be made
> Subject to ruine, in astonishment.

Robert Baron of Gray's Inn, nephew to the Royalist "epistolizer" James Howell, published in 1648 his Εροτοπαιγνιον *or the Cyprian Academy.* It contains an *Elegie,* in part reminiscent of *L'Allegro,*[72] in part of Donne, especially in such details as "Rapacious *Skeleton*" and "Monster fell." The appended *Epitaph* needs no comment, in which the reader is adjured to wish himself "a worme to tast so *choyce a dish.*" Edward Benlowes, the Cavalier religious poet, who in 1652 published his *Theophila,* is led by the metaphysical style into an occasional gruesome image, such as the following purple passage from *The Vanity of this World:*[73]

---

[68] J. T., *Worcester's Elegie*, London, 1638.

[69] Edward Browne, *A rare Paterne of Justice and Mercy*, London, 1642.

[70] Hamlet, V, ii, 347-348: ". . . .this fell sergeant, death, Is strict in his arrest. . . ."

[71] *An Elegie on the Much Lamented Death of Sir Arthur Chichester Knight* [?London] 1643. A copy is to be found in the Thomason Collection in the British Museum.

[72] R. D. Havens, *Influence of Milton,* Cambridge, Mass., 1922, 427-428, etc.

[73] *Caroline Poets, ed. cit.,* I, 424.

Laz'rus, thy skin's Death's sheet, 'twixt that and bone
There's no parenthesis!

Dr. Joseph Beaumont, also a Royalist,[74] composed a poetic version
of *Davids Elegie upon Jonathan,* and in his poem on *Death* has an
occasional mortuary reference to "oughly Bones" and "shameless
Wormes."[75]   Alexander Brome,[76] whose vein is usually light and
somewhat Classical,[77] now and then, as in his *Elegy on a Lady,*
imitates the manner of Donne, and speaks of the "swoln eyes" of
the mourners, and felicitously congratulates the "happy *worms*"
to whose lot the lady will shortly fall.   Payne Fisher, perhaps the
most redoubtable Latinist of the age, brought out in 1665 a number of poems, largely Royalist in sentiment, composed for the most
part in the 1640's, and among others an *Elegie upon Edward late
Earl of Dorset* (1651).   It is chiefly made up of eulogy in the
style of Donne; but the couplet that immediately precedes the final
epitaph is unmistakably funereal in its realistic imagery:

> Thus have I blubber'd out some tears and Verse
> On this Renouned Heroe and his Herse.

During the 1650's Fisher had lapsed, as Waller and many another
did, into a period of occasional Puritan conformity, and composed,
first in Latin, later to be translated into English (1659), his
Threnodia Triumphalis: a Triumphal Funeral Ode on Oliver
Cromwell.   The pages are outlined in a wide black border; but
the poem, perhaps because of its Renaissance Latin beginnings, is
a panegyric rather than a funeral elegy, and phrases the sorrows
of the poet—perhaps because they were not, after all, very distress-
ing—in the comparatively mild terms of "Vexations" and "angry
Wounds."   The minor poets, indeed, who usually constitute a
surer index of tendencies than their more exalted, and more individual, literary brethren, would seem to indicate that, during the

---

[74] Beaumont attended Peterhouse, Cambridge, with Crashaw. He seems to have
written most of his minor poems about
1650.

[75] *The Minor Poems of Joseph Beaumont D.D.,* ed. Robinson, Boston, 1914,
8-9.

[76] His Cavalier proclivities seem rather

clearly shown by his *Royalist* (1646)
and his *Funeral Elegy* (*Poems,* London,
1668, 249).

[77] See his elegies *To his Friend Mr.
W. H. upon the death of his Hawk,* and
*Upon the Death of the Reverend and
learned Divine Mr. Josias Shute* (*Poems,
ed. cit.,* 202 and 251).

1640's, the School of Donne had a wide following,[78] and grew
in elegiac intensity, in part perhaps because of the storm and stress
of the times, in part because of the natural drift of any movement
toward a decadence of extremes, and in part because of the melancholy cast of mind that could not but influence the intellectual and
emotional life of the England over which the Puritans ruled.

The foregoing survey of the three lyric schools that flourished
during the Jacobean and Caroline periods suggests several conclusions. Of the pieces called elegies, many are Classical love-poems;
and, even in those that were occasioned by death, this occasion is
commonly passed over, so that the writer may laud and magnify
the subject's good deeds or indulge in casuistical discussion of
immortality and like theological matter: realistic, funeral descriptions are brief and rare. About a score of elegies contain mortuary passages, most of them very short; and these may be looked
upon as forerunners of the *genre*. Perhaps the first in time, and
one of the most dubious as an example, is William Browne's elegy
on Prince Henry (d. 1612). It is the nearest approach of the
School of Spenser to the mortuary form; and its one mortuary
touch, the "Labyrinth of Woe," is a highly metaphoric description
of the mourners' desolation. The Schools of Jonson and of Donne,
which reached their prime later in the century, have more to offer.
Donne's *Obsequies on the Lord Harrington* (1614), in which the
author imagines himself beside the grave "at night," furnishes a
nearer approximation. Herbert's elegy *Upon the Death of a Gentleman* is too largely composed of the wise saws and pious truisms
of morality and too little of concrete description. A better example is Jonson's poem *On the Death of Lady Jane Pawlet* (1631)
with its ghost, its yew-tree, and its forced, exclamatory style. Other
mortuary landscapes appear in Vaughan's elegy to "C. W. Esq."
(1653) and especially in Cowley's poem on the death of Hervey
(1657), with its tombs and cypress trees and its background of
"a dismal and fearful night." The elegies by Cleveland and by
Bishop King on the beheading of Charles I are not without san-

---

[78] Cf. A. H. Nethercot, *Jour. of Eng.
and Ger. Phil.*, XXIII, 174 *et seq*. It
seems curious that Donne's poetry was
not more dwelt upon by his biographers
and by critics of the time; for his style
was widely imitated. See also G. Williamson (*The Nature of the Donne Tradition, St. in Phil.*, XXV, 418 *et seq*.)
who, strange to say, seems quite ignorant
of the previous work of Nethercot on
the subject.

guine realistic details; and such minor contemporary poets as Baron, Benlowes, Beaumont, and Brome supply vivid images of death and "shameless Worms." Finally the "dying groans" of Waller's verses on the death of Cromwell, give a hint of the death-bed scene, an apt setting for the apparatus of horror. It is to be noted that the School of Spenser, which died out earliest in the century, supplied but one dubious example; that Jonson is but once or twice betrayed into such detail by his inclination toward the realtistic, occasional touch; and that the School of Donne, which furnishes most of the examples, seems at first to stumble on the type by mere fortuity in the search for something new, and to give it freer use only after their style had passed the zenith of its excellence and the Civil War was lending an even more sombre color to their thoughts. Indeed, the three best examples, from all the elegies so far noted, would seem to be those by Vaughan, Cowley, and Waller, all composed in the 1650's, and, in the case of the two latter at least, composed when the authors had, nominally, if not inwardly, become Commonwealthmen, and were presumably celebrating in an appropriate manner subjects appropriate to their new political connections. Most significantly, in his *Elegy on L. K. C.*, who died in 1657, Bishop King notes the variety of elegiac styles used for different sorts or classes of persons, and declares that he will not "Pay diff'rent rites at ev'ry funeral."[79] Is this a Royalist thrust at the elegiac fashions of the Puritans and their tendency to celebrate pious persons of minor distinction; or is it more particularly aimed at Waller and other amenable Royalists, who had made their peace with the Commonwealth and had accordingly varied their poetic styles?

While the Renaissance elegiac type, derived mainly from the Classics, was formulating itself during the sixteenth century, the Christian tradition, descended through the Middle Ages, continued to run a slender course, chiefly in the humbler orders of society that knew little of courtly literary fashions. During the reign of Elizabeth, the poorest classes, who comprised the bulk of the population, being quite unable to read or write, contented themselves perforce with oral literature, traditional folk-poetry sung in the country lanes and in the London streets, and with the spoken and

[79] *Caroline Poets, ed. cit.*, II, 244.   to the station in life of the subject. King himself seems to adapt his elegies

acted drama. The bourgeoisie, who seem to have been the lowest literate class, read their Bibles and religious books to save their souls, almanacs and professional treatises for practical purposes, and for pleasure broadside ballads concocted by William Elderton and his Grub Street fellows and peddled at fairs and public gatherings by such rascals as Shakespeare's Autolycus. To a certain extent all classes shared in the drama and the broadsides—at least all classes that attended markets and fairs, and so saw the plays acted and heard the broadsides sung; and these literary forms, therefore, reflect a general rather than a class point of view, at all events until the increasing Puritanism of the bourgeoisie during the seventeenth century withdrew them somewhat from even these simple pleasures.

The broadside ballads sometimes took their subject-matter from universal themes, but more often, in minute and lurid detail, purveyed the sensation of the hour[80] with all the smug gusto and Sentimental complacence of modern yellow journalism. Their crude wood-cuts and the glaring capitals of their headlines were designed to startle the on-looker into immediate purchase; for broadsides are the ephemera of the poetic genus, and must live their day at once or not at all. The same wood-cut might serve a thrifty bookseller for a whole series of such pieces; and its crudity was occasionally enhanced by slicing off some part that did not chance to be applicable to the case in hand:[81] indeed, a cursory comparison of the broadsides in the Pepysian, Bagford, and Roxburghe Collections shows that an alluring cut might last a whole generation.[82]

[80] E.g., *Tichborn's Elegie, Written with his own hand in the Tower, before his Execution* (1586). Such pieces were presumably concocted by hack writers for sale at the execution.

[81] Cf. the picture at the top of *Fair Phillida* (*Roxburghe Ballads*, ed. Chappell, *Ball. Soc. Publ.*, London, 1871, II, 345) with the Roxburghe pieces II, 210, and II, 644. This last was entered in the *Stationers Register*, Mar. 1, 1675. The iconography of the elegy seems to have had a wide influence: e.g., the arabesque border on the broadside of church-rates of St. Giles Cripplegate (1644) (Guildhall Library, XII, No. 79) and the picture of the skeleton etc., on the affidavit of burial in woolen (1734) (Guildhall Library VIII, No. 24). Cf. the broadside on L'Estrange reproduced in the present volume.

[82] Even the reader who has not access to the originals and must depend on reprints can notice this by comparing the illustrations in the *Shirburn Ballads* (ed. A. Clark, Oxford, 1907), the *Roxburghe Ballads* (ed. Chappell), and the *Bagford Ballads* (ed. J. W. Ebsworth, *Ball. Soc. Publ.*, Hertford, 1878). Cf. *Bagford*, II, 533, *et passim* and *Roxburghe*, II, 345. See also *ibid.*, II, cxcviii. Mortuary borders often came in sections, which were apparently loaned by one printer to another: e.g., the *Elegy* on King William, published by E. Hawkins, has at the top a picture of Fortune riding on

From this lurid iconography of the Elizabethan broadside developed the mortuary pictures of the broadside elegy. Black margins came later: at first, the margin, if any, was likely to be an arabesque, like that on the Lutterell broadside reproduced in the present volume; but, in time, perhaps under the influence of the numerous collected volumes of elegies in the early sixteenth century, such customary suits of solid black were more and more to be seen. Of the elegiac cuts, some are realistic, like the pictures of General Deane's hearse and of Queen Mary's funeral procession, reproduced in the present volume; some are symbolic like the mortuary head-pieces and margins of the broadsides on Captain Bedloe and Sir George McKenzie; and both types came down into the graveyard poetry of the eighteenth century: the one in the first edition of the second part of Young's *Night Thoughts*; the other in the title-page of the first edition of Gray's *Elegy*. This broadside arrangement of a picture with explanatory verse suggests a relationship with the emblem-book, which rose and flourished, beginning in the sixteenth century with Alciati; and at least one broadside entitled *An Embleme of the Times* (1647)[83] points clearly to such a connection; but perhaps this is merely an outward embodiment of the later influence of Quarles.

The astonishing fecundity of the type and its leaning toward the lurid naturally occasioned the composition of many pieces concerning death; but most of these are either mere eulogies of the mighty or "hymning Tyburn's elegiac lines," compact of moralizing and melodrama, in celebration of some recent popular execution. In the Elizabethan and Jacobean periods, however, there are a few "lamentable complaints" that could be termed forerunners of the funeral elegy. The Roxburghe collection in the British Museum contains *A Lamentable Ditty* and *A lamentable new Ballad* on the execution of the Earl of Essex, pieces that are half elegy, half news-item; and there is a self-elegy by "Thomas

a shell, Death, two duellists, etc. The same picture was used, ironically enough, for an elegy on James II, published by Robert Williams. The side-panels of the elegy on King William were taken from an *Elegy* on the Rev. Matthew Mead "Printed and Sold by J. Bradford in Little Britain, over against the Pump, 1699." Apparently Bradford rejoiced in the ownership of these cuts; for in 1707 he used them again for an *Elegy on Sir Cloudesly Shovel*. These broadsides are to be found in the British Museum. Some of them are reproduced in *A Century of Broadside Elegies*, ed. the present author, London, 1928.

[83] It is arranged in imitation of a page in an emblem-book. A copy is to be

Byll, Parish Clerke of West-Felton," that was probably supplied him by some Grub Street hack.[84] *The Stationers Register* lists in 1570 "an lamentable complaynte of a gent for the Death of his moste ffaithful mistres"; and, somewhat later, "A lamentacon for the deathe of master Christofer Watsonne mynister" (1581), and others of the sort.[85] Most of these pieces are funeral elegies only secondarily and by chance; and those that are not merely moral or journalistic are for the most part mere eulogies: *An Epitaph on the death of the Ladie Maioresse* (1570)[86] is a lengthy screed of vaguely Classical Alexandrine couplets; John Phillip did a doggerel eulogy on the Earl of Southampton (1581) with "waileful weedes of woe;"[87] there is *A mournful Dittie on the death of certain Judges*,[88] a collective necrology with a few stanzas devoted to each of the deceased; there is *The Poore People's Complaint* (1585) on the death of the Earl of Bedford,[89] which loaned its tune and style to *The Crie of the Poore* (1596)[90] on the Earl of Huntington; and finally there is a vigorous ballad on the death of Queen Elizabeth.[91] On the whole, however, elegies were the exception rather than the rule in Elizabethan balladry; and Pepys, who seems to have collected omnivorously from the period, has but two or three such ballads and those of a later date.[92]

For the most part, the extant elegiac broadsides of this period survive in the Library of the Society of Antiquaries of London. An *Epitaph* on Edward VI combines a wistful sweetness with mortuary detail that seems at once Puritan and Mediæval:

---

found in the Luttrell Collection in the British Museum, II, No. 68.

[84] Roxburghe Collection, I, Nos. 184, 185, and 136. Cf. the self-elegies of a later date by Puritan divines. Also a hybrid, though composed of different elements, is *Bloody News from Chelmsford* (Lutt. Coll., II, No. 145).

[85] H. E. Rollins, *Analytical Index, Stud. in Phil.*, XXI (Jan., 1924), 121 and 124-125. Rollins also lists "the lamentacon of a gentlewoman upon the Death of hir late Deceased frende William Gryffith gent" (1577); "the Deathe of Sir Roger Williams" (1595); "A lamentacon of a yonge man for the deathe of his mother" (1612); "A Elegie uppon the Death of our sovraigne lord King James &c." (1625); and an "Elegy upon the death of the right hon-

orable Ralph Ffreeman late Lord Mayor of the Citty of London" (1634). See also H. E. Rollins, *Cavalier and Puritan*, New York, 1923, *Introduction*.

[86] *A Collection of Seventy-Nine Black-Letter Ballads and Broadsides, Printed in the Reign of Elizabeth*, London, 1867, 178.

[87] *Ibid.*, 260.

[88] *Ibid.*, 197.

[89] *Shirburn Ballads*, ed. cit., No. LXII.

[90] *Seventy-nine Broadsides*, ed. cit., 228.

[91] *Ballads from Manuscripts*, ed. Morfill, *Ball. Soc. Publ.*, Hertford, 1873, II, 98-99.

[92] Pepysian Library, Collection of Ballads, *A very godly Song* (I, 50); *Death Triumphant* (II, 3); and *The Lamenting Ladies Last Farewell to the World* (II, 38).

> And now that sweet flower
> Hath builded his bower
> In the earth the more is the pitie.
> In whose losse and lacke,
> Is to England a wracke,
> All faithful hartes may morne:
> To se that swete childe,
> So meke and so milde
> So soone subdued to wormes. . . .
>   That swete child is dead,
> And lapped in leade
> And in Westminster lyeth full colde
> All hartes may rewe
> That ever they him knew
> Or that that swete childe did behold. . . .

There is a gnomic broadside in the tone of the morality plays, beginning "Remember Man both night and day, thou must nedes die, there is no nay"; a eulogistic *Epitaphe* on Queen Mary; a *Doleful Ditty* on Lord Darnley, "sometime King of Scots"; a panegyrical biography of the Earl of Arundel (1580); and a no less panegyrical *Epitaph* upon Master Benedict Spinola, a Genoese merchant (1580). The last mentioned of these pieces contains a mortuary cut that seems to be the first example of its kind; and indeed, cuts did not become usual until the middle of the following century. There are Latin elegies on Mary Queen of Scots and on the Earl of Leicester, and a curious sort of prose elegy on Queen Elizabeth; but one feels that the form is sporadic rather than general; and, in all these pieces, mortuary detail is very rare. After the accession of James I, there are broadsides on the death of Sir Edward Stanhope, on Sir Thomas Overbury, and on Hugh Atwell, "servant to Prince Charles," and several pieces on the Duke of Richmond (1624), gotten up with mortuary pictures and black margins; but eulogy gives place to ominous detail in two pieces that are definitely concerned with the bourgeoisie. The *Dismall Day* (1623) by Matthew Rhodes elegizes several score of Londoners who were killed at prayers by the collapse of the building. It starts with a cosmic touch, the "vast chaos of dis-tempre'd [*sic*] Mindes"; it looks on the event as a judgment of "All-powerful God," and describes how the dead and maimed:

> on the ground all bruiz'd and smothered lay
> Some stifled up with Lome, Stones, Dust, and Clay:

And some for helpe and succour loudly calling,
All broken, bruized, and mangled in their falling.

"Tyrant death" appears; and the poet lingers over the improving
scene. Petrowe's *Elegiacall Monument* to John Banks "Citizen
and Mercer of London" (1630), although not exactly mortuary,
is not without something of "direful Mourning." The more aristocratic pieces are generally mere eulogy, such as the elegy on
James I; but the death of the king's grandson in 1629 was celebrated with "words whose force may bend Relentlesse hearts, and
flinty bowels pearse." The fashion for mortuary detail seems to
have been growing in the broadside, as well as in legitimate poetry;
but the style was not fully developed until about the middle of
the century when the Puritans took over the elegiac *genre*.

How far these early broadside elegies are imitations of aristocratic prototypes, how far they are Mediæval survivals, and how
far they are purely independent developments of the Elizabethan
middle and lower classes, is a problem beyond the scope of the
present study; but their Mediæval basis, which *a priori* one would
infer from the general cultural tone of the Elizabethan Commons,
is amply attested in such a one as *Death's Dance*,[93] with gyrating
skeletons in the crude wood-cut and in the doggerel letter-press,
both obviously inspired by the *danse macabre*; and elsewhere the
influence of the *Mirror for Magistrates* points in the same direction.[94]

In despite of Puritanism, broadsides continued to have some
appeal for the middle classes, as is clearly evident in the lines on
the death of Ralph Freeman, Lord Mayor of London, and in the
Elegy on George Watson draper,[95] who is extolled for his learning in the tongues. Their affinity even to the Puritan movement,
moreover, appears in the eulogistic *Verses Made in Memorial of
a learned, painful and pious Minister of this Citty of York, Mr.
Matthew Stainton*.[96] The subject, a clergyman of the Established

[93] *A Book of Roxburghe Ballads*, ed.
Collier, London, 1847, I, 283. See also
Roxburghe Ballads, ed. Chappell, III,
184 *et seq.*, 620, and IV, 75; *Shirburn
Ballads*, ed. *cit.*, No. XVI; *Seventy-Nine
Black-Letter Ballads*, London, 1867, 261;
Pepysian Collection, I, 57; and Luttrell
Collection, I, 174.
[94] *Poems and Songs Relating to George*

Villiers, Duke of Buckingham, ed. cit.,
36, *Upon the Duke*. On the wide influence for Mediævalism of the *Mirror*, see
J. W. Cunliffe, *Camb. Hist. of Eng. Lit.*,
III, 223 *et seq.*
[95] *The Yorkshire Anthology*, ed. Halliwell, London, 1851, 125.
[96] *Ibid.*, 394.

Church,[97] died in 1635; and, as a sharp attack on the Arminian theology of Laud attests, both the author and presumably the "painful and pious Minister" whom the piece celebrates were Calvinists and Puritans. A further sign of such influence appears in *The Great Assize* "By Mr. Stevens, Minister" written on the subject of Judgment Day "in true cobler-puritan style."[98] The pious wood-cuts and mortuary margins, moreover, that occasionally adorn the early elegies and that later become a regular characteristic, suggest Puritan affinities. Curiously enough, however, although Puritanism was usual among the middle classes, and although the broadside was largely read by the middle classes, the broadside, because of the religious scruples of Calvinism, is not generally Puritan, and indeed the singing, if not the printing, of such verses subsided[99] in the mid-century under Puritan persecution. The problem of Puritanism and the broadside elegy may be left for a later chapter; suffice it to say that a few definitely Puritan broadsides were printed during the reigns of Elizabeth and of James.

During the reign of Charles I, the number of broadside elegies hardly increases: the funeral elegy was still the prerogative of the nobility; and the nobility scorned broadsides, and could hardly be expected to requite the balladist with patronage. Elegies, therefore, were either printed in book form as small pamphlets, or printed in collections, like that on Edward King, or not printed at all, but preserved in manuscript among the family papers, like several such pieces in the Rodney and the Egerton manuscripts in the British Museum;[100] but these last are consolatory rather than

[97] At this period of course all except the most extreme Puritans were still within the fold of the Establishment.

[98] *Roxburghe Ballads*, ed. Chappell, I, 394. Some of the pieces that follow may also be Puritan.

[99] Broadside ballads dominated the *Stationers Register* from 1557 to 1640, and are said to have died out during the two following decades (J. W. Ebsworth, *The Bagford Ballads*, Ball. Soc. Publ., Hertford, 1878, *Introduction*). Even the sung broadside, however, was by no means dead in the Restoration period as a number of examples in the British Museum attest (e.g., Lutt. Coll., III, No. 101 *et seq.* on the Popish Plot). There was, however, something of a decline—a decline that was partly due to Cromwell's stringent laws against ballad-singing, partly to the increasing literacy that made prose pamphlets, and somewhat later mercuries and periodical essays, take over the broadside's former functions of entertainment, information, and propaganda. Rollins notes that, during the Commonwealth, the broadside grew less lyrical and more political and journalistic, and its subject-matter more occasional and prosaic. With the development of a simpler prose, such material would no longer be written in verse. (H. E. Rollins, *Cavalier and Puritan, Introduction*.)

[100] Rodney MSS. Add. MSS. 34239, 20, *A Funerall Elegie upon Mrs. Frances Rodney* (d. 1637) by Thomas Hull; one

grievous, and contribute little to the present study. John Taylor, who, though of low degree, received some courtly recognition, penned during the 1620's and '30's a number of elegies, at least some of which were certainly circulated in broadside. His *Muses Mourning: or Funerall Sonnets on the Death of John Moray Esquire*[101] is enhanced by a fine black title-page, but turns out upon examination to be genealogical in theme, Classical in manner, and consolatory in tone. The *Elegy*[102] on the Bishop of Winchester (1626) is a mere versified pious biography with a subjoined panegyric, but it does contain passages on "convulsions, sighs, and sickly groanes" and on "The bells sad toling, and the mourning weede." The broadside elegy on Richard Wyan (1638) is not at all mortuary.[103]

The disapproval of the Puritans for "lewd ballets" more and more obliged the broadside-writers to seek what protection they could get from the opposite party; and this protection, they amply repaid in the person of Martin Parker and his fellows, who during the Civil War spread Cavalier opinions and kept alive the monarchical idea among the Commons. Indeed, the heyday of the Cavalier broadside elegy was during the 1640's when the occasion of death only too often gave them politic opportunities of lamentation. The Earl of Strafford (1641) was well supplied with elegies;[104] and there are at least two "pen'd by his own hand," one moderate and dignified and doubtless of Royalist authorship, and an answering one in crude doggerel in which he is made to repent of his Cavalier principles.[105] *The Apprentices Lamentation* for Sir Richard Wiseman (1642)[106] goes to some length in defending elegiac lamentation, probably in an effort to convict of

by Henry Allen; and *Verses made by Sr Edward Rodney on the deathe [of his] daughter Mrs. Frances Rodney.* See also Egerton MSS. 2877, leaf 106, *Verses in memory of Sr George Frevile Kt, made by his Nephew Tho: Frevile, upon y*[e] *alphabet of his name.* See also Bodleian Lib., Ashmole Coll., 38, No. 162, *Elegie on the Honorable Thomas Coventry, Lord Keeper of the great Seale of England* (d. 1640). The piece is very lachrymose but hardly mortuary. See also Nos. 249 *et seq.* and 387 *et passim.*

[101] John Taylor, *The Muses Mourning,* [London, ?1620].

[102] *All the Works of John Taylor, the Water-Poet,* London, 1630, 323 *et seq.*

[103] John Taylor, *Works, Publ. Spenser Soc.,* 1876. A copy of the original broadside is to be found in Bodleian, Wood. Coll., 429.

[104] See Lutt. Coll., II, Nos. 210, 211, 212. Thomas Herbert did an *Elegie,* listed with a note by Rollins (*Analytical Index,* No. 578).

[105] *The Earle of Strafford his Elegiac Poem as it Was pen'd by his owne hand,* and *Verses Lately written by Thomas Earle of Strafford* (Brit. Mus.).

[106] Thomason Coll. (Brit. Mus.).

ingratitude such Puritans as disallowed the custom. The balladists, like the legitimate poets, now began to explore the remoter
purlieus of lamentation, and were soon lost in mazes of hyperbole
—a condition noted with complacence by the elegist of Lord Brooke
(1643):[107]

> Then let each Mourner, that hath a desire,
> Weep out a part, and weeping so expire.
> Pardon's great Lord, and thy diviner Ghost,
> If by remembring what in thee we lost,
> Out of that honour and love we owe to thee,
> We lose ourselves in an Hyperbole.

A military eulogy of the Earl of Northampton "who died a Con-
querour At the Battaile of Hopton-heath" (1643),[108] although by
a Royalist, turns the lash of satire against dissolute carpet-Cavaliers,
and in its description of the diseases arising from their debauch-
eries, prepares the way for Dryden's famous lines on the pox. But
it was during 1648 and 1649, when the Cavaliers were following
a lost cause, that they turned to the broadside elegy to lament their
downfall and gain for their party what sympathy they could among
the populace. Most of these pieces are eulogies, some more personal, like several on Lord Villiers (1648),[109] some more military,
like some on Lord Capel (1649);[110] some were clearly and directly
political, like those on Pembroke's apostasy[111] and on Sir Charles
Lucas;[112] and, very occasionally, the somewhat artificial exaggeration of grief shows the cloven hoof of the Sentimental, as when
Mistress Abigail Sherard, the daughter of Baron Sherard, was bewailed in the following lines:

---

[107] Lutt. Coll., I, No. 14.

[108] Thomason Coll. This is more properly a tract than a broadside.

[109] *Elegie on the Untimely Death of
Lord Villiers,* and *An Elegie and Epi-
taph, upon Lord Villiers* (Thomason
Coll.).

[110] *Elegie upon that Renouned Hero
and Cavalier, the Lord Capel,* not printed
until 1683 (Lutt. Coll. I, No. 21),
*Mournful Elegy upon Duke Hamilton
and Lord Capell,* and *Obsequies on the
exemplar Champion of Chivalry Arthur
Ld Capell* (Thomason Coll.).

[111] *Pembroke's Passe from Oxford to
his Grave* (Thomason Coll.).

[112] *An Elegie On the Death of Sir
Chas. Lucas;* and *An Elegie On the
Death of Sir Charles Lucas and Sir
George Lisle* (Thomason Coll.); *An Ele-
gie Upon the most Barbarous, Unparal-
lel'd, Unsoldiery Murder of Sir Charles
Lucas and Sir George Lisle,* London,
1648. Somewhat similar are *The Satyric
Elegie Upon the Execution of Nathaniel
Tomkins* (1643) (Thomason Coll.), and
*An Elegie On the miraculously Learned,
and Much Lamented Bishop of Armagh,*
London, 1656.

Sighs do but ease the spleen, and teares the braine. . . .
My soul looks happyest when I hug the griefe.[113]

But of all the Cavalier broadsides, the most significant and the
most numerous[114] is the group written on the death of Charles I.
These poems, the more popular counterpart of the controversial
treatises against which Milton launched his swingeing rejoinders,
were part of a concentrated attack upon Puritanism, an effort to
enlist the popular feelings on behalf of the deposed dynasty; and,
indeed, so nearly successful was it that the Puritan government was
for the moment shaken to its very centre; and, realizing the danger
of a free press in the hands of their adversaries, they proceeded at
once to strengthen the licensing law, to procure answers to the
offending pamphlets, to take unto themselves, as far as they could,
a monopoly of the broadside elegy, and to suppress even the singing
of ballads. The elegies on the execution of Charles I are pitched
to the key of horror; and, as in the pamphlet-poems already noted,
blood is the subject of their lines. Cleveland had set the tone in
his *Elegy* on Laud (1644), that "Most Reverend Martyr," and
continued in the same sanguine style in his lines on Charles I;
and each veriest poetaster followed, or at least faltered, in his steps.
One, in bitterness of soul, addressed the "Bloody Saints":

> His *Blood* was but a draught for to swill up
> Alas, it could not yeeld you each a supp. . . .[115]

On occasion, the printing was even done in red as well as black,
an expensive process that suggests subsidy from political sources.[116]
The royal martyr is presented *in persona propria* to plead his own
cause in *An Ellegy written by Himselfe*[117] and in *King Charles
His Speech*.[118] Extravagant eulogy is thrown against the bloody
background of regicide. Charles is "a God on Earth";[119] and
the Puritans, as wicked as Caligula,[120] as far gone in perdition as

---

[113] *An Elegie and Epitaph for Mistris
Abigail Sherard* (?1648) (Thomason
Coll.). This broadside is full of confu-
sions of fact. See *A Century of Broadside Elegies*, No. 22.
[114] The British Museum has about fifty
such pieces in French, German and Latin,
as well as English.
[115] *An Elegy Sacred to the memory of
King Charles* (Thomason Coll.).

[116] *Chronosticon Decollationis Caroli
Regis &c.* (Thomason Coll.).
[117] *Somers Tracts*, London, 1810, IV,
258-259.
[118] H. E. Rollins, *Cavalier and Puritan*,
New York, 1923, 233.
[119] Brit. Mus. broadside.
[120] Brit. Mus. broadside.

"all the Hissing Convent of Hell."[121] His "Sufferings" are amply
depicted.[122] His flesh will not decay, but will smell of myrrh in
the grave, an odor of sanctity that the Puritans later attributed to
their choicest divines; his death will corrupt the body politic;[123]
and the stanza and allegory of Spenser[124] and cosmic figures such
as Milton later used, are employed to reënforce the initial exhor-
tation: "Howle, howle, distracted Kingdome." Indeed, the courtly
poet might well bewail; for his occupation, like Othello's, was
gone; but the broadside balladist out-Herods him and shrieks his
lamentation from the housetops.

So the Cavalier broadside elegy outdid itself; and, as the Puritan Blue Laws grew more and more stringent, and as the control of the presses grew more and more efficient, Cavalier political
broadsides grew less numerous; and, as the Puritans took over the
elegiac *genre*, Cavaliers ceased to use it for purposes other than
satiric parody. The old ballad, "In sad and ashy weeds," originally ascribed to James I grieving for the death of Prince Henry,
was, to be sure, reprinted, with an apparent ascription to Charles II
bewailing his father;[125] and *The Ladies Lament for the losse of
her Land-lord* is a thinly veiled lament that the House of Stuart
no longer ruled in Whitehall;[126] but, even here, the political motive is somewhat disguised, doubtless for reasons of prudence.
Most of the pieces are personal rather than political in their tendency, and imply their politics merely by the direction in which
they point their panegyric. Of the two elegies on the death of
Sir Paul Pindar (1650), one is an extravagant eulogy by N. Richards,[127] the other more restrained and Classical,[128] looking forward to the Royalist elegies after the Restoration. But Donne's
manner was not at once abandoned; and the beheading of Christopher Love in 1651 was lamented in a prologue and five "acts"
of tropic eccentricities:

> LOVE *lies a bleeding*, and the world shall see
> Heav'n Act a part in this black Tragedie.
> The Sun no sooner spy'd the Head o' the floor,

[121] Thomason Coll.
[122] Brit. Mus. broadside.
[123] Lutt. Coll., I, No. 17.
[124] By F. H.; Brit. Mus. broadside.
[125] H. E. Rollins, *Cavalier and Puritan*, 60.

[126] *Ibid.*, 316.
[127] *Truth's Acrostick*, (Thomason Coll.).
[128] *Obsequies Offered Up to Sr Paul
Pindar, Kt.*, (Thomason Coll.).

But he pull'd in his own, and look'd no more:
The Clouds which scattered, and in colours were,
Met all together, and in black appear,
Light'nings, which fill'd the Ayr with Blazing light,
Did serve for Torches at that dismal night. . . .[129]

Mortuary images even, borrowed perhaps from contemporary Puritan broadsides, occasionally appear, such as death feeding on a corpse and drinking the blood of his victims.[130] The style of Donne, indeed, was falling into such absurd extremes that one can hardly distinguish sincere elegies from parody; and S. H., bemoaning the death of Cleveland,[131] at once praises that poet and, quite needlessly, regrets his own short-comings:

> . . . we can Rant,
> 'Tis true, but not like thee (our Termagant). . . .

The light touch of the School of Jonson occasionally remains;[132] but disease[133] and graveyard worms[134] were becoming more and more the staples of elegiac trade; and, as they became so, serious Cavalier elegies grew continually fewer: some time after the death of Cleveland, "T. P. Gent. of Norfolk" declared him to have been "Never Satisfactorily Deplored";[135] and a Royalist elegist of Dr. John Hewitt lamented the decay of "Elegious Rimes."[136]

Meanwhile, the elegy was becoming more and more the organ of Puritanism: as early as 1651, J. C. associates "common formall Elegies" with the "Geneva Jig" of Calvinism;[137] and, as the Puri-

---

[129] Brit. Mus. broadside. The author seems to have been the Royalist-Presbyterian, Dr. Robert Wilde. See *A Century of Broadside Elegies*, No. 30.

[130] Rodney MSS. (Add. MSS. 34239, Brit. Mus.), elegies on George Rodney and on Sir Edward Rodney, both apparently by F. Atkins.

[131] S. H., *Funerall Elegies, Or the Sad Muses in Sables, singing the Epicediums of Prince Maurice, James, Duke of Lennox, John Earl of Rivers, John Cleveland, the much cry'd up Poet* (Thomason Coll.).

[132] *Elegy on the Princesse Elizabeth* (1655) (Thomason Coll.).

[133] *Affectuumdecidua, in honour of Charles Capell*, Oxford, 1656. For the most part this volume of elegies is Clas-

sical and eulogistic; but Edward Lowe described the eruptions of the small-pox on his body as *"stars* fix'd in the milkie way."

[134] See the self-elegy imputed to Dr. John Hewitt (Lutt. Coll., I, No. 69); and *Certain Considerations Against the Vanities of this World* (1658) (Brit. Mus. broadside).

[135] Brit. Mus. broadside. The author seems to be Thomas Pecke of the Inner Temple, a youthful admirer of Cleveland's. See *A Century of Broadside Elegies*, No. 35.

[136] Lutt. Coll., I, No. 63.

[137] J. C., *Poems with Additions*, London, 1651, 49 *et seq.* A copy is to be found in the Bodleian.

tans carried the old conceits to their utter extremes, and put upon the funeral elegy the realistic mortuary stamp of Quarles, the Cavaliers found the form ridiculous, and, in using it for satire, seem to make a laughing stock, not merely of the butt of their scorn, but of the very elegiac form itself. As early as 1648, two sardonic elegies on the death of Lord Mayor John Warner[138] seem to parody the form: one of them even contains a mock invitation to his funeral feast, and winds up, in the Puritan fashion, with an epitaph. A similar note is manifest in *A Salt Teare: or, the Weeping Onion at the Lamentable Funerall of Dr. Dorislaus* (1649).[139] The prelude stanza of *England's Monthly Prediction*[140] owes part of its effect to parody; the *Sportive Funeral Elegies*, published by "S. F." in 1656, contains a "long burlesque elegy," which is a jovial sort of dirge on the demise of the balladist Martin Parker;[141] and *An elegie upon the death of Mr. Phill Porter who departed this world this present May 1656*,[142] which seems to have maintained a jocular fame down into the eighteenth century, contains, as its "Second Part," an elegy on the author, suggestive of the self-elegies composed by certain Puritan divines. The lively benediction, in the last stanza, of D'Avenant's amusing innovation and of the Inns of Court suggests that the piece was composed by some jocose bencher of none-too-Puritan opinions:

> Now God Bless all that will be Blest,
> God Bless the Inn's of Courts;
> And God Bless *D'Avenant's Opera*,
> Which is the Sport of Sports.

But perhaps the clearest case of ridicule directed against the elegiac form is *The President of Presidents or, an Elegie, On the Death of John Bradshaw* (1659),[143] in which the satiric attitude of the Restoration appears full-blown:

> The wittiest Vengeance man could here invent,
> Must fall far short of such a President.

[138] *An Elegy on the Timely Death of John Warner*; and *An Expostulation with Death and Fate* (Thomason Coll.). The second is ascribed to John Taylor, the Water-Poet.
[139] Thomason Coll.

[140] H. E. Rollins, *Cavalier and Puritan*, 215 *et seq.*
[141] *Ibid.*, 67.
[142] H. E. Rollins, *Analytical Index*, 63. The piece was probably reprinted in *Wit and Drollery*, 1682, and in *Pills*, 1719.
[143] Thomason Coll.

If one omits the moralistic flights of journalism, broadside elegies, during the reigns of Elizabeth and James I, were neither numerous nor especially mortuary in tone. They are to be associated neither exclusively with the Puritans nor exclusively with the Cavaliers; for indeed, these two parties were only in process of formulation, and the homogeneity of Elizabethan literature continued for some time into the following century. The reign of Charles I saw an intensification of the social struggle; but broadside elegies, like the funeral elegies of the poets of the School of Donne, are hardly more than sporadic until about 1640, when the Civil War began to supply the elegiac poet with only too many subjects for his art. The general Puritan disapproval of the broadside ballad turned most of the balladists Cavaliers during this period; and they were not slow to express in their verses their political preferences. During the '40's, perhaps their most common note is one of eulogy for the mighty slain, ending in a shrill scream of horror and a passionate appeal for sympathy at the execution of Charles I. Very similar was the evolution of the School of Donne, from whom the broadside-writers borrowed considerably in matters of style and ornament. During the 1650's, when the legitimate poets had either fled or compounded for their safety, Cavalier broadside elegies grow somewhat less numerous; meanwhile, the Puritans had been taking over the form; and, therefore, the predominant note of the Cavalier elegy becomes that of satire, satire not merely of the Puritans, it would seem, but of the very elegiac form itself. A few Cavalier balladists, without conforming politically to Puritanism, adopted its tone of mortuary realism; and there are some broadsides that have little or no political or social import; but in the main it can be said that the funeral elegy, both in recognized poetry and in the verses of the broadside-writers, rose in the latter years of the reign of Charles I from earlier sporadic beginnings, flourished for about a decade in the hands of the Cavaliers, and then, because of its growing Puritan associations, was more and more abandoned except for purposes of satire. Thus the Puritans, once in power, took over mortuary verse, just as they adopted many of the repressive measures of Royalty such as the law against unlicensed printing, and just as Cromwell found it expedient to assume much of the pomp and circumstance that had previously hedged the person of the king. Thus, whatever glamor occasional poetry could supply in support of the new regime and in praise of its military heroes, was encouraged, or at least tolerated, not perhaps in birthday odes and overt documents of adulation, but at least in funeral elegies the awesome and pious tone of which gave a kind of excuse for this unlawful allowance of the errant Muse, who was thus privileged to repent for the nonce in appropriate sackcloth and ashes. The further testing of such a theory will form the subject of the succeeding chapter on the funeral elegy and the Puritans.

CHAPTER III

THE FUNERAL ELEGY AND THE PURITANS

THE division of literary types according to the social plane in which each had its vogue is at best a parlous thing. Some types, like Elizabethan drama, appealed to all classes, although even here one can point to special plays, such as the court-comedies of Lyly, and dare assert that they were written to one certain taste. Proof, however, in such matters is difficult; and assumption, untrustworthy: both literary and social history follow eccentric evolutions; and synchronous equations between them, even though safely established for a given moment, are subject to constant gradual shiftings, as relative matters of education, creed, or politics, may determine. The literature of the upper class, for instance, is constantly sifting downward into lower social strata: the chivalric romances, composed for noblewomen of the latter Middle Ages, became the characteristic literary diet of the Elizabethan butcher and baker and tallow-chandler, whose delight in Palmerin of England and Amadis of Gaul is so happily depicted in Beaumont's *Knight of the Burning Pestle*; and the Gothic novel, initiated by the fourth Earl of Orford, descended in the Victorian age to be the delight of servant-girls and charwomen. Some literary types, on the other hand, accomplish a social ascent, such as the rise into recognition of folk-poetry and primitive oral literature. Between these two rising and falling movements, radiate, like the spokes in Dame Fortune's wheel, many ironic literary events. But lately, persons were to be found who described Chaucer, the publican of revenues, the finished courtier, the successful diplomat, as child-like and naïve; and his verses have been termed "quaint." Shakespeare, it would appear, wrote and performed his plays to make money, and hoped for fame from his two narrative poems; but posterity neglected his poems for generations while they were delighting in the plays. Milton wrote *Paradise Lost* to "justify the ways of God to men," but to-day is damned for his theology, and is praised, if at all, for his sonorous verse: even the seats of the mighty are subject to the revolutions of the stellar spheres; and the class-interpretation of literature is a study in æsthetic and social relativity, forever changing and forever new. In the seventeenth century, however, so disparate were the traditions of Puritan and Cavalier that there is perhaps some hope of cautiously distinguishing between the two; and, upon the assumption of such a possibility, the present study is conceived.

In the age of Elizabeth, this distinction was not so clear: the Queen had her own reasons for fostering national unity by a fortifying compromise, social, political, and religious; and, during her reign, secessions from this compromise were few and comparatively insignificant. Most Elizabethan Puritans, far from emulating Cartwright or "Martin Mar-prelate," were content to follow the more conservative banner of Leicester in support of the throne, and to assume the easy tolerance of the Renaissance rather than the constraint and rigor of the Reformation. In the reign of James I, however, the king's tactlessness and vacillation in governing Church and State, and at the same time the increasing power of the middle classes and the increasing number of the Puritans, brought the latter into alliance with the enemies of royal prerogative, and by degrees effected a politico-religious cleavage in the ranks of English society.[1] Charles' policy of civil government through ecclesiastical machinery even more sharply accentuated this new social alignment, and drove many, even of rather moderate opinions, into the Puritan camp where they perforce countenanced, if not assumed, the extremes of their associates. Thus, although the Puritan-humanist like Marvell or the youthful Milton, of wide and tolerant mien, still occasionally persisted, most of the party cut every tie that bound themselves to the Court and to its courtliness, and left literature, drama, and the arts severely in the hands of the unregenerate servitors of Mammon.

It is a commonplace of social history that the Puritans for the most part drew their strength from the merchant-class of London and (Oxford excepted) the larger towns in the southeast, the most populous region of England; and that the Cavaliers consisted mainly of the Court, the landed nobles, who attended at least occasionally on its functions, and the peasantry, who tilled the great estates and from personal attachment or blind feudal custom followed their overlords in politics and in war. Religiously, the

---

[1] For further causes of this cleavage see S. N. Patten, *The Development of* *English Thought*, New York, 1899, 128 et seq.

Puritan was an anti-ritualist and a Calvinist, with all the dogmatic severities implicit in that severe confession, Original Sin, Total Depravity, and Salvation of only the predestined few. It was a creed appropriate to a social group among whom life at best was none too comfortable, among whom infant mortality was high, and who in a desperate struggle for political recognition if not supremacy, had turned their hand against the principalities and powers of this world: it was a fighting creed for a battle of long duration and of uncertain outcome. The Cavalier, on the other hand—provided that, like Herrick, his Renaissance proclivities had not quite Paganized his view of life—was an Arminian, who, following in the steps of the Dutch theologian and of Archbishop Laud, denied strict Predestination, opened the way to individual Free Will as determining future rewards and punishments, and gave an especial veneration to the Church as a divine institution founded by Christ on the first day of Pentecost and passed down from the Apostles through successive bishops to modern Christendom. Such a view, implicit in such poets as Herbert and Crashaw, encouraged the fine arts, and in its very ritual found place for them as expressing "the beauty of holiness." This antagonism, social, political, and religious, of townsman against noble and peasant, of Puritan against Cavalier, grew continually more acute down to the period of the Restoration, when England came to realize that the unrestrained rule of neither party was quite to be desired, and a working compromise was gradually developed, politically in the cabinet-system, and religiously in the legal recognition of organized dissent. It is the Puritan side of this division in its relation to literature, and especially to the funeral elegy, that the present chapter will discuss —a side that, during the reign of Queen Elizabeth, was assembling itself in inchoate beginnings; that, without adequate literary or political expression, was accumulating subterranean power during Jacobean and Caroline reigns; that erupted during the 1640's in the Civil War, and for more than a decade without bishops or king triumphantly ruled over England. One strand of the literary history of this English Puritanism, the present study proposes to pursue through the labyrinthine mazes of this tumultuous period.

To define the point of view of any social class is a most difficult matter, especially if that class be submerged politically and be inarticulate in the fine arts; but, even so, something can be done to illustrate the psychology of seventeenth century Puritanism. Mental states may roughly be classified as falling into three groups: the normal, the depressed, and the exhilarated. The first is the common, serviceable state of mind in which most people earn their daily bread and from which they crave release in hours of relaxation. The mental attitude of depression, usually occasioned by a keen sense of physical, mental, or spiritual insufficiency to meet the exigencies of life, is likely, in persons to whom the consolations of religion are possible, to result in a very live faith in supernatural aid and in a fervent dependence upon its comforts. The complementary extreme is a state of exhilaration, amounting at times to intoxication, that arises from a superabundance of energy, a vital balance of trade in which the possessor is overwhelmed by his own riches. Such an one, according to the categories of the old medicine, would doubtless be classified as "sanguine," that is, possessed of a superfluity of blood, the nourishing, vital "humor." He would exemplify the mental state displayed in the exuberance of the Elizabethan drama and so commonly attributed to the Renaissance in general. The second, or depressive type, is clearly represented, in the old medical terminology, by the melancholy man, one in whose physical system black bile predominated. Many such are to be found in the earlier Middle Ages, when human society could hardly cope with the forces of nature and of anarchy about it; and such also were the more rigid Protestants who could scarcely combat the powers of darkness as exemplified in the old religion and in the princes and possessors of the earth with whom they came in conflict: indeed, the Calvinism of the latter seventeenth century, in both England and Scotland, was degenerating into emotional excesses that were generally confused with religious exaltation;[2] and death would seem to have been an especial occasion for such outbursts of religious "enthusiasm."[3] The middle attitude of life, that which seeks and usually finds a sufficiency for its needs, regularly accomplishes this purpose by limiting its require-

---

[2] See, for example, W. E. Alderman, *Publ. Mod. Lang. Assoc. Am.*, XXXVIII, 180 *et seq.*; F. J. Foakes Jackson, *Social Life in England*, New York, 1916. 65, 69, 94 etc.; H. G. Graham, *The Social Life of Scotland in the Eighteenth Century*, London, 1906, Chapter IV, etc.; and the present author, *Bunyan's Mr. Igno-* rance, *Mod. Lang. Rev.*, XXII, 15 *et seq.*

[3] E.g., *The Pattern of True Love* (J. O. Halliwell, *Yorkshire Anthology*, London, 1851, 16), which would seem to be based on fact; and P. T. Hopkins, *Critical History of English Biography*, MSS. thesis, Radcliffe Coll. Lib.

ments, and aims perforce at a nice adjustment of man to nature and of the individual to society. It develops a philosophy of *nil admirari*, and so may be termed Classical; for the idealization of a quiet mean of life is the alpha of Aristotelian ethics and the omega of Stoic apathy and Epicurean ataraxy. Its outward and visible sign is a poised and pleasing decorum, which, in the Neoclassical decadence of a Chesterfield, may degenerate into an empty conventionality without inward spiritual meaning; but at best it represents that perfect balance of humors that, in the old medical theory, was supposed to result in perfect health. To this cult, the age of Queen Anne gave at least lip-service: its high priest was John Locke, and Joseph Addison was its flamen-in-ordinary. The two extremes of depression and exhilaration can easily coexist— often, indeed, appear as reactions one to the other—and, in extreme forms, can together lapse, as they did in the poet Collins, into manic-depressive insanity;[4] but the middle road of restraint, although it may grow as a necessary compromise out of the two extremes, is pleasing to neither; and, to the follower of the Aristotelian mean also, low spirits, at least in the eighteenth century, as the examples of Gray and Walpole attest, seems a tiresome bugbear, and enthusiasm, as exemplified in the Methodists, a vice fraught with dangers of religious anarchy and of civil commotion.[5]

The extent and significance of the prose literature of melancholy during the middle and latter part of the seventeenth century, and especially of the religious reading that bulked so large during the period, has for some time been matter of scholarly record.[6] That such a literature came into being neither for the licentious court of Charles II nor for the illiterate peasantry seems hardly to require proof. One is thus reduced to the assumption that it existed chiefly for the middle classes; and, indeed, evidence is not lacking that such reading was characteristic of the Puritans, who were most numerous among the bourgeoisie. Even in the sixteenth century, the Puritans were of a melancholy cast: they so appear in Sutcliffe's

[4] See Bronson's analysis in the *Introduction* to his edition, Athenaeum Press Series. Melancholia is the older name for manic-depressive insanity.

[5] See A. S. Tuberville, *English Men and Manners*, Oxford, 1926, 10-11; and I. Babbitt, *Rousseau and Romanticism*, Boston, 1919, *Introduction* and Chapter I.

[6] Amy L. Reed, *Background of Gray's Elegy*, New York, 1924, 28 *et seq.* Patten (*op. cit.*, 131) ascribes the melancholy of the Puritans to lack of exercise, improper diet, and like causes. Cf. the Romantic melancholy of a later date.

False Semblant and in Hooker's *Ecclesiastical Polity*.[7] Malvolio is at least serious-minded, and is supposedly mistaken for insane. Burton, diagnosing the Puritans as a professional physician, declared them "certainly far gone in melancholy, if not quite mad."[8] The vogue of melancholy in the Commonwealth is well known.[9] Butler took his Presbyterian hero from Spenser's Sir Hudibras whose "Sterne melancholy" surpassed even his redoubtable courage.[10] Evelyn and Addison, to be sure, suggest that "a religious melancholy, or pious sadness"[11] was sometimes to be found within the pale of the Church of England also; and Anne of Winchelsea's temperament showed what the "spleen" and unhappy changes of fortune could do; but Addison associates melancholy chiefly with dissenting circles, especially of a somewhat earlier day, as his description of the reception of a student by a "very famous Independent minister who was head of the college in those times," amply attests:

He was received at the door by a servant, who was one of the gloomy generation that were then in fashion. He conducted him with great silence and seriousness, to a long gallery which was darkened at noon-day, and had only a single candle burning in it. After a short stay in this melancholy apartment, he was led into a chamber hung with black, where he entertained himself some time by the glimmering of a taper, till at length the head of the college came out to him from an inner room, with half a dozen night-caps upon his head and religious horror in his countenance.[12]

The first question in the examination that followed was whether the youth was prepared to die. The ghastly machinery of the Gothic romance has been imputed to Massinger and his fellow playwrights:[13] should one not also mention the religious theatricality of dissent?

[7] Hooker, *Ecclesastical Polity*, ed. Bayne, London, 1907, II, 129 *et seq.* He points out that the Anabaptists, like the Quakers of a later time, foreswore the intellectual aid of books and would listen only to their own hearts. Cf. the Romantic Original Genius, who would seem to have developed the æsthetic analogue of the Protestant conscience in ethics: both claim to have an inner light that leads to the Good.

[8] Burton, *Anatomy*, London, 1898, 700.

[9] E.g., C. A. Moore, *Mod. Lang. Notes*, XLI, 220 *et seq.*

[10] *Faerie Queene*, Bk. II, Canto ii, St. 17. Butler does not use the word melancholy, but seems to consider it a characteristic, Part I, Canto 1.

[11] Evelyn, *Diary*, ed. Bray, London, n. d., 18.

[12] *Spectator*, No. 494.

[13] Clara McIntyre, *Were the "Gothic Novels" Gothic?*, *Publ. Mod. Lang. Assoc. Am.*, XXXVI, 644 *et seq.*

Even more significant, however, is the evidence, often unconscious, of the dissenters themselves. Samuel Clarke, the chief biographer of Puritanism in the seventeenth century, seems, in the
lives that he chronicles, to find the most overt proof of Election
in a longing for death and a delight in musing upon it;[14] and
Kirkton, in eulogizing the Covenanters, praises not so much any
moral excellence they may have possessed as their capability for
"gregarious excitement."[15] In Addison's own generation, this attitude of mind, though somewhat restrained, was by no means a
thing of the past; and in 1722, Harris, in his funeral sermon upon
his eminent non-conformist colleague, the Reverend John Billingsby, held forth at the grave as follows:

. . . We are surrounded in this Place[16] with the Graves and Monuments
of many of them [Prophets], Elder and Younger; and have seen this
verified in several Instances of late. What is the Voice of this Provi-
dence, when we see an open Grave, and a dead Friend and Brother
before our eyes? What he who being dead yet speak to us? Is not this
the Language to us all; Behold the Fruit of your Apostacy and Sin; see
in me the Sentence of the Law executed, and Righteousness and Faith-
fulness of God to his Word: Dust thou art, and unto Dust shall thou
return; and Death hath pass'd upon all Men, for all have sinned; without Exemption to the best of Men. See the Frailty of Nature, and
Uncertainty of Life. The Natural Tendency to Dissolution, and gradual
Decay in every Constitution; besides the Diseases of Body and Accidents
of Life. Consider your End and the Measure of your Days what it is,
and know how Frail you are. . . . O that you were Wise, and would
understand this, and consider your latter End. Dare not to sleep under
the Wrath of God: Fear the Vengeance of eternal Fire. Death is near;
behold the Judge standeth at the Door. . . .[17]

Boston's *Four-fold State*,[18] the most popular devotional tract of
Georgian non-conformity, treated at length of death in the *ipsis-
sima verba* of the two preceding generations of Puritan elegists;
and Doddridge, the chief dissenting theologian of the age, devotes

---

[14] S. Clarke, *Lives of Eminent Persons*,
London, 1683.

[15] See W. L. Mathieson, *Politics and
Religion in Scotland, 1550-1695*, Glasgow, 1902, II, 157.

[16] This sermon was doubtless delivered
in the dissenters' burial ground at Bunhill Fields in London, just outside Moor-
gate.

[17] W. Harris, *A Sermon Occasioned by
the Death of the late Rev. Mr. John
Billingsly, Preached at Crutched-Fryers,
May 13, 1722*, London, 1722, 43. The
style does not reflect a very high literary
standard.

[18] T. Boston, *Human Nature in its
Four-fold State*, Edinburgh, 1720, 383,
432 etc.

a whole chapter of his *Rise and Progress of the Soul* to the joy of the good Christian in contemplating death and the Last Judgment.[19] In his poem *The Spleen* (1737), Matthew Green enumerates dissenters meetings, along with religious enthusiasm, indulgence in Sentimental "fancy," and other excesses, as the chief cause of melancholy. Isaac Watts describes the ideal dissenting sermon as "a Mixture of the Instructive and the Pathetick" and the ideal preacher as having "paraphrased on the most effecting parts largely" with much "Pathetic Amplification";[20] and there can be no doubt that death and its terrors bulked large in the sermonizing of the seventeenth and eighteenth centuries.[21] Even devotional literature intended for those of tender years was not lacking in mortuary. Watts himself, whose fondness for babyhood appears in his *Cradle Hymn*, and who confessed to a sinful affection for "children with their little hands,"[22] composed, though he was perhaps the sanest dissenter of his generation, the following specimen of appropriate reading for the young:

WHEN I enter into a Church-Yard,[23] I love to converse with the Dead. See how thick the Hillocks of Mortality arise all around me, each of them a Monument of Death, and the Covering of a Son or Daughter of *Adam*. Perhaps a Thousand or Ten Thousand Pieces of Human Nature, Heaps upon Heaps, lie buried in this Spot of Ground;[24] 'tis the old Repository of the Inhabitants of the neighboring Town, a Collection of the Ruins of many Ages and the Rubbish of Twenty Generations.

I SAY within myself, What a Multitude of Human Beings, noble Creatures, are here reduced to Dust! *God* has broken his own best Workmanship to pieces, and demolished by Thousands the finest earthly Structures of his own building. Death has entered in, and reigned over this Town for many successive Centuries; it had its Commission from God, and it has devoured Multitudes of Men.

BUT Nature (alas!) hath fixed the Limits of Youth, Beauty and Vigour; narrow Limits indeed! and when once pass'd, they are unrepassable. The broken Lines of an ancient Painting may be reunited and grow strong, the Features may rise round and elevated and the Colors

---

[19] P. Doddridge, *Rise and Progress of Religion in the Soul*, London, 1745, Chap. XXIX.

[20] I. Watts, *Reliquiæ Juveniles*, London, 1734, 100-102.

[21] See R. Watt, *Bibliotheca Britannica*, Edinburgh, 1824, *sub sermon, death*, etc.

[22] I. Watts, *The Hazard of Loving the Creatures*.

[23] Not without reason did Gray refer to his churchyard as "this neglected spot." See C. J. Abbey and J. H. Overton, *The English Church in the Eighteenth Century*, London, 1906, 426 *et seq.*

[24] Probably Watts had Bunhill Fields, already referred to, in mind.

grow again with sprightly Youth; but our real form grows cold and pale, it sinks, it falters, it withers into Wrinkles; the Decay is resistless and perpetual, and Recovery lies beyond the reach of Hope. This shadow of *Idalio*, touched by your Pencil, lives again, and will see another Age, but the substance dies daily, and is ready to drop into the Dust.

To this Point of Mortality, since 'tis certain and inevitable, let us often direct our Eyes; let our scatter'd Thoughts be recollected from all their Wanderings, and pay a daily Visit to Death. . . . [25]

One might, therefore, expect to find in the Puritan poetry of the early and middle seventeenth century a considerable corpus of melancholic verse; and a survey of the legitimate poetry and the broadside poetasters of Puritanism down to the Restoration in 1660, may not be amiss.

In this period, one might almost assert that recognized Puritan poets, in the nicest sense, are not to be found. The poems of real literary value in Milton's earlier period are an expression of the Renaissance rather than of Puritanism—in fact, such religious poetry as he wrote celebrated Christmas and other feasts of the Church, abhorrent to the stricter sort. Even in the few poems of his middle period, the Puritan ideal is hardly explicit; and the Puritans themselves did not acclaim their Latin Secretary of State as the poetic expression of their movement.[26] Those that tolerated poetry at all would doubtless have thought of Quarles in that character, though Quarles, ironically enough, was an avowed Royalist. Indeed, for the Puritan poets, one must take Marvell, who lives only by a few happy lines, or Hammond, Murford, or James, who cannot be said to live in the general memory at all. The unhappy custom of ascribing the religious poetry of the reign of Charles I to the influence of Puritanism has obscured the fact that the chief religious poets, such as Herbert, whose contemporary influence was probably far greater than that of Milton,[27] and also Crashaw, and Vaughan, were all Royalists in politics and high churchmen appar-

---

[25] I. Watts, *Reliquiæ Iuveniles, ed. cit.,* 107. Children's literature of this sort was not so strange in an age that fed its youth upon the literary pabulum of Quarles' *Emblems.*

[26] The tendency of some historians to look at literature from a modern, or at least a more recent point of view than the age when it was written, has its dangers: such hindsight must not be imputed to contemporaries, who could not know, for instance, that Milton was some day going to publish *Paradise Lost.*

[27] A. H. Nethercot remarks that during the seventeenth century "Herbert's admirers and imitators were almost legion" (*The Reputation of the "Metaphysical Poets" During the Seventeenth Century, Jour. Eng. and Ger. Phil.,* XXIII, 186 *et seq.*).

ently in religion; and, unless one somewhat naïvely identifies all authentic spirituality with Puritanism,[28] it is certainly evident that, even in the treatment of religious themes, the Royalist production considerably outdoes, both in quantity and for the most part in excellence, the poetic output of their opponents. Even the anathemas of the more precise, however, could not quite allay the poetic impulse; and the present study can hardly overlook such authors as combined with the Puritan consciousness sufficient Humanism to produce at least mortuary verse.

The youthful Latin elegies of Milton are, for the most part, elegiac only in meter; those on the deaths of University dignitaries have been aptly termed "impersonal academic exercises";[29] and his *Epitaphium Damonis* on Charles Diodati is in the pastoral style of Mantuan and his Renaissance compeers. Perhaps it is mere chance that introduced such slight mortuary touches as "Magna sepulchrorum regina" and "querebunda Elegeia tristis" into the latter part of *Elegy II* and "Dira sepulchrali More metuenda face" into *Elegy III*. At all events, in the same year, 1626, he composed in somewhat portentous style his elegy *On the Death of a Fair Infant Dying of a Cough*, the stanza-form of which, and possibly some of the imagery, were inspired by Phineas Fletcher:

> Yet can I not persuade me thou art dead,
> Or that thy corse corrupts in earth's dark womb,
> Or that thy beauties lie in wormy bed,
> Hid from the world in a low-delved tomb;
> Could Heav'n for pity thee so strictly doom?
>   Oh no! for something in thy face did shine
> Above mortality, and shew'd thou wast divine.

But at times, like the Cavalier propagandists of the 1650's, Milton chose to color the gruesome Realism and crabbed metaphor of the elegiac *genre* with a satiric, almost comic, tinge; and his two poems *On the University Carrier Who sickened at the time of his vacancy* invest it with a sardonic acidulation. Their humor, indeed, is sometimes too grim to be humorous, as in the reference to the

---

[28] Cf. W. H. Crawshaw, *The Making of English Literature*, New York, Copr. 1907, 163 *et passim*. *The Heath Readings* (ed. T. P. Cross and C. T. Goode, New York, 1927), moreover, refers to the entire mid-seventeenth century as the "Puritan Age" although three-fourths of the selections are Cavalier, and many of them typically High Church Anglican.

[29] J. H. Hanford, *A Milton Handbook*, New York, 1926, 107.

torture of peine forte et dure, prescribed by English law for an
accused criminal who stopped the course of justice by refusing to
plead:

> His leisure told him that his time had come,
> And lack of load made his life burdensome,
> That even to his last breath (there be that say't)
> As he was prest to death, he cried, "More weight" . . .

The *Epitaph on the Marchioness of Winchester* was done, as befitted the subject, in the courtly style of Jonson. It is an elegy
rather than an "epitaph"; and, though it contains one or two
mildly funereal touches, it is, on the whole, light, delicate, and
restrained. *Lycidas*, composed in the tradition of Renaissance pastoralism, with its characteristically Renaissance panegyric on Fame
and its ecclesiastical satire in the tradition established by Petrarch,[30]
has nothing to contribute to the present study. The Classical restraint apparent in *Lycidas*, moreover, seems to have grown on
Milton in later years; and, in the rather small body of verse composed during his second period, although there are several more
or less elegiac sonnets, there is hardly a funereal detail except for
the almost shocking vividness of the lines *On the Late Massacre
in Piedmont*. On the whole, one is surprised to find even so much
mortuary material in Milton: during his second period, he wrote
but little poetry; and, during his earlier years, the funereal was
only occasionally employed by his masters and eminent contemporaries.

Between the School of Donne and other Royalist practitioners
of the funeral elegy on the one hand, and on the other hand the
Puritans, who took over the form about the middle of the century,
stands the person of Francis Quarles. He was himself a Royalist
who suffered for his opinions, and who, with a probable glance at
current occasion, did not hesitate to insert in his free paraphrase
of the Book of Lamentations[31] a reference to "the royal Magazins
of divine And sacred Majesty." His style, moreover, derives largely

[30] See Marion K. Bragg, *The Formal
Eclogue in Eighteenth Century England*,
Univ. of Maine Stud., Sec. Ser., Orono,
1926, 18 and 30.
[31] *Sion's Elegies*, Elegy VI. In his preface *To the Reader* he takes Jerusalem,
the destruction of which he laments, as
the "type of the Catholick Church." One
wonders whether, and how far, these elegies were written as a masked battery
against Puritanism.

from aristocratic prototypes: from the School of Donne,[32] from the influence of Spenser as it came down into the sedulously otiose figures of Phineas Fletcher,[33] and from emblem-writers such as George Wither, who, beneath the picture of a skeleton, lingers over the description of its "sightless eye-holes," "lean crags," and "horrid countenance"[34] as appreciatively as the most searching Puritan or the most "Gothic" Sentimentalist. But Quarles wears these borrowed flowers of rhetoric with a difference; and, in spite of his High Church Anglican antecedents, political and poetic, he became, in the middle and latter seventeenth century, the *beau idéal*, or better perhaps, the *laid idéal*, of Puritan poetry. Many of his pieces are moralized paraphrases of the *Bible*, at times suggestive of the ample didacticism of the eighteenth century, but more religious and less moral and philanthropic in theme. Thus the stories of Jonah, Esther, Samson, and Job are reduced to seventeenth century meditative verse in the best manner of the "painful Pastors."[35]

The *Emblems*, his most renowned performance, is replete with direful images, both in the cuts[36] and in the letter-press;[37] and

[32] A. H. Nethercot includes him in the School of Donne (*Stud. in Phil.*, XXII, 81 *et seq.*, and *Jour. of Eng. and Ger. Phil.*, XXIII, 173 *et seq.*).

[33] The Rev. F. E. Hutchinson (*Camb. Hist. of Eng. Lit.*, VII, 53) derives the style of Quarles from Phineas Fletcher. His cuts and moralizing come from the *Pia Desideria* of the Jesuit, Herman Hugo.

[34] G. Wither, *Poems*, London, 1839, IV, 172, *Emblem VIII*, *Emblem XXI* expresses the converse of the elegiac theme: "Death is no loss, but rather gain, For we by dying life attain." See also *The Muses Dirge* by Richard James, an emblem on the death of James I, with its "heap of bones" and "senseless scull" (James, *Poems*, ed. Grosart, Chiswick, 1880, 113).

[35] See *The General Application* in *Sec. I* of *A Feast for Worms*.

[36] Although the emblem-book and the technique of emblem-writing has a well-recognized pedigree, going back to Alciati's *Book of Emblems* in the early sixteenth century, yet one wonders how great an interaction of influence existed

in England between the emblem and the broadside ballad. Both appealed to the same social class, and so general similarities may arise from this source rather than from direct influence.

[37] E.g., Quarles, *Emblems*, Bk. V, No. VII. The literal style of such passages suggests the plainness of Neo-classicism, which aimed to have a rather broad appeal to the common sense of the average Londoner. This bald objectivity appears even in Quarles' metaphors; and the parallel structure and occasional antithesis of the end-stopped, regularly metrical couplets of the following passage suggest the style of Pope in a cruder stage of metempsychosis:

Why? what are men, but quickned lumps of earth?
A Feast for Worms: A bubble full of breath;
A looking-glass for grief; a flash, a minute;
A painted Tomb, with putrifaction in it;
A map of death; A burthen of a song;
A winters dust; A worm of five foot long. . . .
—*A Feast for Worms, Meditation I.*

Quarles, as if foreboding the rise of Sentimental luxuriation in sadness, warns the pious reader against its delusive joys, perhaps because he had himself observed their effect among his contemporaries:

> But when a noisome grief begins to please
> The unresisting sense, it is a fear
> That death has parley'd, and compounded there. . . .
> We false-joy'd fools can triumph in disease,
> And (as the careless pilgrim, being bit
> By the tarantula begins a fit
> Of life-concluding laughter) waste our breath
> In lavish pleasure, till we laugh to death.[38]

Most immediate, however, to the present subject are his numerous "threnodias" of *Sion's Elegies,* taken from Jeremiah, which contain in passing much downright mortuary description; and Quarles in his paraphrase translation, did not scant the original in this respect. The depiction, for instance, of the afflictions of Judah might serve for the most edifying of death-bed scenes:

> Lingering with Death and Famine, *Judah* groans,
> And to the Air breathes forth her airy moans,
> Her fainting eyes wax dim, her cheeks grow pale,
> Her wandring steps despair to speed, and fail,
> She faints, and through her trembling lips, half dead . . . [39]

And later the effect of sorrow on the bereaved is not ineffectively described:

> Rivers of marish tears have overflown
> My blubber'd cheeks; my tongue can find no tone
> So sharp as silence, to bewail that woe,
> Whose flowing Tides an ebb could never know:
> Weep on (mine eyes) mine eyes shall never cease;
> Speak on (my tongue) forget to hold thy peace;
> Cease not thy tears; close not thy lips so long.[40]

Not unlike in tone, although less happy in effect is his *Alphabet of Funeral Elegies* on Dr. Ailmer. The following passage is redolent of the garnishments of Donne:

---

[38] Quarles, *Emblems,* Bk. I, No. VIII. Miss Reed, *op. cit.,* does not cite this passage.

[39] *Sions Elegies, Thren. I, Eleg. XI*

[40] *Ibid., Thren. III, Eleg. XVII.*

> Envy now burst with joy, and let thine eyes
> Strut forth with fatness; let thy Collops rise
> Pampred and plump; feed full for many years
> Upon our loss; be drunken with our tears . . .[41]

His *Elegy upon the Reverend, Learned, and my honored Friend, Dr. Wilson, of the Rolls* shows a similar provenience. Indeed, if art be exaggeration apropos, elegiac art would seem to be exaggeration malapropos:

> I cannot hold, my day grows dark and dull;
> My troubled Air is damp, my Clouds are full:
> The Winds are still, my stormy sighs are spent;
> I must pour down, my Soul must burst or vent:
> No Azure dapples my be-darkened Skies;
> My passion has no *April* in her eyes:
> I cannot spend in mists: I cannot mizzle:
> My fluent brains are too severe to drizzle
> Slight drops: my prompted fancy cannot showre,
> And shine within an hour.[42]

And even his *Mildredeiados to the Blessed Memory of Mildred, Lady Luckyn* is in the same artless, presumably inspired, style. It is perhaps most notable as associating with the funeral elegy the theme, common to it for the following hundred years, that death is no respecter of rank or virtue, but rather seeks for his arrows a shining mark:

> Quick finger'd Death's impartial, and let's flie
> Her shafts at all; but aims with fouler spite
> At fairer Marks; She, now and then, shoots by
> And hits a fool; but levels at the white,
> She often pricks the Eagle in the eye,
> And spares the carkass of the flagging Kite;
> Queens drop away, when blew-leg'd *Maukin* lives;
> Drones thrive when Bees are burnt within their hives
> And Courtly *Mildred* dies, when Country *Madge* survives.[43]

---

[41] *An Alphabet of Elegies,* termed *Funeral Elegies* in the running head (*Divine Poems,* London, 1674), *Eleg. V.*

[42] Like Polonius, however, Quarles protests that he uses no art at all, "I need no art to set a needless gloss," etc. This is the characteristic Christian doctrine of the inspired, untaught poet-prophet. See also *Emblems,* Bk. V, No. X. Cf. Romantic Original Genius.

[43] The plan of this elegy with its sudden turn in the middle, "Our *Mildred* is not dead . . ." and the apotheosis at the end, is Classical in inspiration, and suggests such eulogistic elegies on the pious as one finds in the latter part of the century.

Indeed, the poetry of Quarles was a magazine of elegiac am-
munition from which any novice might borrow ample equipment
to his purpose; and, having assumed the whole armor of crude
Realism and crass rhetoric, the would-be elegist might assail the
Mount of Helicon, and truly, *vi et armis,* draw tears from the
eyes, not only of the reader, but probably of the Muses also. The
Emblems and the *Divine Poems* muster the entire panoply of grief
from despondent brooding to an anguished, if somewhat unconvincing, frenzy: to the poet this didactic "enthusiasm" was a commonplace of style; and it is easy to see why the sectaries, especially
those of a less restrained psychology, took him to their bosom,
Royalist or no. Almost every theme apparent in the funeral elegy
of later years is anticipated in his works,[44] and like Mary Wollstonecraft, he left but little new for his followers to say: he described death and death-bed scenes,[45] night with its "horrid darkness,"[46] and lamentation that shades into horror, the Last Judgment,[47] the pains of hell[48] and hopes of Paradise[49]—every possible
scene, in fact, but the mortuary landscape, with its yews and cypresses, and mounded earth and charnel-house. On occasion, he
does not stick at borrowing details from loathsome disease,[50] from
the surgical ward,[51] and from the chamber of torture;[52] but, like
most of the Anglican poets who followed Donne, he is too fully
absorbed with immortality to linger over the grave with its cadaver-
ous evidence of death; for, in Quarles, death is not worms and
decay, but the beatific vision, a Christian apotheosis. In his moral
passages, even more fully, he set his stamp upon future elegists:
over and over, he expatiated upon the wretchedness of man and
the brevity and vanity of life; he enunciated the inspired artless-
ness of the elegist; he asserted death's preference for victims of
exalted virtue and high estate; and he meditated upon the hedonic

[44] The present study makes no attempt
to separate the influence of the elegies
from that of the *Emblems* and other
poems; for the same themes and atmosphere pervade them all. Like Matthew
Arnold, Quarles repeats himself at times
almost *verbatim*: e.g., the passages quoted
and *The Feast for Worms* on man's
frailty, and the *Emblems,* Bk. III, No.
VIII, line 31 *et seq.;* and the final couplet of this same emblem is like the

passage on grief quoted from the *Elegy
on Dr. Wilson.*
[45] Quarles, *Emblems,* Bk. III, No. III.
[46] *Ibid.,* Bk. III, No. I.
[47] *Ibid.,* Bk. III, No. XII.
[48] *Ibid.,* Bk. II, No. XIII, and Bk. III,
No. XIV.
[49] *Ibid.,* Bk. V, Nos. V and VI.
[50] *Ibid.,* Bk. I, No. XI, and Bk. III,
No. VI.
[51] *Ibid.,* Bk. III, No. III.
[52] *Ibid.,* Bk. III, No. IV.

calculus of melancholy, its pleasures and pains, and pit-falls for the unwary, the common theme of poets a century or more after his time.[53]

Dowered with such manifest qualifications, Quarles, willy nilly, became for a hundred years the most approved expression of social and religious uplift among those Puritan readers whose powers could hardly presume to the consumption of *Paradise Lost*; and such Neo-classical authors as chose to take a fling at his defects, doubtless had reason to know that among certain classes he was a dangerous literary rival. The fullness of his fame down into the Restoration is amply attested by the number of editions of his works and by such critical comment as the age affords; after the Restoration, the critics, beginning with Cowley, grow cold and finally scornful; but, "among the vulgar," his works still commanded "a wonderful veneration."[54] The early eighteenth century increased, if anything, the vogue of critical detraction; and his reputation fell with that of the other metaphysical poets: five times Pope paid him the compliment of a sneer; and the very number of adverse references suggests that he was still well known and widely read. Scholars, at all events, have found his style not dissimilar to Young's *Night Thoughts*[55] and to Blair's *Grave*,[56] two poems that together with Thomson's *Seasons* would seem finally to have supplanted the *Emblems* in the esteem of the middle classes.[57] Scores of elegiac passages have vague reminiscences of his work; but here, as in other highly conventionalized literary forms, the conventionalization makes one hesitate to write down a single author as the cause of this or that effect; for such senti-

[53] See the passages quoted in the text and footnotes.

[54] The present review of the influence of Quarles is largely based on material assembled by A. H. Nethercot (*The Reputation of the "Metaphysical Poets" During the Seventeenth Century*, *Jour. of Eng. and Ger. Phil.*, XXIII, 173 *et seq.*, and *The Literary Legend of Francis Quarles*, *Mod. Phil.*, XX, 225 *et seq.* The Rev. F. E. Hutchinson (*Camb. Hist. of Eng. Lit.*, VII, 53) seems to be in general agreement. Significantly enough, Quarles seems to have acquired good odor once more among the Romanticists (Nethercot, *Stud. in Phil.*, XXII, 81 *et seq.*).

[55] See T. Campbell, *Specimens of the British Poets*, London, 1841, 187.

[56] See H. A. Beers, *History of English Romanticism in the Eighteenth Century*, New York, 1916, 164.

[57] The use of the *Emblems* as children's literature is an interesting field for investigation. Some of the emblems suggest such a use, e.g., Bk. I, No. III, and Bk. II, Nos. VIII, XI, and XIV. Bunyan's *Divine Emblems* were certainly so used (F. J. Harvey Darton, *Camb. Hist. Eng. Lit.*, XI, 412-413); and at least one eighteenth century child studied Quarles' volume. (See the present author, *William Mason*, New York, 1924, 20.)

ments and language were common to the devotional prose and poetry of the times, and even if abated for a moment, could easily be born anew by spontaneous generation from the middle-class Puritan consciousness.

What other poets of the age Puritanism might call her own can be rapidly surveyed. Richard James (1592-1638), a Middlesex clergyman within the Establishment, represents the earlier phases of the movement in its milder forms. His *Muses Dirge* on the death of James I and his *Funeral Meditation* on Richard Windsore[58] contain one or two mortuary phrases, borrowed probably from emblem-books. Zachary Boyd, Dean of Glasgow University, who in 1640 turned Presbyterian, perhaps for reasons of convenience, prefixed to his *Four Letters of Comfort*[59] an *Epitaph*, which contains "tears of blood," "worms and slime," and other improving touches. Nicholas Murford, apparently a salt-merchant of King's Lynn, committed numerous innocuous elegies[60] that are notable only in that he regularly appended to each one an epitaph, in accordance with the custom that was to grow more and more popular with Puritan poets. In 1656, Samuel Holland did an *Elegy* full of verbose lachrymosity on Anne Gray, daughter of Dr. Nicholas Gray of Tonbridge.[61] William Hammond, who came of a good family of Kent, but who seems to have inherited some tendency toward the precisian from his mother,[62] inserted in his poem *On the Death of my dear Brother* a line about "This awful shade; the horror of the tomb . . .," and gave vent to much moralizing on "Man's frail estate." His *Death*, an ecstatic description of celestial bliss, commences with the Realistic couplet:

> Sunk eyes, cold lips, chaps fall'n, cheeks pale and wan,
> Are only bugbears falsely frighting man. . . .[63]

[58] R. James, *op. cit.*, 113 and 217. At the top is a skull with the Latin motto, "Oritur: Moritur."

[59] The book seems to have come out late in the year, presumably after his change in religion. The title-page of the 1878 ed., presumably copied from the original, depicts a skeleton with an hourglass standing, it would seem, in a graveyard.

[60] N. Murford, *Fragmenta Poetica*, 1650 (ed. Greenland Fishery Museum, King's Lynn).

[61] *The Kentish Garland*, ed. Julia H. L. De Vaynes, II, 568. The piece was originally published on a broadside, a copy of which is in the British Museum. It is reproduced photographically in *A Century of Broadside Elegies*, London, 1928, edited by the present writer, No. 33.

[62] His mother was grand-daughter of that "obstinate and conciencious Puritan," Archbishop Sandys.

[63] *Caroline Poets*, ed. Saintsbury, Oxford, 1905-1921, II, 511. The original came out in 1655.

Andrew Marvell, who like Quarles had a considerable, though smaller, following for over a century,[64] sings in his *Poem upon the Death of the Lord Protector* at times in the mortuary strain: he refers to "the damp of her [Eliza's] last gasps," and describes mankind as "Death's refuge, Nature's dregs," and says that the mourners of Cromwell "with heavy doom, Wander like ghosts about thy lovèd tomb, . . . lost in tears . . ."; and the *Elegy to Lord Villiers*, ascribed to his pen, details to the reader,

> How heavy *Cromwell* gnasht the earth and fell
> Or how slow Death farre from the sight of day
> The long-deceived *Fairfax* bore away,
> But untill then, let us young *Francis* praise:
> And plant upon his hearse the bloody bayes,
> Which we will water with our welling eyes.
> Teares spring not still from spungy Cowardize.
> The purer fountains from the Rocks more steep
> Destill and stony valour best doth weep.[65]

The comparative mildness of such an early Puritan poet as James accentuates the importance of Quarles's influence, and suggests that, but for his example operating about the middle of the century, the funeral elegy might never have become the *reductio ad absurdum* of literary grief.

The Puritan clergy, looking askance as they did upon any elaboration of funeral rites, were especially slow to accept the funeral elegy; and, indeed, the form hardly receives the full impress of Puritanism until the clergy in the 1650's began to celebrate one another in this wise, and, in imitation of their military and civil partisans, began to use the elegies at their funerals.[66] In 1644, the obsequies in Westminster Abbey of the Rev. Dr. Twiss, attended by the whole House of Commons, was not graced by elegies; for, as his biographer tells us, "He needed no *Trophies, Marbles,* nor *Epitaphs.*"[67] In 1651, however, the death of the Rev. Thomas Wilson was celebrated in a long elegy, which may, however, have been written somewhat later.[68] In 1654, the passing of the Rev.

---

[64] See the Rev. John Brown, (*Camb. Hist. of Eng. Lit.*, VII, 210.

[65] Worcester College, Oxford, possesses a copy of an undated edition that is very early, if not an *ed. princ.*

[66] This matter is discussed at length in Chapter IV.

[67] Samuel Clarke, *op. cit., Life of Dr. Twiss.*

[68] *Ibid.*, 40.

Samuel Bolton was lamented in no less than four elegiac pieces; and W. Leigh, one of the poets, though inclined to think that "real Grief makes silent *Obsequies*," remarked:

> To mourn in Verse, and write an Elegie
> Is even grown as common as to die.[69]

In 1655 the death of Ralph Robinson was also celebrated;[70] and, in the same year, the famous Richard Vines had "Many Elegies" of which his biography reproduces some five folio pages. In the hands of the clergy, the elegy lost nothing of the mortuary horror that the Cavalier poets had bestowed upon it in their lamentations over the royal martyr; and such realistic detail and melancholy moralizing as it had before was amply augmented by borrowings from Quarles.

Indeed, an excellent index of the Puritan elegiac style of the period is to be found in a volume of elegies brought out in 1653 on the occasion of the death of Sir Nathaniel Barnardiston, M.P., "renouned for Piety to God, love of the Church," and so forth. He was a Puritan and a bitter opponent to King Charles; and *Suffolk's Tears*[71] would seem to be an anthology of the elegiac Puritanism of Puritan East Anglia. The volume starts with *An Offertory*, apostrophizing the relict of the deceased:

> Thrice Noble Lady, *spare that melting Bead,*
> *Our sorrows want no jewel from your head;*[72]
> *Still let those silver drops, that lightly lye*
> Like little delug'd worlds *within your eye;*
> *Fixed abide* in their own brightest sphear. . . .

The poem revels in the hyperbole of sorrow: each weeper, not content with pocket handkerchiefs, *"brings his sheet"* to wipe the lady's eyes; later come cypress trees, and a "gloomy den of sorrow," hints that the mortuary landscape is emerging from the vast deep and

---

[69] *Ibid.*, 47.

[70] *Ibid.*, 58. Only three years later, the Cavalier elegist of Dr. John Hewitt was noticing the decay of "Elegious Rimes." The relationship of dates can hardly be insignificant: the Cavaliers dropped the form as the Puritans took it over.

[71] *Suffolk's Tears: or Elegies on that renouned Knight, Sir Nathaniel Barnardiston,* 1653. He died in July of that year.

[72] Is the poet aptly comparing the lady to a toad, which, according to the old biological folk-lore, was supposed to have a jewel in its head?

dark abysm of time; and finally angels wait on the lady's eyes "with bottles" to carry her tears to heaven. This is the very luxury of grief! One wonders what Donne, or even Quarles, would have thought of this scion of their example. In the volume generally, the hyperbole of lamentation is, if anything, outdone by the hyperbole of praise; but, in the interstices between the two, the elegists find room for numerous other melancholic themes and for several devices of technique that were to become the commonplace apparatus of the *genre*: among the themes are the power of death and the horror of the tomb,[73] the incompatibility of deep grief with its adequate artistic expression,[74] and the mercenary motives of other elegists;[75] the most notable devices of technique are the use of dialogue between "the Author and his Muse" or between "Death and an Angel,"[76] suggestive of the morality plays, not so long since departed. No less Mediæval is the enumeration of illustrative *exempla* as in Chaucer's *Monk's Tale;*[77] and very Puritan is the appending to most of the elegies of epitaphs, in this volume regularly in Latin. To Mediæval influence, may be added that of Shakespeare[78] and Donne;[79] but perhaps the chief determinant of style would seem to be a combination of Quarles and the poetic incompetence of the author.

Most significant of these pieces and especially worthy of note is the *Elegie* by Christopher Burrell, which was placed early in the volume, presumably to give it special prominence.[80] Burrell first urges the Muse to assume "the sable wings of darkest Night"; and continues his mandatory apostrophe:

> Cover thy head with blackness, do not faile
> Thy brow with mournful shadow now to vaile. . . .

[73] J. C., *Elegie, Suffolk's Tears,* 56, N. B. the reference to "worms and dust," *ibid.,* 32 *et seq.*
[74] Faireclough, *Parentale, ibid.,* 24.
[75] *Ibid.,* 26 and 33.
[76] Christopher Burrell, *An Elegie containing a Dialogue between the Author and his Muse, and between Death and an Angel, ibid.,* 3. Is this a relative of Timothy Burrell whose *Journal* appeared in the *Sussex Arch. Coll.,* III, London, 1850?

[77] T. Marriot, *Elegy at the Funeral,* etc., *ibid.,* 29.
[78] The reference to *"Plague, Sword, and Famine"* suggests the *Prologue* of *Henry V;* and the reference to the "Sargeant's Mace" of Death, recalls *Hamlet,* V, ii, 347 (*ibid.,* 32 and 3).
[79] E.g., Owen, *Epicedium, ibid.,* 45; and Astel's verses, *ibid.,* 49.
[80] *Ibid.,* 3. The tone of this piece and its position in the volume suggest that Burrell was a clergyman, doubtless of the more "painful" sort.

There is a reference to "Rachel's sorrows"; Nature is to "Dissolve her frame" in accordance with the usual pathetic fallacy; and the Muse is to go to "the place where griesly Death doth dwel." Burrell's "House of Death" calls to mind both Vergil and Spenser, but the details of its interior suggest contemporary sermons, and the actual appearance of charnel-houses:

> The chambers there with Coffins planched sure
> Corruptions sap will not let long indure;
> These worn and torn, in time renew'd again,
> The cost of future Funerals maintain:
> The lower floor's of earth, most rooms be ful,
> Loe here the dead mens bones, and there a skul.

> The trophies of *triumphant Death* are there,
> The rooms all hung with whited linnen are;
> The corps intomb'd with juice of Poppy smear'd,
> There rest and sleep in dust, no danger fear'd,
> Till that these bodies, putrifactions prey,
> Be raised up to life at the *last Day*.

This is indeed a mortuary scene, though not yet expanded with an out-of-doors setting. There follows a vivid description of Death as a

> raw bon'd carcass, of his Head the *haire*
> And *flesh* is falne, and left the *skul* all bare;
> His *eyes* no *eyes*, cannot be seen nor see,
> Worm-eaten *nose*, one *jaw*, no *teeth* hath he. . . .

Death's omnipotence over human life receives due emphasis, and the Old Testament allusions betray the chief inspiration of the piece, which, however, winds up with much parleying on the part of the Muse and an apotheosis in the best Classical style. On the whole, a more perfect example of the funeral elegy is hard to find. It goes one step beyond Quarles in its charnel-house details;[81] and there yet remained only the combining of these elements with description of rural nature in the style of Thomson, a combination already anticipated on a small scale in the elegiac writing of Cowley.

[81] An almost equally good example is Underwood's elegy (*ibid.*, 32) in which he invokes a "sullen, melancholly pensive Muse" to arouse "hideous lamentation," and then describes the "*much lamented hearse* . . . In *silent vault* confin'd with *worms*, and *dust*. . . .*"

Quite as curious, though perhaps less significant, are the elegies by "divers Ministers in the City of London" appended to the Rev. Simeon Ashe's *Living Loves*[82] on the death of the Rev. Jeremiah Whitaker. John Sheffield improves the occasion of the last illness of the deceased:

> The racking *Gout* and the tormenting *Stone*,
> In *Kidneyes* Ulsers two, in *bladder* one,
> Made paines sharp, sore, long thick but respit small. . .

These, together with tuberculosis, were the most approved diseases among the pious; and Clarissa Harlowe's death-bed scene, though perhaps of greater duration, was if anything less vivid and realistic than its gruesome prototypes in the Puritan elegy and biography of the three preceding generations. William Lewis, another contributor to the volume, is a specialist in pat hyperbole. London, we are solemnly assured, will "dissolve her stones to tears,"

> whilst every frighted grave
> At this new guest shall charm his mouldering bones
> To eccho to the dead the living moans.
> That so our Levit by both Tomb and City
> May be condol'd with Epidemick pity.

Such volumes demonstrate that during the 1650's, even the special custodians of righteousness had somewhat laid aside their anti-poetic opinions, had taken the funeral elegy to themselves, dowered it with their peculiarly Levitical cast of mind, and placed it for repose in the bosom of middle-class morality.

If, however, the Puritans had been opposed to poetry, they had been especially bitter against the poetry affected by their own social class, the London cits who loved a ballad a life. The opposition between pleasure and principle was one of the cardinal tenets of the stricter sort; and the putting down of ballad-singing was doubtless taken as a sign patent of the social uplift of the age. It is notable that the Puritan clergy do not seem to have indulged them-

---

[82] S. Ashe, *Living Loves Betwixt Christ and Dying Christians*, London, 1654. The volume is taken up with a funeral sermon on the Rev. Jeremiah Whitaker, with elegies appended. See also the elegy on Whitaker by Reynolds (S. Clarke, *Lives of Ten Eminent Divines*, London, 1662, 184 *et seq.*):

Three Messengers were sent to call thee home;
A Stone, an Ulser and a Gangrene too. . . .

selves in broadside elegies until the stringent laws against balladry had taken from the broadside something of its old association of license and jocularity, and until the Cavaliers were abandoning the elegiac form.[83] The weaker brethren, however, among the townsmen had long been susceptible to the seductions of broadside literature; and, as the previous chapter has pointed out, the age of Elizabeth and the early seventeenth century are not without ballads, and even elegiac ballads of a Puritan cast. At times the inclination toward the sensational led the balladists to draw upon the mortuary; and several of the broadsides of a religious, if not a Puritan tone, illustrate this tendency. *The Pittiful lamentation of a damned soule,*[84] though not quite an elegy, constitutes a sort of moralistic litany against various of the seven deadly sins; but the pains of Hell are left rather largely to the reader's imagination:

> No man is able to express the paine
> That, with the devils in hell, I do sustain.
> Wo unto him that there shall remaine!
> Take heed, ye worldlings! in time repent,
> Least ye be dampnèd by God's just iudgment.

Occasionally, as in the satires on His Grace of Buckingham discussed in the last chapter, the Puritans used the broadside elegy as a weapon against their political opponents; and in *Roome for a Justice* they lampooned Justice Waterton "to the tune of *A Sunday Bak'd Pudding*" in elegy and epitaph.[85] The existence, however, of a few such pieces, serious and satiric, hardly makes the broadside the possession of Puritanism, any more than the survival of an occasional broadside elegy before 1640 makes the elegiac *genre* primarily the possession of the middle class.

Indeed, it was only by degrees in the 1640's that the Puritan tendency toward the portentous permeated the funeral elegy. The *Elegiacall Epitaph upon the deplored Death of Colonell John*

[83] Perhaps the earliest examples of elegies on Puritan clergy are the pieces on Stainton, already noted, and on Rogers (Lutt. Coll. I, 125) (1642). These are unique in their time. For the latter, see *A Century of Broadside Elegies,* No. 10. Many of the broadsides cited below are also to be found in this volume.

[84] *Shirburn Ballads,* Oxford, 1907, 260, No. LXIII. The editor dates the piece prior to 1611 because it does not refer to the Authorized Version of the *Bible.* As a matter of fact this version did not come into general use until about 1660; and so his criterion of dating is not very convincing.

[85] Lutt. Coll. II, No. 232.

Hampden Esq. (1643)[86] is one of the first documents in the series of broadsides that culminated in the Puritans' appropriation of the elegiac form and their acceptance, at least in this harmless guise, of broadside literature. The *Elegiacall Epitaph* has an Elizabethan note, suggestive of the manner of Spenser:

> . . . Come *Albion Muses* all, come Maids and Men,
> Come silver Swannes leave singing on the banks,
> Of *Isis* floods[87] and in your painted Rankes
> Yee merry Birds goe solitary sitt,
> Silence and sorrow, does us best befitt. . . .

Such lines were composed in the Puritan tradition of a far earlier date: the stern Puritanism of the '30's and '40's was yet to be stamped into poetic coin. More often the early Puritan elegists studied their art from the School of Donne, which, though in no sense Puritan, was more in the current fashion; and the eulogistic *Elegies on the Death of John Hampden*[88] is composed on this pattern. The death of a hero demanded proper recognition; and poetry cannot be made to order without some model to go upon, even though that model have upon it the stigma of an adversary's use. Two years later, the *Elegie Sacred to the Immortal Memory of the Most Worthy, and most Learned John Pym Esq.* (1643),[89] though hardly mortuary, shows a very happy improvement in the lamentable; and a *Funeral Ellegie, upon the death of Mr. John Pim*[90] goes so far as to indulge in an "Acrostick on his name," a common convention of the later Puritan elegy, and an "Epitaph" in which the worms are advised that Pym's is "sacred clay" that they "cannot rape." In the same year appears a lament upon one of the Puritan clergy done in prose doubtless out of respect to the cloth, *An Elegiacal Commemoration* on the Rev. Josiah Shute.[91] The anonymous author bewails the "departed Prophet in the silent language of a Tear," to the length of eighteen pages; and, in 1644, William Mercer lamented Colonel Luttrell[92] with much

[86] Thomason Coll.
[87] Oxford?
[88] *Elegies* etc., London, 1643. In the Bodleian copy attributed to "J. S." (Josiah Shute?).
[89] Thomason Coll.
[90] Lutt. Coll. I, No. 116.

[91] *An Elegiacal Commemoration of Mr. Josiah Shute,* London, 1643.
[92] Brit. Mus. broadside. See the illustration reproduced in the present volume. The same picture was used, probably at a much earlier date, for a ballad in the *Roxburghe Collection,* ed. Chappell, *Ball. Soc. Publ.,* London, 1871, I, No. 133.

AN ELEGIE,
ON THE DEATH OF THE THRICE VALIANT

and worthy Collonell, *John Luttrell;* VVho in defence of the *King* and *Parliament,* and for the Maintenance of the true Proteſtant RELIGION, was ſlaine the 28. of *January,* 1644. At *Milverton* in *Summerſet-ſhire.*

Wake my Muſe O I wilt thou ſlumber ſtill?
and give free reines unto licencious will.
Canſt thou evade the cenſure of the wiſe?
or thinke to put blind; the quicke ſighed
of all ingenious minds, that in preſence (eyes?
of uſefull recreation, and defence
of Lawfull libertie, thou ſhouldeſt indeed
let thrive and cheriſh, that peſtiferous weed.
Of ſelfe contenting Lazites, nothing breeds
in Lands untill'd, but fire deſerving weeds.
ſhall Th' azure Heaven thoſe ſuch glorious Starrs?
ſuch Mortis periſh by miſchine Warres?

Take all thoſe worthies of whom we read, and then
compar'd; he may be call'd the Man of men,
So truly good, ſo modeſt: grave, and wiſe
ſo upright and ſo iuſt in each mans eyes,
ſo prudent, and to ver ue ſo proprnce
to innocence, a Tower of ſtrong defence.
O'! had the had a longer time to ſtay
and to his fate. had not been forc'd a pray,
Till in the Full fruition and reſpect
of his great favour wee had found th' effect,
and in the ſpring time of his proſperous glory,
not unto us to prov'd ſo tranſitory.

rhetoric, eked out with the picture of a skeleton lying upon the mounded earth of a graveyard.

The first notable outburst of Puritan elegies, however, was at the funeral of the Earl of Essex in 1646. The Puritans seem to have determined that the Earl should lose no pageantry of respect by having joined their party; his obsequies were magnificently celebrated; and broadside elegies, with the countenance, if not the actual encouragement of the authorities, were composed in numbers, and doubtless hawked about the streets for sale to the admiring and lamenting multitude. We are assured that "each Plebian head" did "scan his sighs with pains not scantled";[93] and, in the consequent pieces, both the "sighs" and the "pains" are in some evidence. One of the stricter sort, to be sure, looked askance upon the entire business,[94] cast a slur upon "youthful Elegies," and apparently thought that the funeral savored of the gauds and vanities of this world:

> And are these all the rites that must be done,
> Thrice Noble *Essex*, *Englands* Champion:
> Some men, some walls, some horses, put in black,
> With the throng scrambling for sweet-meats and Sack,
> A gawdy Herald, and a velvet Herse,
> A tatt'red Anagram with grievous verse,
> And a sad Sermon to conclude withall,
> Shall this be stil'd great Essexs Funerall?

Some of the pieces are not especially mortuary; and one is thoroughly Classical;[95] one is a military eulogy;[96] and another expresses its horror chiefly in the accompanying cuts.[97] Twiss is a specialist in the lachrymal, and expands to a whole pamphlet his "inundation of teares";[98] another writer celebrates his "black obsequies" in the *Ultima Thule* of anguish,[99] and yet another lingers over the "gloomy Night Of his dark Vault," and declares that "wee our

[93] *A Funerall Elegy upon the most Honored upon Earth*, signed by Henry Mill, Thomason Coll.

[94] *An Elegie upon the Earle of Essex Funeral*, signed J. W., and attributed to Wilde in the copy in the Thomason Coll.

[95] A MS. elegy by Henry Parker (1646), Thomason Coll., E 358 (1).

[96] *Funerall Elegie upon the deplorable and much lamented Death of the Earle of Essex* (Thomason Coll.).

[97] *Elegy* etc. (Thomason Coll.).

[98] *An Elegy upon the unhappy losse* etc. (Thomason Coll.).

[99] *A Funerall Elegy upon the most Honored upon Earth* etc. (Thomason Coll.).

selves become Congeal'd with Sighs Supporters of his Tombe."[100] Daniel Evance, his chaplain, produced a whole volume:[101] an introductory poem against false elegists, a prose narration of My Lord's illness, death, and burial, and finally *My Lord's Elegy*, embellished with an epitaph and an anagram. The prose piece contains a vivid description of a storm in a forest of cedars, pines, and oaks; and the *Elegy* starts in the cosmic style on which Milton was to set the final seal in *Paradise Lost*, and that was to revive with Thomson and to appear later in Blake and Shelley:

> So *Stars* fall down from Heaven; and the Sun goes out,
> *Mountains* shrink down into the Vales about
> In sudden Earthquakes. . . .

William Mercer, already mentioned for his lines on Colonel Luttrell, combined in even more striking fashion the cosmic, the sylvan, and the nocturnal:

> Cease great *Surveyor* of this glorious Ball
> To shine; you *twinkling Constellations* all,
> Stand in your Spheares. . . .
> You need not more, you heavenly Tapers burn
> Be be as we are; all beclouded over
> With *Sable* Mantles; and do not discover
> Your Orbs a while, but let us live alone
> Dark as Night-Owles, sadly to bemoane
> Our so much losse; and having wept a time
> Give light again; to let us know our crime
> Of guilt. . . .[102]

From this time forth, elegiac commemoration seems to have been a regular Puritan custom. Fairfax had his *Acrostick* and his *Elogie* (1647);[103] Jeremiah Burroughs, "that late faithful servant of God," was lamented in lines that start with "Unconquer'd Death" (1646);[104] Lord Mayor Warner was appointed to the substantial blessings of the Puritan Paradise (1648) and properly eulogized because he took "No recreation, nor no holy-day,"[105] and was ridi-

---

[100] *Elegie Offer'd up to the Memory of his Excellencie* etc. (Thomason Coll.).

[101] Daniel Evance, *Justa Honoraria*, London, 1646.

[102] *An Elegie upon the Death of the Right Honorable, most Noble* etc. (Thomason Coll.).

[103] *An Elogie or Eulogie on the Obits of the Right Honorable Lord Fairfax* (Thomason Coll.). Many writers use the spelling *elogie*, deriving the word, doubtless, from the French *éloge*.

[104] Thomason Coll.

[105] Thomason Coll.

culed in a mock *Elegy* by the Cavaliers. Colonel Rainborowe, who had chosen to be killed rather than kidnapped at Doncaster by a party of Cavalier raiders, was buried with a great public demonstration by the "levellers"; and the existence of at least three elegies of him shows that by 1648 even the extremer Puritans were succumbing to the blandishments of the Muse. One of these broadsides is a mere demand for reprisals;[106] another is a feeble effort to match the Cavalier aptitude for satire;[107] a third is in true Puritan style, a combination of the cosmic and the mortuary:

> Something it was that made the envious Stars
> To mutunie, and discord into Warres,
> In that great Constellation—48.
> Whose brows with curled lashings yet affright
> The reeling Universe. . . .[108]

Later appear "Sable Clouds," the "righteous blood (yet reeking)" of the deceased, and a picture of "blood gorg'd Envy" (Enmity) that may owe something to Spenser, and might quite properly have found a place in Bunyan.

During the 1640's, in short, broadside elegies increasingly assumed the melancholy cast of the Puritan mind, modelled their style on Donne and Quarles, on Cavalier broadsides, and occasionally on the School of Spenser and the tradition that in time should take its name from Milton. The 1650's continued and crystalized this movement; for, as the Cavaliers abandoned the form, the Puritans made it more and more their own. Even a confirmed balladist like Lawrence Price, whose scribbler's itch was accompanied by the more practical ailment of an itching palm, turned sanctimonious as early as 1648 and licentious again about 1659, detailing his poetic tid-bits in the meanwhile with a fine perfervid hypocrisy.[109]

There are a few pieces dedicated to women and children, in which one still finds the light touch of the sons of Ben. Such is the *Elogy Upon Luke Fawne* (1650),[110] ten years old:

[106] *A New Elegie of the Right Valiant Col. Rainsborough* (Lutt. Coll., I, No. 123).

[107] *An Elegie upon the Honorable Colonel Rainsborough butchered at Doncaster* (Thomason Coll.).

[108] *An Elegie upon the Death of that Renouned Heroe Coll. Rainsborrow* (Thomason Coll.). From the rhyme of "forty-eight" and "affright," one judges that this was written by a true Londoner.

[109] H. E. Rollins, *Cavalier and Puritan*, New York, 1923, 57.

[110] Thomason Coll. Attributed to Robert Tutchein.

> We grieve *Our* Loss, not *Thine*; for we're left here
> To the sad Comfort of a *sadder Tear*.

But Samuel Holland's broadside on "Mrs." Anne Gray, aged eighteen (1656),[111] develops the disease-motif, previously apparent in Dryden's well-known lines on Lord Hastings and in one or two broadsides already referred to: she took the smallpox, and so died "A thousand wounds being printed on her face." And there would seem to be a note of morbid Sentimentalism in the elegy *On the Early, but happy death of the very Hopeful young gentleman, Geo. Pitt* (1658). He died of tuberculosis at seventeen; and, we are told,

> He did *espouse* his sickness, was *in love*
> With that which first could seet his soule above. . . .
> He was study'ng whilst he here did stay
> Onely to make *choice* of a *dying Day*.

To-day the enjoyment of ill-health is a modish diversion; in the seventeenth century, it was an act of religious obligation. This pious yearning for illness and death—the Puritan biographers of the time attest to the generality of the attitude—was, however, no consolation to the mourners of the departed who consoled themselves by lavishing a whole poetic fury of tears upon his herse. The *Piæ Juventuti Sacrum* on the same young gentleman,[112] is such an one, and pays for the "bounty" of mourning garments by excessive lamentation: one wishes that some of the other elegists had been as frank in acknowledging the *quid pro quo* that prompted their inundations of tears. Indeed, in the 1650's the Puritan funeral elegy was being applied to both sexes, and to young as well as old, to both clergy and laity; and its characteristics were mitigated by neither age nor sex nor previous condition of righteousness.

The political motive of the Puritans in taking over the funeral elegy is avouched by a number of broadsides on military heroes—not to mention the legitimate poems already dwelt upon. The regicide General Deane was eulogized in an *Elegiack Memorial*

---

[111] Thomason Coll. Mrs. Elizabeth Wilkinson (1654), moreover, had "Divers epitaphs," two of which have come down to us and are long enough to pass as elegies (S. Clarke, *Lives of Ten Eminent Divines*, London, 1662).

[112] The copy in the Bodleian is ascribed to Clem. Ellis.

(1653) with a large wood-cut that shows him lying in state.[113] The panegyric on his Scotch campaigning contains references to "the rugged hills And darksome Groves" of Caledonia, its "craggy Rocks," and to "Dalkeith turrets"—details that look forward to the develoment of awesome Nature-description and of the Gothic motif in literature. Blake, "One of the Generals at Sea," received from the pen of George Harrison an *Elegie* (1657)[114] that, in spite of the appended acrostic, achieves a certain calm dignity:

> Now unto God be Everlasting prayse
> That thus in peace hath finished his dayes:
> And since his fatall thred is quite Spun out,
> Lets draw the Curtains, put the Candles out;
> And let us leave him to his silent Tomb,
> Free from all Troubles, clos'd up in the womb
> Of Mother Earth let him in quiet rest,
> Till he Enjoy the choycest and the best
> Of his desires, in Glory for to see
> His Saviour Christ too all Eternity.

Upon Oliver Cromwell, there is a eulogy by Row, with mortuary details on the omnipotence of death;[115] a miscellany of panegyric and anagrams by Davyes,[116] called *The Tenth Worthy;* and *A Rhetorical Rapture* by Slater,[117] who was presumably Samuel Slater, a Puritan divine:

> Go from this thy brave House of *Somerset*
> To a braver, trimmed with Thee our *Summer set*:
> Sun-like, Go down into thy *Western* Vault;
> *Our Great Generals Bride-chamber* let us call't;
> CROMWELL'S and *Cromwellines* True-Lovers-Knot,
> Till to Glory waked, Their Gloomy Grott
> To rest in, or the Suns cool silent shade;
> Where, Worms do drive a very subtle Trade. . . .

Indeed a strange combining of Elysium and the facts of bodily decay!

Among the clergy there would seem still to have been some lingering doubts, if not about the fitness of writing elegies, at least

---

[113] Brit. Mus. broadside. See the illustration opposite page 112.

[114] Lutt. Coll., I, No. 10.

[115] *Upon the much Lamented Departure* etc. (Thomason Coll.).

[116] Thomason Coll.

[117] Lutt. Coll. I, No. 40.

about the propriety of printing them on broadsides like the "lewd ballets" of the vulgar. Clerical elegies, therefore, until after the Restoration, were more likely to be printed in a volume such as that on Whitaker already discussed; and such copies as may have been used at the funeral services of the deceased were doubtless in manuscript. Indeed, the broadside elegy seems to have been rather forced upon Puritanism by its political allies, and doubtless for political considerations; for it would serve as propaganda among the masses of readers and listeners to whom the purchase of a book was an unknown transaction. This tardiness of the clergy to avail themselves of cheap broadside publication must have kept many of their elegies from appearing in print at all; and in manuscript, such pieces would have little chance of preservation. That the Puritan divines, however, began to use elegies during the 1650's is shown, not merely by the pieces on Whitaker and those already mentioned as inserted in Clarke's lives, but also by the rise of the practice in New England at this period[118] and by the extent to which it flourished in the mother country shortly after the Restoration.

The funeral elegy, it would appear, having sporadically developed during the first half of the seventeenth century, chiefly among the poets of the School of Donne, was intensified in tone by the intenser passions of the Civil War, and for political purposes invaded the broadside, where before it had only occasionally appeared. The Anglican poets, and especially Quarles, sometimes in elegies, sometimes in religious and moral poems of a more general sort, developed mortuary themes. Melancholy however, was neither habitual nor characteristic among the Cavaliers, and appeared only occasionally even in such a writer as Donne, who had a morbid facet to his genius, or in the Royalist poets of the 1640's who had fallen upon evil times. The social group to whom the melancholic humor properly belonged was the Puritans; but the most thoroughgoing Puritans on principle did not express themselves in literature and the arts. Beginning in the 1640's, however, when Puritanism, for the nonce, included many who did not adhere to its stricter tenets, and when its position of authority made it more vocal, it was more or less obliged to express itself in some appro-

---

[118] See Chapter VI.

priate form, and consequently borrowed the funeral elegy from the Cavaliers, accentuated what melancholy was already there, and made the elegy by degrees its own characteristic literary form. This process was complete by 1660, but for the reluctance of the clergy, whose elegies were naturally the most melancholic, to accept the broadside as a medium of publication. The Cavaliers, during the '50's, abandoned these "sad tautologies of lavish passion"[119] to their fate, and fell to ridiculing a literary form that had become a major stage-property of their opponents, and that had never quite conformed to their own blither spirits. Such Cavaliers, however, as submitted to the yoke of the righteous, the courtly Cowley and the humble balladist Price, fell in for the time with the prevailing mode, perhaps for a suitable *quid pro quo*; and he who poeticized and would not be suspect, watered his Pegasus at these tawny Cimmerian rivulets, sluggish and muddy, but at least within the prescribed pale. The funeral elegy, because there was so little else, became for a time, by sheer weight of quantity, the most outstanding *genre* of poetry; but it achieved this bad eminence only at the cost of a literary descent into Avernus: the emphasis shifted from heaven to earth, from immortality to bodily decay; the intellectual arabesque of Donne's metaphor and allusion gave way to the "anfractuous" style (I take the adjective from Quarles) of utter metaphysical decadence, or to a downright and undigested Realism, the gruesome details of which were emphasized by crude wood-cuts and by capitals and italics, as if the moral were chiefly enforced by the horrors, and the horrors, as in cheap modern newspapers, chiefly enforced by the adventitious aid of pictures and typography.[120]

The doubtful quality of much of this Puritan verse has probably contributed toward the current injustice of imputing insincerity to Puritans in general: their æsthetic performance is truly insincere; for artistic insincerity springs from inadequate mastery of medium or form, and the Puritans generally wrote not only prose but verse with their left hands. Religious insincerity is quite a different commodity; and there can be little doubt that the inspired soldiery of Cromwell chopped the stained glass windows out of the English cathedrals with the most ecstatic and fervent devotion. The Puri-

---

[119] Quarles, *Emblems*, Bk. IV, No. XII.   [120] Cf. Miss Reed, *op. cit.*, 249.

tans used the funeral elegy as did the Romanticists of a later date, and as most modern readers use literature in general, as a comparatively harmless outlet for pent-up emotion. This is perhaps of advantage to society; but its literary product, as appears in most modern plays and novels, is often as hollow and ineffectual as the concoctions of the veriest puppet of patronage who would supply condolence and congratulation, as the Renaissance humanists sold panegyric and diatribe, for a price. Although the association with the Puritan middle classes boded no good to the funeral elegy as an æsthetic form, it greatly enhanced its social and historical significance; for the type became the brief chronicle of that subtle psychological evolution that accompanied the gradual rise of the merchant class to the social and political predominance that it finally achieved in the Victorian age; and, until Isaac Watts began to liberate non-conformity from the anti-poetic tenets of Calvin, and secured for the dissenter at least the privilege of a hymnology, the funeral elegy was practically the only poetry that his religion allowed him. Thus, with the decline of English music during the seventeenth century and the increasing control of drama purely in the interests of the corrupt and unrepresentative Court of the Restoration, the funeral elegy, until the following century restored these and other arts to the general consciousness, constituted, except for such minor æsthetic media as devotional writings and mortuary sculpture, the sole artistic expression and literary record of the bourgeois mind.

CHAPTER IV

THE FUNERAL ELEGY IN LITURGIC USE

HOW the fine arts are related to general utility and whether they flourish best when cultivated as an end in themselves or when developed as an auxiliary to some social need, constitute intricate problems; but the fact that they have a social side and that they minister on occasion to a well defined psychological, and at times even to an obviously material human requirement, is inherent in the very nature of art-creation: the individual artist cannot shape and delineate without some urge from within—an urge that he must surely have in common with at least some of his fellows—and usually he cannot spare from the routine of daily necessity the time and energy for this exhilarating but wearisome labor unless compensated by social recognition and reward. Architecture has its obvious physical use; and music, its emotional effect, Apollonian or Dionysiac, which the human mind craves for rest or for stimulation. Sometimes the arts have lent support to some social institution: thus ecclesiastical mosaics and religious painting have helped to sustain, and in return have received patronage from, the Christian Church; and thus have the boast of heraldry and pomp of rule likewise used painting to accentuate an ancient lineage in long picture galleries and to glorify, in the earlier pictures of Turner, their ancient Gothic seats against the glamor of blazing sunsets. Thus, also, much literature has been brought into being to laud and magnify some social institution, the Church, the State, or the noble house: Homer and the Bible and such poetry of Christian tradition as the Mediæval hymns to the Virgin, are religious; the *Æneid* was intended to lend grandeur and perspective to the Roman people as a political entity; and the *Song of Roland*, according to the latest opinion, is an encomium of the crusading exploits in Spain of certain Norman families. Elizabethan drama shows all these tendencies: the religious urge in Bale's *Kynge Johan*; the political, in plays of the Armada period, such as Shakespeare's *Henry V*, and the praise of a single family in *Macbeth* with its mimic genealogy of the House of Stuart. This fertile dramatic age illustrates, moreover, another socio-literary contact, the play that, like *Arden of Feversham*, is an obvious journalistic news-item; and one might even compare the experience of the vulgar who from the pit applauded *Othello*, with the delight of our modern lower classes in the sensational "human interest story." Indeed, the creating of "art for art's sake," although it may be ideal, would seem generally to be an ideal rather than an actuality.

The great volume of elegiac composition of one sort or another during the seventeenth and eighteenth centuries is not surprising: the form satisfied at once the Christian urge for immortality and the urge of the Paganized Renaissance for earthly fame; and, as these two streams met and blended in Neo-classicism, the elegy, quantitatively at least, flourished like the Biblical bay-tree, albeit one that showed many sere and yellow leaves. This "superfœtation," as Dr. Johnson termed it, this "teeming of the press" with elegies, suggests some ulterior motive in the production of such pieces—even granted that a number were doubtless written, *Lycidas* perhaps among them, purely *con amore*. Not a few of the broadside elegies are journalistic in intent, and aim to turn for the author an honest penny by catering to the public's delight in the lurid: such pieces in the nature of the case can seldom be strictly funeral elegies. A great number of the more courtly sort were clearly fathered by the Renaissance system of lay patronage that obliged the writer who happened to be poor in the goods of this world to eulogize some contemporary noble and so gain a precarious livelihood. Such elegies would of course indulge freely in panegyric, and would regularly be modeled on the Classical archetypes so popular among the aristocracy. Some elegies, such as those on Charles I and on Cromwell, and also the satiric pieces on Buckingham, have a distinctly political cast; and, indeed, it would be strange—death has so regularly been the special business of the Church—if one did not find a religious motive underlying the composition of many pieces, especially those of a clearly Christian coloring, such as were the majority of the funeral elegies. Any religious writing, furthermore, is likely to pass over into liturgical use, a tendency exemplified by the borrowings from the *Rig Veda* for Brahman ceremonials and by the inclusion of large parts of the Bible in the missal and in the Book of Common Prayer. The present chapter proposes to examine into the evidences for such uses of the funeral elegy, to ascertain when, how, and in what localities, it was so used, and to study its relationship to other funerary ceremonies and to folk-lore.

The origin of elegiac composition and its employment in funeral services is touched upon by several seventeenth and eighteenth century writers. Both Camden and Hearne refer to "burial songs" in Classical times; and, we are told, among the Anglo-Saxons such pieces were "first song at buryals, and after engraved upon the sepulchres."[1] The fullest treatment of the subject, however, would seem to be that which appeared in a small anonymous volume[2] ascribed to the Rev. John Gill[3] and entitled *An Essay on the Original of Funeral Sermons, Orations, and Odes, Occasioned by Two Funeral Discourses Lately Published on the Death of Dame Mary Page, Relict of Sir George Page Bart.*, London, 1729. The *Essay* reflects the somewhat naïve conception of anthropology and comparative religion that prevailed in the day. The Egyptians are accredited with being the first of all peoples to believe in immortality; the dead were judged at the funeral; and, if no serious accusation was brought, the friends and relatives joined in a eulogy; and thus, we are told, came into being the first funeral orations. The Greeks took over the custom from the Egyptians; the Romans, from the Greeks; and so it entered Christianity as one of the many Pagan accretions added during the Roman Empire. Gill notes that the Romans used songs in the procession to the grave as well as orations at the funeral; and he quotes Macrobius[4] to prove that in most countries singing was a part of the burial of the dead. He admits the existence of some Hebraic precedent for funeral songs, and mentions David's "*Elogium* on *Saul* and *Jonathan*" and "the anniversary lamentation of the daughters of Israel for the daughter of Jephthah";[5] but, perhaps because of his doubt as

---

[1] T. Hearne, *Collection of Curious Discourses*, London, 1773, I, 228. Cf. 233 and 239 *et seq.*

[2] The only copy that the present writer has seen is in the Lib. Boston Athen.

[3] Ascribed by Cushing to the Rev. John Gill, D.D., pastor of the Baptist congregation in Southwark, 1719-1771. The *Discourses* seem to have been by a Mr. Harrison and a Mr. Richardson. Cf. Muret, *Rites of Funeral*, tr. P. Lorrain, London, 1683, which, however, contains nothing on seventeenth century England.

[4] The reference would seem to be to Macrobius' commentary on Cicero's *Somnium Scipionis*, Lib. II, iii, 6. Cicero refers to such a custom among the Greeks and the Romans (*Leges*, II, 24, 62); and Horace (*Carmina*, II, 20-21), Festus (ed. Miller, 163, *Paul. Diac.*), Suetonius (*Augustus*, 100), and others refer to it among the Romans.

[5] See II *Samuel*, i, 17 *et seq.*, and *Judges*, xi, 40.

to the propriety of such pieces,[6] he is inclined to derive the custom from Pagan sources, and thinks that the Biblical cases cited hardly "give countenance to these [sic] kind of performances." Undoubtedly the recitation or singing of elegiac verses at funerals is very wide-spread among both civilized and barbarous peoples; and one should certainly be wary of ascribing the origin of the Christian custom to any single source.

So far as England is concerned, one is not obliged of necessity to impute the origin of funeral poetry to either Hebrew or Classical tradition. Many of the English and Scottish ballads are obviously elegiac; and modern scholarship finds in folk lore the beginnings of the dirge and similar poetic types.[7] At all events, even as late as the nineteenth century, the singing of songs, especially during the procession from the church to the grave, seems to have been not uncommon in Yorkshire and other northern counties where such customs would most easily linger. The old *Lykewake Dirge*, the language of which bears the mark of authentic archaism, would appear to be the earliest of such pieces; and the *Lamentation of a Sinner*, sung at Redcar in Cleveland, accompanied by an ancient, perhaps Pagan, ritual, would seem to be another example, although here the singing took place on the way from the public breakfast to the church, rather than on the way to the grave.[8] It is written in a loose ballad quatrain similar to that of the *Lykewake Dirge*; and its common appearance in the *Prayer Book* at the end of the metrical Psalms suggests that the *Lamentation* was the Anglican counterpart of the more ancient *Dirge*. Sometimes this singing, in more Protestant fashion, took the form of psalmody;[9] and, at Whitby, that time-honored seat of Christian observances, "many of the old inhabitants had an aversion to being hearsed, choosing rather to be 'carried by hand,

[6] Gill thinks that although the custom has been "cleared of many things that would smell too rank of Paganism," yet he observes with concern the Classical models of many elegies and the quantity of "fulsom flattery" that they contain (*ibid.*, 14); he will allow the "singing of psalms before the corps, at the burial of the dead," but is rather disapproving of "our elegiac Verses and Odes." One of the peculiarities of traditional Protestantism is that, while it insisted that prose sermons and prayers be composed especially for the occasion, it also insisted that all the poetry in its services follow with a *verbatim* ritualism the very words of the *Bible*.

[7] See R. Adelaide Witham, *English and Scottish Popular Ballads*, Boston, Copr. 1909, xvii. Cf. Louise Pound, *Poetic Origins of the Ballad*, New York, 1921, 29, 101, 133 etc.

[8] *Publ. Folk Lore Soc.*, XLV, 308.

[9] *Ibid.*, XLV, 309-10.

and sung before,' as it was the mode of their families in time past."[10] The most recent variation of the custom would seem to be the singing of "favorite hymns" on the way to the grave.[11] In at least a number of communities, therefore, since the Middle Ages, the people have been accustomed, whatever may have been the momentary rulings of the Church or State, to accompany the burial procession, singing more or less appropriate words of a more or less popular nature; and the deep-laid human desire for the katharsis of musical expression has doubtless tended in all ages to operate on crowd-psychology in times of grief.

In the Middle Ages, the pageantry of Christian consolation had been highly developed. Funerals with bell, book, and candle, with dirge and procession, with high, and even solemn high, masses for the dead, were not uncommon among the nobles and even the rich burghers; and "trentals," the celebration of thirty masses for the dead, were remembered even as late as Sidney's *Dirge* as having regularly accompanied a funeral.[12] In the same passage, Sidney mentions the dirge also as part of the funeral rites; and, indeed, a brief survey of even a limited collection of Elizabethan lyrics shows that the dirge and the "lament," usually of a consolatory cast, had by that time become accepted art-forms, and were still being written, whether used in the actual service or not.[13] In Elizabeth's reign, the funeral sermon was "put in the place of trentals";[14] and, although much pomp and circumstance remained —the passing bell, the draping of the house in black, the hired mourners who howled dismally and threw bay and rosemary into the grave, the feasting, as mentioned in *Hamlet,* and even wakes in the remoter shires[15]—yet proof of the use of either the dirge or the funeral elegy during this period is hardly to be found. The funerals of the gentry were, or were supposed to be, fully supervised by the Heralds' College;[16] but such records as the present

---

[10] *Ibid.,* XLV, 311.

[11] *Ibid.,* LXIII, 243 and XLIX, 135.

[12] This *Dirge,* beginning "Ring out your bells, let mourning shews be spread," was first printed with *Certain Sonnets,* 1598.

[13] E.g., F. E. Schelling, *Book of Elizabethan Lyrics,* 4, 15, 27, 52, 92, etc. See also Sir W. Besant, *London in the Time of the Tudors,* London, 1904, 153-154.

[14] *Adm. ap. Whitgift Def.,* 727, quoted in Hooker's *Ecclesiastical Polity,* ed. Bayne, London, 1907, II, 401, note 2.

[15] See P. Macquoid in *Shakespeare's England,* ed. Lee, Oxford, 1916, II, 148 *et seq.*

[16] See A. H. Nason, *Heralds and Heraldry in Jonson's Plays,* New York, 1907, 70 *et seq.*

writer has had access to[17] would seem to indicate that no money was directly paid for the composition, reading, or singing of any elegy during any part of the ceremony at the church or at the grave. Neither Dethick[18] nor Tate[19] refer to elegies; Hooker, although in defending funeral sermons he refers to the elegiac pieces in the *Bible*, makes no mention of such a custom either among the Anglicans or the sectarian bodies of his day;[20] and certainly there was no elegiac tribute at the grave of Ophelia, although the "maimèd rites" may account for this omission. Nevertheless, in spite of all this negative testimony, poetic lamentation of some sort, as the custom of the following century and the number of pieces composed on the death of Sidney would seem to imply, may well have had some sort of use at Elizabethan funerals; and some of the broadside laments in the *Shirburn Ballads* doubtless date from the sixteenth century.[21] There would seem to have been a kind of standardization of grief among the poorer classes for whose needs the booksellers supplied stock broadsides for stock occasions, such as the death of a husband or a child. Such pieces were as vivid and specific as their general use would allow. They seem to aim to console the survivors rather than to celebrate the dead; and, although written to be sung to common ballad tunes, may, or may not, have been used at the funerals. Possibly the more aristocratic vogue of funeral elegies sprang from this humble source, but the present writer is inclined rather to impute some other origin, such as the example of the Mediæval Church.

The seventeenth century is a period of bitter liturgical conflict; and, therefore, it is necessary to give separate treatment to the ritualistic Anglicans, who followed the Book of Common Prayer, and to the different Puritan bodies who preferred various forms of extempore petition and admonition to the Almighty. Evidence of the exequial use of elegies among members of the Church of England is largely to be gleaned from contemporary poets. Cunningham, in his edition of Jonson,[22] notes that "in many parts of

[17] See James Dallaway, *Inquiries into the Origin and Progress of the Science of Heraldry*, London, 1793. Dallaway quotes extensively from the official records of the College.

[18] Sir William Dethick, *Antiquity of Ceremonies used at Funerals anno 1599*, included in T. Hearne, *Collection, ed. cit.*, I, 199 *et seq.*

[19] Francis Tate (1560-1616), *Antiquity, Variety and Ceremonies of Funerals in England anno 1600*, in Hearne, *op. cit.*, I, 215 *et seq.*

[20] Hooker, *op. cit.*, II, 401.

[21] *Shirburn Ballads*, ed. A. Clark, Oxford, 1907, No. XXXV, note.

[22] Ben Jonson, *Works*, ed. Cunningham, London, 1903, III, 355 n.

the Continent, it is customary, upon the decease of an eminent person, for his friends to compose short laudatory poems, epitaphs, etc., and affix them to the hearse or grave with pins, wax, paste, etc."; and he adds that the practice was once "prevalent" in England, and cites as proof, among other pieces, Bishop King's *Elegy on Donne*:

> Each quill can drop his tributary verse,
> And pin it, like a hatchment, to his hearse.[23]

Bishop King, in fact, has several allusions to the custom, the earliest in 1612;[24] later, though less clearly, he mentions it in his *Elegy on the Bishop of London* and elsewhere;[25] and, in the *Exequy*, a lament on his wife, he refers to "a strew of weeping verse" that is to take the place of "sweet flowers to crown thy hearse." The term *exequy* itself,[26] borrowed from the Latin *exequiæ*, a train of followers, although loosely used for funeral rites in general, seems originally to have referred—and perhaps still did in the Latin-minded consciousness of the seventeenth century—especially to the funeral procession.[27] The term *epicedium* also, used occasionally in elegiac titles, has been so explained as to suggest that such poems formed a part of the funeral rites;[28] and Puttenham

---

[23] *Caroline Poets*, ed. Saintsbury, Oxford, 1905-1921, III, 218. Among others, Cunningham cites Eliot's *Poems*, 39:
Let others, then, sad Epitaphs invent,
And paste them up about thy monument. . . .
Shirley in *The Witty Fair One*, V, III, *Dram. Works*, 1833, I, 357, introduces a herse bearing mocking elegies. One reads:
How he died some do suppose,
How he lived the parish know;
Whether he's gone to heaven or hell,
Ask not me, I cannot tell.
This play was licensed for presentation Oct. 3, 1628, and published 1633. Cf. Nason, *James Shirley, Dramatist*, 41, 75, 184-191.
[24] *Caroline Poets*, ed. cit., III, 216.
[25] *Ibid.*, III, 246.
[26] It seems to have come through the OF. *exequies*, which appears in English sometimes as a singular, sometimes as a plural. See *N.E.D.* The original Latin sense seems to have been preserved in the occasional sense of "funeral train" or

"bier." The word *exequy*, from its use in King's poem, has been given yet another sense, "funeral hymn or elegy" (*Century Dict., s. v.*); and, if this sense existed, it would clearly establish the wide prevalence and long continuity of the use of elegies in funeral rites; for semantic changes arise only when the old concept and the new are closely associated in the minds of many speakers over a long period of time. The use of *exequy* in the sense of "elegy" is very doubtful: *N.E.D.* repudiates it, and explains King's use in the regular sense of "funeral rites."
[27] In the passage quoted from Sandys (1615), it seems clearly to mean "funeral procession."
[28] E.g., Henry Peacham, *The Period of Mourning in Memory of the late Prince* (Prince Henry), 1613, reprinted by F. G. Waldron in *The Literary Museum*, London, 1792. The first part of the poem is styled "a Epicedium," which the editor explains in a note as a poem "proper to the body while it is unburied." An epitaph follows.

says that "Funerall songs were called Epicedia"[29]—a statement that, with its context, clearly shows that the word implied some sort of performance or use at a funeral.[30] Numerous references to the custom, however, are to be found that do not depend upon the exact interpretation of *exequy* or *epicedium*. John Taylor the Water-Poet clearly refers to it at the end of his first "sonet" on the death of John Moray;[31] and, though his description of the Duke of Richmond's funeral has no mention of elegies,[32] yet there is an extant broadside attributed to his pen entitled *True Loving Sorrow attired in a Robe of Griefe; presented upon the . . . Funerall of the Duke of Richmond* (1624). To lament Lord Nottingham, moreover, he wrote a "poor unworthy artlesse Verse," so that it might "In duteous service wait upon his Hearse."[33] An anonymous elegist bewailed Sir Edward Rodney in a verse "That should be offer'd on this honor'd Hearse!"[34] Drayton's "fulsome coffins" and other passages in his *Elegie upon the death of Lady Clifton*, seem fairly clear;[35] and Cleveland's *Elegy upon Doctor Chad-[d]erton* (1640), which was occasioned by his long-deferred funeral, begins with an apostrophe at once sprightly and reverend:

Pardon dear Saint, that we so late
With lazy sighs bemoan thy fate,
And with an after-shower of verse
And tears, we thus bedew thy hearse.

In the broadside *Funerall Elegie* on Major Edward Grey (1644),[36] the poet wishes his lines to "deck the Pomp and mournings of his Herse"; and there are clear references to the custom in the pieces on Sir Arthur Chichester[37] and on Dr. Oldsworth, Chaplain to

[29] G. G. Smith, *Elizabethan Critical Essays*, Oxford, 1904, II, 50-51.
[30] In the passage quoted, Puttenham, as was usual with Renaissance critics of specific forms of verse (G. G. Smith, *op. cit.*, I, xxx and xlvi) is referring to Classical poetry and Classical customs; but this helps to establish the sense of the word in English.
[31] John Taylor, *The Muses Mourning*, [London, ? 1620].
[32] *All the Works of John Taylor*, London, 1630, 334-335. The probable date of composition is 1624.

[33] *Ibid.*, 327.
[34] Rodney MSS., Brit. Mus., Add. MSS. 34239, p. 19.
[35] Drayton, *Minor Poems*, ed. Brett, Oxford, 1907, 103. Lines 117-118 seem clearly to point to such a custom.
[36] Lutt. Coll., I, No. 52.
[37] *An Elegie on the Much Lamented Death of the Right Honorable Sir Arthur Chichester Knight*, London, 1643. A copy of this pamphlet is to be found in the Thomason Coll., Brit. Mus.

Charles I.[38] Stanley in *The Exequies* (1651) refers to the use of elegies "To charm the terrors of my hearse";[39] and indeed, there can be no doubt that during the first half of the seventeenth century the use of funeral elegies in the procession to the grave was among Anglicans a common custom.

After the Restoration, the Royalists continued to make a great funeral an opportunity for display—a pageantry of lamentation that extends down into the eighteenth century:

> And such indifferent greifes attend their Rights
> As they were not their Funerals, but our Sights.
> Herse, Scutchins, Darknesse, the pale tapers blaze;
> All that invites our first, or after gaze;
> The Nobles, Heraulds, Mourners sable-clad;
> These make a solemn pomp, but not a sad.[40]

So wrote Martin Lluelyn on the death of the Duke of Gloucester in 1660; and the same funeral was likewise celebrated with a multiplicity of elegies, two of them significantly entitled, *Loyal Tears Poured on the Herse*[41] and *Some Teares Dropt on the Herse*[42] of the deceased. There was also a *Cordial Elegy & Epitaph*[43] upon the Duke that was designed to "deck" his hearse "With Cordiall briney Teares, and Tragick verse." As the reign of Charles II advances, however, the references to elegies upon the hearse of the deceased become vaguer and more metaphoric, and seem to arise from poetic convention rather than an actual

---

[38] *An Elegie in Memory of Dr. Oldsworth* (Thomason Coll.). There also the *Stipendariæ Lacrymæ, or, a Tribute of Teares Paid upon the Sacred Herse of Charles I*, the Hague, 1654. This place of publication was probably printed on the broadside to escape Puritan censorship; the date, however, is probably correct, and it shows that the piece could not actually have been put upon the King's hearse: such expressions, therefore, were becoming a convention, and are not necessarily to be taken literally.

[39] *Caroline Poets, ed. cit.*, III, 139-140.

[40] M. Lluelyn, *An Elegie on the Death of the Most Illustrious Prince Henry Duke of Gloucester*, Oxford, 1660 (Thomason Coll.). Some idea of the pomp of funeral processions of the day may be gleaned

from the broadside of Queen Mary's funeral reproduced in the present volume and from an Elegy on Matthew Mead (1699) (Brit. Mus. broadside) though the former is too closely modelled on a coronation broadside of James II (Guildhall Lib., London, Pamphlets, 1685-87, No. 20) to be of value as detailed evidence. The exact arrangement of the procession can, however, be learned from *The Form and Proceeding of the Funeral of Queen Mary II*, printed by the authority of the Lord Marshall. (Guildhall Lib.) No reference is made to elegies.

[41] Lutt. Coll., I, No. 54.

[42] Thomason Coll.

[43] *A Cordial Elegy & Epitaph upon Henry Duke of Gloucester*, London, 1660 (Thomason Coll.).

continuance of the custom. Waller attributes this rite to the Muses, thus removing it at least one degree from actuality:

> Thus mourn the Muses! on the hearse
> Not strewing flowers; but lasting verse
> Which so preserve the hero's name,
> They make him live again in fame.[44]

Indeed, the convenience of the oft-repeated rhyme of "hearse" and "verse" probably helped to keep the custom alive in poetic metaphor. One writer speaks of "Incense to" the hearse of the Duchess Dowager of Albemarle (1669);[45] another wishes to "pay Tribute to" the hearse of William Whitmore Esq. (1678);[46] and yet another hopes that his "sad Verse" will "attend" upon the hearse of Charles II (1685);[47] and a similarly vague reference appears in an *Elegy* on James II (1701),[48] in which Britain is exhorted to attend his funeral "with tributary Verse." Indeed, during the latter part of the century, there would seem to be but two straightforward and literal references to the custom, neither of them unquestionably Anglican in reference: in the triple acrostic on "Valiant Sprague,"[49] the writer wishes to "Hang these dull Pendants on his Funeral Herse"; and, in 1688, perhaps under the influence of restored Roman Catholicism, there comes to light *A Paraphrase on a Hymn, Sung when the Corps is at the Grave, By T. S., Fellow of Maudlin College, Oxon.*[50]

A considerable amount of negative evidence points to the discontinuance of the custom among Anglicans during this period. The funeral processions pictured on the broadsides, some of them large and realistic, like that of Queen Mary reproduced in the present volume, do not show broadside elegies attached to the hearse;[51] sometimes elegies were not written for a fortnight or

[44] Waller, *Of an Elegy Made by Mrs. Wharton on the Earl of Rochester.*
[45] *On the Death of Anne* etc. (Lutt. Coll., I, No. 3).
[46] *An Elegie on* etc. (Lutt. Coll., I, No. 159).
[47] Lutt. Coll., I, No. 29.
[48] *An Elegie on the Death of* etc. (Brit. Mus. broadside).
[49] *An Achrostical Epitaph* (Bodl. Lib., Wood Coll., 429). The fact that both of these pieces came from Oxford suggests that the custom lingered in that academic atmosphere, and doubtless elsewhere in the provinces.
[50] *Poetical Recreations, Part II, by several Gentlemen of the University, and others,* London, 1688, 1.
[51] The pictures at the headings of broadsides are for the most part very crude and sketchy; and none of those showing funeral processions gives clear evidence of elegies attached to the hearse or the trappings of the horses. See for example

more after the subject's decease,[52] and rather often on persons who were lost at sea[53] or who died in foreign lands;[54] and, as the following elegist remarks, poets would seem to have been rather less in haste than previously to celebrate the virtues of prospective patrons:

> Are all the *Poets Dumb*? And is there *None*
> Whose *Tears* may fill our empty *Helicon*?
> So as to fix a Never-dying Verse
> On Pious *Devonshire's* deserving Herse.[55]

The prose literature of the period, likewise, does not show traces of the use of elegies at funerals. The three funerals described at any length in Evelyn's *Diary*, although two of them make particular reference to a sermon followed by a funeral oration, say nothing of elegies, epitaphs, or other poetic embellishments;[56] and, in a lower social stratum, and likewise Anglican in observance, Timothy Burrell, in noting the expenses of his sister's funeral, though he gave the generous sum of £2, 3s, for the sermon,[57] makes no mention of any money paid out for elegies. The anonymous *Directions to Fame*,[58] moreover, although it refers to insincere elegiac hyperboles as a commonplace of literature, omits all reference to the use of elegies at funerals; and the *Diary* of Pepys seems to have nothing to offer: that convivial gentleman did not linger upon the sadder aspects of life. It seems highly probable,

---

Roxburghe Ballads, ed. W. Chappell, *Ball. Soc. Publ.*, 1871, II, 210, 345, and 644; and *Bagford Ballads*, ed. J. W. Ebsworth, *Ball. Soc. Publ.*, Hertford, 1878, I, 319 and II, 539. After the Restoration, the illustrations are generally less crude, and so should serve better as an index of the actual facts. See also *A Century of Broadside Elegies*, London, 1928, Nos. 3, 17, 19, 25, 87, and 90.

[52] E.g., *An Elegy on Sir Matthew Hale* (1677) (Brit. Mus. broadside). E. Arwaker voiced the same idea (*An Elegy on General Tolmach*, London, 1694), and also an anonymous elegist of the General (*An Elegy in Commemoration of* etc., Bodl. Lib., Wood Coll., 429).

[53] E.g., *In Memory of the Truly Loyall, and Valiant Capt. John George* (1690) (Brit. Mus. broadside), lost at sea near Cape Sable.

[54] E.g., *On the Ever to be Lamented Duke of Lorraine* (1690) (Brit. Mus. broadside).

[55] *An Elegy on the Truly Honorable, and most Virtuous, Charitable and Pious Lady, Countesse of Devonshire* (1675). As patroness of Waller and other poets, she especially deserved poetic celebration. See also a broadside elegy on the actor Charles Hart (Lutt. Coll., I, No. 62).

[56] See the *Diary* under the dates of Jan. 2, 1641, the funeral of his father; Feb. 12, 1692, the funeral of his father-in-law; and Jan. 6, 1692, the funeral of Robert Boyle.

[57] *Sussex Archæological Coll.*, III, London, 1850, 155 and note 106.

[58] *Directions to Fame about an Elegy on the Late Deceased Thomas Thynn*, London, 1682, 26-27. Perhaps this piece is satiric.

therefore, that, during the latter seventeenth century, the custom of using elegies at funerals was dying out among the members of the Established Church.

In short, the use of funeral elegies among seventeenth century Anglicans as a strew for the hearse during the exequies or funeral procession, or as an ornament attached to the hearse like heraldic hatchments, is a fact beyond question; and, at least occasionally, these pieces were sung, or possibly recited. Such obsequies seem generally to have been the prerogative of the great rather than of the humble; but, of the latter, the records are so scanty that one hesitates to make final pronouncement. The omission of all mention of such a custom from heraldic records and expense books of the time would seem to show that this epicedial compliment was an extra-heraldic ceremony, and was not directly paid for, as were the funeral baked meats and the services of the torch-bearers and the hired mutes—who were not mute! The decline of the custom after the Restoration seems to be fairly well established by the evidence of the elegies themselves and by contemporary descriptions of funerals. Such a ceremony does not entirely savor of the Catholic Middle Ages; for the earliest poems of the sort incline toward the eulogy rather than the dirge; it may perhaps be an outgrowth of folk ways, but the Renaissance borrowed such novelties as it introduced from aristocratic rather than popular sources; perhaps the use sprang up by spontaneous generation, and the very vogue of elegies begot their use at funerals: there remains the hypothesis, obviously supported by the very names of some of the early pieces, *elegy, epicedium, exequy,* and the like, that the use of such pieces at funerals sprang largely from Classical example; and, although Gill may well have been wrong in attributing a Roman origin to the Mediæval dirge, he was quite possibly right in pointing to such a provenience for the Renaissance courtly elegy, with its Stoic restraint and its characteristically Renaissance promise of eternizing the subject in the annals of earthly fame.[59]

Queen Anne funerals were far from lacking in mortuary pomp; but elegies are not mentioned as an adornment of the hearse, at least among the upper classes:

---

[59] The Roman *nenia* or *nænia* were also largely eulogistic.

Strait at th' Alarm the busie Heraulds wait,
To fill the *Solemn Pomp*, and *Mourn in State*:
'Scutcheons, and Sables then make up the show,
Whilst on the Hearse the Mourning streamers flow
With all the rich Magnificence of Woe.[60]

Indeed, with the English aristocracy, the custom rose and fell about coincident with the use of the term "funeral elegy" and with the popularity of the School of Donne. Among Anglicans of the lower classes and perhaps in the provinces, it may have lingered; and the miser in Ned Ward's *Wealthy Shop-keeper* (1700), leaves £200 to the Blue-Coat Hospital,[61] "Hoping their Boys will sing me to my Grave"; but more courtly writers refer to the custom, if at all, only in the vague terms of poetic convention; and Pope was merely metaphoric when in his *Elegy* he mentioned the "hallow'd dirge . . . muttered o'er thy tomb." The use of a "Hearse with 'Scutcheons" still survived at least into the time of Gay; but, though he several times mentions elegies in the *Trivia*,[62] he gives no record of their use at funerals. Walpole does not speak of elegies as a part of the "pompous parade for the burial of old Princess Buckingham,"[63] nor some years later, at the elaborate funeral of George II,[64] which he described with indiscreet jocularity of detail; and, although, at the funeral of the Duc de Tresmes in 1739, he noted that there were "no plumes, trophies, banners, led horses, scutcheons, or open chariots," yet he did not apparently look for funeral elegies.[65] Goldsmith in his essay *On Eulogies of the Great Dead*, somewhat vaguely remarks:

It was formerly the custom here, when men of distinction died, for their surviving acquaintances to throw each a slight present into the grave. Several things of little value were made use of for that purpose,—perfumes, relics, spices, bitter herbs, camomile, wormwood, and verses. This custom, however, is almost discontinued, and nothing but verses alone are lavished.

The custom, therefore, of throwing verses into the grave seems

---

[60] *Elegy on the Lamented Death of Sir Cloudesly Shovel* (Brit. Mus. broadside).
[61] The pieces, however, sung on these occasions by the boys of Christ's Hospital, in commemoration of their benefactors, were hymns rather than elegies. See the words and music dating from 1687 and later years preserved in the Guildhall Library, London (Broadsides, V, 50, 51, 52 etc.
[62] Gay, *Trivia*, II, 379 *et seq.*, and III, 255 *et seq.*
[63] Walpole, *Letters*, Oxford, 1903-1905, I, 336.
[64] *Ibid.*, IV, 455.
[65] *Ibid.*, I, 26.

somewhat to have persisted down into the middle of the eighteenth century, several generations after the aristocracy had abandoned it. At the Universities also, it was continued. *The Paraphrase of a Hymn* by "T. S., Fellow of Maudlin College, Oxon.", already discussed, shows that the ceremony of singing the corpse to the grave lingered at Oxford at least as late as 1688; and, at Cambridge, almost a hundred years later at the burial of Dr. Chevallier, Master of St. John's College, (d. 1789):

The corpse was carried in the usual manner round the court, and when it entered the ante-chapel, . . . the crowd was tremendous. To the pall was pinned . . . various compositions in English, Greek, and Latin, furnished by the members of the Society, expressive of their deep regret.[66]

An irreverent wag snatched from the pall "several of the papers that were attached to it," and read them to his friends, finding that some of the pieces were scandalous lampoons, and that the Latin lines abounded in false quantities: certainly these "elegies" were not intended to be read or to be sung publicly! The custom, therefore, in some quarters at least extended its period of decline far down through the eighteenth century.[67]

In general, however, even as early as the reign of Queen Anne, in fashionable, urban circles, the evidence for affixing elegies to the hearse of the departed is quite negative. Nothing of the funeral elegy appears in the satiric and obscene *Description of Mr. Dryden's Funeral*,[68] though all the bardlets of London are represented as being present:

> Some groan'd, some sob'd, and some I think there wept,
> And some got drunk, loll'd down, and snor'd and slept.

But none seems to have written, read, or sung, funeral elegies. Steele's *Funeral, or Grief a-la-Mode*, although it has a fair share of verse and dwells at length on funeral arrangements, mentions no elegy in connection with Lord Brumpton's funeral. There

[66] Henry Gunning, *Reminiscences of Cambridge*, London, 1855, I, 184 *et seq.*
[67] Certainly "epitaphs," some of them by no means short, were much cultivated by the lower orders. See J. Ashton, *Social Life in the Reign of Queen Anne*, New York, 1925, 416; and a MS. thesis by Percie T. Hopkins, *A Critical History of English Biography in the Eighteenth Century*, 1924, Chapter II (Radcliffe College Lib.).
[68] *A New Collection of Poems Relating to Affairs of State*, London, 1705.

were certainly no funeral elegies at the funeral of Frederick, Prince of Wales, in 1751.[69] Neither Young[70] nor Birch[71] in their long biographies of Tillotson suggests the use of elegies at his funeral, although, like all the conscientious biographers of the day,[72] they devote much space to showing that their subject made a good end. The funeral ceremony in general was growing if anything more ostentatious and costly, with ghastly funeral rings, and even black funeral stationery,[73] individual candles for the mourners, and undertakers' invitations and hand-bills, as if the last rites were a benefit performance for some popular actor; but elegies seem to have formed no proper part to these proceedings, although Ashton suggests that such pieces "got up in charnel-house style" were sometimes printed and sent to friends.[74] This was, perhaps, the last relic among the *élite* of a former observance; for not only fashionable life, but fashionable death also, must follow the current decorum. Among Anglicans of the better class, in short, the use of the elegy at funerals seems to have arisen in the spacious days of Elizabeth and to have died out under Charles II, though it lingered among the lower classes and at the universities for perhaps another hundred years.[75]

The melancholy bias of dissent and the portentous devotional prose that grew out of it prepare one to expect among dissenters not only the considerable production of mortuary verse surveyed in an earlier chapter, but also a wide use of it at funerals. The dissenters certainly expanded the funeral sermon to its amplest proportions; and, during the seventeenth century, elegies were undoubtedly a part of the mortuary rites among many Reformed bodies on the Continent.[76] Two counteracting influences, how-

[69] See *Scots Mag.*, XIII, 204 *et seq.*

[70] Edward Young, *Life of Tillotson*, London, 1717, 119, etc.

[71] Thomas Birch, *Life of Tillotson*, London, 1752, 344.

[72] See Miss Hopkins' thesis already referred to.

[73] See Sir W. Besant, *London in the Eighteenth Century*, London, 1902, 270 *et seq.*

[74] Ashton, *op. cit.*, Chapter IV.

[75] The Methodist Movement seems to have transmuted the custom into the use of special hymns ([C. and J. Wesley], *Funeral Hymns*, third ed., London, 1753).

Several of these pieces were occasioned by the death of specific individuals; and such elegies as one finds appended to Methodist biographies may have been so used (e.g., John Gillies, *Life of Whitefield*, London, 1772, 275 *et seq.* and 338).

[76] John Durel, *View of the Government and Public Worship of God in the Reformed Churches beyond the Seas*, London, 1662, 48. The Protestant Drelincourt wrote Durel that the custom of having "the Ministers silent at dead mens burials" was "unsufferable."

ever, militated against this elegiac tendency in England. Directly under the influence of Calvin, and ultimately perhaps of Plato's *Republic*, Puritanism saw no good in poets or poetry, and pointed a special finger of scorn at current balladry. The Presbyterians, furthermore, who formed the largest single body of organized dissent in England, reacted so sharply against trentals and prayers for the dead in Purgatory that they were opposed to any sort of burial rite; and their *Directory for Publique Worship of God*,[77] based on Calvin's liturgy at Geneva, sent to its last account the soul of the departed quite unhousel'd and disappointed: indeed, the *Directory* declared that funeral rites, if there were any, were purely the affair of the State; and even the Scotch Episcopalians in the days of their triumph under Charles II, reduced the funeral liturgy to its lowest terms. After the establishment of Presbyterianism in 1688, the *Directory* became law in Scotland, and must have stood as an important example to the English Calvinists:

When any person departeth this life, let the dead body, upon the day of Burial, be decently attended from the house to the place appointed for Public Burial, and there immediately interred without Ceremony.

And because the customes of kneeling down, and praying by, or toward the dead Corps, and other such usages, in the place where it lies, before it be carried to Buriall, are Superstitious: and for that, praying, reading and singing both in going to the Grave, . . . have been grossly abused, are no way beneficiall to the dead, and have proved many ways hurtful to the living, therefore let all such things be laid aside.

Howbeit, we judge it very convenient, that the Christian friends which accompany the dead body to the place appointed for publique Buriall, do apply themselves to meditations, and conferences suitable to the occasion: And, that the Minister, as upon other occasions, so at this time, if he be present, may put them in remembrance of their duty.

That this shall not extend to deny any civill respects or differences at the Buriall, suitable to the rank and condition of the party deceased whiles he was living.

The prohibition of singing on the way to the grave probably refers not so much to any contemporary, mid-seventeenth century custom, at least so far as the Scotch Lowlands were concerned, as to the chanting of dirges in pre-Reformation times: indeed, so

---

[77] *A Directory for the Publique Worship of God, Throughout the Three Kingdoms of England, Scotland, and Ireland,* London, 1644. This was authorized by the Westminster Assembly.

thoroughly was the *Directory* followed in Scotland that it would appear to have been, at least in the Lowlands, a codification of established practices rather than an enforced innovation. During the seventeenth century, the minister was "seldom present" at a funeral;[78] and, even later, his only part was to say a protracted and edifying grace over the banquet, which was "lavish and prolonged," with much drinking and carousal. Then followed the progress to the grave, broken only by the dolorous sound of the kirk bell tolled either from a convenient tree or in the hands of the beadle at the head of the procession.[79] On the return of the mourners, their sorrows received further solace from another feast called the "dredgy,"[80] after which they got home if they could. Sturdy beggars and vagabonds for miles around assisted at these mortuary festivities; and one is not surprised to learn that the cost of a fine funeral was "sometimes equal to a year's rental," and that the very poor hoarded for a life-time to provide a feast that would attract at least a respectable line of mourners. In 1705, the body of the Countess of Cromarty, after lying in state, was carried by water to another of her residences attended by "many noblemen and gentlemen in several boats at twelve o'clock at night, with a great many flambeaus, and all the time firing guns." Again she lay in state, and finally was "interr'd very splendidly."[81] In the Highlands, funeral ceremonies lasted for days, with a midnight procession attended by wailing pibrochs and with coronachs sung by the clansmen:[82] indeed, Alexander Robertson of Struan, dying as late as 1749 at the age of eighty-one, was attended by two thousand mourners for full eighteen miles to the family tomb. The

[78] Morer, *Account of Scotland*, 1702, *Tour Through Great Britain*, IV, 247. Most of the details on Scottish funerals, the present author has drawn from H. G. Graham, *Social Life in Scotland in the Eighteenth Century*, London, 1906, 52-54, 259, and 300 *et seq*. During the eighteenth century, the minister was more commonly present, and certain of the kirk dignitaries had to be there to attend the ceremony of "kysting," to see that the body was clothed in Scottish woollen in accordance with the law subsidizing that industry. For a discussion of the Scottish elegies, see Chapter VIII.

[79] Graham, *op. cit.*, 54. See also *Notes on the Folk-Lore of the North-East of Scotland*, London, 1881, *Publ. Folk-Lore Soc.*, VII, 212; and J. E. Simpkins, *Folk-Lore concerning Fife*, London, 1914, *Publ. Folk-Lore Soc.*, 171.

[80] If this word, as Graham suggests, is a corruption of *dirge* (*op. cit.*, 300-301) then the second collation would be the dirge-feast, an expression that gives further proof of the regular use of dirges in former times.

[81] See J. Maidment, *Scotish Elegiac Verses*, Edinburgh, 1842, 22, quoting the *Edinburgh Courant*.

[82] J. E. Simpkins, *op. cit.*, 173.

poor crofters, however, seem to have been laid to rest with scant ceremony. In 1773, Boswell, though somewhat ambiguously, describes a funeral which he and Dr. Johnson attended in their Highland tour, in which grave-digging seems to have been the only formality:

I observed in this churchyard [Durinish], a parcel of people assembled at a funeral. The coffin, with the corpse in it, was placed on the ground, while the people alternately assisted in making the grave.[83]

In the Lowlands, the upper classes, at least occasionally, may have followed the custom, probably introduced from England, of affixing poems to the hearse of the departed. Although there is no mention of such poetry at the re-interment of Lord Montrose in 1661, the appended description of Sir William Hey's funeral refers to the corpse as borne in procession "garnished with Escutcheons and Epitaphs";[84] and the Scotch supply a few references to such a custom, which can hardly all be mere echoes of an English poetic convention. One author in the third person bewails his helplessness in the face of death:

> But ah! what can hee doe? bring to thy hearse
> Teare-blubbered Threnody's lugubrious verse. . . .[85]

In 1691, R. A. brought out in broadside *An Elogie On the Death of the Learned and Honorable Sir George McKenzie,* in which he exhorts his imaginary fellow-poets:

> Let's Funeral Rites be celebrate in Verse,
> And let us straw our Wishes on his Herse
> [Who] After enjoying long and happy Fate,
> Is now interr'd with Honour and in State.[86]

The times were troublous, and it is not always easy to draw lines between the Episcopalian nobility and the Covenanting com-

[83] Boswell, *Journal of a Tour to the Hebrides*, ed. Morley, London, 1891, V, 173.

[84] *Relation of the Funerals of Lord Montrose* etc., *Harl. Misc.*, London, 1746, VII, 286 *et seq.* As Montrose was a Royalist, this may have differed somewhat from the usual Presbyterian funeral, even of a nobleman.

[85] G. Lauder, *Aretophel on the death of Lord Buccleuche, Fugitive Scottish Poetry of the Seventeenth Century,* Sec. Ser., Edinburgh, 1853, No. 9, 18.

[86] Lib. of Univ. of Edinb. See frontispiece of the present volume. See also an *Elegie* on Lord Tyrconnel (1691) and a *Threnodie* by S. P. Sc. on King William (1702) (Nat. Lib. Scot. XXIV).

mons of Scotland; but, in so far as the elegy was ever used in actual funerals, it was probably by the former: the term "funeral elegy" was chiefly employed by the Anglican clergyman, Ninian Paterson; and the Presbterian Blair, on the other hand, son and grandson of clergymen, though he revels in the description of a funeral, omits from *The Grave* all mention of elegies in any exequial use. The funerary use of the elegy, then, can hardly be said to belong to Presbyterian Scotland, though English Presbyterians were presumably less rigid.

The strictness of Presbyterianism in this, as in numerous other regards, was doubtless due, in large measure, to the keen-sighted efficiency of its organization, especially in Scotland. In England, many dissenters, like Milton, found this scheme of things no better than the Anglican Establishment. The Independents, Baptists, and indeed the English Presbyterians themselves, although in origin all these bodies were thoroughly Calvinistic in their opinions, were more subject to the inner light of their individual consciences or feelings, and so could the more easily depart from the strict letter of Genevan dogma. Among the Independents, or Congregationalists, each separate group, following the lead of its chosen preacher, was almost a law unto itself: indeed, the congregations had little in common except their objection to the practices, and to the restraint, of both the Anglican hierarchy and the Presbyterian assembly. This contrifugal tendency, individualism in religion, analogous to Romantic solitariness in æsthetics,[87] makes a general study of their funeral rites peculiarly difficult; but some early record of their opinions still remains; and it is possible to inquire into the customs in vogue during the Protectorate and also in Congregational New England. Originally and basically, the Independents were as anti-liturgic as any other dissenters: Barrowe's *Brief Discovery of the False Church* (1590) describes the Book of Common Prayer, in comparison with their own extempore performance, as "old, written, rotten stuff" and "stinking patchery";[88] the seventeenth century abounds in such declarations, directed even against the Lord's Prayer; and Cotton, in his *Modest and Clear Answer to Mr. Ball* (1642), inveighs against the use of all liturgic forms.[89]

[87] I. Babbitt, *Rousseau and Romanticism*, New York, 1919, Chap. III.

[88] B. Hanbury, *Historical Memorials relating to the Independents, or Congregationalists*, London, 1839, I, 44-45, 106 etc. This is a valuable anthology of documents.

[89] *Ibid.*, II, 157 *et seq.*

The Confession of 1616, moreover, placed funerals on exactly the same plane as did the Presbyterian Directory:

Concerning making of Marriage, and Burying the Dead, we believe that they are no actions for a church-minister; because they are no actions Spiritual, but Civil.

Apparently Independent marriages were not looked upon as made in heaven; and the minister was directed to take no part in such doings.[90] The pious and reverend John Carter (d. 1634), moreover, was so godly that he would not have even a funeral sermon preached over his body, for fear that some undeserved praise might then be spoken;[91] and Richard Mather, probably for like reason, looked askance upon eulogistic sermons, and refused to preach them.[92]

But the Protectorate (not to say *reign*) of Oliver Cromwell produced among the Independents something of a change, perhaps not in the letter of the law, but, more important, in the general attitude toward outward and visible signs of authority: the illiterate masses during the Renaissance required of their rulers a certain dignity and state, and without it would hardly recognize them as rulers. Thus the comic opera of court-ceremonial was most necessary to the stability of any government; and, indeed, the importance of any single act, the reception of an ambassador, the marriage of a princess, or the obsequies of a general or statesman, was adjudged by the vulgar and also by the courtiers themselves, from the amount of pomp and circumstance used on the occasion.[93] To the entertainments of bull- and bear-baiting and to the theatre and the magnificence of the masque, the Protectorate could hardly give open countenance, especially after the vitriolic denunciations of Prynne and his fellows; but funerals at least might be made an occasion of gloomy, if not quite religious, grandeur; and the Puritans accordingly seem to have developed to the full a decorum of

---

[90] *Ibid.*, I, 300. See especially paragraph xxii.

[91] S. Clarke, *A Collection of the Lives of Ten Eminent Divines,* London, 1662, 20.

[92] S. Clarke, *Lives of Eminent Persons,* London, 1683, 129.

[93] Not for nothing did the Venetian ambassador, the representative of the wiliest state in Europe, dispatch to his government minute descriptions of the court-functions in the reigns of Elizabeth and James. Every least action and command of the sovereign was interpreted in the light of current international politics.

An Elegiack Memoriall of the Right Honourable Generall DEANE, &c.

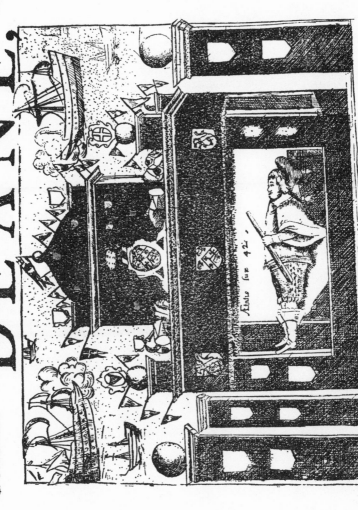

Aetatis suae 42.

R E dumb ye Muses who speake rightly Him
Needs the high Accents of a Seraphim,
A Cherub quill, & so perhaps his Verse
He in himselfe drew the Epitome

A Princely soul he had, though Country-borne,
That greatnesse could chastise, teach, use, and scorne.

And darksome Groves that *Caledonia* fills ;
Whil'st the fell Natives stand aloof and gaze,
From craggy Rocks, in a profound amaze,

funerary magnificence.[94] At first, this was probably merely a matter of extempore lamentation, as one judges from the description of the obsequies of Mr. Samuel Cook:

His Funeral was extraordinarly celebrated, not only by voluntary confluence of the greatest number of people . . . But by multitudes of Gentlemen and Ministers, *all striving to out-mourn each other,* standing about his Hearse with tears. . . . [95]

But mere tears were not sufficiently spectacular and impressive, even with the additional attraction of lachrymose rivalry; and various extrinsic aids were sought to heighten the effect. The accompanying illustration, taken from a contemporary broadside, conveys an approximate notion of the "hearse" upon which General Deane lay in state in 1653. Ireton's official funeral, the previous year, had been emblazoned with every ceremonial device;[96] and the Latinist, Payne Fisher, composed a florid poem upon the "much lamented" general "at whose Tombe, and to whose Memory this Funerall Elegy is offered and Wept."[97]

Indeed, even early in the 1640's, the exequial use of funeral elegies is unquestionable. The death of John Hampden in 1643 was celebrated with a whole pamphlet of complimentary verses, one at least of which declares itself intended for use at his funeral:

> Yet give me leave (Renouned dust) to send
> My grateful Muse in mourning to attend,
> And strew some Cypress on your Martial Herse;
> There her milde griefe, in elegiacke verse,
> Shall tell the stupid Age 't hath lost, in thee,
> More worth than e're can be repair'd in three.[98]

At least one of the pieces on the death of Pym (1643) was composed to "trouble the herse" of the departed;[99] Captain William Mercer's elegy on Colonel Luttrell (1645) professes to "add one

---

[94] The Commonwealth Period was especially important in training the middle classes in the practical business of government, thus preparing them to coöperate in the cabinet system in the reign of Charles II.

[95] S. Clarke, *Ten Eminent Divines,* 46. The italics are not in the original.

[96] Evelyn, *Diary,* ed. Bray, 219.

[97] "T. M., Junior, Esq." [Payne Fisher], *Elegy upon the death of the Late Lord Deputy of Ireland,* London, 1652.

[98] *Elegies on the Death of that Worthy and accomplish't Gentleman Colonell John Hampden,* London, 1643.

[99] *An Elegie Upon the Much Lamented Death* etc. (Thomason Coll.).

mournefull verse Upon his lifeless, much lamented hearse;"[100]
and, the following year, the same poet celebrated the interring of
Sir Henrie Mervyn's body at Westminister and exhorted his compeers to write eulogies "up his Chest."[101] Perhaps the most notable
example of burial rites *in extenso* were those of the Earl of Essex
in 1646. It took four weeks after his death to complete the
arrangements for a magnificent military funeral;[102] a special hearse
was erected at Westminster for his lying in state, decorated with
"Mottoes," some of which have come down to us, and would seem
to be proper enough elegies:[103] one of them even addresses the
funeral procession as if the mourners were actually present, and
suggests that it was intended to be recited or possibly even sung.[104]
The eminent Richard Vines delivered, and later published, the
funeral sermon, which significantly enough was largely taken up
with an extended apology, with much Biblical reference, for
funeral lamentation.[105] The whole affair had a distinctly political
tone: Parliament came in a body, and the army was well represented; and a precedent was established that could hardly be gainsaid, even though some question might still remain as to the most
godly variety and degree of lamentation. One fears, however,
that the unlearned wept their dead without consulting the latest
theological authority.

During the 1650's, the custom was widely followed. *An Offertory, Presented at the Funerals of the Right Honorable, Edward
Popham, Admirall, &c.* (1651) contains clear references to it.
The memorial volume to Sir Nathaniel Barnardiston, discussed in
the preceding chapter, gives evidence that some, if not all, of the

---

[100] *An Elegie on the Death of* etc.
(Brit. Mus. broadside).
[101] *An Elegie In Memorie, and at the
Interring of the Body of the most famous
and truely Noble Knight* etc. (Lutt.
Coll. I, No. 81).
[102] *A Brief and Compendious Narra-
tive Of the renouned Robert, Earle of
Essex,* London, 1646, 12.
[103] See *A Perfect Relation of the memorable Funerall of the Right Honorable
Robert Earle of Essex,* London, 1646;
and Daniel Evance, *Justa Honoria,* London, 1646. Copies of both of these
pamphlets are to be found in the Thomason Coll.

[104] *An Elegy upon the unhappy losse
of the Noble Earle of Essex,* London,
1646.
[105] *A Hearse of the Renouned, the
Right Honorable Robert Earle of Essex,*
London, 1646. Such a stand on the part
of the Presbyterian Vines suggests that
the English Presbyterians were less rigid
in the matter of lamentation than were
their Scotch brethren. Vines, however,
does not specifically advocate elegies, and
perhaps refers merely to sermons. See
also Obadiah Sedgwick, *Elisha his Lamentation,* London, 1654; and Samuel Clarke,
*An Antidote against Immoderate Mourn-
ing,* London, 1659.

poems it contains were attached to his hearse during the funeral procession: Marriot entitles his piece an *Elegy at the Funeral* of his subject; and such passing expressions as ". . . . thus late my verse, In *black* and *white* attends your sacred hearse . . ."[106] seem clear references to the custom. Richard James declared that funeral elegies were composed "with courteous intent" as an honor to the "hearse" of the departed;[107] a broadside *Funeral Elegy Upon the Death of George Sonds Esq.* (1655) admits that it was intended "to consecrate and to adorn his Hearse." Indeed, there can be little doubt that the custom flourished during the Commonwealth Period.

After the Restoration in the welter of non-conformity, evidence is scarcely procurable; but it seems clear that non-conformity did not, like the Establishment, give up the custom. Possibly there were restrictions upon the publication of such pieces;[108] but the number that were printed shows that they could not have been "silenced" even as much as were dissenting sermons. Puritan funerals could hardly have been as elaborate as before; but elegies were at least sometimes employed. The attitude of the occasional elegist toward his art and its purpose is well summarized in a broadside *Elegie Sacred to the Memory of Sir Edmund-bury Godfrey Knight; Barbarously Murthered* (1678).[109] The writer is clearly a Whig, if not a Puritan:

> An elegie! forbear: who ere *profanes*
> This *lasting Name* with cheap unhallowed strains,
> Commits a *Murther* second to their Guilt,
> By whose *infernal Hands* his Blood was spilt.
> So vast a *Merit*, and so strange a *Fate*,
> Must not be *Blazon'd* at the common Rate;
> With *mercenary* Rhyme, Set-forms of Praise,
> Or stale Applauses which bold Flatterers raise
> To pin upon some Herse, whose waiting throng
> *Mourn* onely 'cause the party liv'd *so long*.
> Those *customary Sighs* have here no part;
> We weep *in earnest*, and untaught by Art.

[106] *Suffolk's Tears*, London, 1653, 18, 28, 39.

[107] Richard James, *Poems*, ed. Grosart, 216-217.

[108] See *On the Death of Mr. Calamy* (Lutt. Coll II, No. 29):

And must our Deaths be silenced too!
    I guess
'Tis some dumb Devil hath possesst the
    Press;
Calamy dead without a Publication!

[109] Lutt. Coll., I, No. 53.

Thus do all the elegists blacken their neighbors' faces in the naïve expectation that the process will whiten their own. The reference to pinning the elegies upon "some Hearse" suggests, in its bald literalness, that the funereal use of elegies was an actual current custom. Some broadsides contain an announcement of the time and place of the interment, like that on the noted Independent minister, the Rev. George Cokayne (1691)[110] or bear the legend that they are printed "for the Use of the Friends of the Deceased."[111]   An *Elegiack Essay*[112] on "the Rev'rend Gouge" shows that in 1700, elegies were still used in funeral processions, but at the same time suggests the decline of the custom:

> Shall but One muse accompany his Hearse,
> Singing his Praise in Elegiack Verse?

And in lamenting the "Faithful and Laborious" Baptist divine, Mr. Benjamin Keach (1704), the elegist wishes to spread his "lowly Verse, as grateful Tributes round thy mournful Hearse."[113] During the latter seventeenth century, the natural fondness for music reasserted itself; and "rude strains in the vulgar tongue" became audible from Independent chapels.[114] The melancholy elegiac mood was not passed over; and Isaac Watts, who gave the dissenters their first real hymnology, called one of the five lyrics of *Death and Heaven* an *Ode at the Interment of the Body, supposed to be Sung by the Mourners*.[115]   In 1745, Doddridge even went so far as to append to his *Sermon Occasioned by the Heroick Death of the Honorable Col. James Gardiner* an *Hymn Sung after the Sermon*;[116] and the non-conformist Defoe seems to have taken the elegy as one of the essential trappings of death.[117]   In view of all this evidence, therefore, it seems safe to conclude that, in spite of the Confession of 1616, the Independents, from the time that

[110] Lutt. Coll., I, No. 43.

[111] *To the Memory of Mr. Caleb Skinner and Mr. Hezekiah Middleton* (1688) (Brit. Mus. broadside).

[112] *Elegiac Essay on the Death of Thomas Gouge*, London, 1700, 4. A copy of this pamphlet is to be found in Harvard Univ. Lib.

[113] *An Elegy on the Much Lamented Death of* etc. (Brit. Mus. broadside).

[114] W. J. Courthope, *History of English Poetry*, London, 1895-1910, V, 329.

[115] I. Watts, *Poetical Works*, London, 1807, I, 161 *et seq*. See also T. Gibbons, *An Elegiac Poem to the Memory of the Rev. Isaac Watts*, London, 1749. Watts, we are told, "sung of Gunston . . . o'er the closing Grave."

[116] P. Doddridge, *Sermon* etc., London, 1745, 34.

[117] D. Defoe, *Farther Adventures of Robinson Crusoe*, ed. Maynadier, Philadelphia, 1903, 9.

they began to take over the elegy in the 1640's, regularly used it in their funeral services down into the eighteenth century, long after Anglicans of the better class had foregone the custom.[118]

New England supplies several interesting documents in support of such a view. One of the earliest New England elegies is suggestively entitled *A Funeral Tribute*[119] though the piece was probably used during the procession or at the grave rather than during the funeral rites—if, indeed, funeral rites were permitted in seventeenth century New England! In two of his elegies, Cotton Mather seems clearly to refer to the custom of attaching such verse to the hearses of the eminent departed. In his lines *To the Reader* prefaced to his elegy on Oakes, he says: "And Norton's Herse do's Poet Wilson trim With Verses"; and later: ". . . I cannot but thy Herse bedew With dropping of some *Fun'ral Tears!*" And still later he refers to his composition as "a Verse to wait upon thy Grave." In his lament on Nathaniel Collins, printed in Boston in 1685,[120] he describes the hearse as adorned with bad "Funeral verses," and alludes to elegiac writing as "A *Paper* winding sheet to lay him out!" The exact title of this piece, *Funeral Tears at the Grave*, etc., suggests that elegies were used at the interment and perhaps thrown into the earth after the body. The continuance of this custom at an even later date is implied in the title of a broadside, with a fine mortuary border, published in 1708: *Carmen Miserabile, A Solemn Lachrymatory for the Grave of Jonathan Marsh*. Although some of these broadsides adopt the immediate tone that implies performance at the funeral, and are written in a sing-song stanza form,[121] yet the setting of such pieces to music would seem to have been rare,[122] and probably did not take

---

[118] The Baptists were perhaps slower to accept the elegy and its funereal use; but the verses on Keach show that they were following the custom at least in the reign of Queen Anne.

[119] Benjamin Thompson, *A funeral Tribute to the Honorable dust of that most charitable Christian, John Winthrop*, a Boston broadside (1676), listed in Evans (*American Bibliography*, Chicago, 1903, item 224). The Independents (or Congregationalists) had of course made their form of worship the established church in most of the New England provinces. For a discussion of the New England elegies, see Chapter VI.

[120] C. Mather, *An Elegy on Nathanael Collins*, ed. Hunnewell, *Publ. Club of Odd Volumes*, Boston, Mass., 1896, No. 3.

[121] E.g., J. Burt, *A Lamentation Occasion'd by the Great Sickness . . . in Springfield* (1712) (Lib. Mass. Hist. Soc.), and S. Danforth, *An Elegy in Memory of Thomas Leonard* (1713) (Lib. Boston Athen.).

[122] S. A. Green (*Proceed. Mass. Hist. Soc.*, VIII, 387) says that elegies were commonly circulated in MS., and sometimes printed on broadsides. Large numbers have doubtless been lost.

place until the example of Watts had long since paved the way. A single broadside, however, dating from about 1750, clearly indicates that such a use at least occasionally existed; and the more secular and less melancholy atmosphere of the text suggests that the piece, and probably also the custom, belong to the decadence of the funeral elegy. Indeed, *The Mournful Lamentation For the sad and deplorable Death of Mr. Old Tenor, To the Mournful Tune of Chevy Chase*,[123] seems almost a travesty of its seventeenth century forebears. The continued use of elegies at Congregational funerals in New England clearly supports the opinion that such pieces were so used during the same period by the same sect in the mother country; and it seems difficult to avoid the conclusion that the Independents, having assumed the elegy and its funerary use during the Commonwealth, continued them down into the eighteenth century, some generations after the general body of Anglicans, for whom the Prayer Book supplied a sufficient ritual, had abandoned them.

Strictly speaking, there was never a liturgic use of the funeral elegy; but the evidence points to its employment as a ceremonial accretion, hardly recognized officially by ecclesiastical authority but based on Classical and Mediæval precedents and somewhat on the customs of the folk, and developed in response to the Renaissance impulse for at least a short-lived earthly fame. The attaching of elegies to the hearse before, or during, the funeral procession seems, in the seventeenth century, to have been common among members of the Anglican Communion who were sufficiently eminent to claim such an honor. The dissenters, to whose melancholy cast of mind such a custom should have appealed, were somewhat restrained from following it by their disapproval of poetry, of set liturgical forms, and of funeral liturgies in particular: the Presbyterians, consequently, at least in Scotland, hardly used the elegy; the Independents, on the other hand, though quite as opposed in theory, yet, partly because they were less strictly organized, and partly because their period of rule during the Commonwealth required more of pageantry and parade, developed funerary ceremonial, lapsed into the funerary use of elegies, and seem to have continued this use down into the eigh-

[123] See *Proceed. Mass. Hist. Soc.*, XLIII, 256.

teenth century, when the Anglicans, perhaps because they began to see in it the hall-mark of dissent, had abandoned the practice. The rise, in the late seventeenth century, of an original hymnology removed at least one objection to the funeral elegy; and, in the person of Isaac Watts, dissent combined song and funeral poetry, and once more, in a sense, returned to the pre-Reformation days when the body was borne to the grave to the singing of a dirge. In America, although Congregationalism was more fully organized than at home, a similar, though slower, change seems to have come into being. The age-long tendency of art to associate itself with the social life of the people, and especially with the three great institutions, the family, the church, and the state, is fully illustrated in the history of the funeral elegy, although one sometimes thinks of the form as a mere traditional combination of literary conventions. The use in funerals of such verses, especially when written by poets of a melancholy cast whose Pegasus could not soar beyond the details of immediate realism, undoubtedly augmented the mortuary tone already apparent in some of the religious poems of Donne; and thus the taking over of the elegy into funerary use by the Puritans accentuated the element of mortuary description; for the immediacy of death would naturally suggest to the hard-driven poet the depiction of the last illness, the dying moments, the funeral, the grave, and the bodily corruption, of the departed; and to all this he could append appropriate moral truisms to adorn the gruesome tale. During the eighteenth century, however, British dissent, under the influence of wider educational facilities and of the rise of Deism, was growing colder; and, as the economic position of the middle class improved, especially during the reigns of William and Mary and the Hanoverians, their attitude toward the affairs of this world grew brighter, and was somewhat reflected in a corresponding change toward the affairs of the next. Addison, in a passage already quoted, records the new tendency toward optimism;[124] and, as early as the 1730's, even the close-knit Presbyterians found in their numbers not only some who denied the more rigorous tenets of Calvin, but even ministers holding Arian views.[125] At the same time, dissenters were widening

---

[124] According to Bunyan, this change was taking place even as early as the reign of Charles II. See the present author, *Bunyan's Mr. Ignorance, Mod. Lang. Rev.*, XXII, 15 *et seq.*
[125] See Lecky, *History of England in*

their artistic interests and turning to other media for expression, so that, during the early eighteenth century, the funeral elegy by degrees, ceased to constitute the chief æsthetic expression of the dissidence of dissent, and, as a funebrial auxiliary, was outgrown and discarded.[126]

the Eighteenth Century, New York, 1892, I, 360.

[126] These changes are discussed at length in Chapters VII, IX, and X.

CHAPTER V

THE FUNERAL ELEGY IN THE REIGN OF CHARLES II

IN general, the Renaissance saw a decline in the political prestige of the trading classes. After a protracted struggle during the Middle Ages against lay and clerical overlords, the townsmen had won for themselves, by about the beginning of the fifteenth century, the most coveted privileges and immunities. In this struggle, the king had been their chief ally: they supported him with taxes and loans; and he in return gave them chartered rights against their aristocratic neighbors, and afforded what protection he could to their commerce on the king's highway and on the high seas.[1] Both were combined against the lay nobles who wielded the power of the sword in most localities and against the great ecclesiastics who could call down spiritual terrors and threats of vengeance from abroad. The power of the nobles, however, considerably diminished after Crécy and Poitiers had shown the efficacy of cloth-yard arrows against full-panoplied knights, and after the invention of gunpowder had made the baronial castle insecure. The great ecclesiastics, moreover, fell during the reign of Henry VIII: the priors and the abbots were no more; and the bishops were now appointed by the king and not from Rome. Thus, during the sixteenth century, royalty was the cogent factor in the state; the nobles and clergy were reduced to courtiers; and the king needed no alliance with the trading classes to maintain himself. Tudor despotism had come in; and the towns, by imperceptible degrees, experienced a political decline. The foundation of the Royal Exchange and the increase of foreign trade in the reigns of Elizabeth and James were, to be sure, a certain economic compensation; but colonial expansion brought with it a sort of Nemesis: the younger sons of the county families, and even of the nobility, had in earlier times become London merchants, and so had lent dignity, culture, and social position, to that calling; now they sought adventure in foreign parts; and, furthermore, the

[1] See Mrs. J. R. Green, *Town Life in the Fifteenth Century*, N. Y., 1895.

monastic schools, which had previously put education within the reach of the moderately well-to-do, were now dissolved, and new foundations like that of the Merchant Taylors of London, gave but slight compensation.[2] Thus, by degrees during the seventeenth century, was inaugurated the social principle of the vulgarity of trade and the utter separation of the commercial orders from the cultivated aristocracy.

Partly because of this loss of social prestige in an age when the court was all-powerful and when court-favors depended largely upon the courtliness of the petitioner, and partly because the royal power, instead of supporting, was often in opposition to their pre-rogatives and desires, the towns and the townsmen, although they were possessed of increasing riches, found their political influence at a rather low ebb, until in the 1830's, the middle classes com-bined with the proletariat, forced the passage of the Reform Bills, and, without quite shattering it to bits remolded the scheme of things nearer to their hearts' desire.[3] The Civil War and the Commonwealth constitute their chief protest against this inter-mediate period of decline; and the citizens and trained bands of London took a prominent part. The country as a whole, however, neither desired nor was ready for a Puritan[4] plutocracy[5]: at the Restoration, all society hastened to repudiate what had gone be-fore;[6] and the reign of Charles II witnessed, in some respects, the lowest point that the bourgeoisie reached, the nadir in the swing of the pendulum between the fifteenth and the nineteenth cen-

---

[2] The increasing acceptance during the earlier and middle seventeenth century, of the anti-artistic tenets of Puritanism by the bourgeoisie, constitutes a symptom of this decline in social *savoir faire*. On the monastic dissolution and the Renais-sance as the "revival of ignorance," see the Rev. R. H. Benson, (*Camb. Hist. of Eng. Lit.*, III, Chapter III).

[3] See Sir W. Besant, *London in the Eighteenth Century*, London, 1902, 37, 51, 230, *et seq.* The line between no-bility and trade grew very sharp, *ibid.*, 408-409.

[4] The present chapter continues some-what to use the word "Puritan," and in-cludes under the term not only the two thousand divines that were excluded from their livings by the Act of Uniformity in 1662 and their followers in dissent,

but also some others, especially in the towns, who might with an equal consis-tency have followed their example, but were restrained by either inertia or con-venience, and so constituted the extreme Low Church of the Establishment. Cf. C. H. Firth, *The Stuart Restoration, Camb. Mod. Hist.*, New York, 1908, V, 98 *et seq.*

[5] See S. N. Patten, *The Development of English Thought*, New York, 1899, 128 *et seq.*; and R. Lodge, *History of England, 1660-1702*, London, 1918, 1 *et seq.*

[6] In spite of the King's efforts at con-ciliation and toleration, consonant with the Declaration of Breda, the Parliament that sat from 1661 to 1679 was intensely reactionary. See Firth, *op. cit.*, 97.

turies.[7] Money, to be sure, they still possessed, and indeed were accumulating more of it at the expense of their Dutch rivals; but down to the end of the century when improved banking and insurance began to place mercantile affairs on a firmer foundation, the probability that any individual merchant could keep his gains was so slight that—unless he invested in landed estates, and forsook the counting house to join the squirarchy—he had little chance of passing on to his posterity either his money or the traditions of culture that accumulate with it; and, even in the eighteenth century, there was some justification for the plea implicit in Burke that, without a legally constituted and protected nobility, culture and the arts and even the settled government on which they were based could not exist.[8] Thus, in the reign of Charles II, the middle class, though wealthy and on the whole prosperous, was socially uncouth and politically discredited.

The decades of the 1640's and '50's constituted a crucial period in the history of the funeral elegy. Before 1640, such commemoration was largely the prerogative of the Cavalier nobility; it emanated usually from poets of repute, and the pieces were printed in their works or in volumes of miscellaneous authorship got up to commemorate the death of some individual. During the '40's two changes take place: the Cavaliers develop the elegy for political propaganda, encouraging hack poets to bring out broadsides to curry favor for their cause among the London cits; and the politicians of Puritanism, likewise, over-riding religious scruples, perceived in the *genre* an advantage to their own cause, and employed it as a counterpoise to the royal dignity that no longer reigned from Whitehall, and as an element of impressive grandeur in funerals of state; and, like the Cavaliers, they printed their pieces on broadsides for dissemination among the lower orders. By degrees, even the Puritan clergy accepted the funeral elegy; and, though they still held off from broadside publication until after the return of the Stuarts, they did not scruple to use such verses at one another's funerals. Meanwhile, the Cavaliers, having failed to win over for the royal martyr the sympathy of the broadside-reading public, abandoned the elegy to their adversaries, and

---

[7] See W. E. H. Lecky, *A History of England in the Eighteenth Century*, New York, 1892, I, 8-9. Under Charles II, many of the city corporations most hos-tile to the Crown were accused of petty irregularities, and so lost their charters.

[8] See especially Burke's *Reflections* and his *Letter to a Noble Lord*.

employed it, if at all, in parody or ridicule. Thus the funeral elegy, from sporadic use by the balladists and the poets of the School of Donne, became in the course of twenty years the semi-official expression of Puritanism, and the brief chronicler of its heroes and its saints; and, although at the Restoration, journalistic broadside elegies of an indeterminate party cast again became common, yet the Puritan tradition did not subside; and in aristocratic circles, the funeral elegy, in anything like its older forms, was ignored or made light of, and was little used by any poet who did not wish his loyalty called in question.[9] An earlier chapter has shown how Cowley and Waller, who had previously fallen into the atrabilious style, promptly fell out of it again at the Restoration;[10] and, even as early as 1650, Denham felt it necessary to offer excuses to himself and to his polite readers for the "privilege" of a "Tear" on Lord Hastings.[11] After 1660, the display of too much feeling, especially of the sorts affected by the Puritans, was neither good politics nor good manners: the accusation of "enthusiasm" must at all costs be avoided; and most persons, including the poets, chose to hunt with the hounds.[12] The courtly elegy, therefore, although widely cultivated during the quarter-century of Caroline rule, fell into the form of a somewhat flat and forced Pindaric ode without either the mortuary detail of the Puritan pieces or the assurance of Salvation of the School of Donne. Thus "metaphysical" influences for a time subsided;[13] and elegiac melancholy, along with Puritanism, though both still persisted as a strong undercurrent in the body social, was submerged and, on the surface of both literature and society, but little apparent.

Dryden, like Cowley and Waller, represents the sharp change in poetic style immediately consequent upon the Restoration. His youthful *Elegy Upon the Death of Lord Hastings*, following in the tradition of the broadside eulogy of Lord Northampton (1643) previously discussed,[14] is chiefly known for its ingenious description

[9] See Firth, *op. cit.*, 99-100.
[10] See Chapter II.
[11] Denham, *Elegy on the Death of Henry Lord Hastings*, written in 1650, *Oxford and Cambridge Miscellany* [ed. Fenton] London, [c1707].
[12] Even the dissenters of a former generation were growing more decorous; and their objection to the "enthusiasm" of the Quakers is not insignificant. See, for example, Bunyan's writings against them, especially *Some Gospel Truths (Works,* London, 1859, I, 77 *et seq.*).
[13] See A. H. Nethercot, *The Reputation of the "Metaphysical Poets" During the Seventeenth Century, Jour. of Eng. and Ger. Phil.*, XXIII, 173 *et seq.*
[14] Thomason Coll. See Chapter II.

of the small-pox; and, like Fracastoria's famous Latin poem, it
gives ample symptomatology of a "foul disease":

> So many spots, like næves,[15] our Venus[16] soil?
> One jewell set off with so many a foil?
> Blisters with pride swelled, which through his flesh did sprout
> Like rosebuds, stuck in the lily skin about.
> Each little pimple had a tear in it,
> To wail the fault its rising did commit. . . .

Here surely was a young elegist *sans peur*, if not quite *sans re-
proche*; and Donne himself hardly winged a more unerring paradox in the face of convention. The following quotation, in its
cacophony of metrical emphasis, is also suggestive of Donne; and,
in its final metaphor, of Crashaw's *Weeper*:

> Must then old three-legged grey-beards with their gout,
> Catarrhs, rheums, aches, live three ages out?
> Time's offals, only fit for the hospital,
> Or to hang an antiquary's rooms withal!
> Must drunkards, lechers spent with sinning, live
> With such helps as broths, possets, physic give?
> None live but such as should die? shall we meet
> With none but ghostly fathers in the street?
> Grief makes me rail, sorrow will force its way,
> And showers of tears tempestuous sighs best lay.
> The tongue may fail; but overflowing eyes
> Will weep out lasting streams of elegies.[17]

Dryden's quatrains on Cromwell constitute a Renaissance military
eulogy replete with Roman allusions recently gleaned in the school-
room: Cromwell was apparently too mighty to be bewailed in any
mere private or Christian character. At the Restoration, Dryden
very hopefully renovated his elegiac style, along with his opinions,
to accord with the stellar revisitation that England was about to
enjoy. He still employed generous proportions of panegyric and
of Classical reference, especially in the pastoral *Amyntas*; but the
touch is lighter, almost whimsical, with smooth passages of poetic
fioritura. His lines *To the Memory of Mr. Oldham* especially

---

[15] Spots or small excrescences of the
body.

[16] "Venus" refers to Lord Hastings as
the perfection of beauty.

[17] It is significant that Oldham, imitating this poem in his elegy on Charles
Morwent after the Restoration, did not
choose to borrow the passages here quoted.

possess this quality of polished fineness. His *Threnodia Augustalis, a Funeral-Pindaric Poem to the Happy Memory of King Charles II* —although written almost equally in congratulation and eulogy of his successor—is nevertheless somewhat more than the "prostrate and anxiously rhetorical obituary from the blazoning pen of a commissioned laureate"[18] that one might expect: Dryden never quite lacks dignity. It is written in irregular stanzas after the manner of Cowley; and, ostensibly for that reason, got no praise from Dr. Johnson.[19] The first strophe, with its "lethargy in mighty woe," has a few mildly mortuary touches; and it is perhaps significant that Johnson found supreme merit in Dryden's similar ode on Mrs. Anne Killigrew, which barely mentions the tomb and only in connection with the Resurrection. Dryden's post-Restoration elegies may indulge in some necessary reference to death; but they neither rejoice in it as a release and a consolation, as did the early Cavaliers, nor find in it an awful warning, as did the Puritans: they ignore it as much as possible, and pay to it only such passing notice as the theme of the poem requires.

A similar attitude obtains in the elegies of Matthew Stevenson, whose *Bellum Presbyteriale* vouches for the Royalist orthodoxy of its author's politics. The *Elegy upon my Worthy Friend Mr. Isaak Lawton*[20] is consolatory to the point of almost flippant optimism. He goes on record as favoring a decorous and proper death-bed scene (perhaps like that of Charles II!); and rather scorns those "sullen Souls" that

> . . . at Deaths unwelcom [*sic*] doom,
> Break like an Earthquake from the trembling womb,
> And with unknown Convulsions, tear, and wrest,
> As Devils took their leave of the possest.

Perhaps the passage was intended as a delicate mortuary compliment to the Puritans. Many of his pieces are quite appropriately included in *Norfolk Drollery;*[21] but here and there the influence of Donne,

---

[18] This happy characterization of the generality of elegies of the day is taken from G. L. Kittredge, *Chaucer*, Cambridge, Mass., 1915, 39.

[19] Johnson, *Life of Dryden*. See *Lives of the Poets*, ed. Hill, Oxford, 1905, I, 438.

[20] M. Stevenson, *Poems; or, a Miscellany of Sonnets, Satyrs, Drollery, Panegyrics, Elegies*, etc., London, 1665, 108 et seq.

[21] M. Stevenson, *Norfolk Drollery*, 1673, reprinted in J. O. Halliwell, *Norfolk Anthology*, Brixton Hill, 1852. The elegy on Rant was perhaps intended as Puritan satire.

or possibly of Quarles, is apparent in lines that date perhaps from
the pre-Restoration period. His verses *Upon a Gentleman drown'd,
and lost in the River Wharfe in Yorkshire* have a vermian reminiscence of ante-bellum poetry:

> It signifies just nothing when Heaven calls,
> Let Worms, or Fishes, be our *Cannibals*.
> My fancy yet, the nobler Fish prefers
> Before the Worms, those crawling Sepulchres.

But the gruesome images seem to be employed with the conceited
cleverness of Donne rather than the morbid emotionalism of the
Puritan elegists. The consolation, to be sure, is chilly enough;
but it is apparently intended as consolation rather than as edification. His elegy *Upon a Lady at York dying in Child-Birth*
contains the conventional reference to "ashy Death mounted on
his pale steed; That Prince of terrors . . ."; and his *Epitaph
upon Mr. Robert Dey*, the Norwich apothecary, although penned
in a most elaborate style, has only the mildest mortuary elements.
The exact date of the writing of these poems is uncertain, but their
style suggests early composition. It is, however, quite possible that
in the remote regions of Yorkshire and in a Puritan stronghold
like East Anglia, the older fashions might linger. In either case,
Stevenson's *Elegy upon Sir Henry Wright* (d. 1663) has quite a
different tone; and, although it indulges in the conventional hyperbolic metaphor of sorrow—*viz.* "Tempests of sighs and Hurricans
of tears"—yet, on the whole, it is restrained and decorous and
optimistic. In short, Stevenson would seem to have suffered the
metamorphosis common among bards in 1660; and these rapid and
noticeable transformations apparently indicate that the degree of
emotion and the devices of ornament, at least of the elegy, are a
matter more of convenience and less of inspiration than is by some
allowed, and that poetic style is not always "the man himself."

Any great change of literary atmosphere is more surely illustrated in the many conventional poetasters of an age than in its
few, and more individualized, poets; and certainly the general run
of courtly writers, Anglican politically if not religiously speaking,
did not indulge in the mortuary even as much as their forebears
of the 1620's and '30's: indeed, they seem to make a point of
avoiding it. They cultivated poetry "on several occasions" as a

decus, an ornament to the bare events of life; and to them the gloomy was not ornamental. There is *The Exclames of Rho-dopæa*[22] on the death of the Marquis of Montrose, a performance as Royalist in theme as it is Classical in manner. There is the *Elegy on James Bristow, Late Fellow of All-Souls,* Cowleian Pindarics by one Edward Palmer,[23] whose lines would have been more felicitous had he taken his subject with a few more grains of rather more Attic salt. The mob of gentlemen who supplied amusement, poetic and otherwise, to the court of the merry monarch wrote elegies, but very seldom in an elegiac style; and the irregular Pindarics by which most poets beguiled the time usually displayed their poetic fire rather in the light of an *ignis fatuus.* A poem *To the Memory of the Duke of Buckingham,*[24] is written in the dignified tone of current fashionable Stoical restraint:

> When the dread summons of commanding Fate
> Sounds the last Call at some proud Palace Gate;
> When both the Rich, the Fair, the Great, the High;
> Fortunes most darling Favorites must die;
> Straight at the Alarm the busie Heraulds wait,
> To fill the solemn Pomp, and mourn in State,
> Scutcheons and Sables then make up the Show,
> Whilst on the Hearse the mourning Streamers flow,
> With all the Rich Magnificence of Woe.

Most of the elegies, however, are designedly either trivial or satiric. Lord Roscommon's airy poem *On the Death of a Lady's Dog* links the tradition of Herrick with Gray's *Ode* on the drowning of Horace Walpole's cat. The *Elegie on Colonel Blood* (d. 1680),[25] that entrancing blackguard who hardly needs the pen of Sir Walter Scott to immortalize his career, is clearly satiric, both of its subject and of the elegiac form. The Colonel usually followed the fortunes of the Puritan party; but his biography forbids one to describe him as a Puritan and his politics were as reliable as those of Defoe. At the end of the elegy proper is appended an *Epitaph* that, with more truth than poetry, holds him up to scorn as an

[22] *Various Pieces of Fugitive Scottish Poetry,* Sec. Ser., Edinburgh, 1853, No. 32.

[23] Palmer, *Elegy on Bristow,* Oxford, 1667.

[24] *Chorus Poetarum: or Poems on Several Occasions By the Duke of Buckingham, the late Lord Rochester,* etc., London, 1674, 75.

[25] *Roxburghe Ballads,* ed. Chappell, Ball. Soc. Publ., Hertford, 1889, VI, 78.

egregious turn-coat. The poetic joke-books of the age, moreover, such as *Wit and Drollery*[26] and *Rome Rhymed to Death*[27] contain satiric, sometimes obscene, elegiac parodies. Oldham, to be sure, once forsook his Sicilian Muse to follow the Bible rather than Bion; but his rendition of *David's Lamentation for the Death of Saul and Jonathan*[28] is merely another irregular Pindaric, with as little of the mortuary as the original allowed; and his elegy *On the Death of Mrs.* [Mistress] *Katharine Kingscourt, a child of Excellent Parts and Piety* belongs to the same class as Prior's charming lines *To a Child of Quality Five Years Old*. Samuel Butler's *Pindarick Ode to the Happy Memory of the Most Renouned Du Val*, seems written under the influence of the author's Hudibrastic style. Indeed, the England of Charles II and especially the courtiers of that "merry" reign were too deeply disillusioned to care for the immediate contemplation of death: they ate, drank, and drowned the sorrows of human mortality in the much bruited cask of malmsey—or, even more effectively, in draughts of fashionable French brandy.

The literary performance of Thomas Flatman, miniature-painter and poet, has long since been epitomized in Rochester's famous triplet; and it is all-too-generally applicable to his all-too-numerous funeral odes on the nobility and the royalty of his time:

> Nor that slow drudge in swift Pindaric strains,
> Flatman, who Cowley imitates with pains,
> And rides a jaded Muse, whipt, with loose reins.

Flatman's Pindarics are neither inspiring nor inspired; but they contain a few happy phrases that are subject for the present study, and that serve to remind the reader that the poet embarked upon his elegiac career during the Commonwealth.[29] He begins the first strophe of his poem *On the Death of the Earl of Ossory* with "Emasculating sighs, and groans around"; and the ode *On the Death of the Earl of Albemarle* has a pertinent strophe on "Death's

---

[26] *Wit and Drollery*, London, 1682, 40 et seq., *On the Death of Joseph Wright*.
[27] *Rome Rhymed to Death* "by the E[arl] of R[oscommon], Dr. Wild, and others of the best Modern Wits," London, 1683, 78 and 107. Wilde was, of course, a noted Puritan though a Royalist in politics.

[28] Written, September, 1677. He characterizes London as "The Charnel-House of Gallantry" and the "Golgotha of Worth."
[29] See the collection of Oxford verses on the death of Charles Capel, 1656.

grisly shape" in the battle-field. The lines *On the Death of my Dear Brother Mr. Richard Flatman* do not aspire to soaring on main wing, and, because they attempt only a middle flight, escape the calamity of Icarus. He has "melancholy thoughts of Death" in the second line, and later something of his brother's "last Agony"; but the general tone is restrained and not ineffective. Flatman, however, like Donne and others of his forebears, incorporated his most mortuary materials in certain non-elegiac poems, such as his *Dying Tears*, and his *Dialogue between Death and a Lady*, both of which seem to have had something of a vogue as broadsides.[30] His *Dooms-Day Thought*, composed, appropriately enough, in the *Götterdämerung* of the Commonwealth, is too significant to be omitted from any anthology of gloom; it begins with cosmic horrifics, which later sink to an elegiac note:

> Go to the dull church-yard and see
> Those hillocks of mortality,
> Where proudest Man is only found
> By a small swelling in the ground.
> What crowds of carcases are made
> Slaves to the pickaxe and the spade!
> Dig but a foot or two to make
> A cold bed for thy dead friend's sake,
> 'Tis odds but in that scantling room
> Thou robb'st another of his tomb,
> Or in thy delving smit'st upon
> A shinbone or a cranion.[31]
>   When th'prison's full, what next can be
> But the Grand Gaol-Delivery?
> The Great Assize, when the pale clay
> Shall gape, and render up its prey;
> When from the dungeon of the grave
> The meagre throng themselves shall heave,
> Shake off their linen chains, and gaze
> With wonder when the world shall blaze. . . .
>   What shall we do then, when the voice
> Of the shrill trump with strong fierce noise
> Shall pierce our ears, and summon all
> To th'Universe' wide Judgement Hall?
> What shall we do! we cannot hide,

---

[30] *Roxburghe Ballads, ed. cit.*, IV, 360, and II, 189. There seems no doubt that Flatman's appeal was chiefly to his fellow-citizens of London.

[31] Cf. the grave-diggers' scene in *Hamlet*; but Flatman's source may have been, not literary, but the actual condition in the burying grounds of his day.

Nor yet that scrutiny abide:
When enlarg'd conscience loudly speaks,
And all our bosom-secrets breaks;
When flames surround and greedy Hell
Gapes for a booty (*who can dwell*
With everlasting Burnings!), when
Irrevocable words shall pass on men;
Poor naked men, who sometimes thought
These frights perhaps would come to nought!
What shall we do! we cannot run
For refuge, or the strict Judge shun.
'Tis too late *then* to think what course to take;
While we live here, we must provision make.

Saintsbury is clearly right in assigning Flatman's "sense of Death" to an earlier generation;[32] but it is notable that after the Restoration, the plenitude of his mortuary stream subsides to a rather slender trickle, especially in the elegies designed for the perusal of the great.   In his earlier years, his chief inspiration, outside the seventeenth century poetic tradition, seems to have been *Ecclesiasticus*; in his later Lucretius; and the change is significant.

Except for Flatman, who generally was not in the courtly tradition, there is almost nothing in the legitimate poetry of this period that is material for the present study; and the Pindaric formula on which the poets planned their commemorative works was far from mortuary.   The broadside verse of the reign of Charles II would seem to fall into three classes: such pieces as were written to inveigle patronage from the great, and so were largely composed of vapid eulogy; such pieces as were written for sale to the general public and are therefore largely journalistic in the more doubtful sense of that dubious adjective; and pieces composed by sorrowing friends especially on non-conformist divines of eminent piety.   Broadside elegies of the first of these classes commonly belong to the second also; but the third class, though printed for general sale, is rather distinct.   The ballad-reading public was still largely the bourgeoisie; and ballads of the second and third groups intended for their consumption were mainly concocted of sensational and moralistic ingredients: in the clerical elegies, moral reflections were an immediate development from the exemplary life

[32] *Caroline Poets*, ed. Saintsbury, Oxford, 1905-1921, III, 280.

of the subject; and his sickness, death, burial, and bodily decay, supplied the spice of the sensational.

The two first mentioned types, the eulogies of the great and the tid-bits of journalism, though very numerous, may be rather rapidly dismissed. The mere eulogies often betray themselves as pseudo-Classical, even in their titles, *Epicedia*,[33] *Threnodia*,[34] *An Heroick Elegy*,[35] *Minerva's Check to the Author Attempting to write an Elegy upon the Earl of Orrery*,[36] and the like. They imitate, or try to imitate, the fashionable style of restrained emotion, and seldom speak with feeling but in jest. Of the six or more elegies[37] that celebrated the death of the Duke of Gloucester in 1660, but one contains lines that could at all be called mortuary, so immediate was the change in literary fashions:

> . . . what! do impetuous showers
> Of tears from th' *Weeping Clouds* (preventing ours)
> Distill; Or doth the *Day's bright Lamp* straight burn
> Dull as a torch to light us to his Urn?
> Is the dismantled Skies Bright Azure—Black?[38]

Such use of the pathetic fallacy may seem extreme; but, in bewailing the Earl of St. Albans,[39] the modest poet carried the figure to the point of wishing to "Arrest the Envious Course of Day and Night." At the close of his *Epitaph*, he declares: ". . . if yet some Vertuous be, They but the Apparitions are of Thee." Such elegies are marked by interminable eulogy that contrives to be at once exaggerated and conventionally cold. Some, like the mathematician, Sir Jonas Moore,[40] are praised for learning; some, like Lord Pembroke,[41] for everything in general; some, like the Duke

---

[33] *Epicedia or, Funeral Verses Upon Mr. Hmphrey[sic] Colles*, (1661) (Bodleian, Wood Coll., No. 429). Death appears as usual as a "cruel Sergeant"; there are notes to the references to Horace; and the Establishment is praised as the *via media* between Rome and the "Phranticks."

[34] Arthur Bret, *Threnodia On Prince Henry, Duke of Gloucester*, Oxford, 1660 (Thomason Coll.).

[35] *An Heroick Elegy Upon Sir Edmund Wyndham* (1681). (Lutt. Coll. I, No. 161.)

[36] Lutt. Coll., I, No. 111.

[37] See Lutt. Coll., I, Nos. 54 and 55; and *A Cordial Elegie & Epitaph*, London, 1660, and *Some Tears Dropt on the Herse* etc., and the *Elegie* by Martin Lluelyn, (Thomason Coll.).

[38] *An Elegie upon the Universally Lamented Death* etc. (Thomason Coll.).

[39] *An Elegy on the Death of the Earl of St. Albans* (1684) (Lutt. Coll., I, No. 146).

[40] *To the Memory of my most Honoured Friend Sir Jonas Moore, Knight* (Lutt. Coll., I, No. 106).

[41] *An Elegy on the Right Honorable William Earl of Pembroke* (1683) (Lutt. Coll., I, No. 119).

of Norfolk,[42] for their Royalist politics, which apparently constitutes their chief title to celestial bliss. Pindarics, though the usual
elegiac form among the courtly poets, are rarely found on broadsides;[43] and. this difference accentuates the contrast between the
literature of the masses and the literature of the select; and, though
a number of the broadside elegies show Classicism and restraint,
few of the pieces apparently intended for politer consumption follow either the mortuary realism of Quarles or the mannered curi-
ousness of Donne.[44] Occasionally the meteorological is called into
use[45] and often the Classical: the rake Rochester was sung as "the
Muses Darling, and the Son Of Great Apollo."[46] Samuel Holland, on the other hand, who apparently had faith in Bishop Burnet's efforts to reform the prodigal, declared that my Lord's
"pointed Wit" was his "worst of Crimes," and gave him a fine
repentance with "Death-cold Horrors," "gloomy Clay," and "re-
doubled *Sighs* and Floods of *Tears.*"[47] Since retribution failed
to overtake this noble example of vice, the Puritans were doubtless
determined that at least repentance should. Most of these elegies
are marked with the anxious importunity of Grub Street, for the
poets of assured position published in books; and at least one piece,
a lament for Lord Dorchester (1681),[48] notable for its extreme
Royalism of politics and poetic style, was signed "By Jo. Crouch,
once his Domestick Servant."[49] Indeed, the broadside elegy was
a common vehicle for aristocratic adulation.

A few women, famous or infamous, as the case might be, received the passing tribute of a sigh; but women were hardly taken
seriously by Restoration society: in the upper classes, they existed
only to make love; and in the lower, only to make pasties and

---

[42] *An Elegy on the Death of Henry
Howard, Duke of Norfolk* (1684) (Lutt.
Coll., I, No. 104). This piece does con-
tain "a Dismal shriek."

[43] *Pindarique Elegy On Dr. Willis*
(?1675) (Bodleian, Wood Coll., No.
429). Such pieces, however, are very
rare. One wonders why a physician happened to be singled out for this particularly aristocratic mode of poetic remembrance.

[44] *An Elegie on Charles Stuart, Duke
of Richmond* (1673) (Lutt. Coll., II,
No 251).

[45] *An Elegie on the Death of the Duke*

of Cambridge (1677) (Lutt. Coll., I,
No. 13).

[46] Lutt. Coll., I, No. 124. There was
also a conventional elegy on Lord Salisbury (1683) (Lutt. Coll., I, No. 135).

[47] Brit. Mus. broadside. Holland had
elegized on Mrs. Ann Grey in the Commonwealth period, and he doubtless carried over his style from that age.

[48] Lutt. Coll., II, No. 36.

[49] One fears, however, that he had long
since fallen upon the evil ways of hack-
writing; for in 1664, he had published
a broadside eulogy on Lord Tiveot (Bodleian, Wood Coll., No. 429).

pickles. The departed fair of the reigning house were likely to be wept in rather heavy Neo-classical style, as befitted royalty.[50] Madam Mary Carlton was sung with a lighter wit;[51] "Old Madam Gwinn," with a panegyric on the virtues of brandy;[52] and "my pretty Infant-Cousin Mrs. Jane Gabry," in the light style of Prior.[53] That "Most Accomplish'd Virgin Madam Elizabeth Hurne" (1683) was laid to rest with a decorous eulogy and a neat epitaph, the smug finality of which might have been in Byron's mind when he wrote his mordant panegyric on Don Juan's mother:

> As for her Church, she most Discreetly chose,
> That which the *Pope* and *Presbyter* oppose,
> And in its Bosom took her soft Repose.[54]

Various distinguished professions, moreover, shared in these honors. The military were loaded with such compliments, though for them the older and less modish style of Donne and Cleveland was oftener employed; and the law-lords, physicians, and others of the learned, could practice no posthumous evasion. General Monck was honored by at least three panegyrics and a satire (1669),[55] the one by "T. J. Master of Arts," in the metaphysical manner.[56] The expeditions in defence of Tangier and against the Barbary pirates occasioned several such pieces;[57] and Albemarle,[58] Sandwich,[59] Ossory,[60] Prince Rupert,[61] and Colonel Edward Cook,[62]

[50] Henry Bold (Oxon.), *Elegy On the Death of Her Highness Mary Princess Dowager of Aurange* (1660) (Brit. Mus. broadside); *An Elegy On the Lamented Death of the most Illustrious Princess Anne* (1671) (Lutt. Coll., I, No. 168); *On The never too much lamented Death of the most Illustrious Princess Henrietta Maria* (Lutt. Coll., I, No. 113). The elegist has confused Queen Henrietta Maria and her daughter the Princess Henrietta Anne.
[51] *An Elegie* etc. (1673) (Lutt. Coll., I, No. 20).
[52] *An elogie on Old Maddam Gwinn* (1679) (Lutt. Coll., I, No. 51). The person referred to was the mother of the famous Nell. This piece, as well as a number of the others here mentioned, is to be found in *A Century of Broadside Elegies*, ed. the present author, London, 1928.
[53] Lutt. Coll., I, No. 58 (1672).

[54] Lutt. Coll., I, No. 67 (1683).
[55] *On the Death of* etc.; *A Great Cry and Little Wool* (satire); *George Monck* (Lutt. Coll., I, Nos. 97, 98, 99).
[56] Lutt. Coll., I, No. 100 (1670).
[57] *Death's Envious Triumph* on Lord Rutherford (1664) (Lutt. Coll., I, No. 132; *Elegie* on Lord Tiveot (1664) signed "Jo. Crouch" (Bodleian, Wood Coll., No. 429); and a series of pieces on Captain Thomas Harman (Lutt. Coll., I, Nos. 64, 65, and 66), and *An Elegy on Captain William Harman* (Brit. Mus. broadside).
[58] *On the Death of His Grace* etc. (1670) (Brit. Mus. broadside).
[59] Lutt. Coll., I, No. 138 (1672).
[60] *An Elegy to Thomas* etc. (1680) (Lutt. Coll., I, No. 109).
[61] Lutt. Coll., I, Nos. 127, 128, 129 (1682). The first is a trifle Puritan in tone; the last is a proper military eulogy.
[62] Lutt. Coll., I, No. 41. See also such

were written into the annals of broadside fame. Grub Street found
the learned also worthy of its polite attentions: Sir Edmond Saun-
ders, Lord Chief Justice of England, was thoroughly elegized;[63]
and the "Immortal Scroggs" was not forgotten.[64] The "most
Eminent Doctor of Physick Sir John Mickle[th]waite" was aptly
lamented in a poem on the pains of illness[65]: indeed, as we descend
a little from the court circle, mortuary details are more likely to
appear, even though the subject, like Micklethwaite, beguiled the
Royalist times by trying to look like them as much as possible.
Actors occasionally received their due meed of praise;[66] the poet
D'Avenant was celebrated;[67] and so was "Mr. James Bristow,
Late Fellow of All-Souls," Oxford.[68] But there are few, if any,
of these pieces that can be called real funeral elegies.

Most significant is the rarity of broadside elegies on the Anglican
clergy, especially when one bears in mind their numerousness in
comparison with the non-conformist divines. The present writer
has been able to find in the whole quarter-century of the reign of
Charles II, but five elegies on members of the Episcopal Bench;[69]
and the recipients of three of these compliments, Bishops Sanderson and Henchman, were well known as Low Churchmen. Indeed,
one of the elegies on the latter, with its worms fed on "Carkasses,"
its objection to "Set forms of Tatter'd Verse," and its praise of
the Bishop's *"Primitive Zeal,"* is unquestionably by a Puritan admirer. The broadside on the Bishop of Worcester (1662) has
something of the conceits of Donne; but, in general, the verses
are chilly with decorum, without the ardor of a fresh inspiration.
The lines on My Lord of Norwich call attention to the paucity

pieces on De Ruyter (1676) (Lutt. Coll.,
I, No. 133); on Sir Christopher Minns
(Oxford, 1666); and on "Valiant Sprague"
(1673) by E. M. (Bodleian, Wood Coll.,
No. 429).

[63] *An Elegy on the Death* etc. (1683)
(Bodleian, Wood Coll., No. 429. See
also Lutt. Coll., I, Nos. 136 and 140).

[64] Lutt. Coll. I, No. 137.

[65] *An Elegy to Commemorate and Lament* etc. (1682) (Lutt. Coll., I, No.
80).

[66] *Elegy on Mr. Clun* (1664) (Lutt.
Coll., I, 44).

[67] *An Elegy Upon the Death of Sr
William Davenant* (Bodleian, Wood
Coll., No. 429). This piece may well

be by Killigrew. See *A Century of
Broadside Elegies, ed. cit.,* No. 49.

[68] *An Elegy on the Death of* etc., Oxford, 1667. In the Bodleian copy, this
is ascribed in a seventeenth century hand
to "Edw. Palmer."

[69] *An Elegy On the Much Lamented
Death of Dr. Sanderson* (1662) (Bodleian, Wood Coll., No. 429) (Bishop of
Lincoln); *Elegy* on the Bishop of Worcester (1662) (Lutt. Coll., I, No. 57);
*Elegy Humbly offered to the Memory of
Dr. Humphry Henchman, Bishop of London* (1675) (Lutt. Coll., I, No. 60; see
also No. 31); *An Elegy On the Renouned Edward, late Bishop of Norwich*
(1684) (Lutt. Coll., I, No. 103).

of elegies on the Bishop; and the piece on My Lord of Lincoln contains the significant declaration: "This Age's unable, or unfit to grieve." Only two of the numerous London clergy were properly eulogized—one with a slur on "Enthusiasts,"[70] and the other as "a Mighty Loyalist."[71] Dean Lingard (1671) was set to rest in the usual free Pindarics;[72] James Heath, the Royalist hack-poet, among his other lamentable pieces, did *An Elegie upon Dr. Thomas Fuller* (1661). Like most of these Anglican elegies, the piece is restrained; but the writer did succumb to metaphysical temptation in the witty line: "Bliss covets to be FULLER and compleat."[73] The Loyalist divine Nathaniel Strange (d. 1665) was mourned in the style of Donne, which seems to have lingered a little during the 1660's, and was given *An Acrostick*, an *Anagram*, and much punning eulogy—but no mortuary details.[74] The present writer, in short, has been able to find hardly a dozen broadside elegies on members of the Establishment; and, of these, only the pieces upon Low Churchmen have anything of mortuary detail: the funeral elegy had become an organ of dissent, and the orthodox would have none of it.

The cold, critical temper of the Restoration Royalists made them especially apt at the composition of satire; and it is worth noting that, as in the 1650's, their satires of the Puritans were often expressed in parodies of the funeral elegy; and the opening lines of the mock-elegy on "the Famous Thief *Thomas Sadler*" (1677)[75] clearly associates Puritanism with the elegiac Muse. Charles II was hardly safe upon the throne before a bitter invective *On the Death of that Grand Impostor Oliver Cromwell*[76] used the elegiac form to stigmatize the late Lord Protector as a "Scarlet Hypocrite"; and the *Æternitati Sacrum* (1662)[77] likewise employs the

[70] *Bishops-gate Lamentation For the Loss of their late Rector Mr. Robert Clark* (1678) (Lutt. Coll., I, No. 32).

[71] *An Elegy on the Death of the Reverend, Learned, and Pious William Bell, D.D. Vicar of S. Sepulchres* (1683) (Lutt. Coll., I, No. 11).

[72] *An Elegy and Funeral Oration on the Rev. Richard Lingard, D.D., Dean of Lismore*, London, 1671. (Bodleian, Wood Coll., No. 429).

[73] Bodleian, Wood Coll., No. 429. Fuller, of course, belongs to the generation of the immediate followers of Donne,

as does his elegist James Heath, who is also the author of the pieces already mentioned on Dr. Sanderson and Dr. Gauden.

[74] *A Memorial on the Death of that faithful Servant of Jesus Christ, Nathanael Strange* (Lutt. Coll., I, No. 149).

[75] *Groans from New-Gate or an Elegy on the Famous Thief* etc. (Lutt. Coll., I, No. 134).

[76] Thomason Coll. The piece is dated 1661, but more probably was issued in 1660.

[77] Lutt. Coll., I, No. 37.

elegy for political satire. Dr. Robert Wilde, the one time Presbyterian eulogist of General Monck's "Iter Boreale," which had ended in the Restoration of the Stuarts, died of apoplexy in 1679; and the event was celebrated in an outburst of rather unseemly ridicule to remind the world that the "Northern Journey" and the Restoration it accomplished had not concluded quite as the Presbyterians could have wished. *A Wipe for Iter Boreale Wilde*[78] taunts the departed with his unfulfilled expectations; and *A Dialogue Between Death and Dr. Wyld* seems to be written in ridicule[79] of such edifying Puritan dialogues as Flatman's *Death and the Lady*; and the piece is probably in no worse taste than some of the originals that it parodies:

Death) No *Roring* Christmas shalt Thou keep, now *Rore*
Bold Wit. Wyld) Oh! oh! Hhohh! Well! I'le cry no more,
Alas it is for *Thee* and not for *Me* to *Rore*
A *Deadly* Blow! But where's thy *Sting* There lies
The *King* of *Terrors* cow'd out! In Sacrifice
(An *Eucharist*) *Lord*, take this *Soul* to Thee,
By *Death* Thou hast *slain Death, Redeemed Me.*
　Grave take the *Carcass*, at the reck'ning Day
With *Interest* the *Principal* repay.
Take *Worms meat* (they'l scarce lick the *puncked* Face)
Bring't up in *Glory*, though sown in *Disgrace*,
In never-fading *Beauty* it shall rise,
And be transplanted int'yon Paradise.
They'll *Digg* the *Kernels* out (the Eyes) Digg on!
One *Breakfast* makes the Head a *Skeleton.*
They'll *tease* the Hands, and Toes, and Paunch (their Fence)
Intolerable *Pains* have *numb'd* all Sense.

The death of Thomas Merry of St. Anne's Lane (1682)[80] was made the occasion of an obscene satire of Lord Shaftesbury and the Whigs, which even that confirmed reader and collector of broadsides, Narcissus Luttrell, describes in manuscript in his copy as "a Tory thing." The executions of Stafford (1680),[81] of

---

[78] *A Wipe* etc., signed by "I. M." (Brit. Mus. broadside).

[79] *A Dialogue* etc. (Brit. Mus. broadside. See also Lutt. Coll., II, No. 61). There is just the barest possibility that this was all intended seriously as a proper enough lamentation!

[80] *An Elegy on the Death* etc. (Lutt. Coll., I, No. 82).

[81] Lutt. Coll., I, No. 148. The piece is dated 1681. It is moralistic rather than strictly satiric.

Algernon Sidney (1683),[82] and of Lord Russell[83] and Sir Thomas Armstrong (1684),[84] were all duly celebrated by the Tories in mock-elegies more notable for vituperative rigor than delicacy of taste. The Earl of Essex, "Who Cut his own Throat in the Tower," (1683) was twice honored;[85] and *An Elegy On the much Lamented Sir William Waller, Who valiantly Hang'd Himself at Rotterdam* (1683)[86] was properly styled by Luttrell "an abusive scandalous thing": the Whigs are reviled as disloyal—and they certainly were not enthusiastic over the prospect of James II as king—and dissenters are vilified as intriguing hypocrites. The Tories even parodied individual Puritan broadsides, as in *The Elegy On the Reverend Presbyter Mr. William Jenkins, Who finished his Obstinacy the 19th of January in the Goal of Newgate . . . In a Dialogue between Despair and Comfort: In Imitation of a former Elegy, in dialogue between Faith and Sense. Seiz'd and supprest by Authority* (1685).[87] The parody even rejoices in an acrostic epitaph. Certainly as late as the 1680's, the funeral elegy was generally associated with non-conformity; and, in the tense political struggles that occupied the last years of the reign of Charles II, the ridicule of its short-comings was a common weapon in the hands of the Tory pamphleteers. The Puritans attempted to answer, for the most part in heavy moralizing;[88] and, occasionally, they let loose bitter invective against Socinians and Quakers;[89] but their verbal artillery was too heavy to be useful in satire. Perhaps the most characteristic piece on this side is the

---

[82] *An Elegy on the Death of Algernon Sidney; Who was found Guilty of High Treason* (Lutt. Coll., I, No. 147).

[83] Lutt. Coll., I, Nos. 130 and 131.

[84] *An Elegie on the never to be forgotten Sir Thomas Armstrong Knight* (Lutt. Coll., I, No. 4).

[85] Lutt. Coll., I, Nos. 35 and 50.

[86] Lutt. Coll., I, No. 156.

[87] Lutt. Coll., I, No. 75. See also *An Elegy* on Lord Shaftesbury (1683), which was shortly reprinted in double columns with a Tory "libell" attributed to Dr. Oats (Lutt. Coll., I, Nos. 143 and 144).

[88] See *An Elegy Upon March's* one of the two *publick Sworn Informers against Protestant religious meetings in the City of London* (1675); and an *Elegy* on Thynne (1681) (Lutt. Coll., I, Nos. 83 and 151).

[89] E.g., an *Elegy* on "the Reverend Fowler's dust" (1677) (Lutt. Coll., I, No. 45); and a *Poem* dedicated to Baxter (1680) (Lutt. Coll., I, No. 6). Hobbes was attacked in an elegy, but it may not have been written by dissenters (Lutt. Coll., I, No. 68). The expression of extreme dissenting views seems to have been dangerous; and *A Poem Dedicated to the Lasting Honor of Mr. Richard Baxter* (1682) claims to be a reprint of an Amsterdam broadside, and veils its satire rather carefully. See also the thinly veiled satire of the enemies of Shaftesbury in the *Elogy against Occasion Requires upon the Earl of Shaftesbury* (1681) (Chetham's Lib., Halliwell Coll. 46), a piece that anticipated his death by two years in order to attack his Tory enemies.

broadside "By Geo. Gittos" on "Tom of ten thousand," the partisan of Monmouth:

> . . . Did we not see at that Outrageous Blow,
> The Powder-Smoke into thick Vapours grow,
> Mixt with the Clouds, their obscure Shadows hurl'd
> Their Mourning-Mantle, muffled up the World;
> Ev'ry Ear fill'd with Clamours, and the Sky
> Seem'd to lament this Bloody Tragedy?
> The middle Element was fill'd with Groans,
> And Mother-Earth quak'd at her Peoples Moans:
> All Women wept, all Mankind grieved sore,
> Salt tears ran trickling like the Common Shore,
> And Children with their Infant-Voices rore.[90]

Such a piece satirizes the enemies of Shaftesbury only by the most indirect implication; and, when the Puritans tried to be more direct, they became merely vituperative.

The court circle and the upper classes of society, then, in the works of recognized poets, and even in the broadside pieces, supplied but few mortuary elegies; and those few were regularly written on individuals who had some sort of Puritan connection. Among the Puritans themselves, in spite of their old disapproval of poetry, and in spite of their political and social submergence, funeral elegies both in books and on broadsides flourished vigorously. Dr. Robert Wilde, already mentioned as the subject of satire, who had been ejected from his living under the Act of Uniformity in 1662, had included in his *Iter Boreale* an elegy *To the Memory of Mr. Jeremy Whitaker, Powerful in Prayer and Preaching, Pious in Life, Patient in Sickness*.[91] It is sufficiently extreme to be taken at first glance for a Cavalier satire; but there can be no doubt that Wilde, if he wrote it, really meant his hyperboles to be taken at their face value. He praises his subject for his prayers against the enemies of Puritanism, and gives a special section "on his preaching." We are told to "Weep over him":

> 'Twould wash away the Stone (which covers him)
> And make his Coffin (like an Ark) to swim.
> Now wipe thine eyes (my Muse) & stop thy Verse

[90] *An Elegy On the Famous Thomas Thin* (1681) (Lutt. Coll., I, No. 150).
[91] R. Wild, D.D., *Iter Boreale*, London, 1668, 31. *Ed. princ.* 1660. This elegy may have been composed at Whitaker's death in 1654.

(Thy Ink can only serve to black his Hearse,)
Yet (stay) i'll [*sic*] drop one Tear, sigh one more sigh. . . .

The elegy by N. W.[92] on Dr. Willis, the noted London physician, although one can be sure of the religious views of neither the poet nor his subject, would also seem to spring from the non-conformist conscience: it refers to "mortal Dust," "silent Taper," "crawling Worms," "dampish Echo," and "The silence and disorders of the grave." Mrs. Anne Wharton, whose husband's[93] Puritan up-bringing and Whig politics would seem to indicate her own religious proclivities, following in the lead of Donne and Quarles, did a poetic version of the *Lamentations of Jeremiah*,[94] with much exclamatory grief and an abundance of rhetorical passion. The demarcation, however, between Puritan funeral elegies and Cavalier Classical elegies cannot always be absolutely drawn. The Rev. John Rawlet, for instance, whose conscience apparently allowed him to submit to conformity at the Restoration, stands as a literary expression of a great number of Low Church divines, and exemplifies the narrowness of the line that, even in this age, divided that party from non-conformity. The touch of Donne seems still to linger in his lines *On Death*,[95] in which he finds the grave preferable to

Juleps, Blisterings, and Phlebotomy,
And other medicinal Artillery.

His *Midnight Meditations*, on the other hand, points forward to Edward Young, with its moralizings on sin and "that King of Terrors, Death," who comes in "dismal shape" to "affright Thee with the horror of eternal night." Rawlet would seem to cultivate such subjects as a pious discipline, and not, like so many later writers, for the sweetness of melancholy and the titillation of the emotions. He represents Puritanism within the Established Church.

There are, moreover, a considerable number of broadsides of a

---

[92] N. W[est?] *Mago Sæculi. The Image of the Age*, Oxford, 1676, 98 *et seq*.

[93] The first Marquis of Wharton, 1648-1715. Mrs. Wharton's maiden name was Lee. She died in 1685.

[94] *Miscellanea Sacra*, collected by Samuel Phillips, third ed., London, 1707, II, 73.

[95] John Rawlet, B.D., *Poetick Miscellanies, London*, 1687. Rawlet died in 1686; and it consequently seems fair to assume that the pieces included in the volume were done during the reign of Charles II, although a few may be juvenilia written during the Commonwealth.

more or less mortuary character, for the most part obviously associated with Puritanism. The more general poems of this type are
well illustrated in *Death Triumphant*:

> Death is a raw-bon'd shrimp, nor low nor high,
>   Yet he hath power to make the highest low . . .
>
> Death is worms Caterer, who when he comes
>   Will have provision, though the Market starve;
> And knows before where he intends to come,
>   And on which carkass he intends to carve.
> As he awakes the sin belulled Drones,
>   And cuts them off, as rightly they deserve;
> Its he that all things to subjection brings,
> And plays at Foot-ball with the Crowns of Kings.
>
> Two empty lodges hath he in his head,
>   Which hath two lights, but now his eyes are gone.
> Cheeks had he once, but they are now hollowed,
>   Beauty he had, but now appears there none;
> For all those moving parts are vanished,
>   Presenting horror, if but look'd upon;
> His color sable, and his visage grim,
> Most ghastly looks do still attend on him.
>
> Fleshly he was, but now it's pickt away . . .
>
> If we shed tears they're bootless for his eyes,
>   Instead of sight are molded up in clay:
> If we essay to pierce his ears with cries,
>   Vain is our labour, fruitless our essay:
> For his remourseless ears all motions flies,
>   Nor will he give the Prince a longer stay.
> His payment must be present, and his doom
> Return to earth, thy cradle and thy tomb.[96]

There follow several like stanzas of free ottava rima on the power
and the universality of death. A similar theme, though developed
with less of mortuary description, appears in the pentameter couplets of *The Midnight Messenger or, a Sudden Call from an
Earthly Glory to the Cold Grave. In a Dialogue between Death*

---

[96] Andrew Jones, *Death Triumphant*,
fifth ed., London, 1674. The *ed. princ.*
may belong to the Commonwealth period,
but the reprinting of it after the Restoration shows that there was still a sale.

*and a Rich Man, who, in the midst of all his Wealth, received
the tidings of his Last Day, to his unspeakable and sorrowful
Lamentation.*[97] Even closer to the elegiac type are the *Dying
Words of a Young Man*[98] in most wretched sapphics, and *The
Dead-Man's Song Who Lived near Basing-Hall in the City of
London.* The man dies; his "Carcass" is "brought from Bed,
And laid upon the Ground"; his relatives weep; and the funeral
preparations are made. He then describes heaven, then the horrors
of hell, "a cole-black Den," and finally gives the devil his due:
"An ugly Creature . . . And in a Cauldron of Poison Filth His
ugly Corps was wash'd . . . " Truly, most of these elegists would
seem to be possessed by training of all the graces of elegiac convention, and by nature of a "pretty wit," not incomparable to that
of Audrey in *As You Like It.*

Just as there was a miscellany of Tory broadsides upon the
deaths of eminent persons of various professions, so the Whigs also
celebrated their notables. To the pieces on Shaftesbury already mentioned,[99] one may add broadsides on Sir William Jones (1681),[100]
with its slur on 'th'undermining Tories," and Mrs. Rebecca
Palmer (1667),[101] whose one delight was in *"Th'Assemplies of
the Saints,"* and who achieved salvation by "Closet-Cries and tears."
There is at least one alderman, Sir Nathanael Hern (1679),
whose loss we are warned properly to "Improve";[102] and at least
three lord mayors are wept in appropriate strains by the City.
Robert Viner (1674) received the usual inflated encomium,[103]
probably from the pen of Settle; Sir Richard Ford (1678) was
buried with the consoling assurance:

> Though Time and the devouring *Grave* may strive
> To Riot on thy Flesh, thy *Fame's* alive.[104]

And to the elegy on Sir Joseph Sheldon (1681) was appended an
epitaph, with the usual reference to worms:

[97] Harvard Lib., Medlicott Coll. Is
this an English or an American broadside?

[98] Harvard Lib. An American broadside?

[99] See also *Elegy* on Lord Shaftesbury
(Brit. Mus. broadside).

[100] *An Elegy On the truly Honored and
greatly Beloved Sir William Jones* (1682)

(Brit. Mus. broadside). There is also
one dated 1681, Lutt. Coll., I, No. 72.

[101] *An Elegie On the Death of Mrs.
Rebecca Palmer* (Brit. Mus. broadside).

[102] Lutt. Coll., I, No. 70.

[103] *Carmen Encomiasticum, or, an Elogium to Sir Robert Viner*, Lutt. Coll., I,
No. 154.

[104] *London's Sighs for Sir Richard Ford*
(Lutt. Coll., I, No. 46).

Reader *look down and* Weep *to see*
Death *Triumphing in Victory*:
Whose Greedy Maw *has here Devour'd,*
That which Alive *we all Ador'd.*[105]

But such pieces form but the trappings and the suits of woe: the real essence of Puritanism lay in its clergy; and the real essence of Puritan lament is to be found in those numerous and affecting pieces upon painful and pious divines, often penned by members of their own sect and profession.

Indeed, at the Restoration, the dissenting ministry had quite succumbed to the blandishments of the elegiac Muse: they not only wrote elegies and used them at the funerals of the most godly but even printed them on the despised broadside for the delectation of the faithful. Such pieces contain as many mortuary passages as all the other broadside elegies of the period combined; they are far more numerous than elegies of any sort on members of the Establishment; and one can hardly escape the conclusion that elegiac melancholy, during the reign of Charles II, was the particular and proud possession of this Brahman class of non-conformity. Sometimes, to be sure, as a sort of conventional survival, an elegist takes space to apologize for the elegiac *genre*, and refers the precise reader to David's lament over Jonathan, as does the celebrant of Norcot; but most of the sects seem to have taken elegies for granted; and such verses were written on Independents like Venning and Owen, on Baptists like Loveday, Bampfield, and Jesse, and even on Presbyterians like Calamy and Wadsworth, although the Covenanters in Scotland still stood out against such prelatical practices.[106] Very occasionally, the authors of these pieces, like the broadside eulogist of Baxter, hold themselves within the bounds of a certain decorum of grief, and, like the Cavaliers of the 1630's, dwell on the joys of heaven; or, like the Royalists of their own day, on the virtues of the departed;[107] but, as a general rule, they seize the occasion to tear any passion they have to very tatters; and

---

[105] *Elegy on Sir Joseph Sheldon* (Lutt. Coll., I, No. 145).

[106] There is even a pseudo-Quaker Elegy on the Death of Charles II signed "W. P.", in the pious hope that the unwary reader might suppose the author to be William Penn.

[107] See *An Elegy on the Rev. Lazarus Seaman* (1675) (Lutt. Coll., I, No. 141). No. 142 is also on Seaman, but is more tearful-sad. He seems to have been noted for his mild tolerance.

indeed, so amply was the grief of the mourners poured on paper that, if modern psychology be right in declaring that the expression of an emotion destroys it, then both poets and readers, after such a catharsis, must have felt quite comfortably resigned to their bereavement.

Grief, indeed, sometimes individual and lyric, sometimes in gregarious sympathy, was developed to an extreme. The author of *Bochim, Sighs poured out by troubled Hearts*,[108] an elegy on John Vernon, (1667), exhorts the righteous: "Saints! fill your Bottle with repenting tears," and even works himself to such a fury that he dares refer to "Backsliding England"—a passage that might well have sent him to the pillory or to jail. The *Elegy* on Dr. John Owen (1683)[109] combines lamentation with theological panegyric:

> His *Fame* will Live to lat'st Posterity,
> In's *Theo-Christo-Pneumatology*.

Certainly that elegist was not among those of little faith! The eminent Calamy (1667)[110] was duly celebrated with the usual "Universal Groan" of "Afflicted *London*"; and the poem catalogues his virtues, and describes his last illness and his "many Fasts to keep off Judgments." The *Elegy* on Samuel Loveday starts with a note of pseudo-lyric ecstasy; and even pseudo-lyric ecstasies were rare about 1677:

> My tears so overflow, I scarce can guide
> My trembling Hand. O stop, you swelling Tide
> Of brinish Tears! Alas! my Heart does break:
> So strong's my Grief, although my Muse be weak.[111]

He then urges his listeners to "Let floods of Tears Run from the Conduits of your moistened Eyes." The piece ends with a poetical advertisement of the sermons of the deceased, which we are advised to "feed on" by day:

> And when the sable Curtains of the Night
> Are closely drawn, then feed by Candle-light.

Possibly the broadside was written—or at least printed—by his pub-

---

[108] Lutt. Coll., I, No. 153.

[109] Lutt. Coll., I, No. 108.

[110] Lutt. Coll., II, No. 29.

[111] Lutt. Coll., I, No. 71.

isher. The elegist of Ralph Venning (1674), luxuriating in his grief, asks leave to

> Water his *Herse*, since my *Big-bellied eyes*
> Long for Deliv'ry at his Obsequies.[112]

And elsewhere he describes the affliction of others of the godly, in good set terms:

> Hark! how our *Sion* with *Heart-piercing* Groans,
> Her *chariots* and her *Horsemens Loss* bemoans,
> See! how each *Pious blubber'd* Cheek doth wear
> The sad *Ennamell* of a Briny Tear;
> Each soul turns a *Close Mourner* in its Cell;
> And ev'ry *Tongue* becomes a *Passing Bell*:
> Must *good Men* still dye *first*, and is there gone
> Another *Cedar* in our *Lebanon*?
> Are Holy *pow'rfull 'Preachers* snatch'd so fast?

The melancholy consumptive, James Janeway, who escaped from this Vale of Tears in 1674 at the age of thirty-eight, was bewailed with two elegies,[113] both of them enthusiastic and affecting performances. Quotation from one will perhaps suffice:

> Ah! Whither, whither, into what Abyss
> Of sorrow, and unfatom'd [*sic*] Grief is this
> In which my Soul is plung'd? what Seas
> Of terrour cau[s]ing (what strange) thoughts are these?
> What ai[l]es my Heart, that thus with fear it quakes?
> What! have the Furies with their hissing Snakes,
> And flaming Torches, left their dark abodes?
> What! hath black *Dis* and the Infernal Gods,
> Let loose those Hellish Fiends, confin'd to lye
> In that Infernal plac Eternally?
> Ah? No: great JANEWAY'S dead. . . .

The same *fortissimo* is continued—one can hardly say *sustained*—in the succeeding passages on the sorrow of the mourners, and the experiences of damned souls in Hell.

But these cis-diluvian deluges of tears, not only gave a pleasing satisfaction to the mourner, but also assured him Salvation, as it

---

[112] *Elegy on the Death of Mr. Ralph Venning* (Lutt. Coll., I, No. 155).

[113] *An Elogie with an Acrostick and an Epitaph On Mr. James Janeway* (Lutt. Coll., I, No. 76). See also No. 77.

were, by the quart; and thus, in the popular mind, was developed
an identity between pleasure and virtue which is doubtless account-
able for the popularity of such views in the philosophy of Shaftesbury and Hutcheson. The *Elegy* on Norcot (1676) by E. K.,
evidently one of his flock, is an excellent case in point:

> . . . The narrow Sluices too of dribling eyes,
> Should be too streight for those great Springs [of grief] that rise.
> But since our Vessels fill us to the top,
> Lets empty them, for every sin a drop.
> For it lets wish we were compos'd of Snow,
> Instead of Flesh, yea made of Ice, that so
> We might in sense of sin and it loathing,
> Melt with hot love to Christ, yea thaw to nothing.
> And should our sins deprive our Souls of him,
> Let tears run from our Eyes till Couches swim.[114]

Surely this description of excessive grief was no mere poetic convention; and dissenting funerals must have been carnivals of the
macabre. Nor must one forget the happy case, already discussed,
of Mrs. Rebecca Palmer, who climbed to the Celestial City by the
avenue of tears.

Some clerical broadside elegies, however, were notable not merely
for superlative lamentation but also for cultivation of other mortuary themes. Death as "the King of Fears" is the subject of the
elegist of Henry Jesse (1663).[115] Francis Bampfield, who died a
prisoner in Newgate because he refused to be silenced, was elegized
in extenso (1684) with the usual couplets.[116] The piece starts with
the grief of the author's Muse; then come the "skilful Mourners"
(had mourning then become a skilled profession in dissenting circles?); and these were exhorted to reveal their grief "In doleful
lines"; the corpse, all "wan" and "stupid cold," is described, its
hands and eyes and "lovely Countenance"; God is invoked; the
mourners grieve; and the piece ends with a fitting *Requiescat in
pace*. The *New Poems upon the Death of that Eminent Servant
of God, and truly Pious and Learned Minister of the Gospel, Mr.*

[114] *Elegy on the Death of that most
Laborious and Painful Minister of the
Gospel, Mr. John Norcot* (Brit. Mus.
broadside).
[115] *A Pillar Erected to the Memory of
that Holy, Humble, and Faithful Servant*
of Christ, Mr. Henry Jesse (Brit. Mus.
broadside). See also Lutt. Coll., I, No.
74.
[116] *An Elegy on that Faithful and Laborious Minister of Christ Mr. Francis
Bampfield* (Lutt. Coll., I, No. 5).

Stephen Charnock (1680)[117] starts with the fear of God's judgment, and ends in an acrostic and an epitaph. The double lament on Pledger and Wells (1676)[118] pictures a mortuary landscape almost in the terms of Baudelaire's *paradis artificiel*: a parched land "Hard as Adamants compacted Parts"; and, against this background, introduces "Devouring Death" and the "All-consuming Tomb." Later there follows a "Lamentable storm Of *Sighs* and *Groans*, whilst overflowing Eys dissolve their yielding *Balls* in Deluges." Great quantities of eulogy, apt and inept, may be passed over; but the fertile topic of the pains of illness demands at least some rapid illustration. "The Reverend and Pious Mr. Thomas Wadsworth" (1676)[119] would certainly seem to have merited a martyr's crown for his sufferings. He is described as dwelling in heaven,

> Where living, He shall Live and never Dye,
> No more Tost, nor Groan through Pain and Crye;
> For *Kidney*, *Ulser* and *Stone* in *Bladder*,
> Hath proved to him a Happy Jacob's Ladder.

There follows a passage on his joys in heaven in the select company of other non-conformist divines; and the piece ends with a eulogy of his private life and of his power as a preacher. Surely these elegies on dissenting ministers show that Calvinism was the special repository for mortuary melancholy and associated literary themes, even when the Court was most given up to a brilliant but profligate levity and lightness of mind.

A discussion of the pieces on the death of Charles II forms a fitting conclusion to an investigation of the Caroline funeral elegy. The tributes of Dryden and of Flatman have received sufficient characterization; but some minor poets, and the broadside poetasters also, require notice. John Whitehall, following in the courtly tradition, brought out *Short Remarks*[120] on the subject in the inevitable irregular Pindarics. Arwaker also wrote some pseudo-Pindaric strophes called *The Vision*,[121] notable chiefly for their de-

---

[117] Lutt. Coll., I, No. 33.
[118] Lutt. Coll., I, No. 118.
[119] *An Elegy on* etc. (Lutt. Coll., I, No. 157).

[120] John Whitehall, *Miscellaneous Poems*, London, 1685.
[121] E. Arwaker, *The Vision: A Pindarick Ode Occasion'd by the Death of King Charles II*, London, 1685.

velopment, though in somewhat Classical style, of the mortuary
landscape:

> Behold a *Grove*, whose *Melancholy* shade
> Appear'd for *Sorrow's* last retirement made,
> Where in confus'd disorder grew,
> Bidding Defiance to the Sun's bright Eye
> The *Mournful* Cypress and *Unlucky* Yew;
> So closely interwov'n they were,
> His Mid-day Beams were Strangers there,
> Nor durst into its dismal Secrets pry.
> Here, in the *darkest* of the Solitude
> My Soul, which fearless did intrude,
> Saw on the Margin of a Murm'ring Brook,
> By a faint light almost expired,
> An *Awful MATRON*, Mournfully retir'd. . . . [122]

There follow "the damp unwholesome Ground" and some allegorical touches reminiscent of Spenser: indeed, it seems plain that
the poet was writing out of his time. Two other odes, moreover,
suggest that the very end of the reign witnessed a reaction of poetic
style preparatory to the change that was to take place under William and Mary. "J. H., Esq.,"[123] whose use of initials suggests
that, *mirabile dictu*, he expected no emolument for his poetic pains,
compiled the usual Pindaric ode, without form and void, from the
usual non-entities of pathetic fallacy and Classical reference; but
the picture of his "Melancholy Muse"—compare Cowley, whose
Pegasus was troubled with a like distemper—overwhelmed with
"the horror of the Dismal News," and "gasping laid" quite properly "Beneath a Doting Willows Shade," is not impertinent to the
present study. Even more significant is the *Pindarick Ode* by "Sir
F. F., Knight of the Bath."[124] It describes the effect of the king's
death on the populace:

> *Horror* and *Cryes* fill all around.
> *Distracted* looks, and *Throbbing hearts*,
> In every dismal place are found. . . .

[122] The "Awful Matron" is the Church
of England—a strange irony if the stories of the King's final conversion to
Roman Catholicism be true. But perhaps
the Anglican Church was sorrowing over
the accession of James! It had reason to.

[123] J. H. Esq., *A Pindarick Ode on the
Death of King Charles the Second*, London, 1685.

[124] Sir F. F., *A Pindaric Ode on the
Sacred Memory of Our late Gracious
Sovereign King Charles II*, London,
1685.

MEMENTO MORI

AN ELEGY

Upon the Unfortunate Death of

Captain William Bedloe,

Who Departed this Life, on FRYDAY the Twentieth of AUGUST. 1680.

HOw fickle is the State of all Mankind ?
And how are all our Joys with Grief combin'd ?
Scarce can one say he lives, and doth enjoy
The Bleſſings of this World, without allay,
But ſome unhappy Chance diſturbs our Peace,
And all our Pleaſures in a moment ceaſe.
The truth of which, Great Captain *Bedloe's* Fate
Confirms more than a thouſand Inſtances of late.
He who through various ways hath boldly ran,
Boggled at nothing cou'd be done by Man :
At firſt miſguided by his Popiſh Zeal,
To ſerve his *Holineſs* in any ill ;
On which the Jeſuits put a Gloſs of good,
And whoſe Perniciouſneſs wan't underſtood.
How eager was his bold Endeavour ſtill,
By any means the Proteſtants to kill ?
Until at laſt, being by Heav'n inſpir'd,
He wiſely from his former ills retir'd,
And as a Second *Saul* he fiercely ſtrove,
As once his Hate, to manifeſt his Love
To's Native Country and Religion too,
Which former Miſts wou'd never let him do ;
And when Converted, All that e're he knew,
He boldly told, and nought but what was true.
To him our Engliſh Nation much does owe,
Who vent'ring all he had at one great throw,
Valued not his Dear Life, ſo he might ſave
The Kingdom's Ruine, and the King from's Grave.
He was the Man, who many Plots reveal'd
Gainſt the King's Life, which elſe had been conceal'd ;
He was the Man 'Gainſt Bribes ſo Armour proof,
That to be Falſe thought no Price great enough.
In vain the Romiſh Zealots 'gainſt him ſay,
That hopes of Wealth made him their Plots betray ;
For cou'd he have been tempted by them to prove
Falſe to his King, and 'gainſt his Country move :

Their proffers large wou'd not have been in vain,
If he wou'd for ſome Perſon's ſake refrain
To give in Evidence, but he withſtood
All the Temptations, to a ſeeming Good.
Having at laſt been bleſt with a kind Wife,
The only ſolid Comfort of Man's Life :
And hoping now to live at Peace and Reſt,
And be for ever by his Country bleſt ;
Was ſtrangely ſeiz'd with a dire Malady,
And by a ſtrange unheard of Propheſy
He fanci'd all along, that he ſhould dye
By that Diſeaſe, yet then he perſever'd
In what he had ſaid, and not one Tittle err'd,
As he was then even in a dying State,
From what he ever did oth' Plot relate ;
And before Witneſſes at's parting Breath,
The Truth of 's Depoſitions ſeal'd with Death :
Now at his Loſs, let this ſad Nation mourn,
And drop with Grief ſome Tears upon his Urn :
Let us his ſudden Death juſtly bemoan,
Had he liv'd longer, he had more made known.
Dear Dr. *Oates*, I muſt Digreſſion make,
And beg you wou'd in this great Loſs partake.
You've loſt a Friend that much did value you,
Becauſe like him, all you have ſaid is true.
Go on, Good Doctor, and whilſt here you live,
And this the Nations Loſs you do ſurvive.
Witneſs the Truth, and be not you diſmai'd
By threatning Papiſts, neither be afraid
Of Popiſh Plots againſt you, for ther's One
That ſits upon the Bright Celeſtial Throne,
Will Guard you, and this Nation will Protect
From all the Plots of the Proud Romiſh Sect.
22. 9. 49
F I N I S.

LONDON, Printed for *John Gay*, at the *Flying-Horſe* between St. *Dunſtan's* Church and *Chancery-Lane.* 1680.
25. Aug.

The poet indulges his own grief in an appropriate spot, among *"Ruins,* that to Religion Sacred were of *yore,"* and thus takes perhaps the first step in bridging the gulf between the idyllic and the Gothic romance. Here all things "please" his "Melancholy fancy," a pleasure that he expresses in terms of the pathetic fallacy:

> I softly with my load of Grief, retreat:
> Where ev'ry Rock and ev'ry Tree
> Would (I knew) *condole* with me;
> Only stern Fate would *unrelenting* be.
> Thus then with many a Tear and Groan
> My *Dead,* my Sacred PRINCE I did bemoan.

The rest of the piece is given over mainly to eulogy; but the passage quoted is notable for its combination of the Gothic and the Sentimental, for the poet clearly suggests that he is deriving pleasure from his gloomy surroundings. Gothicism is to be found also in some of the broadside woodcuts of the period; and more than once appears the elegiac heading of a castle, or at least of turrets: such a heading adorns the Whig eulogy of Captain Bedloe reproduced in the accompanying illustration, and also a Puritan-sounding broadside on the death of Charles II.[125] Indeed, the numerous broadside elegies on the "Merry monarch" emanating as they did from a variety of social classes and from persons of all shades of opinion, illustrate the whole gamut of elegiac styles. The death of a noble is chiefly the concern of his noble relatives; the death of a king is matter for national mourning. Some of the pieces are merely the customary eulogy;[126] and one especially drives panegyric to the last strident gasp, and rings true only in the lines:

> My Muse (of all *Apollo's Tribe*) the Worst,
> To Thy *Great-Sepulchre* comes only First;
> Thy *God-like Acts* let *Abler* Pens *Paint* forth
> (In Words, *worth Dying for,* Declare *thy Worth.*)[127]

P. K., to advertise his virtuosity, did two pieces: a double acrostic, and a tortured thing in the last decadence of the style of the

---

[125] Lutt. Coll., I, No. 30. The elegy on Captain Bedloe is in Lutt. Coll., I, No. 9.

[126] *Elegy on the Most Lamented of Princes* (Lutt. Coll., I, No. 31); and

England's Sorrow (Lutt. Coll., I, No. 34).

[127] *An Elegy upon his late Majesty* (Lutt. Coll., I, No. 24).

1630's.[128]   The author of *Susperia* sighs like a furnace, with a woeful broadside:

> . . . Ah! Words where are ye! Ah! what must I borrow
> Language from Tears to Represent my Sorrow!
> Drop then ye friendly Streams, till like a Flood,
> (More Elegant than Words) be Understood,
> Our Universal Grief; to Mourn thus, you,
> Better than Groans, or Elegies, can do.[129]

There is a surprisingly enthusiastic *Pindarick Ode* that lingers dolefully over the "Paleness and tears and pensive looks" of the mourners, and ends with the declaration that "The valiant wise and just, Are attributes that Dirt and Worms must have";[130] and lastly there is *The Whole Nations Lamentation*, to the tune of *Troy Town*, a black-letter broadside with a eulogy followed by a description of the funeral:

> And thus they to the Abby went,
>   to lay him in his silent Tomb,
> Where many inward Sighs was spent,
>   to think upon their dismal Doom:
> Whole showers of Tears afresh there fell,
> When they beheld his last farewell.[131]

Indeed, one would expect more of the mortuary in these royal elegies; but perhaps the Puritans did not consider His late Majesty a sufficiently exemplary character to demand their fullest poetic commemoration.

The elegies of the reign of Charles II for the most part fall into fairly distinct groups: Pindaric eulogies upon the nobility, that are hardly to the purpose of the present study; more or less journalistic broadsides composed for popular consumption; and definitely Puritan pieces written in commemoration of noted non-conformists. The first and second are flaccidly conventional and flat; the third are effusions of raw melancholy labored into an exclamatory similitude of passion, not quite unlike the prose style in which Shaftesbury later phrased his popular philosophic *pronunciamenti*.[132]

---

[128] *A Mournful Elegy* (Lutt. Coll., I, No. 25; see also No. 29).
[129] Lutt. Coll., I, No. 28.
[130] *A Pindarick Ode Upon the Death of* etc., Oxford, 1685.

[131] Roxburghe Coll., I, 282.
[132] W. E. Alderman (*The Style of Shaftesbury, Mod. Lang. Notes,* XXXVIII, 209 *et seq.*) discusses his emotional rhetoric, and gives a summary of the history

These innumerable minor elegists, who in a travail of cold convention or of lugubrious lament, discoursed most eloquent nothings and presumably hoped to be heard for their much speaking, might *in toto* inspire an acidulous critic to an elegiac *Dunciad;* and, indeed, as the panorama of the subordinate poets of the age—as of most ages—displays itself before the brief chronicler of the bathos of the time, he finds himself more and more drawn to sympathize with the attitude and opinion of the satirists.   But historical significance is independent of artistic bathos; and the present chronicler finds in both the ignoring of death by the Cavaliers and its cultivation by the Puritans, the reaction of two social classes to a common background of pessimism and disillusion. The age seemed out of joint: some made it tolerable by debauchery; some, by religion.   But the courtiers looked life in the face and smiled sardonically; whereas the Puritans looked away from it to death; and, as long as their religious inhibitions were strong enough to forbid their cherishing any great certainty of infinite bliss, they were compelled to focus their attention on the grave, which thus, oddly enough, came to be a symbol of escape from the *Weltschmerz* of living.   Thus Court and Commons both saw the world through the tiny orifice of a pin-hole camera; and neither, in the classic phrase of Arnold, saw life steadily and saw it whole.   Even the realism of aristocratic comedy is narrow in subject, cynical in outlook, and hectic in tone;[133] and the middle-class elegy, in quite a different way, is also narrow, disillusioned, and hectic. The difference between them would seem to have been largely a matter of the degree of emotionalism, a difference illustrated in the contrast between the reigning comedy of manners, and the comedy of sentiment that later arose.[134]   Indeed, the rakes seem to have had almost a monopoly of the cultural and analytical faculties; and

of opinion, but does not suggest why he used such a style or where he found it. Its existence in the poetry, sermons, and devotional books of the dissenters and of the Whig Low Churchmen, followers of the former Lord Shaftesbury, might well explain the adoption of it by the philosopher, and would certainly help to show why it was so rapidly taken up by the eighteenth century.   Goldsmith notes this vogue in *The Bee;* see also other references in Alderman.

[133] Cf. B. Dobrée, *Restoration Comedy,* Oxford, 1924, 13 *et passim.*
[134] See A. Nicoll, *A History of Early Eighteenth Century Drama,* Cambridge, 1925, Chapter I; and J. W. Krutch, *Comedy and Conscience after the Restoration,* New York, 1924, 153 etc. See also a review of the latter work by the present author, *Mod. Lang. Notes,* XLI, 332 *et seq.*

the vulgar, of "enthusiasm" and (if anyone in the age possessed such a thing) of virtue.

In the poetry of Puritan lament, the very number and exaggeration of the images of grief make the authenticity of the emotion suspect. Even Bennett and Bogue, whose whole *History* is an apology for English non-conformity, admitted the truth of Clarendon's charge that "hypocricy and fanaticism contributed to form the character of the [Commonwealth] period."[135] The serious, not to say gloomy, demeanour that the Commonwealth imposed upon society must, for many persons, have carried with it a taint of insincerity; few men can make melancholy the business of years without either reacting violently to the other extreme, or learning, like Jaques, to suck a bitter-sweet savor from its cultivation. The violent reaction was expressed in the court of the restored Stuarts; whereas dissent assumed the mantle of Jeremiah, and found that the rôle of the disconsolate was not without its consolations. Indeed, Puritan writers, and doubtless readers also, during the reign of Charles II, were apparently beginning to enjoy the lugubrious and the horrific, very much as some persons are said to "enjoy ill-health." There was not necessarily conscious hypocrisy in this. Quite naturally, the enormity of sin and the dangers of damnation would constitute, in an otherwise uneventful life an interesting— nay, absorbing—experience; and, as such a sensitiveness to sin was commonly supposed to be a "test" of Election to a heavenly reward, it must have been piously cultivated along with the appropriate sensations of exalted emotion that might be supposed to accompany such a blessed state. As long as these emotions were the natural and naïve repercussion of spiritual experience, they had a psychological genuineness; but, when they were found to be not unpleasing, and were sedulously developed *ad hoc*, they became spurious and Sentimental; for Sentimentalism is the cultivation of emotion for its own sake.[136] That the Caroline period saw some such change in the religious psychology of the middle classes, or at least the inception of such a change, seems indisputable: Birch, who had reason to know the age, refers to it almost as a matter of course;[137]

---

[135] D. Bogue and J. Bennett *History of Dissenters*, London, 1808-1810, 21.

[136] I follow the definition as given by Sir Leslie Stephen (*English Thought in the Eighteenth Century*, London, 1912, II, 436) and W. A. Neilson, *Essentials of Poetry*, Boston, 1912, Chapter III.

[137] T. Birch, *Life of Tillotson*, London, 1752, 360.

and Bunyan, who was certainly acquainted with English non-conformity in his generation, pictures it in *Pilgrim's Progress*, in the person of Mr. Ignorance, whose heart assures him of his natural goodness, and who comes down a pleasant green lane to a Salvation of which he has not the slightest doubt.   Bunyan, who had no patience with such folly, has him cast into hell.   Hopeful, moreover, declares that there were "whole families, whole streets," full of such people, even among the very Elect; and one can hardly avoid the conclusion that the vogue of eighteenth century "sensibility" had begun.[138]   The great popular appeal of the Quakers, in this their early, or "enthusiastic" period, points to the same conclusion.   The sudden stage-success of Cibber's *Careless Husband*[139] just before the end of the century, and the association of Sentimentalism with the bourgeoisie in both drama and novel,[140] all are unmistakable evidence that such an undercurrent had long been gathering force; and in Scotland[141] and in Geneva,[142] though somewhat later, a similar evolution from Calvinism toward the optimistic is apparent.   Indeed, Calvinism, through strong under affliction, seems to have been a rather unstable socio-religious compound when it fell upon better days, and was subject to a decomposition that released into the general atmosphere a flatulent Sentimentality.

The funeral elegy reflects this development: as its style sought novelty in the extremes of poetic hyperbole and forced comparisons, the divergence between poetic statement and actual fact widened more and more; and so the sincerity of the authors was put to a constantly increasing strain.   Indeed, the poets do protest too much; and, in a fashion, they cry *peccavimus* themselves by accusing one

[138] See the present writer, *Bunyan's Mr. Ignorance*, Mod. Lang. Rev., XXII, 15 et seq., and P. S. Wood, *Pub. Mod. Lang. Assoc.*, XLIII, 182 et seq.

[139] See E. Bernbaum, *Drama of Sensibility*, Boston, 1915, Chapter I. See also A. Nicoll, *History of Restoration Drama*, Cambridge, 1923, 251 et seq.

[140] See Helen Sard Hughes, *The Middle Class Reader and the English Novel*, Jour. Eng. Ger. Phil., XXV, 362 et seq.

[141] See H. G. Graham, *The Social Life of Scotland in the Eighteenth Century*, London, 1906, Chapter X.

[142] In Geneva the change officially took place in the early eighteenth century under Turretin and Vernet, the latter a friend of Rousseau whose evolution toward the Sentimental seems to have reflected that of his native city. See P. M. Masson, *La Religion de J. J. Rousseau*, Paris, 1916. See also L. Cordier, *J. J. Rousseau und der Calvinismus*, Langensalza, 1915; and A. Dide, *La Protestantisme et la Révolution Francaise*, Paris, 1910.   Is not the genesis of Romanticism to be sought in the Calvinistic Switzerland of Rousseau and Gesner and in the Calvinistic middle class of England? See Finch and Peers, *Origins of French Romanticism*, London, 1920, 17 et seq.

another of mercenary motives and of lauding fools and chronicling small beer. A few of the writers even give direct and unblushing expression to the Sentimental complex: the theological dogma of justification by tears, as expressed in the elegies on the Rev. John Norcot and the pious Rebecca Palmer, reflect the transition of this development; and the Puritans who see in lamentation for the dead a joyful relief, if not a positive delight for themselves, had started upon the agreeable path of accommodating pleasure and virtue. The Cavalier elegies are too cold and objective to arouse any emotion beyond the resentment of boredom; but the Puritan pieces, with their lingering reminiscence of each sad *memento mori,* would seem to furnish a fertile field for the cultivation of Sentimentalism, and show that their public was prepared for, if not already embarked upon, the impending revolution in thought and taste.

CHAPTER VI

THE FUNERAL ELEGY IN THE AMERICAN COLONIES

TO separate the poetry peculiar to each of several social classes and religious groups is the chief preliminary concern of any socio-literary investigation; and, even in seventeenth century England, the lines of demarcation are sometimes indistinct. In America, however, different colonies represented with a rather remarkable fullness and exactitude the different social and religious backgrounds of the mother country; and, as a glass prism separates the sunlight into its heterogeneous colors, so the geographical boundaries of the New World rather definitely distinguished between the various elements that blent into the social system of the old. Many of the colonies were founded as a religious refuge for a given sect; and, as sectarian divisions generally followed the lines of social classes, the natural result was the predominance of one certain point of view in a given colony. Some settlements, to be sure, like New York, were cosmopolitan from the first; and some, like Quaker Pennsylvania and Roman Catholic Maryland, legalized a toleration far in advance of their time. In general, however, the southern colonies of Virginia and the Carolinas were settled by aristocrats who transplanted the Church of England to their shores, without bishops, to be sure, but with a parochial system, a theology, and a general atmosphere, that were closely akin to those they had always known. New England, on the other hand, was settled almost entirely by Calvinists who were drawn for the most part from the *bourgeoisie*. In Massachusetts and Connecticut, the two most prominent colonies of this region, the Independents had established Congregationalism as a state church, an establishment that survived the Revolution and continued well down into the nineteenth century; and those who refused to conform might suffer on occasion as severe legal penalties as any dissenter endured in the reign of Charles II. New England, and especially Massachusetts, can, therefore, be taken as representing, and continuing to represent, down to the rise of Unitarianism in the 1830's, a Calvinistic orthodoxy almost as complete as that of Geneva in its palmiest days; and the Southern colonies, except Georgia which was not colonized until the time of the Wesleyan Movement, may be taken as illustrating the Cavalier element in seventeenth century English society; and the middle colonies, as showing rather a mixture of all sorts and conditions, with a considerable number of Dutch, Swedes, and French Huguenots.

In view of this condition, it is significant that the funeral elegy seems to have been unknown in the South, that it appears only very occasionally in the central group of colonies, and that in New England it flourished practically to the exclusion of all other poetry.[1] At first glance, one might be surprised that the southern colonies' did not cultivate the Pindaric eulogies that were produced so abundantly at the court of Charles II; but the absence of urban life with its literary inclinations and the absence also of a Grub Street with interested motives in the production of such pieces, combine to explain the lack of elegiac eulogy in the scheme of plantation life. The colonies between Virginia and Connecticut supply only occasional broadside elegies, such as the verses *To the Memory of that faithful Minister of Christ, Thomas Lightfoot, who fell asleep in Jesus, November 4th, 1725;*[2] and the lines suggest that Lightfoot was probably a Calvinist. The abundance of such pieces in New England, however, at a time when it had little other poetry,[3] and especially among the Congregational ministers, who boasted that they represented the Protestantism of the Protestant religion and

[1] See W. P. Trent, *History of American Literature*, New York, 1903, 16. One cannot even be sure that the lines on Mrs. Hannah Lee (1750) (*Gent. Mag.*, XX, 231) were strictly American. In either case, they are not on the whole mortuary.

[2] It was printed in Philadelphia, in 1725. The New York Pub. Lib. has a photostat. O. Wegelin (*Early American Poetry*, New York, 1903) mentions also two other late Philadelphia elegies: *An Elegy on the Death of that ancient, venerable and useful Matron and Midwife, Mrs. Mary Broadwell who rested from her Labours, Jan. 2, 1730*; and *An Elegy on the much Lamented Death of the Ingenious and Well-Beloved Aquila Rose* (1723). The latter is by the printer Keimer. Wegelin also notes that the son,

Joseph Rose, collected the elder Rose's *Poems* in 1740, and subjoined pieces written "to his Memory after his Decease." The *Elegy on Mary Bradstreet* is also mentioned by C. R. Hildeburn (*List of Publications Issued in Pennsylvania, 1685-1759*, Philadelphia, 1882).

[3] J. F. Hunnewell (*Early American Poetry*, Boston, 1896, *Publ. Club of Odd Volumes*, IV) says that before 1717 elegies were "abundant" and that "little else" was produced. W. C. Ford (*Publ. Mass. Hist. Soc.*, LXXV, Introductory Note) extends the period of abundance to 1750. J. Sabin (*Dictionary of Books relating to America*, 1868-1892, III, 129-130) and O. Wegelin, *op. cit.*, show, furthermore, that the elegy was by no means discontinued after 1750.

the dissidence of dissent—these facts afford no small support to the theory already advanced that the funeral elegy *per se*, particularly during the latter seventeenth century, was essentially the possession of the Puritans of the middle classes, certainly in New England, and presumably in Old.

In content, these elegies are generally like their counterparts of the Commonwealth period. They were usually printed on broadsides with poor typography and crude pictorial embellishments; and their headings show the skull and cross bones, the hour-glass, and the skeleton with a scythe, against the usual background of rather imperfectly inked-in black. Their first appearance would seem to be in 1647, about the time that the poetic type in England was first being associated with Puritanism. The earliest example is, appropriately enough, upon the death of a divine, the exemplary Thomas Hooker; and, with its Biblical allusion, its hyperbole of panegyric and of grief, its personifications suggestive at once of the moralities and of Neo-classicism, and its lingering and mournful pathetic fallacy, it constitutes a fairly characteristic, if somewhat meek and mild example of the poetic type:

> Come sighs, come sorrows, let's lament this Rod,
> Which hath bereav'd us of this Man of God:
> A Man of God, which came from God to men,
> And now from them is gone to God agen.
> Bid Joy depart, bid Merriment be gone;
> Bid Friends stand by, sit sorrowful alone.
> But ah! what sorrow can be to suffice,
> Though Heaven and Earth were filled with our cries,
> The Clouds were turned into drops of tears,
> The Mourning for to last an Age of Years?[4]

At an early date appeared in America the elegiac convention of the elegy written, or supposed to be written, by some person of eminent piety immediately before his death, and printed presumably as a monitory depiction of the most approved death-bed decorum. The composition of the following poem in octosyllabic couplets, like some yet to be cited,[5] is significant as delineating a

[4] Nathaniel Morton, *New England's Memoriall*, Cambridge, 1669, 127. W. C. Ford says that the elegies collected in this anthology originally circulated as broadsides (*Broadsides, Ballads &c.*, Boston, 1922, xi.).

[5] *Cf.* J. S.'s epitaph on the Rev. Jonathan Mitchel, Morton, *op. cit.*, 196.

tradition of pensive pieces written in this meter, and also as admonishing the literary critic to beware of ascribing such pieces, without grounds more relative than this, to the influence of Milton's *Il Penseroso*; for the limited technique of the writers, and perhaps also the rise of Neo-classical fashions, threw the funeral elegy regularly into pentameter or tetrameter couplets. The *Verses found in pocket of Mr. Thomas Dudley at his Death July 31, 1653* show that the funeral elegy had grown somewhat in grace and in mortuary detail since the effort six years before on the death of Hooker:

> Dim eyes, deaf Ears, cold stomach shew
> My dissolution is in view.
> Eleven times seven near liv'd have I,
> And now God calls, I willing die:
> My Shuttle's shot, my race is run,
> My Sun is set, my Deed is done;
> My Span is measur'd, Tale is told
> My Flower is faded and grown old. . . .[6]

In 1657, furthermore, at Cambridge, Massachusetts, was printed a broadside entitled *A Copy of Verses Made by that Reverend Man of God Mr. John Wilson, Pastor of the First Church in Boston: on the sudden death of Mr. Joseph Brisco, who was translated from earth to Heaven Jan. 1, 1657*;[7] and it seems fair to assume that many more such pieces have perished; for broadsides are but transient things, and many laments, furthermore, were doubtless still-born in manuscript. The notable success of Michael Wigglesworth's *Day of Doom*, first published in 1662, shows that by then the literary mood was already popularly established; and, although the sermons of the day doubtless had a main part in fostering this vogue, elegiac literature also probably had some share in preparing the way, and undoubtedly furnished the necessary precedent for the practice, dangerous to Puritan eyes, of putting even religious material into verse.

Long before *The Day of Doom*, however, Anne Bradstreet—hailed by her London publisher, 1650, as "the Tenth Muse lately

[6] *Ibid.*, 139.

[7] See C. Evans, *American Bibliography*, Chicago, 1903, item No. 48. Evans would not seem to be very complete in his listing of broadsides; for he finds no other elegies until that of Increase Mather on Richard Mather, 1670, No. 150.

sprung up in America"—was penning poems allied more or less closely to the funeral elegy. Wife of one governor and daughter of another, Anne Bradstreet had spent her girlhood browsing in a goodly Elizabethan library and her womanhood not without contact with the more cultured of the early colonists—scholars and gentlefolk. In 1638, she wrote *An Elegie upon that Honorable and Renowned Knight, Sir Philip Sidney*; in 1641, *In honour of Du Bartas*; and, later, *In Honour of that mighty Princess Queen Elizabeth*. Of these poems, the first and second each concludes with an epitaph; the third concludes with two. Among Mrs. Bradstreet's other poems are verses in memory of her father who died in 1653, her mother, who died in 1643, a grandchild who died in 1665, and two other grandchildren and a daughter-in-law who all died in 1669. To the posthumous edition of Anne Bradstreet's poems, John Norton appropriately appended *A Funeral Elogy, upon that Pattern and Patron of Virtue, the truely pious, peerless & matchless Gentlewoman Mrs. Anne Bradstreet, right Panaretes, Mirror of Her Age, Glory of her Sex, whose Heaven-born-Soul leaving its earthly Shrine, chose its native home, and was taken to its Rest, upon the 16th. Sept. 1672.*

The last four decades of the seventeenth century saw the custom of elegiac broadsides firmly established in New England. In his elegy on Urian Oakes, [8] Mather summarized by items the mortuary bathos of his age. After defending the propriety of elegiac writing, he proceeds:

> Cotton *Embalms great* Hooker; Norton *Him*;
> *And* Norton's *Herse do's* Poet-Wilson *trim*
> *With Verses*: Mitchell *writes a poem on*
> *The Death of* Wilson; *and when* Mitchell's *gone,*
> Shephard *with fun'ral Lamentations gives*
> *Honour to Him: and at his Death receives*
> *The like from the* [like Maro][9] *Lofty Strain*
> *Of admirable* Oakes!

The clerical poet still occasionally feels called upon to defend the writing of elegies; but, in 1685, Mather spoke the final *ipse dixit*

[8] C. Mather, *A Poem Dedicated to the Memory of the Reverend and Excellent Urian Oakes*, Boston, 1682. Oakes was President of Harvard College, and died in 1681. The poem has been edited by Hunnewell in *Early American Poetry*, ed. *cit.*

[9] Hunnewell's emendation.

of orthodoxy, and declared that "apology" for the funeral elegy
was "altogether superfluous."[10] Perhaps because apology proved to
be more necessary than he had supposed, or more probably because
he was merely following an established poetic convention, he took
occasion twenty years later again to defend the custom, citing the
most exalted Christian precedent.[11] But unquestionably the poetry
of death was acceptable, even when he wrote his first apology, to
the severest of the New England Puritans; and his later statements
are probably no more than clerical repetitions of an accepted truism.

Among the lesser elegists, the most outstanding was probably
Urian Oakes, who enjoys the distinction of having been ranked as
Mather's poetic equal.[12] The elegy on his fellow-pastor, Thomas
Shepard, is a characteristic performance. Like Polonius, the mod-
est author protests that he uses no art at all; but, by the fortieth
stanza, he throws trammels to the winds, revels in the distress of
"Poor Widowed *Charlestown*," and luxuriates in "grisly Death"
and the lamentations of Cambridge and especially of Harvard.
The final apotheosis of Shepard takes up only two stanzas of the
fifty-two!

A considerable number of pieces by minor elegists of the Caroline period have survived. Thomas Tileson's octosyllabic *Elegy on
John Foster* contains the theme, already noted in Quarles, "That
God does thus our choice ones Slay," and complacently looks forward to "A dreadful flood of wrath in vieu."[13] There are at
least two anonymous elegies on Governor Winthrop, the second
aptly described as "Another Black Parenthesis of Woe."[14] The
passing of the Rev. Jonathan Mitchell produced

> A Mourning great, each Eye distilling Streams;
> Sad Sighs and Sobs in most men's mouths their Theams. . . .[15]

And the octosyllabic quatrains on Wilson significantly stress the

[10] C. Mather, *Funeral Tears on the Rev. Nathanael Collins*, Boston, 1685, Preface. See also *Early American Poetry*, ed. cit., No. 3.

[11] *Elegy on the Early Death of Seven Young Ministers* (1706).

[12] W. B. Otis, *American Verse, 1625-1807*, New York, 1909, 60.

[13] Foster's death in 1681 dates the piece. It was reprinted by S. A. Green in *John Foster*, Boston, 1909, 40. There is also a *Funeral Elegy* to Foster, also in octosyllabics, in the *Pro. Mass. Hist. Soc.*, VIII, 392 *et seq.* See also Wege-lin, *op. cit.*, who lists an elegy on Foster by Joseph Capen.

[14] *Ibid.*, 125 *et seq.*

[15] *Elegy on the Rev. Jonathan Mitch-ell* (1668) in Morton, *New Englands Memorial*, Cambridge, 1669, 192-193.

close relations between the Colony and the dissenters of the mother country.[16] Edmund Weld's *Funeral Elegy By way of Dialogue Between Death, Soul, Body and Jesus Christ,*[17] composed in a sort of loose Pindaric measure, ends with a pat nicety that is not quite undignified, and yet is very much in the Puritan tradition, since the time of the morality plays:

> Blest be thy glorious Majesty
> That looks on such a worm as I;
> Thou did'st me from the Dungeon rase [*sic*]
> That I might ere advance thy praise
>   When I did dwell,
>   In lower Hell,
> Love everlasting fetched me thence:
>   Else I had been,
>   Through Satan's spleen,
> Forevermore excluded hence. . . .

The pentameter couplet, although used with far more *enjambement* than English Neo-classicism would have allowed, more than occasionally appears, as, for instance, in the lines signed by F. D., *To the Memory of the Learned and Reverend Mr. Johnathan Mitchell, Inhumed July 10, 1668*:

> The Countries Tears, be ye my Spring; my Hill
> A general Grave; let Groans inspire my Quill
> With an Heart-rending Sense, drawn from the Cries
> Of Orphan Churches, and the Destinies
> Of a Bereaved House: Let Children weep
> They scarce know why; and let the Mother steep
> Her listless Hopes in Brine; the Private Friend
> O'rewhelmed with grief falter his Comforts end
> By a warm Sympathie let Feaverish Heat
> Roam through my Verse unseen; and a Cold Sweat
> Limning Despair, attend me; Sighs diffuse
> Convulsions through my language, such as use
> To type a Gasping Fancy; Lastly shroud
> Religious Splendor in a Mourning Cloud,
> Replete with Vengeance for succeeding Times
> Fertile in Woes. . . .[18]

---

[16] *On the Revd Mr. John Wilson* (1667); *ibid.*, 187.

[17] The date of the original broadside would seem to be 1668; but it was re- printed in 1751, a proof of its popularity. The N. Y. Hist. Soc. owns a copy. See Ford, *op. cit.*, No. 948.

[18] See N. Morton, *op. cit.*, 193 *et seq.*

The gentle reader is instructed to "Reade his Tear-delug'd Grave," and there learn the "present Woe and future Miserie" of the mourners; and the piece ends with an epigrammatic epitaph. The writer seems to take a pleasure in piling a horrific Pelion upon an already quaking Ossa; and, like Lear's elder daughters, he finds it suspiciously easy to heave his heart into his mouth. Some pieces are notable, as are contemporary epitaphs, chiefly for their somewhat startling Realistic details. Joseph Capen apparently considered the following couplets a suitable introduction to a serious eulogy:

> Here lie the relict Fragments, which were took
> Out of Consumption's teeth by Death the Cook.
> Voracious Apetite dost thus devour
> Scarce ought hast left for worms t'live on an Hour
> But Skin & Bones no bones thou mak'st of that
> It is thy common trade t' eat all the fat.[19]

What monsters ensue, when a bard cudgels both his Pegasus and his brains! Surely such versification and such sentiments are far removed from the poetry of court-life—even the court of Charles II—and the leaders of Puritanism, for all their Cambridge degrees, had hardly acquired that sense of the appropriate that is the essence of gentility: Puritanism, and the poetry of Puritanism, though they might be sincerely religious and deeply learned in the learning of the day, were not things of the aristocracy. The following fragments, from an elegy on the Rev. John Reiner, are perhaps equally worthy of quotation:

> . . . But when that doleful word REINER *is dead*,
> I heard, Lips quiver'd, Belly trembled,
> My spirits fail'd, Corruption seiz'd my Bones,
> My face grew pale, my heart as cold as Stones. . . .
> Some smarting Wounds we had receiv'd before,
> This lays us welt'ring in our Blood and Gore,
> Under the fifth Rib stuck; you that pass by
> Stand still and see, and sigh to see us dye.[20]

The original is printed so largely in italics (omitted here) that one hardly knows which sort of type was intended to give emphasis.

[19] Dated 1681. See Green, *op. cit.*, 36.

[20] *Lamentations Upon the Reverend Mr. John Reiner*, Dec., 1676. The original broadside is to be found in the library of the Boston Athenaeum. For Reiner, see Green, *op. cit.*, 128.

With so admirable an opportunity to improve piety with praise, it seems strange that the reverend authors should expend so much of their literary effort on the mere details of mortality and of affliction: indeed, the edifying gloom of the living was seemingly accounted of more moment than the Salvation of the dead. Doubtless they were fearful, like their co-religionists of the 1630's, of anticipating the divine judgment and perhaps giving the deceased more than his due meed of praise. Be the reason what it may, the more precise brethren turned their eyes downward to the grave rather than upward to eternal bliss.

Cotton Mather's own elegies deserve more than passing mention. He supplied several of his memorial volumes on deceased colleagues with elegiac supplements, pieces of ponderous hyperbole ingeniously labored into a spurious appearance of the *furor poeticus*. His *Funeral Tears on the Rev. Nathanael Collins* furnishes a taste of his quality.[21] After a short prologue in verse, the lament proper begins with a bibulous metaphor quite appropriate to a region that was prospering from the trade in Jamaica rum:

> I sigh the *Fate* for which our broached eyes
> Spend floods of *brine;* at which a dire surprise
> Of a soul-chilling horrour doth invade
> The *Soul* not *stone* before; at which are made
> In serious minds as many *wounds* as were
> To *Caesar* given.   Reader, shake to hear;
> *The* DEATH *of* COLLINS *tis.*

Extravagant pseudo-Biblical pictures follow, and a description of Lady "Sympathie," as vivid and about as attractive as one of Spenser's seven deadly sins:

> Grov'ling in Ashes, with dishev'led hair,
> Smiting her brest, *black'd* with a *mourning* dress. . . .

Later the poet breaks into quatrains of shrill panegyric, and with forced fingers rude rifles the science of his age in search of fresh figures modelled after, very far after, the vivid conceits of Donne. Such ingenuity hardly expresses, but rather skirts the periphery of, sorrow, telling how or why to be sad, but in itself expressing no sadness.

[21] Mather's elegies were reprinted in *Early American Poetry, ed. cit.*

The elegy on the Reverend John Wilson, included in *Johannes in Eremo* further illustrates Mather's learned eulogistic style, which in this piece he spices with parenthetical footnotes:

> Might *Aarons* Rod (such *Funerals* mayn't be *Dry*)
> But broach the *Rock*, t'wood gush pure *Elegy*,
> To round the Wilderness with purling *Layes*,
> And tell the *World*, the Great Saint WILSONS Praise.
>
> Here's ONE, (*Pearls* are not in great clusters found)
> Here's ONE, the *Skill* of *Tongues* and *Arts* had Crown'd
> Here's ONE (by frequent *Martyrdome* t'was Try'd)
> That could forego *Skill*, *Pelf*, and *Life* beside,
> For CHRIST; Both ENGLANDS *Darling*, whom in Swarms
> They Press'd to See, and Hear, and felt his *Charms*.
>
> Tis ONE, (when will it Rise to Number Two?
> The World at once can but ONE *Phoenix* Show:)
> For *Truth*, a PAUL; CEPHAS, for *Zeal*; for *Love*,
> A JOHN; inspir'd by the Celestial *Dove*.
> ABRA'MS true Son for *Faith*: and in his *Tent*
> *Angels* oft had their *Table* and *Content*. . . .

One wonders how safely it can be assumed that "All bad art springs from genuine feeling," and whether there was not something spurious in the sentiments that underlay such writing. The poet seems to force himself to a certain heat of emotion; and is not the artificial cultivation of emotion for a social or even a religious purpose somewhat akin to the artificial cultivation of emotion for the sake of meretricious pleasure? In short is not emotionalistic religion rather close to emotionalistic ethics; and is not the emotionalizing of ethics Sentimentalism?

Perhaps the lines on Clark, one of "seven young ministers" on whom Cotton bestowed literary and theological immortality, achieve the apex of mortuary impropriety. The picture of his *"Wasted Flesh"* melted away by "Flaming *Zeal*" is all too consciously clever; and the comparison to a "Fat Cloud"—not quite in the manner of Shelley!—constitutes a metaphor without price:

> My CLARK was One, And such a *Clark* as he
> *Synods* of *Angels* would take *Theirs* to be.
> *Faintly to Praise* a Youth of such Desert,
> Were but to Shoot indeed vile *Slanders* Dart.

See but his *Wasted Flesh*; T'was Flaming *Zeal*
That Melted him: The Flame is burning still.
Methinks I see his Ravish'd Hearers wait
And long to hear still his next *Heav'nly Treat*.
Look; the Fat Cloud, what *Oracles* he pours
On Thirsty Souls in most *Expedient Showres*! . . .
Botanists, Boast your *Palm-tree*, whence arise
More than Three Hundred rich commodities.
Write *Persian Poet*, that brave Tree to Praise,
As many *Songs* as in the year be *Dayes*.
My CLARK more *Vertues* had; So must the Tree,
Too rich for Earth, to Heav'n transplanted be.

The present writer trusts that it is unnecessary to quote also from the elegiac eulogy on the learned Cheever, which Mather published in his *Corderius Americanus* (1708).

The closing years of the seventeenth century are well reflected in Mather's elegies: they show no considerable tendency toward Neo-classical restraint; and, although there is no lack of emotionalism, they are saved from the Sentimental by at least something of a genuine religious motive. Ichabod Wiswell wrote a eulogy (1693) in ballad stanzas on the Rev. Samuel Arnold, followed by an "Anagram." The eulogy begins:

When Lights go out, Darkness succeeds,
Is this sad Marshfield's Case?
Ah! little, little, little know
We who succeeds in Place.[22]

A rapid reader might suppose that the first two lines referred to the flight of the soul from the body. But nothing of the sort. They have to do merely with the problem of filling Arnold's Marshfield pastorate. The Puritans were nothing if not practical, a bourgeois trait evident in Cromwell himself, who, while he prayed, saw to it that the powder was kept dry. The anagram also makes its first concern the loss to the parish, and not the death —and, one might presume, Salvation—of a pious Christian. Certainly Arnold himself dared to look forward with hope, if not with certainty, to Salvation, as he suggests in an elegiac autobiography written in rough pentameter couplets "not long before his Death";[23] but perhaps his friends were not quite so sure. His

[22] Lib. of Congress broadside.   [23] Lib. of Congress broadside.

lines are comparatively restrained, for excessive eulogy or excessive lamentation would hardly have been in place; and they seem to have a Classical touch in his desire after death to "soar and mount aloft, With Egale's wings," like a Roman emperor. Edward Thompson's *Elegiack Tribute to Seaborn Cotton* (1686) is written in rather broken and ill-rhymed couplets, but is interesting for its occasional attempts at musical felicity:

> If tears & fears or moans, or groans were verse
> How would I, could I, should I grace ye herse . . . [24]

The New England elegy of the latter seventeenth century generally uses pentameter couplets, but with the rough emphasis and run-on lines of Donne rather than with the polished smoothness of Pope; and it is quite as likely to be written in ballad-stanzas or in octosyllabics. The elegiac themes show no great change: the mortuary landscape is not developed beyond the occasional touches evident in Commonwealth elegies; and the exaggeration of emotion seems to spring more from the decadence of the "metaphysical" style and from the peculiar tone of New England Puritanism than from actual Sentimentalism. Certainly the word-play, the odd allusion, and the hyperbolic metaphor of these pieces show that long after the Stuart Restoration the Puritans were still enjoying what Addison chose to stigmatize in *The Spectator* as "the little Gothic ornaments of epigrammatical conceits, turns, points, and quibbles." The literary and social aristocracy have never applauded the tastes of the middle classes, although these tastes are commonly derived from themselves.

During the reign of Queen Anne, the funeral elegy hardly abated its productivity, though it sometimes mitigated its tone. The *Carmen Miserabile, A Solemn Lachrymatory for the Grave of Jonathan Marsh* (1708),[25] which ekes out its mortuary effect with a skeleton, an open grave, and other pictorial felicities, is most notable for its tolling death-knell and its vivid personification of death:

> A Groaning Eccho tolleth in mine Ear,

[24] A MS. of this elegy is in the possession of the Mass. Hist. Soc. of Boston, Winthrop Papers, 7b. A copy of the broadside is to be found in the library of the Boston Athenæum. See also Ford, *op. cit.*, 44.

[25] Lib. Boston Athen.

> A Ghastly Visage fill'd with *Panick* Fear
> Draws nigh; desist th'approach, hood-vail your Eyes
> And wane but the faint accents of your Cries.

Benjamin Thompson's lines (1708) on the death of a Boston schoolmaster, with the familiar title of *The Gramarian's Funeral*,[26] reminds one of the sixteenth century university drama. It personifies the eight parts of speech who, wearing *"Mourning Gowns,"* bewail the passing of the deceased. Thompson seems also to be responsible for *A Neighbor's Tears Sprinkled on the Dust of the Amiable Virgin Mrs. Rebekah Sewall* (1710),[27] a turgid piece, its lines bombasted out to fit the requirements of meter and rhyme. Under a proper mortuary cut, it presents to the edified reader the usual ideas of death the "fell Sergeant," borrowed through elegiac tradition ultimately from *Hamlet*, and of death the regicide, taken from an ubiquity of lamentations:

> Heav'ns only, in dark hours, can Succour send;
> And show a Fountain, where the cisterns end. . . .
> Death, that stern Officer, takes no denial;
> I'm griev'd he found your door, to make a trial.
> Thus, be it on the Land or Swelling Seas,
> His Sov'raignty doth what His Wisdom please.
> Must then the Rulers of this World's affairs,
> By Providence be brought thus unto Tears?

In the seventeenth century, the funeral elegy had been almost entirely the prerogative of the clerical theocrats. As the foregoing examples attest, the following century showed a widening of elegiac subject-matter; but so ingrained was New England society with Calvinism that the atmosphere of the broadsides does not greatly change. Following the lamentation for "the Amiable Rebekah Sewall" and one on Mrs. Mary Gerrish at about the same time,[28] appeared other pieces on women, with a larger and larger element of eulogy: Madam Elizabeth Hutchinson (1712) was elegized as an example of "Honor and Virtue";[29] and Madam Hannah Sewall (1717) was honored with a panegyric upon her

---

[26] Lib. Mass. Hist. Soc.
[27] Boston Pub. Lib.
[28] Although it has the curious title of *Profit and Loss*, it is largely eulogistic.

A copy is to be found in the Library of the Boston Athenæum.
[29] Lib. Boston Athen.

"Greatness and Goodness."[30] But the Puritan Muse did not always melt into mere eulogy before the picture of exemplary womanhood; and, although the writing of elegies may sometimes have degenerated, as it certainly did in England, into a mere bid for ecclesiastical or other patronage, yet there were still those who used the form whole-heartedly for the edification of their fellow men. Such a one was the author of another elegy on Mrs. Mary Gerrish, a composition in the best Puritan tradition of the seventeenth century: The "King of Terrors" appears in official guise; and, we are told,

> That bare-bones Scithe Cuts with Impartial Stroke
> The tender Lily, and the Sturdy Oake. . . .

Does not the Puritans' gloating over this idea arise from the comforting thought that their social betters were after all no better than they?

During the eighteenth century, the elegiac Muse honored not only Boston and also Cambridge but also the provinces. As early as 1687, John Cotton had elegized upon the subject of John Alden of Duxborough.[31] Samuel Danforth wrote a panegyric on Thomas Leonard of Taunton,[32] and was in turn bewailed in company with Peter Thacher of Milton. Jonathan Burt composed a *Lamentation Occasion'd by the Great Sickness & Lamented* DEATHS *of divers Eminent Persons in Springfield*;[33] but, with this transplantation and widening of application, the more colorful elements of the New England elegy began to fade into the light of common day. As it grew more indiscriminate, its zest departed: perhaps life in the new country was growing so agreeable that death was a less congenial contemplation, even to the Elect. Thus slowly began to appear indications of an innocuous Neo-classicism, a sweet, supine, Leodicean thing, neither hot nor cold. It was not the stuff of which early Christian martyrs were made, but it was amply loqua-

[30] Copies of this and the following broadside are to be found in Boston Pub. Lib.

[31] Wegelin, *op. cit.*, also lists poems *On the Much Lamented Death of the Reverend Mr. Noadiah Russel, Late Pastor of the Church of Christ in Middletown* [Conn.], New London, 1714; and poetic *Memoirs of the Life and Death of the Pious and Ingenious Mrs. Jane Turell* (1735).

[32] Lib. Boston Athen. See also *A Poem on the Death of Peter Thacher of Milton and Samuel Danforth of Taunton* [Boston, ?1724].

[33] Written in 1712, printed 1720. Copies of this and the following piece are to be found in the Lib. Mass. Hist. Soc.

cious in directing others along the ways of the righteous; and the didactic Pegasus, whose wings, like the auk's, have long since grown puny from disuse, and who therefore ambles flat-footed along the ground, happened upon the funeral elegy, claimed it as his own, and found it more succulent than asphodel.

Perhaps the most perfect combination of the didactic and elegiac styles, in a generalized elegy such as contemporary poets were beginning to produce in England, is to be found in a series of tabloid *Meditations on the uncertainty of Mans Life, Of the Torments of Hell and the Joys of Heaven, Occasioned by the Sudden DEATH'S of sundry Persons in the County of Plymouth* (1708). The first meditation restates the old theme of the brevity of life, but is notable for its nine-line stanza, ending, like Spenser's, in an Alexandrine. The second has an epigrammatic verve in happy contrast to the usual *rigor mortis* of elegiac style:

> I am but dust; to dust I shall Return;
> Naked I came, and Naked shall I goe:
> Friends or Relations can't the time ajourn,
> But when He calls, it must be even so.
> I to the Grave may goe within a trice,
> Where is no work, no knowledge, no device.

The theme of *vanitas vanitatis* also supplies some more or less pointed apothegms. This Neo-classical style of sententious generality occasionally gives place to vividness of mortuary detail; but the blight of abstraction saps something of its pristine vigor:

> In Hell no comfort is, there's nought but grief,
> Anguish and torment, pain without relief.
> Eternal Torments where the Worm nev'r dyes:
> And where the Groan's and everlasting Cryes
> Of Damned Souls: is still augmented hire,
> By scorching flames of everlasting fire;
> The Abyss of Torme[nt] . . . than nothing worse,
> Prepared for those tha[t Je]hovah Curse.
> O Lord! direct me in the way that I,
> Should walk: and let me keep it till I dye:
> Then let my Soul this place of Torments miss,
> And Rest Above in Joy and Peace, and Bliss.

In place of the final apotheosis so common in the elegy, the last two meditations are taken up with a description of heaven and a prayer for eternal Salvation. Indeed, a little elementary revision could make of the final part a very respectable hymn:

> O Thou Inspirer of these Souls of ours!
> Great God of Light, by thy Almighty pow'r,
> Remove the darkness that doth us invade;
> And cleanse these Souls of ours which thou hast made.
> We are defil'd with Sin, polluted foul,
> Throughout in Body, Spirit and in Soul.
> So that in us (that is) *within our Flesh*,
> *There dwelleth no good thing*: O God refresh
> Us therefore, from the fountain of Thy Grace;
> Who fillest Heaven and Earth and every Place,
> And cause these Souls of ours, tho' dead in Sin,
> To Live, and Breathe, and grow & thrive again:
> That when our days shall end on Earth, and we
> Enter the List into ETERNITIE:
> Our Souls may Live Above, and rest in Heaven with Thee.

Thus do the *Meditations* display a Neo-classical refinement of the funeral elegy, and develop from the earlier form the extended moralistic poem comparable to the graveyard effusions of Blair and Young; and the final apotheosis faintly anticipates the lyric revival as it appeared in the hymns of Wesley and Cowper. The Neo-classical elements may perhaps be attributable to British influence; but the touch of emotional lyricism would seem to be an independent development of New England Puritanism along the same lines as the Puritanism of the mother-country. It is, however, unsafe to generalize from a single example.

For the most part, the restraining influence of Neo-classicism is but slightly apparent; and the lyricism, if it can be said to exist at all, belongs to the Elizabethans rather than to the dawn of Romanticism. As far as elegiac literature is concerned, Wendell is generally right in his contention that the culture of New England in the early eighteenth century was not materially different from that of the mother-country a hundred years before when most of the colonists had emigrated;[34] and this is true even of some pieces that are more recent than the reign of Queen Anne. The *Elegy* by Josephus Nash on Dr. Thomas Hastings (1728)[35] begins with "the Grave that swallows all," and then turns to

[34] B. Wendell, *Literary History of America*, Boston, 1898.

[35] Boston Pub. Lib.

eulogy with an occasional spice of the putrescent. The *Funeral Elegy, By way of Dialogue Between Death, Soul, Body, World and Jesus Christ*[36] suggests in the rough doggerel of its dialogue the old morality plays, and the following speech by Death would seem to be based on the well-known passage in *Hamlet,* "this fell sergeant, death, Is strict in his arrest":

> Ho, ho prepare to go with me,
> For I am come to summons thee:
> See my Commission seal'd with Blood,
> Who sent me, he will make it good.
> The Life of Man
> Is but a span;
> Whose slender Thread I must divide
> My name is Death,
> I'll stop thy Breath,
> From my Arrest thou can'st not hide.

Josephus Nash, whose lines on Hastings have just been mentioned, wrote also an *Elegy*[37] on "the Reverend & Excellent Mr. Solomon Stoddard" (1729). The piece has some characteristic lines on the power of death:

> It's Sword will pierce the rich and royal Race,
> And who from Scarlet, Dunghills do embrace.
> Anointed ones, cloath'd with Salvation,
> Of Aaron's house in white, Death feeds upon,
> Whose feet are beautiful, who tydings bring,
> Of peace and joy from our Immanuel King.
> To pit's descent still must they walk, and have,
> Their Heritage within the shady Grave. . . .

The later lines are given over to eulogy, which was becoming a larger and larger ingredient of elegiac verse. About 1738, the Rev. Mr. Byles addressed an elegy to Governor Belcher "on the Death of his Lady"[38] with the conventional depiction of death, the leveller of all, and a rather vivid couplet on the rites of burial:

> Cold to the Tomb see the pale Corpse convey'd,
> Wrapt up in Silence and the dismal Shade.

[36] Lib. Penn. Hist. Soc.
[37] Boston Pub. Lib.
[38] Dr. John Winstanley, *Poems Written Occasionally,* Dublin, 1742, 50 *et seq.* The poem was originally printed in Boston in 1730 (Wegelin, *op. cit.,* 15). Wegelin also notes elegies by Byles on Queen Caroline (1738) and on Governor Belcher's brother-in-law (1726).

Perhaps because of the Calvinistic revival of Jonathan Edwards, the elegies, as one approaches the mid-century, are, if anything, more mortuary than those of the reign of Queen Anne; and, in 1743, even a woman could be elegized in lilting ballad stanzas on "Tyrant Death" and the "Midnight Darkness" of the grave and the direful Last Judgment.[39] The religious revival of the period was, like most such revivals today, an eruption of artificially stimulated emotion that could not, in many cases, have been very deep; and a mutilated broadside entitled *An Elegy Occasioned by the sudden and awful Death of Mr. Nathanael Baker,*[40] "A Young Man just upon the point of Marriage" (1733), illustrates the religious psychology of at least one poetaster who attempted to "raise a melancholy Fire," with "Strains of Woe, that shall be adequate." "Oh! boundless Grief," he exclaims, "Oh! Tears that can't be pent," and then rather naïvely declares:

> It seems to me my song should give relief,
> If I could imitate his Parents Grief.
> But that I know is far beyond my Pen,
> Or Rhet'ric of the sons of mortal Men;
> We can't express by Words, they can't reveal,
> The Floods of Grief, the Agonies they feel.
> O this our Son, in all his Strength and Pri[d]e
> When Youth and Beauty in their Lustre s...e
> Is hurl'd away to Shades of Death, and Gloom.
> How melancholy is the mournful Room? . . .
> All his acquaintance bathe his Urn with T[ears,]
> A sprightly Youth in midst of blooming Years. . . .
> He feeds the Worms that can't be bribed t[o] . . .

The poet then passes to "the Grave, from whence he cannot Rise," and to his fiancée's "doleful Strains." The consolation at the end is rather cold; for the poet seems to feel that, except for the possibility of hell, our death is but a sleep and a forgetting—or, at all events, like many Puritan elegists, he writes as if such were his creed. If this piece be not Sentimental in its avowed cult of the melancholic, it is at least so similar to Sentimentalism as to defy immediate distinction.

[39] *An Elegy Occasion'd by the Death of Mrs. Ruth Edson,* Boston, Pub. Lib. Cf. a contribution from New England to the *Gentleman's Magazine* (V, 549) in which there is a fine whiff of brimstone for those who "too late" had "humbly worship'd their tremendous God."
[40] Lib. Dedham Hist. Soc.

A delightful comment on the funeral elegy in New England is contributed by young Benjamin Franklin, 1722, to his brother James' ribald sheet *The New England Courant.* In this letter (now known as No. 7 of the "Do-Good Papers"), Franklin suggests that the reason why good poetry is so scarce in New England of the day, is "purely because we do not afford that Praise and Encouragement which is merited." He cites a recent elegy upon the much lamented death of Mrs. Mehitebell Kitel; calls it "the most *Extraordinary* Piece that was ever wrote in New-England"; finds "no English Author, ancient or modern, whose Elegies may be compar'd with this"; and quotes from, and comments on, the piece at length. He concludes with "A receipt to make a New-England Funeral Elegy":—

For the Title of your Elegy. *Of these you may have enough ready made to your Hands; but if you should chuse to make it your self, you must be sure not to omit the words Ætatis Suæ, which will Beautify it exceedingly.*

For the Subject of your Elegy. *Take one of your Neighbours who has lately departed this Life; it is no great matter of what Age the Party dy'd, but it will be best if he went away suddenly, being* Kill'd, Drown'd, *or* Frose to Death.

Having chose the Person, take all his Virtues, Excellencies, &c. and if he have not enough, you may borrow some to make up a sufficient Quantity: To these add his last Words, dying Expressions, &c. if they are to be had; mix all these together, and be sure you strain them well. Then season all with a Handful or two of Melancholly Expressions, such as, Dreadful, Deadly, cruel cold Death, unhappy Fate, weeping Eyes, &c. *Have mixed all these Ingredients well, put them into the empty Scull of some young* Harvard; (*but in Case you have ne'er a One at Hand, you may use your own,*) *there let them Ferment for the Space of a Fortnight, and by that Time they will be incorporated into a Body, which take out, and having prepared a sufficient Quantity of double Rhimes, such as* Power, Flower; Quiver, Shiver; Grieve us, Leave us; tell you, excel you; Expeditions, Physicians; Fatigue him, Intrigue him; &c. *you must spread all upon Paper, and if you can procure a Scrap of Latin to put at the End, it will garnish it mightily; then having affixed your Name at the Bottom, with a Mœstus* Composuit, *you will have an Excellent Elegy.*

N. B. *This Receipt will serve when a Female is the Subject of your Elegy, provided you borrow a greater Quantity of Virtues, Excellencies, &c. . . .*

The funeral elegy died hard in New England. There is a

rather colorless lament on "that worthy Friend [Quakeress?] Priscilla Coleman, deceased" (1760);[41] there is a *Funeral Elegy
Occasion'd by the Tragedy at Salem* (1773)[42] in which ten persons
were drowned, which begins with an invocation to the Muse and
ends with "dismal Urns"; and, even in the early nineteenth century, a very Sentimental perversion of Gray's *Elegy* celebrated the
death of the Rev. Joseph Buckminster,[43] that promising young
scion of the Romantic Muse. The elegist revels in sadness and
sympathy, and finds it "sweet . . . To weep around thy consecrated urn." Was such a point of view entirely borrowed from
England? Was it not also, to some extent, an authentic American growth from an analogous stem? Indeed, the New England
funeral elegy shows shreds and patches of Sentimentalism; but, in
New England, the absence of a Cavalier leaven and also the religious revival of Edwards delayed the disintegration of Calvinism,
so that the colonies were importing early Romantic poetry from
England before they had time to develop any considerable quantity
of their own; but the rapid spread of the Romantic attitude suggests that the soil had for some time been prepared for its reception.

The contrasting influences of the Neo-classical and Romantic
schools in eighteenth century America are exemplified in the two
principal poets of the American Revolution—John Trumbull,
1750-1831, and Philip Freneau, 1753-1832. The former was
so far a Neo-classicist that he made but three contributions to
elegiac poetry: *On the Vanity of Youthful Expectations, An
Elegy* (1771); *An Elegy on the Death of Mr. Buckingham
St. John* (1771); and *An Elegy on the Times* (1774)—all in
the stanza of Gray's *Elegy* and all somewhat reminiscent of the
Grave Yard School.[44] Philip Freneau, however, notwithstanding
his predominantly satiric mood, is at times sufficiently a romanticist
to be a very good example of the belated influence of the British
funeral elegy on American poetry. His *The Desert Farm House*,
seemingly written as early as 1772, is in the stanza, and often
almost in the structure, of Gray's *Elegy*. His long romantic poem
The House of Night, composed seemingly in 1776 and first pub-

---

[41] Boston Pub. Lib.
[42] Lib. Boston Athen. See also Wegelin *op. cit.* and Sabin *op. cit.* for other
late elegies.
[43] Lib. Boston Athen.

[44] See *The Poetical Works of John
Trumbull, LL.D.*, 1820, reprinted in *The
Colonnade*, Volume XIV, 1922, pages
499, 511, and 519.

lished in August, 1779, is written in the same stanza except that the first and third lines do not rhyme; and narrates the last illness, parting words, death, burial, and epitaph of *Death personified*! His poem *The Jamaica Funeral*, 1776, is not indeed a funeral elegy; but it gives an interesting sidelight upon funeral customs: a satiric account of the funeral feast and services and sermon—concluding with a dance! More or less in the elegiac tradition are his stanzas *To the Memory of the Brave Americans* who fell at Eutaw Springs, 1781; *Elegy on Mr. Robert Bell*, 1786; *On the Death of Colonel Laurens*, 1787; *On the Death of . . . Joseph Reed*, 1785; *Elegiac Lines*, 1788; *On the Death of Dr. Benjamin Franklin*, 1790; *Stanzas to the Memory of General Washington*; *To the Memory of Edward Rutledge, Esq.*; *To the Memory of the late Ædanus Burke, Esq.*; *Stanzas on the Decease of Thomas Paine*; *In Memory of James Lawrence, Esquire*; and *On the Death of General Ross*. Freneau is also the author of an *Epistle from Dr. Franklin, deceased, to his Poetical Panegyrists*, on some of their Absurd Compliments, 1790[45]

In the New World, the funeral elegy was clearly the possession of the Puritan colonists of New England who had been drawn largely from the British middle classes. The elegies were generally printed on broadsides, and were analogous to the English broadside pieces on non-conformist ministers during the Commonwealth and Caroline periods: they were not the offspring of the Pegasus of Grub Street in union with the all-too-human cupidity for solid pudding, but rather the compositions of pious and respectable Independent clergymen on their deceased colleagues. They were clearly intended, not so much to arouse pleasure, even of the most impeccable sort, as to promote edification of the spirit; and, if the æsthetic discomfort occasioned by the perusal of such pieces have any salutary effect upon the soul, they may certainly be said to have achieved their purpose and to constitute, therefore, according to this oft-repeated criterion, great and effective literature. But the present study is not concerned chiefly with matters *de gustibus*; and there is perhaps difference of opinion. The funeral elegy appeared in New England almost immediately upon its accept-

<hr>

[45] See *The Poems of Philip Freneau*, ed. Pattee, I, 212, 239; II, 101, 260, 283, 288, 328; III, 36, 232, 234, 235, 238, 243, 286, 313, 356; and, for the *Epistle from Dr. Franklin*, III, 36.

ance by the Puritans of the mother country; and it retained its most archaic characteristics longer than did the parent stock. Unlike its English and Scotch prototypes, it was taken over first by the clergy, perhaps because only the clergy were sufficiently eminent to be worthy of its celebration. By the beginning of the eighteenth century, however, the traffic in rum and slaves had brought wealth and distinction to some of the laity, and the subject-matter of the funeral elegy is duly extended and the element of eulogy duly enlarged. The *Meditations* of 1708 illustrate the generalizing of the elegiac theme, as in English graveyard poetry; but, in general, the New England elegy shows but slightly the effect of Neo-classicism; and, although highly emotional in the great religious revival of Jonathan Edwards, shows no very clear traces of Sentimentalism until the nineteenth century: perhaps the disintegration of Calvinism under the influence of rationalizing Neo-classicism was a necessary prologue to the rise of the Sentimental. One fact, however, clearly emerges from an investigation of the funeral elegy in the American colonies: the form belonged to the Puritan clergy; and its rigor of macabre detail was not even slightly lessened until it began to be applied to social groups that were not professionally imbued with the tenets and the tone of Calvinism.

Calvinism was more intense and more universal in New England than in Old; it was farther removed from extraneous influences and from the immediate shock of new scientific discoveries and of rival philosophic systems. Thus its disintegration was more prolonged: its anti-artistic bias for the most part lingered; and Sentimentalism seems to have developed much later, and rather as a borrowing from Europe than as a native evolution: in England, a Sentimental overflow of optimistic emotion seems to have been evident in society before it entered the realms of philosophy or literature; to America, it apparently came first as a philosophy, especially a political philosophy to justify the American Revolution, and was derived by Jefferson from French sources.[46] Even later

[46] Jefferson's authorship of most of the Declaration of Independence is, of course, well known. The continued existence of slavery and of indentured servants in practically every colony and of religious and other restrictions or suffrage show how purely theoretical was the statement that all men were created free and equal; and it is significant that the Constitution of the United States, composed after the Revolution, when the revolt from England no longer required justification, and written as a practical legal document rather than as a popular manifesto, displays almost none of the Sentimental theories of the earlier Declaration.

appeared its literary expression, Romanticism, likewise theoretical, a poetic manner imitated from prototypes, rather than the expression of a dynamic urge inherent in society; for the Industrial Revolution came late to America; and its stress and strain in the new country was far less than in the old. Indeed, American Romanticism is generally sedate, decorous, and restrained, like a Horation imitation of Sappho. Thus New England, during the eighteenth century for the most part continued ·to express the psychology of the mid-seventeenth; and one need not feel surprise that the profound and rapid cultural evolution that took place in England during the hundred and fifty years after 1660 is scarcely reflected in America until the nineteenth century.

CHAPTER VII

THE FUNERAL ELEGY AND THE NEO-CLASSICAL COMPROMISE

ALTHOUGH the Restoration of Charles II saw the middle classes decline to a subordinate position in the state, nevertheless, even this period of reaction shows the inception of political and religious compromise.[1] The restored monarchy was Parliamentary, not personal;[2] and Charles, realizing that a successful and continued reign required conciliation, had given, in the Declaration of Breda, the most solemn guarantees of constitutional freedom and religious toleration: thus, although the newly convened Tory Parliament cared nothing for dissent or for the trading classes, the king himself became in a sense the champion of both,[3] and even allowed himself to be led by the latter into a commercial struggle with the Netherlands.[4] As Parliament more and more assumed the direction of affairs, especially after the fall of Clarendon in 1667, the party system came into being, the Whigs developing from the former Commonwealthmen, and representing trade and non-conformity; the Tories, as successors to the Cavaliers, representing the squirarchy and the Established Church.[5] The Council, to be sure, was still framed at the pleasure of the King; but Charles was too astute a politician not to give each party at least some representation among its members; for royalty must divide if it would rule. Thus was established a machinery for political compromise that proved strong enough to give England a settled government during this difficult period, and to act as a buffer between the tumultuous populace and the more stable power of the crown: stability, in fact, was England's greatest

---

[1] C. H. Firth, *The Stewart Restoration, Camb. Mod. Hist.*, New York, 1908, V, Chapter V, 92 *et seq.*

[2] *Ibid.*, 102-104; and R. Lodge, *History of England, 1660-1702*, London, 1918, 6 *et seq.* "The first duty imposed upon the monarch was to hold an even balance between the two sections of the coalition, the cavaliers and the presbyterians." The following references to the *Camb. Mod. Hist.* and to Lodge, are inserted, not so much to prove the accompanying statements, which for the most part are common knowledge, but to assist the reader to go farther into political detail if he cares to do so.

[3] Firth, *op. cit.*, 100 *et seq.*

[4] *Ibid.*, 108.

[5] *Ibid.*, 95, and W. E. H. Lecky, *History of England in the Eighteenth Century*, I, Chapter I.

need; and England achieved it chiefly because the disturbances of the mid-century had clearly shown the horror of religious civil war and the ultimate uselessness of such ventures, and partly because Charles was willing to accommodate himself to kaleidescopic changes, provided he was not obliged to "take up his travels again." Thus, although Whig and Tory hated one another with but slightly diminished animosity, peace and settled government were on the whole maintained; and such intrigues as the "Popish Plot"[6] and such abortive rebellions as the Pentland Rising[7] made no headway against them. Indeed, so well-knit was this arrangement that, even after the accession of James II, unpopular though he was for both religious and personal reasons, the rebellion of Monmouth could easily be crushed, for the great Whig families refused to enlist in his cause, and, in spite of the unfriendly attitude of the king,[8] preferred to cast in their lot with the organized government.

The reign of James II was too brief to have any direct social effect, and is important to the present study chiefly for the reactions that it generated in later periods; for it forced the Tories to relax their strict theory of Divine Right and to give a practical acquiescence to the idea of political compromise. James attempted to be at once widely tolerant in religious, and narrowly personal in political, rule: to almost every shade of religious opinion in his day, tolerance was abhorrent; for it seemed outrageous that ignorant and ill-advised persons should be allowed to effect their eternal damnation according to their own perverse wishes—and especially so, if, in the process, they endangered the safety of the state. Thus tolerance, *per se*, was generally looked upon askance by the religiously sincere, who could be made to live peaceably with their differing neighbors only because two generations of experience had shown that it was impossible for even the most well-intentioned person to save his neighbor's soul *vi et armis*. Tolerance, therefore, was anathema: its extremes terrified the Roman Catholics, who feared the inevitable reaction; it alienated from the Crown its staunchest supporters, the Established Church; it even alienated the dissenters, who preferred themselves to live under disabilities rather than to see the disabilities on Roman Catholics removed.[9]

---

[6] Lodge, *op. cit.*, Chap. VIII.
[7] *Ibid.*, 187 *et seq.*
[8] *Ibid.*, 250 *et seq.*
[9] *Ibid.*, 257 *et seq.* and 268 *et seq.*

The refusal of the dissenters to join with James against the Church of England won them somewhat the respect and gratitude of that body.

The political policy of James, moreover, the severities of Jeffreys, the arrogance of the king and his high-handed dealings with Parliament and with the bishops, were likewise abhorrent to all classes. Thus, after a brief and undistinguished reign, he found himself forsaken by the Tories, in spite of their doctrine of non-resistance to the worst of kings, and opposed openly and bitterly by the Whigs, who, even some months before he fled the country, were busy arranging for William of Orange and Mary to reign in his stead.[10]

The "Bloodless Revolution" of 1688 brought to the throne William and Mary pledged to constitutional sovereignty and owing their new dominions chiefly to the efforts of the Whig party; and thus the balance of power in the new reign was largely in favor of the middle classes.[11] William, furthermore, was a foreigner,[12] and for that reason easily liable to unpopularity;[13] he was deeply involved in Continental affairs,[14] and disliked English domestic politics, although to achieve his purposes abroad he became an adept in their manipulation[15]: thus William and Mary, although they might chafe under its restrictions, had reason to abide by the Bill of Rights[16] and the other Parliamentary restrictions placed upon their power. Religiously, King William, himself a Dutch Calvinist, sympathized with the English Calvinists, and could see no valid reason why the less radical dissenters should not be received within the fold of the Establishment;[17] and commercially, he had learned from the rich burghers of Amsterdam to sympathize with the mercantile point of view. Thus many ties of character, principle, and gratitude bound him to the Whigs. But he was not by any means purely a Whig sovereign; for that party was most anxious to curtail the royal power,[18] and in the ensuing years was

[10] *Ibid.*, 276 *et seq.*

[11] Cf. E. Legouis and L. Cazamian (*Histoire de la Littérature Anglaise,* Paris, 1924, 748 *et passim*), who recognize the rise of the bourgeoisie after 1688, but see no notable literary effect until well on in the eighteenth century (*ibid.,* 765).

[12] Lodge, *op. cit.,* 307 *et seq.*

[13] N. B. the defense that Defoe felt called upon to write of him in *The Trueborn Englishman.*

[14] Lodge, *op. cit.,* 365 *et seq.* He was therefore of necessity absent a great deal from Westminster. Moreover, his health

was poor (*ibid.,* 449), and the dampness of Whitehall is said to have disagreed with him.

[15] *Ibid.,* 451.

[16] *Ibid.,* 305 and 312.

[17] *Ibid.,* 310-311. See also the Rev. H. M. Gwatkin, *Religious Toleration in England, Camb. Mod. Hist.,* V. Chapter XI.

[18] Especially in the Act of Settlement. See H. W. V. Temperley, *The Revolution and the Revolution Settlement in Great Britain, Camb. Mod. Hist.,* V, Chap. X, especially 274 *et seq.*

not always ready to vote funds for the defense of his Protestant interests on the Continent. The Tories, moreover, by the somewhat dubious legal fiction of considering James' flight an abdication, could bring themselves to give a certain, if not a very whole-hearted, support to the Crown, for the Crown had always been the corner-stone of their political theory; but they could hardly rally to the cause of William and Mary as they had to the Restoration of Charles II. Thus the reign of James II brought about two ultimate social effects: a general improvement in the position of the Whigs and non-conformists, and a strengthening of the idea of political, and thus of social, compromise. Economically, the new reign was generally favorable to the merchant-classes; and, in spite of the large accumulation of national debt and the heavy cost of current wars, the nation, at least in the latter years, was prosperous: new markets were being won abroad;[19] and the genius of Montagu and of Somers had reformed the debased currency and founded the Bank of England,[20] thus giving a new stability to trade, and eventually making possible the rise of the great commercial houses that in generations to come outrivalled in wealth and culture the old landed nobility. The influx of the Huguenots, moreover, after the revocation of the Edict of Nantes, established the manufactory of fine cloth and of many other staple articles in England; and, finally, the foreign policy of William started England upon that series of French wars that crystallized the patriotism of the country, gave all Englishmen immediate common ties, and so put the domestic compromise on a firm foundation.

The change from a strictly legitimate to a conveniently Parliamentary sovereign required a revision of the old political philosophy of the Renaissance summarized in the theory of Divine Right; and, since nations, as well as individuals, must rationalize a departure from established habit, and justify it in their own eyes, if not before the world, an apologist arose who framed a political justification, and, in doing so, associated it with far-reaching implications, psychological, religious, and social. The

[19] Cf. Ibid., 264.

[20] Lodge, op. cit., 402 etc. It must not be forgotten that the Bounty Act of 1689 gave an economic establishment at least equally valuable to the Tory landed gentry; thus a certain balance was maintained.

political philosophy of John Locke[21] substituted Social Contract for Divine Right, and gave, for all practical purposes, the final answer to Hobbes, who had looked upon the generality of men as too degraded to bear any part in government. The experience of the Commonwealth and the condition of education and of society in general did not recommend to the serious observer in the 1680's the extreme of republicanism; and Locke took a middle ground, advocating a government of checks and balances, just such a government as the party and cabinet system was already providing.[22] The historical significance of this theory appears in its practical acceptance in later times by both the radical Chatham and the conservative Burke, and in the nineteenth century by both Whigs and Tories, whose party differences had to do merely with the adjustment of the balance.[23] The real basis of Locke's philosophy, however, was his psychology, and especially the idea of the *tabula rasa*[24]: the mind is capable of acquiring only such ideas as it can glean through the senses; there are no innate ideas; and in an age when psychology recognized only the conscious mind and little within that beyond the idea-creating intellect, the theory of the *tabula rasa* clearly implied that all men were born free and equal in the crudest sense of that expression. Such a theory removed the chief justification for hereditary rights, and implied that any clever tradesman, with equal opportunities for study and travel, could be as useful to the state and to society as a Cavendish or a Russell: it made for individualism and ultimately for democracy. The primitive psychology of the age, moreover, which underestimated both the natural differences in men's several abilities and also the force of ingrained habit as determining conduct, somewhat fallaciously implied that the education, politically, philo-

[21] Significantly enough, Locke's father had served as Captain in the Parliamentary army; and, in the reign of Charles II, he had himself held a minor secretaryship under the Whig government of Lord Shaftesbury. S. N. Patten (*The Development of English Thought*, New York, 1899, 160 *et seq.*) finds Locke's philosophy to be the outgrowth of Puritanism. The present writer would rather look upon it as the adjustment of Puritan to Cavalier.

[22] See Locke, *Treatise on Government* (1690).

[23] Cf. Patten (*op. cit.*, 118): "Since the time of Locke there has been practically no development of political thought [in England]." This was generally true until the rise of Socialism and the Labor Party.

[24] See Locke, *Essay on the Human Understanding* (written 1670-1687, published 1690). It met with immediate celebrity. Locke was closely associated with the policies and the government of William and Mary.

sophically, and otherwise, of society would not be difficult; and Addison's experiment in the *Spectator* seems to be an early step in the same movement as Godwin's Perfectabilianism and Huxley's Board Schools. The opinion, furthermore, that the senses were the sole source of mental data encouraged the empirical attitude of science, advocated long since by Lord Bacon and put into actual practice by Newton, Boyle, and their fellow-members of the Royal Society.

Upon religion, however, the effect was dissipating and chilling: how can we know God if all our knowledge comes through the senses; and how, indeed, could the prophets and apostles have known him? Without some sensuous experience, how can we even be sure that he exists, unless we are willing really to conceive of him as utterly above natural as well as human law? Such premises forced the ordinary mind to face a three-fold dilemma of heterodoxy: agnosticism, or deism, or a pantheistic assertion that God *is* Nature and that our senses can, and do, experience him.[25]   All three answers to the problem have found ready advocates; but Toland, who, though disclaimed by his master, posed as the immediate follower of Locke, turned the thought of the age in the direction of Deism[26]: according to this view, God becomes merely a First Cause of the Universe, which he set going by immutable laws as one might wind a clock—and then left it.   Such a view takes all efficacy from prayer, all probability from the miracles of the Bible,[27] and all human consolation from

[25] Deism in a modified, semi-orthodox form seems to have been the answer of the early eighteenth century, Pantheism of the late eighteenth and early nineteenth centuries, agnosticism of the Victorian age. Such a High Church thinker as William Law escaped from the dilemma by questioning the first premise; the Pantheists escaped by denying the second. Most people, however, especially outside London, were little touched by the controversy, and followed by habit in the religious observances of their forefathers, leaving to their ecclesiastical betters to give a reason for the faith that was in them. British society in the eighteenth century represented every shade of religious condition, from the extreme "enlightenment" of Gibbon and Hume to the mysticisms of Law and of Wesley,

from the pre-Christian folk-customs in outlying districts and the utter irreligion that Hannah More found in the Mendip Hills to the highly developed ceremonial of Roman Catholicism. But Christianity in some form, and especially Anglican Christianity, still dominated the central bulk of society; and even such skeptics as Bolingbroke and Hume conformed to the Established Churches of their respective countries.

[26] See Sir Leslie Stephen, *History of English Thought in the Eighteenth Century*, London, 1902, I, Chapters II and III; and G. H. Hibben, *The Philosophy of the Enlightenment*, New York, 1910.

[27] This was the storm-centre of eighteenth century Christian apologetics. See Stephen, *op. cit.*, 228 *et seq.*

religion. In short, this compromise, between Christianity and science is almost entirely on the side of science; for it dispenses with the two latter members of the Trinity, and recognizes God the Father only in the character of a Creator. On the other hand, it led to certain immediate social benefits: to a tolerance,[28] derived from laxity if not from conviction, to a hatred of religious "enthusiasm" as overthrowing poise in the individual and bringing tumult into society,[29] and to a willingness for practical, if not always logical, adjustment of differences. Locke, therefore, in religion, in politics, in society, set the seal of philosophic consecration upon cool restraint and devious compromise. Like Burke, he thought of. the particular terms of the compromise developed in his day as final, and would doubtless have resisted change, as did Burke, for fear of revolution[30]: thus he and his generation saw society as a finished and consummate entity. In all these qualities, restrained, cold, static, the compromise philosophy of Locke represents the tone and tenor of English Neo-classical culture. It is by no freak of chance that he was the most widely quoted thinker in eighteenth century England, not to mention the Continent; that he influenced alike the Tory Bolingbroke and the Presbyterian Reynolds, whose *View of Death*[31] is modelled on his thought; that, indeed, he provided the axiomatic basis on which practically every other system, political, social, or philosophic, was erected for more than a hundred years.[32]

The cultural effects of political and social adjustments are apparent only slowly and by degrees. The literature of the reign of Charles II reflects, in the *Term Catalogues*[33] of the period, the lingering disparity between Royalist and Puritan; but the social

[28] See Locke, three *Letters on Toleration*, 1689-1692, and a fourth unfinished and printed posthumously in 1706.

[29] This largely explains the unpopularity of the Methodists with the intellectuals of their day: men remembered that religious enthusiasm had generated religious civil war in the seventeenth century. Wesley's Tory and High Church conservatism held his movement within the pale of established institutions both politically and even religiously.

[30] Cf. Chatham, and the younger Pitt in the 1780's, both of whom advocated Parliamentary reform, which would have radically changed the balance of power as indeed it did in the 1830's.

[31] J. Reynolds, *View of Death, A Philosophical Sacred Poem*, London, 1725. But Reynolds' death in 1703 gives the composition of the poem a much earlier date.

[32] The present author takes Locke, not as the *cause*, but as the *expression* of Neo-classical thought. The existence of such a reasoned and plausible apology, however, certainly strengthened the movement.

[33] See the *Term Catalogues, 1668-1709*, ed. Arber, London, 1903-1906. See Arber's introduction; also Amy L. Reed, *The Background of Gray's Elegy*, New York, 1924, 28-29.

groups, even of the most widely divergent views, cannot maintain a constant and peaceable intercourse without acquiring at least some mutual understanding; and thus, after a time, a centripetal social tendency obtained, and literature and the other phases of culture became more centralized, more uniform, and began to reflect the restraint and the necessary conventional decorum that the social compromise imposed.   This decorum, although it became the practical ethics of the day, was founded neither on logic,[34] nor on religious sanction: like the sovereignty of William and Mary, it was based chiefly upon the convenience of the high contracting parties; but it came to assume a sanctity in the eyes of the general public as "common sense," the epitome of social propriety, analogous to common law in political, and the Book of Common Prayer in religious, spheres.   The Cavalier ideal had been the Renaissance version of Classicism, the polished and charming courtier, an ideal suited to an age of absolute monarchy and expressed in the "courtesy books" of the sixteenth century, in treatises such as Machiavelli's *Prince*, and in belletristic works such as the *Euphues*, the *Arcadia*, and the *Faerie Queene*.   It was a cultural ideal with an intellectual bias that turned more and more scientific during the seventeenth century: men were born to boorishness and ignorance; the former might be remedied by Classical elegance; the latter, by Classical and scientific learning.   The Puritan ideal had been the Reformation version of Christianity, the righteous and prayerful Christian, an ideal suited to an age of religious turmoil and expressed especially in the severe system of Calvin.   It was a religious ideal with an emotional bias as discussed in a former chapter.[35]   Mankind was born to sin, with every instinct naturally perverse, and could hope for Salvation only by Grace bestowed from above and evident in a severe righteousness of conduct. Both ideals were strenuous and disciplinary; but they were not quite mutually exclusive; and the person of Joseph Addison, the

---

[34] The present author must to some extent take issue with the very grounds of the debate on the Neo-classic and the Romantic between Professor Babbitt (*The New Laocoön*, New York, 1910, and *Rousseau and Romanticism*, New York, 1919) and Professor Lovejoy (*Publ. Mod. Lang. Assoc. Am.*, XXXIX, 229 *et seq.*); for both seem to regard these developments as primarily philosophical, and so presumably governed by logical law: the present author considers them primarily phenomena of culture-history, and so subject to historic evolution, in which logic plays only a subordinate part.

[35] See Chapter III.

Christian gentleman[36] and ideal type of the reign of Queen Anne, shows a combining of elements from each: the Renaissance-Cavalier ideal gave polish and intellectuality based on Classical models; the Puritan ideal gave an intense interest in morals and conduct. The decorum established by this compromise governed, or was supposed to govern, every aspect of social life and every department of literature. In poetry, the Puritan ideal usually dictated matters of content; the Cavalier, matters of form.[37] Middle-class morality and religion must be maintained;[38] at all events, the notorious cultivation of their opposites must be at least publicly eschewed. In matters of form, attention must centre on symmetry and imitation of the analogous literary type approved by Classical authority. Thus, moral truisms modelled on Classic, or at least pseudo-Classic, forms constitute the typical poetry of the age[39]: satire after Horace or Juvenal, and the didactic poem after Horace or Vergil. Gay's *Trivia* and Prior's society verses show the more Cavalier side of the compromise; and Blackmore's *Creation* and the hymns of Isaac Watts show it inclining toward Puritanism. The cultural aspects of Neo-classicism were not fully in evidence until the reign of Queen Anne; but the latter seventeenth century shows signs of the development: Collier insisted that the ethics inherent in aristocratic comedy coincide more nearly with the moral principles of orthodox Christianity; the dissenters, on the other hand, were relaxing their zeal against poetry and some were even singing hymns in their meeting-houses;[40] and the poetry of

[36] The present writer is simplifying the problem; for the diverse and conflicting reactions of cultural phenomena require some simplification if the main line of development is to be explained.

[37] This was very natural, for the Puritans had no English poetry, except the elegy, of their own. Literary form, moreover, was a matter of little concern to them.

[38] The Cavaliers, as their earlier courtesy-books and later comedies show, were interested in manners; but the satire and the didactic poetry written on such subjects after the rise of Neo-classicism, commonly treat them from the point of view of morals. Even Pope found it prudent, as the century wore on, to assume this virtue, if he had it not (T. R.

Lounsbury, *The Text of Shakespeare,* New York, 1906, 468 *et seq.*); and even the translations of the period were clipped and doctored in order to accord with it. (See the present author, *The Theory of Translation in the Eighteenth Century, Neophilologus,* VI, 241 *et seq.*).

[39] In prose, the Classics supply less abundantly appropriate types for imitation; and, as in painting, the Renaissance was called upon to supply archetypes, for such forms as the essay and the picaresque novel.

[40] The Independents seem to have started hymn-singing as early as this. (See W. J. Courthope, *History of English Poetry,* London, 1895-1910, V, 329). The Baptists, according to H. S. Skeats (*History of the Free Churches,* London,

death, the one type of verse cultivated in distinct yet unbroken succession at once by Puritan and Cavalier, should at least in some fashion reflect the new social development. The reign of Charles II witnessed courtly Pindaric strains full of eulogy and Classical allusion, and also Puritan elegies on sorrow, illness and the grave: in the reign of William and Mary, the line was less clearly drawn; the seventeenth century was passing, and the Neo-classical compromise was beginning, even in literature, to minimize the old social cleavage.[41]

The plenitude of elegies during the period under consideration leads their historian to the conclusion that few if any persons of even the most moderate distinction were allowed to die unwept, unhonored, or by any means unsung: certainly no *fin de siècle* weariness affected the current annalists of grief. The stream of Cavalier eulogy abundantly continued; and, though a number of pieces show a mingling of Puritan influence, there are many that upheld the old tradition unchanged. In the *Poems* of Charles Cotton, who, like Lovelace, united military with poetic activities, death, when it appears at all, is a happy release, as it was to the Royalist poets of the School of Donne;[42] and the broadside elegies on Captain George (1690) and on Admiral Carter (1692)[43] are the

[1891], 74) did not begin singing in church until about the mid-eighteenth century; but they had begun to write funeral elegies at least as early as the reign of Charles II.

[41] Cf. Patten, (*op. cit.*, 191 *et seq.*), who sees the eighteenth century as a compromise between Catholicism derived from the Roman Empire and Puritanism derived from the Old Testament, Catholicism gave "a love of order, a desire for security, and a willingness to submit to society"; Protestantism gave "toleration, willingness to compromise, love of liberty, a demand for representation." The present author does not find in Protestantism *per se* either tolerance or a willingness to compromise: these qualities arose as a result of the religious wars of two centuries, which showed that neither side could hope for absolute victory in most of the countries of northern Europe. W. J. Courthope (*op. cit.*, V, 363 *et passim*) seems likewise to associate Neo-classicism with the Revolution of

1688 and its attendant political compromise. J. G. Robertson (*Studies in the Genesis of the Romantic Theory in the Eighteenth Century*, Cambridge, 1923, 235) would seem, on the other hand, to find in Neo-classicism a purely aristocratic phenomenon and to ascribe its rise to the influence of France. French influence was undoubtedly strong after the Restoration, but the present writer is inclined rather to agree with Patten and Courthope. But perhaps this disagreement hinges merely on one's definition of Neo-classicism.

[42] Charles Cotton, *Poems*, London, 1689, 266 and 313. The Cavalier spirit of many of these pieces is doubtless due to their having been written at an earlier date.

[43] *In Memory of the Truly Loyall and Valiant Captain George* (Brit. Mus. broadside). *An Elegy on the Death of that brave Sea-Commander, Reer-Admiral Carter* (Brit. Mus. broadside).

conventional military tributes, such as flourished during the Civil
Wars and the reign of Charles II.   It is significant that the death
of Dryden, who stood quite apart from the court of William and
Mary, was celebrated with a volume of elegies which, in all its
fifty-five pages, contains hardly a mortuary detail.[44]   Thomas
D'Urfey, dramatist, frequenter of the Stuart court, and writer
of burlesque songs, published his *New Poems* in 1690; and the
elegies in the volume show no funereal details, and can be said
to point forward to the new social compromise only in their tendency to generality and abstraction.[45]   The Anglican classicist,
Morgan, celebrated the death of Robert Boyle, somewhat inappro-
priately, in lines that suggest the intellectual ingenuity of Donne;
but they are spun out over-long without the excuse of authentic
emotion or of artistic *finesse*.[46]   Among these writers in the Cavalier tradition is Robert Gould, whose place as servant to Lord
Dorset locates him in a social stratum below the middle class.   His
numerous elegies on Waller, Dryden, and ladies and gentlemen
of rank, are restrained and eulogistic.[47]   His poem on *Madam
Pool's Son and Heir* has, to be sure, a fairly realistic description
of death's "Ghastly Aspect"; and his elegy on Queen Mary has
"Despair and Horror"; but he lets pass a fine opportunity for the
grisly, and neglects to describe "Death's still Mansions."   His
fondness for "Funeral Eclogues," moreover, and his hymns on
festivals of the Anglican calendar, show him at once a Classical
imitator and a follower of the Establishment.   His writings suggest that the literary expression of the common people, so far as
it had disengaged itself from folk-song and balladry, was allied
rather with the aristocracy than the middle classes, a situation that
is not surprising in view of the close relation between the owners
and the tillers of the land, who had traditionally shared the same
social, economic, political, and religious opinions.   When in the
early eighteenth century, moreover, the lower classes once more

---

[44] *Luctus Britannici*, London, 1700.

[45] Thomas D'Urfey, *New Poems, con-
sisting of Satyrs, Elegies and Odes*, London, 1690, 91, 177, etc.   D'Urfey came
of Huguenot stock; but neither his biography nor his poetry suggests such a precisian ancestry.

[46] M. Morgan, *Elegy on the Death of
Robert Boyle*, London, 1692.   Such a

celebration of Boyle's death is a bit incongruous: he himself suffered from melancholy in his youth; and the "meditative school" that followed him has been
cited as an influence on Pearshall's *Contemplations* and like eighteenth century
lucubrations (*Crit. Rev.*, VI 213 *et seq.*).

[47] Robert Gould, *Works*, London, 1709,
222 *et seq.*

emerged into formal literature in the person of Stephen Duck, the thresher-poet,[48] the resulting compositions regularly followed the Neo-classical tradition of the aristocracy, not religious melancholy or the Sentimentalism of the bourgeoisie. Thus Sentimentalism would seem to be peculiarly the characteristic of the trading classes; and neither the older poets who continued to produce in the courtly manner of an earlier reign nor their humble imitators who sprang from the soil illustrate those characteristics that chiefly concern the present study.

Many elegies of the Puritan tradition also, show little variation from the style and themes of their Caroline progenitors. The unnatural repression of grief enforced by the Westminster *Directory* had in fact so far given way that even John Nesbitt, an Independent minister noted for his Protestant zeal, might conscientiously declare:

We can't part with such in whom we have Pleasure, without Pain; nor can such as have been united in Affection, part without a Sigh and a Groan. To have no Sense of what we suffer, or to part with our Friends as we sustained no Loss, is Stupidity, and not Submission; but while you feelingly complain to God, to show your Affection, beware of complaining of him, or censuring his dispensations.[49]

Under the influence of this declaration of freedom from silence, Nesbitt describes death as a "Banquet of Worms" and a "King of Terrors," and quotes aptly and copiously from Commonwealth divines. Even dissenters of strict Presbyterian inclination, apparently agreeing with Nesbitt's point of view, regularly take for granted their right of indulgence in the elegiac tear. Robert Fleming's *Elegy to the Memory of the Reverend Mr. John Sinclare*[50] does not lack the diction of conventional solemnity:

What mean our *Tapers* to go out so fast,
And leave us in this *dismal* Night agast?

[48] Rose M. Davis, *Stephen Duck, the Thresher-Poet, University of Maine Studies,* Orono, Maine, 1927.

[49] John Nesbitt, *A Funeral Sermon Preached at the Merchant's Lecture, upon the Death of the Reverend Mr. Thomas Gouge,* London, 1700.

[50] Robert Fleming, *The Mirrour of Divine Love Unvail'd, Whereunto is added* a *Miscellany of several other Poems,* London, 1691, 55 *et seq.* Sinclare's death in 1687 gives the piece an approximate date. At the end is an *Acrostick to the Memory of Mr. George Reed,* suggestive at once of the abecedarian Psalms and of the acrostic *penchant* of the Renaissance.

Soon the reader arrives at "dusky *grief*"; but the elegy as a whole
is not more distinguished than its fellows. The *Elegy* (1691) on
Sir Thomas Pilkington, three times Lord Mayor and opponent of
King James II, rejoices in a description of his funeral ceremones; [51]
the *Elegy* (1691) on the Rev. George Cokayne, a dissenting minister of note, urges the reader to make it his "constant care,"

> To walk amongst the Tombs while we are here;
> That Death might not be a surprise to none. . . . [52]

Thus we are to "mortify the deeds of the Body." The *Elegy* on
Dr. William Bates (1699), "the *Nonconformist's* (nay, all *England's*) Crown," among other mortuary touches, assures us that
"the *Stone*, the *Gout*, the *Colick*" did "rend his Body here." [53]

The Rev. Matthew Mead was several times blest with commemoration (1699). One of the pieces is aptly called *An Ocean
of Pious Tears;* [54] and the opening eulogy and final apotheosis are
but a frame for the main subject, the grief and horror of the
mourners; and the lamentation of his wife, his children, and his
congregation, appear in itemized account. Perhaps the following
lines are the most quotable:

> And here his *Children*, they poor Babes, behold
> His worthy Carcass, and their Hands unfold,
> With weeping Tears, and nashing Teeth, they cry
> 'Gainst *Death* their Father's furious enemy.

Perhaps, however, the best example of the Puritan elegy that still
retains its Puritan characteristics is Browne's *Elegiack Essay to the
pious memory of the late Matthew Mead, Minister of the Gospel
at Stepney; Who departed this Life Oct. 16, 1699.* [55] It starts
with something of the mortuary landscape:

> . . . the *Chill Hours* of the Gloomy Night,
> Whose pow'rful Shades had chas'd the *chearing* Light;
> With *Sable Attoms* fill'd the low'ring Air. . . .

[51] *Bagford Ballads,* ed. Ebsworth, *Ball.
Soc. Publ.,* Hertford, 1878, II, 489.
[52] Lutt. Coll., I, No. 43.
[53] *An Elegy On the much-lamented
Death of Dr. William Bates* (Brit. Mus.
broadside). This piece and several of
the other broadsides cited in this chapter
are reproduced in *A Century of Broadside Elegies,* ed. the present author, London, 1928.
[54] Brit. Mus. broadside.
[55] M. Browne, *An Elegiack Essay,* London, 1699.

But the author, "All wrapp'd in *Melancholy Thought*," can find
no peace, for "MEAD'S *gone from Earth*":

> Gone ever, whom we *ever shall deplore*,
> *For ever gone*, whom we did all *adore*,
> MEAD, dearest MEAD, alas! is now no more.
> Long since I heard the *News*, yet scarce wou'd give
> It *Credence*, but believ'd great MEAD did live,
> And until *now* cou'd not consent to grieve.
> But t'other Day walking a *silent Grove*,
> I found a sweet Recess, a *dark Alcove*,
> Seem'd made by Nature,[56] fit to Contemplate
> The Turns and Destinies of Rigid Fate:
> Where on my Hand my Head supinely laid,
>   *Methought I heard a Mournful Accent spread*,
> *Which Eccho-like in murm'ring Whispers said*:
> *Drop, drop a Tear for* MEAD, *Great* MEAD *is Dead*. . . .

Then follows the still expected eulogy with the usual apotheosis
at the end. The *Elegiack Essay* is a transition piece, expressing
the old motive of the grief of the mourner; but the poem is cast
in the first person so that the grief is subjective and lyrical; an
expressive background of "Nature" is employed; and the writer
finds the "Recess" of melancholy "sweet"; in short, the second
of the passages quoted has distinctly the touch of the Sentimental.
This piece, like so many of the elegies on ministers, was probably
written by one of his own congregation; and one ventures to
wonder whether its Sentimentalism was in any way derived from
the preaching of the good man himself. Puritanism, by intensi-
fying both heaven and hell, made wickedness infinitely bad, and
goodness correspondingly good; and in 1697 "the celebrated Mr.
Matthew Mead" had even declared that the Holy Ghost in an
actual personal manner inhabited the souls of the righteous—a
dogma that would surely invest the righteous with such a moral
infallibility as would furnish a broad and solid basis for Sentimental optimism; and, as wickedness seemed to grow more and
more wicked, most men comfortably took it for granted that they
belonged to the happy number of the Elect.

Many writers, both of the older generation and of the younger,

---

[56] This would seem to be a late occurrence of the Elizabethan construction of
the omission of the relative pronoun in-
troducing a restrictive clause.

some sprung from a Puritan background, some from a Cavalier, show a blurring of the old lines of demarcation. Such Low Churchmen of the Establishment as John Rawlet, discussed in a previous chapter,[57] had provided, even in the reign of Charles II, a middle ground. John Potenger (1647-1733), who, though sprung from Puritan antecedents, nevertheless prospered under the restored Stuart rule, published in 1691 his *Pastoral Reflections on Death*,[58] uniting, as did his biography, the portentous tendencies of the Puritans with the Classicism of the Renaissance. Strephon and Damon improve the occasion with amœbean moralizings as they sit

> Beneath a gloomy Yews unhealthy Shade
> Whose noxious Covert's shunn'd by Bird and Beast. . . .

Damon is considering suicide because of Myrtillo's death; and Strephon describes the "King of terrors" with his "icy Hand" and "Agonies." Rapin in his *Discourse on Pastoral Poetry*[59] had allowed funerals as a fit subject for the eclogue; but surely he had not anticipated anything quite of this sort. Even the love-elegy, descended through the tradition of Ovid and Catullus,[60] takes on occasionally "intruding horrors" and "mournful griefs";[61] and the Classical translator Philip Ayres, in his *Lyric Poems Made in Imitation of the Italians*, invokes Death in funereal tones that he might, to be sure, have found in the literature of Italy, but that rather suggest a less distant origin.[62] Prelates like the Bishop of Chichester (1689)[63] and soldiers like Lord Dartmouth (1691)[64]

---

[57] See Chapter V. The *Pindarique Elegy* by "N. W." on Dr. Willis might also be mentioned as combining Classical form and mortuary detail.

[58] John Potender (Pottenger), *Pastoral Reflctions on Death*, London, 1691. For its position in the history of the pastoral, see Marion K. Bragg, *The Formal Eclogue, Univ. of Maine Studies*, Orono, Maine, 1926, 34-35. A similar combination of the pastoral and the mortuary appears in the *Carmen Pastorale Lugubre*, London, 1700, by J. F[owler?], Gent., on the death of William Duke of Gloucester (Lambeth Palace Lib.).

[59] Rapin's famous *Discourse* was translated by Thomas Creech and printed with his translation of Theocritus, Oxford,

1684. For its influence on pastoral poetry, see Miss Bragg, *op. cit.*, 31 *et seq.*

[60] Miss M. P. Aiken of the University of Maine is engaged upon a study of such influences upon the elegy.

[61] See a love-elegy in couplets by "Dispair," *Athenian Mercury*, Aug. 20, 1695.

[62] Philip Ayres, *Lyric Poems*, London, 1687, 52.

[63] *An Elegy on the Death of that Worthy Prelate, Dr. John Lake, Late Lord Bishop of Chichester* (Brit. Mus. broadside). He was one of the seven Bishops confined in the Tower by James II.

[64] *Elegy on Lord Dartmouth* (Lutt. Coll., I, No. 39).

were celebrated in a mildly mortuary tone, and the Duke of
Grafton (1690) with "tears like Rivers." [65]   Not merely were
mortuary touches introduced into Classical elegies and into elegies
on the upper classes, but poets whose antecedents were Puritan,
like D'Urfey and Potenger, sometimes wrote in the Cavalier tradition.   Such, for instance, is Nahum Tate's *Pastoral Elegy* on
Ormond,[66] done in restrained and even couplets, and perhaps the
anonymous *Elegy* on Henry Care (1688).[67]   Poets of Cavalier
antecedents, likewise, lapse into the Puritan tradition, like the
fellow of "Maudlin" College,[68] who composed for a lykewake
dirge such stanzas as the following:

> Condemn us not unto the pains of Hell,
> Where Horror reigns, and endless Torments dwell;
> From whence no ransome ever can be made,
> Since we our bless'd Redeemer have betray'd.

A View of Death, by the Presbyterian, John Reynolds, written
under the inspiration of Locke, reduces the terrors of the "proud
remourseless king" to mere exclamatory moralizing.[69]   Perhaps,
however, the most striking example is John Hopkins' *Victory of
Death,* a Pindaric ode-elegy on Lady Cutts.[70]   The form is Classic, but the detail goes far beyond Classic reserve in such matters.
Early in the poem appear the conventional "gloomy Cypress Trees"
and "Mansions" of Death:

> No Ray of their bright God can here
> Amidst this solid Gloom appear,
> Their melancholy Thoughts to clear.

Then follow Death's "overshadowing Night" and "horrid Groans
of Ghosts," and "Tombs, and Groans . . . a vast Crop of Death"
with "Streams of Blood opprest with Bones."   The goddess "beck-

[65] *An Elegy On the Death of His Grace
the Duke of Grafton,* signed "J. F."
(Brit. Mus. broadside).

[66] Nahum (Nathan) Tate, *Pastoral Elegy in the Memory of the Duke of Ormond,* London, 1688. See also his *Elegies,* London, 1699.

[67] *An Elegy Upon the Most Ingenious
Mr. Henry Care* (Bodleian, Wood Coll.,
No. 429).

[68] *Poetical Recreations by Several Gen-
tlemen of the Universities and Others,*
London, 1688, Part II, 1. See also the
*Elegy on the D. of N. D., Doctor of
Physick, ibid.,* 7.

[69] J. Reynolds, *A View of Death,* London, 1725.

[70] Her husband Baron Cutts (1661-
1707) seems to have varied his politics
from Royalist to Whig.

ons with a bloody Hand"; and the gates open, although overspread "with putrid Rust" and "all besmear'd with Blood of Lovers dead"; and, as they open, they sprinkle the ground with "flakes of clotted Gore." The diseases bear Death's bloody crown, which is a skull "o'erflowing with black, putrid Gore," somewhat in the manner of Spenser's House of Pride.[71] Later there is a very moving charnel-scene, at the end of which Death is "drunk with blood." The poem concludes with the joys of heaven.[72] Details of the author's biography are meagre; but his father had enjoyed ecclesiastical patronage under Charles II, and his brother was a friend of Dryden and Congreve, and wrote in the approved Restoration style. Surely it is not insignificant that John Hopkins, of Royalist antecedents, writing on a noblewoman whose husband was but lately a courtier of the merry monarch, should, in the latter years of the century, fill his poem with mortuary detail that, a generation earlier, would have stamped him as a Puritan, and quite possibly have been taken as an insult by the family to whom he addressed his lines.

If further proof of this literary change be necessary, a glance at the special classes of funeral elegies will perhaps supply it. The revival of interest in David's lament over Saul and Jonathan is not without importance. The twenty-five years of the reign of Charles II seem to have produced but one poetic paraphrase, that of Oldham in 1677; the decade of the 1690's saw the publication of at least three such pieces. The first is entitled a *Funeral Elegy,* and was written by the Presbyterian Robert Fleming.[73] If the Old Testament authority, however, made such a paraphrase attractive to the non-conformist mind, the subject-matter—and perhaps also its former use by Dr. Beaumont[74]—recommended it no less to the opposite party; and, in 1694, appeared a *Paraphrase of David's Elegy on Saul and Jonathan,*[75] used in place of the first lesson at Morning Prayer on January thirtieth, the day dedicated

[71] *Faerie Queen,* Bk. I, Canto iv. Cf. the *Elegie* by Christopher Burrell in *Suffolk's Tears,* discussed in Chapter III, and E. Arwaker's *Vision* in Chapter V. May one infer that Spenser's influence lingered especially among the middle classes, as had Malory's in an earlier day? His Puritanism would have recommended him to their taste.

[72] John Hopkins, *The Victory of Death,* London, 1698.
[73] Robert Fleming, *The Mirrour of Divine Love,* London, 1691, 195.
[74] Joseph Beaumont, *Davids .Elegie upon Jonathan,* probably written about 1650. See Chapter II.
[75] *The Athenian Mercury,* February 13, 1694.

to St. Charles, King and Martyr. It has no especial mortuary details; but the first lines express the tone of the lamentation:

Mourn *Isreal*! Mourn, admit of no Relief,
To thy intolerable Grief!

Not content with these paraphrases, an anonymous writer did another only four years later.[76] It begins with "Grief and Amazement" *in excelsis*, but on the whole is not distinguished.

The elegies on the death of Queen Mary in 1695 furnish an interesting comparison with those on Charles II ten years earlier, and show at least some advance in the variety of mortuary effects. Of the several poems on the earlier monarch by Dryden, Flatman, Whitehall, Arwaker, and others, most contain no mortuary touches at all, and the rest content themselves with a mildly melancholic landscape or a general reference to *"Horror* and Cryes"; and even the broadsides supply only some "inward Sighs" and an odd reference to "Dirt and Worms." The elegies on the deceased Queen would seem to have been legion, many in manuscript, and many that "few, besides the Printers, e're have seen";[77] and their number suggests that the elegy was entirely in favor as a poetic form at court. *The Mourning Poets: or, an Account of the Poems on the Death of the Queen* has praise for the performances of Congreve, Motteux, Stepney, Dennis, and a few others, but only condemnation for "th'unworthy rest," who "coppy still, and copy for the worst":

For who can read, tho he delights to toyl,
All the good Paper which our Scribblers spoyl?
Yet to move Sadness let *their Works* be bad,
And sure they'll prove, unless the Reader's mad,
Grave, woful, dismal, lamentably sad.
What bulky Heaps of doleful Rhyme I see!
Sure all the world runs mad with Elegy;
Lords, Ladies, Knights, Priests, Souldiers, Squires, Physicians,
Beaux, Lawyers, Merchants, Prentices, Musicians,
Play'rs, Footmen, Pedants, Scribes of all Conditions.

Certainly this catalogue suggests the ubiquity of lamentable composition. Most of these elegies would seem, fortunately, to have

[76] *Odes and Elegies upon Divine and Moral Subjects*, London, 1698, 29.   [77] *The Mourning Poets*, London, 1695.

perished; but at least two or three of those that remain deserve some mention. Henry Park, Curate of Wentworth in Yorkshire, and, like most of the inferior clergy, a High Churchman, if one may infer it from his self-designation as "sacerdos," produced his *Lachrymæ Sacerdotis, A Pindarick Poem upon the Queen*,[78] in which he represents death as *"The raw-bon'd Archer"*; and later, in the very passage that asserts the divinity that doth hedge a king, he seems to identify the dead individual with the dead body, as any Puritan might have done:

> They [rulers] likewise soon or late
> Must bend their consecrated Heads to fate,
> Wrapt up in dull Narcotick Lead,
> A fit reception for the cold and Dead. . . .

Even Talbot, in his very proper *Instructions to a Painter*,[79] urged the artist to express the "dismal Pomp" of the Queen's death and burial. Most significant, however, is the *Funeral Elegy*[80] by William Walsh, collaborator with Vanbrugh and literary mentor to the youthful Pope. King William appears as "that Load of Woe . . . By Grief, by Horror, by Despair possest"; and his edifying thoughts are set forth *in extenso*, with "Death's Altar" for a fitting background and "Doleful Ecchoes from the Groves." Richard Steele, moreover, first won the patronage of Lord Cutts by his exequial piece on Queen Mary entitled *The Procession*.[81] It contains one fine hyperbole, "The *Mourning World* attends her to the Tomb," and at least one very bad one, the pathetic depiction of the *"Generous* steed" who "heaves into big *Sighs* when he would Neigh," a somewhat unconvincing epiphany of equine solicitude when one calls to mind that animals commonly sniff and show uneasiness at the smell of blood or of dead flesh. There are, furthermore, two pastoral broadsides on the deceased Queen,[82] one of them notable for combining the bucolic with the mortuary landscape;[83] for some such combination forms the basis of the

---

[78] Henry Park, *Lachrymæ Sacerdotis*, London, 1695.

[79] J. Talbot, *Instructions to a Painter*, London, 1695.

[80] William Walsh, *Funeral Elegy upon the Death of the Queen*, London, 1695.

[81] A vivid idea of this procession can be gained from the heading of *Great Britain's Lamentation*. The illustration in the present volume is greatly reduced in size. On the literal accuracy of this picture, see Chapter IV, note 40.

[82] *Great Britain's Lamentation* (Brit. Mus. broadside).

[83] *A Funeral Eclogue Sacred to the Memory of Queen Mary*, London, 1695.

Great BRITAINS Lan

Of that most Incompa

MARY of ever Blessed Memory, Queen of *England*, *Scotland*, *France*, and

of Her Age, she Reigned Five Years 8 Months and 17 days. And was conc

by the Nobility, Judges, and G

S
One single blow has all our Triumphs pall'd:
Who can from Grief's Extreamities refrain!
Or in due Bounds the swelling Tide contain?
Who can behold this dismal Scene pass by
With an unmov'd and unrelenting Eye?
LONDON, Thou Pride and Glory of our Isle,
Though in Thy Bosom both the *Indies* smile;
Oh ne'er forget that unauspicious Day,
Which thy best Treasure rudely snatch'd away,
Thy busy *Change* Be for a season dumb,
No sawcy Mirth within thy Mansions come;
Let all thy Sons in Mourning Weeds appear,
Each Face show Sorrow, and each Eye a Tear,
To express their Duty, let all Hearts combine,
And on this Black, this sad Occasion join.
   Mourn drooping Britain, Mourn from shore to shore,
   Thy best adored MARIA is no more.
Ye Beauteous Virgins that in moving Strains
Were us'd to sing her Virtues on the Plains:
Ye Shepherds too, who out of Pious Care,
Your Rural Sports and MARIE's Name to wear;
This is no time for Ornaments of Pride,

of your Reeds, that lately tun'd your j
On the sad Willows now neglected ly:
But bring, oh bring, the Treasures of your F
That short-liv'd Wealth, which unbid Natu
The Mourning Hyacinth inscrib'd with Woe
The beauteous Lillies that in Vallies grow;
And all the Flowers that scatter'd up and dov
Or humble Meads, or lofty Mountains crow
Then gently throw them all upon Her Herse,
To these join lasting Bays, and living Verse,
   Mourn drooping Britain, Mourn from shore
   Thy best adored MARIA is no more.
Ye dauntless Hearts, that for your Country
All Dangers scorn, and wade through Seas o
In heavy silence, march around Her Tomb,
And then Lament your own and *England's* De
For Death has by this single stroke done more
Than when Ten Thousand slain he stalks in g
Ye pensive Widows, who by Fortune crost
In Foreign Fields have your dear Husbands lo
Now give a free and open vent to Grief,
Banish all Hopes, and think of no Relief;
That Bounteous Princess, who so justly knew
What was to blooming Worth and Merit due

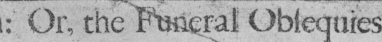

: Or, the Funeral Obfequies

NT PRINCESS,

arted this Life the 28th. of *December*, at *Kensington*, 1694. In the 32th. Year

to *Westminster-Abby*, in an open Chariot of State, on Black Cloath

uesday the 5th. of *March*, 169⅘.

e lov'd on Valour still to arme,
l to recompence the Soldiers Toil;
nalicious Fate wou'd have it so)
as! to the dark Shades below.

drooping Britain, *Mourn from shore to shore,*
belov'd MARIA *is no more.*

ch Heads, and likewise you that wait
Altar in a lower state,
Loss of so Divine a Prize,
all the sluces of your Eyes;
ritude Her Memory preserve,
m true Religion ne'er it did serve:
ady Pomps Her Mind cou'd not allure,
e Word, and in Her Faith secure :
d Scriptures were Her daily Care,
xercise and Food was Pray'r :
Joy, Her Pious Breast employ'd,
ll dying liv'd, and living dy'd.
1 ye now so great a Pattern find?
1 ye meet so bright, so pure a Mind?
drooping Britain, *Mourn from shore to shore,*
belov'd MARIA *is no more.*
ugh proud Fate has done her utmost spite,
d all our Hopes in endless Night;

Though ravenous Death has seiz'd the richest Prey,
That ever did a Regal Scepter sway;
Her Name shall Live, and still continue fair,
Fragrant, as Rich *Arabia's* Spices are:
While *Albian* in Triumphant State shall reign,
Queen of the Isles, and Goddess of the Main.
While silver *Thames* in wanton folds shall play,
And Tribute to the *British* Ocean pay,
While haughty *Lewis* shall remain abhorr'd,
And *William* be by all the World ador'd.
Our grateful Tongues Her Virtue shall proclaim,
Through all the distant Provinces of Fame:
Still in our Hearts shall Pearless *MARY* Reign,
Though dead, Her Station there she shall maintain.
Then Shepherds leave at last your mournful Lays,
And turn your Songs of Grief to Songs of Praise.

Licensed according to Order.

London: Printed for J. *Whitlock* near Stationers Hall. 169⅘.
Price, 1d.

pensive Nature-descriptions so numerous during the following century. Celadon retires into an "obscure Grotto," "All Gloomy as his thoughts," and then indulges in "little Rivulets of tears." This poetic hybrid would seem to have been very taking with royalty; for Oldmixon, in his *Funeral Idyll* on King William, turned the pathetic fallacy to similar mortuary uses.

Perhaps the most striking indication of the gradual blending of Cavalier and Puritan ideals in the Neo-classical compromise appears in the satiric elegies of the period. During the reign of Charles II, the elegy was again and again parodied by the Royalists in ridicule of their opponents, who occasionally replied with affecting laments or heavy, moralistic vituperation. During the reign of William and Mary, perhaps because even the Tories were thankful for the help of the dissenters against James II, perhaps through the natural mellowing of opinions, the elegy is seldom used for satire at all; and, when it is satiric, the form as such is not parodied, and dissent is not the subject of attack. The broadsides show an occasional elegiac lampoon, such as *The Whores Lamentation for the Death of Sir W[illiam] T.*,[84] and an obscene *Elegy on the Death of Dr. Thomas Staffold*.[85] There are two anti-Jacobite pieces, one on Sir John Fenwick,[86] beheaded in 1697, and one on James II,[87] probably by a dissenter; but they might better be described as moralizing apropos than as satire in the stricter sense. There is, finally, an anonymous *Elegy on the Death of Trade*,[88] which was clearly written from the point of view of, and presumably by, some member of the merchant class, and was probably not intended to ridicule the elegy as such: funereal detail was becoming a part of the accepted decorum of the day, approved alike by nobles and bourgeoisie. It yet remained for the upper class, during the eighteenth century, to take it up as the fashionable pose and give it a positive vogue.

In assigning causes to the rise of the religious lyric, Professor Courthope attributes it partly to the influence of High Churchmen and especially to the Non-Jurors,[89] whom he looks upon as sharing

---

[84] Brit. Mus. broadside. An attack on Sir William Turner.

[85] Bodleian, Wood Coll., No. 429.

[86] *Elegy Or, final farewell to Sir John Fenwick, Baronet* (Brit. Mus. broadside). He was beheaded in 1697.

[87] *Epitaph on King James II* (Brit. Mus. broadside).

[88] *Harl. Misc.*, London, 1744, II, 274 et seq. The original elegy appeared in 1698.

[89] W. J. Courthope, *History of English Poetry*, London, 1895-1910, V, 327 et seq.

in the emotionalism of dissent. His theory is perhaps borne out by some types of lyric and by such a personality as Lord Nottingham, the Tory leader in the reign of Queen Anne, whose dark complexion and melancholy bearing won him the nickname of Don Dismallo; but among such characteristic Non-Jurors as Jeremy Collier and William Law, one looks in vain for a lingering love of the lugubrious; and the funeral elegies that can with certainty be assigned to this group, show, even in this age of transition and compromise, a general restraint and absence of the mortuary. The *Pindaric Ode Sacred to the Memory of the Most Reverend Father in God Dr. William Sancroft*, the Non-Juror Archbishop of Canterbury,[90] is a true Pindaric with strophe, antistrophe, and epode, in regular form, one of the few scattered down the decades from Ben Jonson to Thomas Gray.[91] It starts with an invocation to the Muse, a bit ponderous, and continues in a tone purely panegyric. It has, to be sure, an appended epitaph, but neither epitaph nor ode contains anything of the horrific or even of the mildly melancholic. The Reverend John Norris (1657-1711), the Platonist whose High Church inclinations are implied in his attack on the Quakers, the Deists, and even on Locke, has, in *The Parting*,[92] written on a generally elegiac subject that should have called forth what gloomy images he had in his poetic repertoire; but the only association with the mortuary that it supplies is the line about "angel's visits short and bright," which was later borrowed by the atrabilious Blair and later still by the Romantic Campbell in his *Pleasures of Hope*. The Non-Juror Joseph Perkins, self-styled "Latin Laureate," in his *Elegus* to Wheeler and other Latin elegies, is merely complimentary in tone.[93] Of the two broadside "Epitaphs" for James II, the satiric piece already mentioned, presumably Whig in origin, is noticeably more mortuary than the one written by one of his own followers.[94] Perhaps in this group should also be included the *Elegy on Lord Finch* (1682),[95] which is certainly not mortuary, and the poems of Anne Finch, wife of the Non-Juror Earl of Winchelsea, whose fondness for the country and whose

[90] *A Pindaric Ode* etc., London, 1694. Sancroft died in 1693.

[91] For bibliography on the subject, see the present author, *William Mason*, New York, 1924, 147-148.

[92] John Norris, *Miscellanies*, London, 1687. The book had a considerable vogue.

[93] Joseph Perkins, *Elegus in Obitum Era, Wheeler Equitis*, London, 1697.

[94] Brit. Mus. broadsides, the former "Printed for Robert Williams," the latter, "Printed for H. H."

[95] Lutt. Coll., I, No. 49.

bluestocking inclinations[96] won her the covert sneers of her contemporaries.[97] Her melancholy, which was mild as compared to
that which these pages have chronicled, would seem to have arisen
partly from the "spleen,"[98] which in turn was doubtless derived
from bad living conditions, diet, and so forth, and partly from
her unhappiness at the overthrow of James II.[99] In spite of all
this, however, her elegies are but slightly mortuary in tone. In
the lines *Upon the Death of Sir William Twisden*, she develops
from the pathetic fallacy a sort of mortuary landscape; the elegy
Upon the Death of King James the Second, although it possesses
an unusual degree of sincerity both artistic and personal, is not at
all mortuary; and the poem *On the Death of the Honorable Mr.
James Thynne* has the quiet restraint of one who looks, not to the
decay of the body, but to the resurrection of the dead and the life
of the world to come:

> Then lay the fading Reliques which remain,
> In the still Vault (excluding farther Pain). . . .

Like many of the Cavalier religious poets of the School of Donne,
such mortuary details as Anne Finch's poems supply are chiefly to
be found in her non-elegiac meditative pieces; and of these the
lines *To Death* contain perhaps the best example; but here the
point of view is neither Puritan nor Sentimental but rather, as in
her more strictly elegiac work, a lingering echo of the late Elizabethans:

> . . . sure I must
> Encrease thy gloomy Kingdom in the Dust.
> My soul at this no Apprehension feels,
> But trembles at thy Swords, thy Racks, thy Wheels;
> Thy scorching Fevers, which distract the Sense,
> And snatch us raving, unprepar'd from hence;

[96] The world of Neo-classicism was not
only an aristocratic world, but also, intellectually at least, a man's world. Women of character did not frequent the
coffee-houses; and, until the opening of
Elizabeth Montagu's salon in 1750, women were generally outside the intellectual pale.

[97] See the *Poems of Anne, Countess of
Winchelsea*, ed. Myra Reynolds, Chicago,
1903, lvii. Her recognition dates from
the second quarter of the eighteenth century (*ibid.*, lxx). Miss Reynolds thinks
her "hardly strong enough to be counted
one of the influences in bringing about
Romanticism."

[98] *Ibid.*, xlii *et seq.*

[99] *Ibid.*, xxix-xxx. It is also just possible that she derived some of it from
association with Mrs. Elizabeth Rowe,
who was an ardent Calvinist.

> At thy contagious Darts, that wound the Heads
> Of weeping Friends, who wait at dying Beds. . . .

Indeed, a latitudinarian like Robert Boyle would apparently in the days of his agnostic youth, more easily fall under the shadow of melancholia than these Anglican High Churchmen, who saw in the death of a worthy Christian a joyful apotheosis. Theirs is the view of Donne and Herbert, and the latter poems of Vaughan;[100] to them death did not mean the judgment of a wrathful God visiting his predestined doom upon sinners who vicariously fell from Grace before they were born; nor yet was it the death of the body, with worms and skulls and putrefaction: to them, death was immortality; and the death of the righteous, an immortality of bliss.

Not merely the mortuary and moralistic content, but, to some extent, the form also of these funeral elegies shows the influence of the Neo-classical compromise. During the first half of the seventeenth century, no especial distinction in form had been apparent between Cavalier and Puritan elegies: a number were in regular stanzas, those in the ballad quatrain being influenced, no doubt, by the *Lykewake Dirge* and the *Lamentation for a Sinner;*[101] some, like Cleveland's lines on Dr. Chadderton,[102] were in octosyllabics; and many, especially of the broadsides about the mid-century, were composed in pentameter couplets, either run-on and broken for emphasis, like those of Donne, or metrically regular with little *enjambement,* like those of Jonson. After the Restoration, the Cavaliers usually employed the amorphous strophes of the Cowleian Pindaric or sometimes the Jonsonian couplet, and more than occasionally snatched a grace from the conventions of pastoral poetry. The funeral elegy of Puritan authorship, on the other hand, and the broadside poets of Grub Street, commonly held to the couplet in the manner of Donne, octosyllabics as in Flatman's *Dooms-Day Thought,* and very occasionally a stanza-form, as in the broadside *Death Triumphant,* though even here the *ottava rima* is treated with such freedom as to be scarcely recognizable. The

---

[100] The Roman Catholic poets took a similar view, e.g., Southwell's *Image of Death*, and the work of Habington, and the later poems of Crashaw.

[101] See Chapter IV.

[102] See Chapter II. Several elegies, moreover, in octosyllabics by Bishop Corbet were published posthumously in 1647; but these are in a lighter vein.

technique of the fixed stanza-paragraph, as in Spenser's *Faerie Queene* and the Elizabethan sonnets, was becoming a lost art, not to be revived until the mid-eighteenth century, though the influence of Spenser and the Elizabethans, in matters of content, was by no means dead among the middle classes. The reign of William and Mary saw a uniting of the Cavalier and the Puritan traditions; and, indeed, one is surprised at the apparent facility with which this cultural union took place, and the speed with which it is reflected not merely in the content, but even in the form of literature. The Pindaric ode-elegy, as in Hopkins' lines on Lady Cutts, still persists, though likely to contain a larger element of the mortuary; but the form that most gained by the compromise is clearly the heroic couplet, especially the regular couplet that had descended from Jonson. Rougher heroics still appeared; but their roughness suggests the incompetence of the poet rather than the intentional metrical emphasis of Donne. This Jonsonian measure was to predominate, almost to the exclusion of all others, for two generations; and among the many reasons that may be assigned for its predominance—the ease of its composition, its immediate appeal, its epigrammatic felicity, the critical bias in favor of "heroic" poetry and therefore of an "heroic" measure—one should also mention that it had been, since the mid-seventeenth century, the verse-form that Puritan and Cavalier had most notably pursued in common. The Puritans seldom wrote Pindarics; neither Puritan nor Cavalier often employed octosyllabics; and the Cavaliers avoided the regular stanza-forms of balladry: surely this mutual preference had some influence in establishing the preëminence of the heroic couplet when Royalists and dissenters met on common ground and resolved their cultural differences.[103]

Miss Reed, in noting the chief literary influences on the melancholic prose and verse of the reign of Queen Anne, lists "Lucretius, Vergil, Horace, Seneca, Martial, Ecclesiastes, Job, the Psalms, reinforced by the influence of Milton."[104] In a general way, such a list, augmented by *Hamlet* and a few other Elizabethan plays[105] and by the poets of elegiac tradition, English and to some

---

[103] The Cavaliers, as usual, dictated in matters of form. There was also a simplification in diction and sentence-structure and an increased interest in the general so that a wider class of readers might enjoy literature. See Spingarn, *Critical Essays*, Oxford, 1909, I, xlv.

[104] Amy L. Reed, *op. cit.*, 126.

[105] K. Müller, *Robert Blair's "Grave" und die Grabes- und Nachtdichtung*, Weimar, 1909.

degree Latin, and by contemporary religious prose, might serve as
a statement of the literary background of the elegy. There is,
however, a certain distinction between these influences: Lucretius,
in particular, and most of the other Latin authors, could hardly be
cited as the inspiration of the early Puritan elegists; and the more
obvious Classical influences seem to combine with the mortuary
only after the Neo-classical compromise had begun to take effect
in the reign of William and Mary. On the other hand, the aristocratic poets of the Restoration show little influence of the Bible
or of Milton. Furthermore, after the Restoration, the mantle of
Donne and more especially of Quarles, incongruous as such a fate
may seem for two Anglican Royalists, fell upon the Puritan poets;
that of Jonson, Denham, and Waller, upon the minstrels of the
Court. Toward the close of the century, the influence of Jonson,
especially in metrics and style, survived, in part perhaps because of
the spread of Classical education, in part, because it was more susceptible to the restraints of compromise than the quaint oddities
of metaphysicality. The influence on the funeral elegy of contemporary devotional prose, of sermon, prayer, meditation, and
pious biography, although doubtless considerable, is difficult to define: it is, "God woot, a large feeld to ere," full of folk, but without a ploughman. Miss Reed does hardly more than call attention
to its existence; and great patience, in both the etymological senses
of the word, will be required of its historian. Suffice it to say that
the conclusion of Burnet's *Life of Rochester*, if versified, would
make a fairly characteristic, though restrained, funeral elegy;[106]
and, if such a Broad Churchman as Burnet supplies such an example, how much more might be expected of less restrained biographies, with their death-bed scenes and detailed descriptions of
funerals—not to mention prayers and meditations on the threats
of hell and hopes of paradise! On the whole, however, as far as
the reign of Queen Anne is concerned, and to some extent that
of William and Mary also, Miss Reed is right in grouping together
somewhat indiscriminately Classical, Biblical, and other sources;
for Neo-classicism had a wide tolerance for anything and everything—so long as it did not too much savor of "enthusiasm."

But while Neo-classical ideals were impressing themselves upon
both the content and the form of poetry, the power that was to

---

[106] Dr. Gilbert Burnet, *Some Passages   of the Life and Death of John Earl of
Rochester*, London, 1680, 159 *et seq.*

occasion its downfall was developing *ab ovo*; for certain elements of Puritanism could not enter into the new order of things, elements that, of necessity, continued to persist.   Indeed, the savor of emotionalism lingered somewhat about the dissenters; melancholy had long since marked them for her own; and the mark was not easily erased.   The touch of the Sentimental in the elegy has already been noted in the foregoing pages: the treatment of nature by "the matchless Orinda" mildly suggests it; but especially the hyper-melancholy of the Puritan elegists renders many of them more than suspect.   Indeed, Browne, in his *Elegiack Essay* on the Rev. Matthew Mead, frankly declared that he found a melancholy environment "sweet"; and he was not alone in his predeliction.   After the death of Charles II, the cult of the inconsolable was beginning to spread even to persons of whose Puritan antecedents there is no patent proof.   Sir F. F. found that Gothic ruins in a desolate setting "please" one's "Melancholy fancy"; and Charles Goodall the younger, lamented the death of Ormond[107] in good set terms weighing delight and dole:

> Under a fatal Yew, as I was laid,
> Pleas'd with the dismal melancholick Shade,
> *Democritus* in a black *Veil* appears
> Democritus his Ghost in *flouds* of *Tears*.
> *Horrour* my Senses in *confusion* seal'd,
> The *icy current* of my *Bloud* congeal'd.

Here are the phrases and the very trick of italic emphasis common to Puritan elegies since the beheading of Charles I; but the author is "Pleas'd" with his melancholy; and one wonders whether he found the *"icy current"* and the *"Horrour"* quite uncongenial. Mrs. Jane Barber addressed the reader in a complacently "Querimonious Song";[108] and apostrophized Sorrow anent her brother's death as her "faithfull'st Lover," and, more than this, declared that "All thoughts of him [the brother] are only Pimps to thee," a metaphysical metaphor that suggests that she found Sorrow a pleasant companion!   A broadside balladist, lamenting the accidental drowning of two rich merchants at Blackwall (1688)[109] revels in his tears:

---

[107] Charles Goodall, *Poems and Translations*, London, 1689, 121.

[108] Mrs. Jane Barber, *Poetical Recreations*, London, 1688, 18, 19, 47.

[109] *On the Memory of Mr. Caleb Skinner, and Mr. Hezekiah Middleton; Merchants* (Brit. Mus. broadside).

> Patience a while, unruly Tears! My Pen
> Must weep, and you shall have your turns again.
> Come all you artless Passions, Grief and Love,
> Frustrated Hopes, and Sickly wan Despair;
> Beat all your Throbing Breasts and rend your Hair;
> Till everything but Destiny you move . . .

Such lines with their vivid personifications, might almost be taken for a lost, and very inferior, stanza of Collins' *Ode* on the passions. There follows something of Neo-classical pastoralism, and then a somewhat too vivid description of the corpses as they were recovered from the Thames, their "Dear Lips":

> Livid and Black, and all Deform'd they're grown,
> And Death and Horrour revel in their Face!
> Bloated and swoln their Eyes, and dull and dead,
> Mud in their Hands, and Weeds about their Head.

Sentimentalism, with its exalted faith in human nature, often during the eighteenth century, associated itself with very practical philanthropy; and it is significant that in a broadside on Alderman Turner (1693),[110] amidst the mourners' sorrowings with the usual exclamation points and rhetorical questions, is the following eulogistic passage:

> So Charitable, that though he's Dead,
> His Works of *Charity* Live in his stead.
> An *Hospital* he lately did Erect,
> The Hungry *Christian* to Feed and Protect;
> Besides a *Chappel*,[111] wherein twice a Day
> A Minister is ordered to Pray;
> Wherein full Forty *Poor* he doth Maintain.
> Oh! that our Sighs could him recall again!

If, indeed, "Grief has always been the subject of the *Elegy*,[112] the *genre* of the funeral elegy was beginning to be cultivated because of its propensity for grief. It had arisen in the School of Donne, probably from an urge for novelty; had been taken over by the Puritans about the mid-century to lend pomp and circumstance to

---

[110] *An Elegy On the Death of Sir William Turner, Knight, and Alderman of the City of London* (Brit. Mus. broadside).

[111] Meaning, of course, a non-conformist meeting-house.

[112] Sir William Temple, *Of Poetry* (1690), J. E. Spingarn, *Critical Essays, ed. cit.*, III, 89.

funerals; had declined at the Restoration, and given place to the free Pindaric eulogies patronized by the Court; had risen again with the middle classes in the reign of William and Mary, and somewhat combined with its Pindaric rival in a literary expression of Neo-classicism; and, almost simultaneously, had begun to change from an expression of exaggerated, though perhaps sincere, religious feeling, into an instrument for the cultivation of sweet sadness and pensive Sentimentality.

Perhaps no single figure better summarizes the tendencies of the time, Puritan and Cavalier traditions converging into Neo-classicism, and Sentimentalism diverging from this compromise, than the person of John Pomfret (1667-1702). His poem *The Choice* (1700) widely read for two generations and praised by Dr. Johnson in his life of the author, has been accepted as typifying the Neo-classical ideal; and, indeed, it "harmonizes with the prevalent mood of its contemporary readers."[113]   His *Pastoral Elegy* on Queen Mary[114] is a conventional amœbean eclogue expressive of polite grief on the part of a man who would seem to have vowed himself a disciple of *nil admirari*.   A very different tone appears in his "Pindaric essay," *A Prospect of Death*,[115] in which he perverts the favorite elegiac form of the Court poets to a moralistic and mortuary use in the Puritan manner.   He depicts the horror of the grave, describes a death-bed scene, and vividly portrays the "insupportable Torments" of dissolution—the "clammy Sweat," "Blood inactive," and "dying Eyes" that roll heavily about, "Their light just going out."   Such a piece suggests the Puritans of the 1650's; but at times his mood is reminiscent of an even earlier date, with a consolatory touch not unlike the Cavalier religious poets of the reign of Charles I.[116]   Quite different again is his poem *To his Friend Under Affliction*: he exalts melancholy, and sees not only moral uses in "a timely Grief" but also an æsthetic value:

> The finest Musick of the Grove we owe
> To mourning Philomel's harmonious Woe. . . .[117]

[113] E. Bernbaum, *English Poets of the Eighteenth Century*, New York, 1918, *Introduction*, xvii.
[114] J. Pomfret, *Poems*, London, 1736, 48 *et seq.*

[115] *Ibid.*, 112 *et seq.*
[116] *Ibid.*, 60.
[117] *Ibid.*, 57.

To this decorous clergyman, death may suggest consolation, as it did to the School of Donne in the early seventeenth century, or the horror of the grave, as the Puritans expressed it in the Commonwealth and in later funeral elegies, or a few correctly conventional remarks in pseudo-Classical—in this case, pastoral—form, as among the courtiers of Charles II; or lastly, the thought of death may awaken a subdued ecstasy, sad yet exquisite, like the sadness of music. Thus do the reactions of former ages persist in poetic convention; and truly Pomfret, taken piecemeal at least, harmonized with all the prevalent moods of contemporary readers. The divergent lines of class-literatures, with the exception of the Sentimental, were coming together again; and a single poet could epitomize, though with small regard for consistency, every attitude toward death known to his generation.

CHAPTER VIII

THE FUNERAL ELEGY IN SCOTLAND

AMONG Scotch Presbyterians and Episcopalians alike, the funeral elegy, as an earlier chapter has indicated, would seem never to have achieved more than occasional liturgic use; and, perhaps on that account, even the composition of such poems is a late development, and one apparently subsidiary to English example. Presbyterianism, probably because of its close-knit organization in which elders and ministers were made informers against each other, and partly perhaps because persecution in Scotland was more severe and prolonged than it was to the south of the Tweed, retained the full vigor of its Protestant prohibitions for a generation longer than did the English dissenting bodies. In England, moreover, non-conformity was a house of many mansions, Presbyterians, Independents, Baptists, Quakers, and others; and so the necessity of coöperation in the face of a common adversary forced upon each sect at least some tolerance of mutual differences. In Scotland, Presbyterianism, though comprising several shades of opinion, monopolized the opposition to the Episcopalian Establishment; and persecution, in consequence, produced an intensification of the bitter Covenanting spirit. Thus the Puritan spirit in England, rather by accident and certainly without intention, produced toleration; whereas, in Scotland, it inbred its inherent narrowness and its anti-æsthetic dogmas. Scotch funeral elegies, therefore, are rare until about 1680; and such as do exist during this early period are more or less certainly Episcopalian in origin. Practically all the Scotch elegies, earlier or later, have come down to us only on broadsides; and, of the broadsides that belong in the 1680's when the movement had its inception, a considerable number would seem to be mere reprints from the London trade. Presbyterianism, however, after its triumph in the reign of William and Mary, became more tolerant, and toward the close of the century allowed, if it did not encourage, the composition and sale of broadside funeral elegies, but never seems to have given them any place in the burial of the dead, perhaps because of a lingering disapproval, or perhaps because the custom was already obsolescent in England. Indeed, the *genre* was never quite incorporated into recognized Scottish poetry: it seldom appears in the printed volumes of standard poets; and it was usually written in English dialect. In this precarious middle ground, neither native nor exotic, neither aristocratic nor popular, the funeral elegy managed to flourish for more than a generation during the reigns of William and Mary, Queen Anne, and George I, and then, by slow inanition, died out at about the same time as its English prototype. The Scotch elegies are generally shorter than the English, more often merely adulatory or political in theme, and, as compared with those of the English dissenters, rather less mortuary; for in England the elegy largely grew out of Calvinism, and in Scotland, largely in spite of it. As one would expect in the poverty-stricken North Country of the period, the format of the broadsides is cruder than in England; the ink and paper are of poorer quality; and the type is often broken. A black border about half an inch wide was usually their only embellishment. This border was set up in sections a few inches long; and, as some of the printers took no special care to set them evenly together, the different parts were liable to tilt at various angles, like tombstones in an old graveyard. Pictorial devices were sparingly introduced, and these of the crudest: indeed, the *Elogie* on Sir George Mc Kenzie, reproduced in the present volume, is one of the most ornate and best printed. The wretched format of most of these pieces, one would suppose, must have neutralized the complimentary message of the verse; but, in Scotland, apparently, the industry of mortuary literature never attained sufficient dimensions to justify any great outlay of capital—or perhaps the Scotch preferred to lament their dead with thrift rather than with elegance.

The earliest Scotch elegies occur sporadically, beginning in the reign of James VI, and, like the elegies of contemporary England, have nothing of the mortuary about them. They generally show the influence of Spenser, particularly of the *Amoretti*, and they lack the solid black borders that graced their successors.[1] In 1594, M. W. F. brought out a broadside *Epitaphe upon the Death of*

---

[1] Sometimes, as in the broadside elegies on Bowes and Seton, there is a geometrical border, like that surrounding the *Elogie* on Colonel Luttrell reproduced in the present volume. The broadside on Seton is photographically reproduced in *A Century of Broadside Elegies*, ed. the present author, London, 1928, No. 91.

*Sir John Seton of Barns Knight, ane of the Lords of our Soveranes
privie Counsell and Session,*[2] an Italian sonnet in modified Scotch
dialect; and probably in the same year appeared *A Funeral Sonet,
Written upon the death of the honorable and maist virtuous Gentlewoman, Elizabeth Dowglas, spouse to M. Samuel Coburne,
Laird of Temple-Hall.*[3] Fowler's *Epitaph* on Robert Bowes,
Queen Elizabeth's ambassador to Scotland, who died in 1597, is
thoroughly Spenserian in both diction and versification. Fowler
himself had lived at foreign courts in his younger days; and the
writing of broadside elegies was doubtless the exotic product of
his travels:

> Build up, O England! Statues, Arches BOWES,
> And Tombes, and Pillars, to his living fame,
> Who was the wisdome of the valiant BOWES,
> And solid honour of that ancient name.
> And you white Swannes of Thames, and Tweide, proclame
> Your grievous losses, and his high desert,
> Who both his courses and his cares did frame. . . .
> All dangers from your baubes aye to divert. . . .

The removal of the Scottish court to London in 1603 seems to
have prevented the rise in Scotland of a courtly elegiac school;
and the turbulence[4] and poverty of the country would hardly promote the cultivation of the arts. Thus the funeral elegy, for
more than half a century, is only sporadic, and because of the
religious bias already referred to, occurs regularly in association
with the Episcopalian and Royalist cause. In 1653 appeared the
Funerals[5] of Bishop Forbes of Aberdeen, a small volume of Latin
and English elegies, similar to the contemporary English collections. The poems are short and Classical rather than mortuary.
In 1649, the Cavalier propaganda of grief at the execution of
Charles I seems to have spread to Scotland; and *The Scotch Sol-*

[2] Copies of the earliest elegies are to
be found in the Library of the University of Edinburgh. M. W. F. doubtless
stands for Mr. William Fowler (or
Fowlers). Alexander Gardyne's *Garden
of Godlie and Gothic Flowers*, Edinburgh, 1609, and *The Poetical Recreations of Mr. Alexander Craig*, Edinburgh,
1609, contain similar elegiac sonnets.

[3] Fowler signs himself "Secretarie to
the Queenes Majestie of Scotland," that
is to Queen Anne, the consort of James
VI. The piece consists of two Spenserian sonnets.

[4] See W. L. Mathieson, *Politics and
Religion in Scotland, 1550-1695*, Glas-
gow, 1902, Chapter XVII; and G. H.
Graham, *The Social Life of Scotland in
the Eighteenth Century*, London, 1906,
Chapter IV.

[5] *Funerals of the Right Reverend Fa-*

diers Lamentation,[6] in its appeal for vengeance to the princes of Europe, would seem to reflect the growing emotionalism of the elegy during the 1640's:

> What doe you weep? Alas, it is in vaine
> Him to deplore!
> These weeping marbles by their teares complaine,
> You must doe more.
> You must weep blood; these stones by teares doe call
> For vengeance, you by blood must right his fall.

About ten years later appeared a broadside elegy by T. S. *On the Most Noble James, Earl of Annandale*,[7] the restrained brevity of which suggests the epitaph rather than the lament.

The Scotch elegy can hardly be said to have developed before the 1680's; and, as it was even then seldom in Scotch dialect and seldom printed outside Edinburgh, it bears the mark of a distinctly foreign innovation. The earlier examples, moreover, are regularly associated with the Episcopalian system that the Stuarts forced upon their Scotch subjects; and no elegies appear in the Scottish section of Clarke's contemporary hagiology,[7] or in the *Biographia Presbyteriana*,[8] in connection with the obsequies of the numerous martyrs of the 1680's. A single elegy is, indeed, subjoined to the *Life of Renwick;* but it is merely a political poem upon a convenient occasion. Mungo Murray's verses *On the Death of the Illustrious David Earle of Wemyss* (1679)[9] combine Classical allusion with "A *Floud* of *Tears*" and "murmuring *Tydes*" and "*Hollow-Rockie-Caves*," very much as the noble earl who formed their

---

ther *in God Patrick Forbes of Corse, Bishop of Aberdene*, Aberdeen, 1635. Elegiac literature during most of the century is rare in Scotland. G. Lauder's *Aretophel (Fugitive Scottish Poetry of the Seventeenth Century*, Sec. Ser., No. 9, Edinburgh, 1853) at times touches upon the mortuary vein. Maidment includes several pieces in English and Latin in his *Scotish Elegiac Verses*, most notably Johnston's elegy on Lord Kinnoul (1634) and Mungo Murray's on the Earl of Perth (1675); but they seem regularly to be Episcopalian, and have few mortuary touches.

[6] But few elegies survive from this period; and indeed this and the follow-

ing piece on Lord Annandale should perhaps be accounted English rather than Scotch; for the unique copies of both broadsides are in the British Museum in the Thomason Collection.

[7] Samuel Clarke, *Lives of Eminent Persons*, London, 1683, 207 *et seq.*

[8] *Biographia Presbyteriana*, Edinburgh, 1827. The original broadside on Renwick's death was "composed immediately after his Execution at Edinburgh, 17 Feb., 1688."

[9] This and the three following broadsides are to be found in the National Library of Scotland, Pamphlets vol. XXIV.

subject combined Covenanting principles with a Caroline earldom:

> As *Great-Men* do, their *Vassals* charge and call
> Them to attend anothers Funerall;
> *Neptune* bids *Triton* warn each *Christal-Spring*
> A *Floud* of *Tears* into *Forths Firth* to bring,
> To wait *His* murmuring *Tydes*, upon Wemys Shore
> That Noble *Earles* Death still to deplore,
> Whose *Hollow-Rockie-Caves*, with Eccho's may
> Teach *Swans* to weep, in an unwonted way. . . .

More truly Royalist and less vivid with nature-description, is Murray's elegy on the "Horrid Murder" of Archbishop Sharp, a clarion call to vengeance: indeed, the early Scotch elegies, like those of the period of the Civil War in England, were often political in motive. Some of them, moreover, were either imported from England, or were Edinburgh reprints of London broadsides or pamphlets. Such, it would seem, were the *Elegy On the Earl of Essex: Who Cut his own Throat in the Tower* (1683) and the lines on General Tolmash; and such were *The Duchess of Monmouths Lamentation for the Loss of Her Duke* (1683)[10] a protracted depiction of her "endless torments" to arouse sympathy for the Whig cause, and *The Duke of Monmouth's Answer.* The Tories as usual met sentiment with satire; and in 1684 ridiculed the elegiac form in *An Elegie On the never to be forgotten Sir Thomas Armstrong Knight* (1684);[11] and, although there was some bickering on both sides, the elegy as such in Scotland was as yet mainly associated with the Episcopalian cause, as it had been in England before 1650. James Cuningham's Latin elegy on Charles II takes pains also to lament his father, the "Royal martyr"; and the more mortuary note of Cuningham's piece on Umphrey Milne (1695) suggests that Cuningham's religion changed with the times.[12] *England's Mournful Elegy for the Dissolving of Parliament*,[13] with its satire of Roman Catholicism, need not be Presbyterian; and certainly no Presbyterian wrote the measured eulogy on Pope Innocent XI[14] that appeared presumably on the occasion

[10] Nat. Lib. Scot., XII. An undubitable case of Scotch reprinting of an English broadside is *Britain's Sorrowful Lamentation* on Queen Mary (*Roxburghe Ballads*, London, 1871 etc., VII, 768).
[11] Nat. Lib. Scot., I.

[12] Copies of these two broadsides are to be found in the Signet Library, Edinburgh.
[13] Nat. Lib. Scot., XXII.
[14] Nat. Lib. Scot., I.

of his death in 1689. How many of these pieces were reprints, and how many originated in Scotland is hard to say; but, even as late as 1708, the caustic broadside on Partridge, the almanack-maker, apparently from pure motives of journalism, was reprinted in an Edinburgh broadside.[15]

Not all the Scotch elegies of this period, however, were English reprints; for, in the person of Ninian Paterson, Scotland possesses a poet—at least a poet of a sort—who devoted his chief literary energy to elegiac composition, and who, as early as 1685, defended the sorrowful Muse by the most approved Christian authority:

> Witness the *Sacrid Scriptures*, it's no wrong
> To vent a *Lamentation* in a Song.[16]

His *Obsequies to the Memorie of that Reverend, Learned, and Devoute Prelate, Alexander, Late Lord Bishop of Rosse*,[17] who is described as "A Prelate wise, devout in words and deeds," clearly shows Paterson an Episcopalian and a Royalist. The details of his life are obscure; but we know that he was born in Glasgow about 1636, attended the University, took his degree in 1659, and held various livings in the Episcopalian Establishment, until in 1674 he was deposed for immoral conduct. The latter part of his life seems to have been spent in vain pleadings for the relaxation of the sentence against him. He had married in 1668, and had at least two children. In December, 1688, he died.[18] His first published work would seem to be the *Epigrammatum libri octo. Cum aliquot Psalmorum paraphrasi poetica*, Edinburgh, 1678, probably written in the hope of gaining patronage that would restore him to favor, or perhaps merely to turn an honest penny for the support of his family. Doubtless from like motives, he turned out in 1683 a controversial pamphlet called *The Fanatick Indulgence granted anno 1679*, and about the same time, a few occasional pieces. At about this time also, he started upon his career as desultory elegist to the Scotch nobility: possibly he now hoped to accomplish through the nobles what the clergy, for their own

---

[15] Signet Lib. Cf. Bagford Coll., III, No. 74.

[16] *On that Devout, and Industrious Gentleman, George Monteith, Merchant in Edinburgh*, broadside, Nat. Lib. Scot., XXIV.

[17] Nat. Lib. Scot., XXII.

[18] See H. Scott, *Fasti Ecclesiæ Scoticanæ*, Edinburgh, 1866-1867, Part I, 115 et passim; Part II, 278. Cf. Maidment (*op. cit.* xxiv), who seemingly believes Paterson to have been innocent.

good reasons, had refused. His verses are hardly to the modern taste; but the brief chronicler of his life finds him "an elegant poet"; and, though denied even the twilight immortality of the *Dictionary of National Biography*, yet he is perhaps the most striking figure in Scottish poetry between Drummond of Hawthornden and Allan Ramsay.[19] Besides the two broadside elegies already mentioned, he composed military panegyrics in the conventional English style on General Dalziel and on "Brave Cleaveland's Corps laid in a Darksome Grave,"[20] and did a *Funeral Elegie* on Lady Lee (1686), a rather heavy Classical performance. Also Classical are his lines *To the Memory of Sir John Nisbet of Dirletoun;*[21] and the gruesome crudity of the mortuary symbols that serve as a heading is in strange contrast to the restraint of the text. Occasionally Paterson forms his style upon that of his predecessors of the reign of Charles I; and his first dated elegy on the death of Major Cockburn (1683), written perhaps before he realized that the mortuary tone had become the property of non-conformity, is his most characteristics example:

> This world's a boyling gulph of griefs and fears,
> The Rendevouz of anxious sighs and tears:
> This worm of five foot long, this moving span
> Compos'd of sin and dirt, we call a man,
> Is the tost passenger. . . .[22]

Occasionally this motif reappears later in his work as in the elegy (1686) on Thomas Robertson, "Bailie and Builder of Edinburgh": "This World's a Boiling Gulf of Griefs and Fears. . . . ",[23] and in the elegies on Sir Andrew Ramsay (1688) and on "The Incomparable Gosford." Ninian Paterson, indeed, would seem to deserve the credit, if credit it be, of naturalizing the mortuary elegy to Scottish soil; and, from his example, his followers learned to heap the shrine of luxury and pride with incense kindled not

---

[19] Cf. T. D. Holmes (*Lectures on Scottish Literature*, Paisley, 1904, 39), who says that the "rhythmic voice of the country was stifled" for the century preceding Ramsay. See also T. F. Henderson, *Camb. Hist. of Eng. Lit.*, XI, Chap. X, 204.

[20] Nat. Lib. Scot., XXII. The following elegy is in XXIV.

[21] Signet Lib. Four of Paterson's pieces are reproduced in *A Century of Broadside Elegies*, Nos. 94, 95, 96, and 97.

[22] *Elegy On the Much Lamented Death of the Valiant Major William Cockburn*, Nat. Lib. Scot., XXIV. Signed "N. Paterson": some of these broadsides are signed merely by initials.

[23] Nat. Lib. Scot., XXIV, contains this and the two following broadsides.

so much at the altar of the Muse as at the hearthstone of pecuniary necessity.

The decade of the 1690's presents a fair quantity of elegiac material, though the influence of English archetypes is still apparent. The *Elogie On the Death of Sir George Mc Kenzie*[24] by R. A. seems to be modeled in both style and iconography on English sources; and the *Elegie Upon the Earl of Angus*, who was killed in battle in 1692, is an essentially English poetic necrology, printed on a large sheet with a skull and cross-bones and motto at the top. The broadside *On the much to be lamented Death of the Worthy Umphrey Milne* (1695)[25] would seem to illustrate the acceptance of the form by the Presbyterians for other than satiric purposes. Milne is eulogized "Though he was called EPISCOPAL"; and the tone with which the poem begins is that which the present study has usually found associated with Calvinism:

In Gloomie Shades of darksome Night, where Phoebus hides his Head,
I heard an Echo cry aloud, that Umphrey Milne was dead;
My stupid Senses rose aloft, and wakened with a Cry. . . .
O Monstrous Dearh [Death] and Bloody Foe, thou Enemy of Man! . . .
Death with his fearful bloody Syth. . . .

Of a lighter type is the lament upon "that Incomparable Princess, Queen Mary," signed by "Mr. C—," who somewhat airily passes over the unpleasant facts of her demise in the single line: "Dissolv'd in dust the fair MARIA lyes." Equally lacking in mortuary tone is the eulogy of the pedigree, character, and personal appearance of Captain George Melvil (1699), whose Episcopalian politics are clearly implied in the poem.[26] Of quite a different cast, on the other hand, are two broadsides on Lord Reath and Lord Crawford, both written in iambic heptameter, signed "J. D.," and dated 1698.[27] The latter elegy shows the author to have been a Presbyterian, and his religious views seem to have colored his poetic style. The *Elegie On the Much to be Lamented Death of Alexander Lord Reath, One of his Majesties Privy Council* starts

[24] This and the following broadside are to be found in the Lib. Univ. Edinb.

[25] Signed "J. D.," probably James Donaldson. See *A Century of Broadside Elegies*, Nos. 99 and 100. This and the following broadside are to be found in the Signet Lib.

[26] Signet Lib.

[27] Signet Lib. The similarity in versification and tone suggest that the same "J. D." was also the author of the elegy, already discussed, on Umphrey Milne.

with a panegyric and lamentation of the deceased, followed by an apostrophe to "You Seraphims and Cherubims," which leads one to suppose that the author, though a true blue Presbyterian, was not able to read his Bible in Hebrew. At the end, the survivors of the departed are left with the following consolation:

Tho Friends should make the Rivers run with Tears that's shed below, He will not rise for all their Cryes, till the last Trumpet blow.

The *Elegie* on Crawford lapses from a Classical overture into a free fantasy in the minor key:

But Death that fearful Bloody Foe, Grand Enemie of Man, Has bent his Bow, and with a Dart from Earth now has him tain: Death's Commission's very great, he bears a Bloodie Shield. The Motto on his Scutcheon is, Ye Mortals all come yeild. . . .

The general metrical effect of these long couplets is to break into the jog-trot of the ballad quatrain, a stanza about as appropriate to devout lamentation as are the dance-rhythms of the average Evangelical hymn to the pious sentiments of its text.

During the two or three decades after 1700, the funeral elegy attained its highest point of popularity: the peerage, the law-lords, the military, and the clergy had their elegies, as in England during the Restoration. Some of these pieces were by ministers; some, one may suppose, by hack writers; at least two, by students of the universities.[28] During the middle decades of the century, the custom seems to have declined, partly perhaps because it was declining even among the dissenters in England, partly because Allan Ramsay and others were supplying Scotland with a more authentic literature, and partly because Neo-classicism was not favorable to melancholy, and Romanticism sought other motives for its cultivation than the immediacy of death. The Scotch elegies generally run true to the types already familiar in seventeenth century England; and of these the most common was the eulogy of a peer or other notable from whose family some remunerative patronage might be expected. Such pieces have little occasion for mortuary detail; but sometimes the author betrays himself into a dour phrase

---

[28] *On the Death of Mr. Brand Student in the University of Edinburgh*, 1717, Signet Lib.; and *Elegy on the Rev. Mr. John Anderson*, 1721, Signet Lib.

or two that demands recognition. The *Elegie On the universally Lamented Death of Mr. Alexander Scheills* (1700),[29] whose dying at Jamaica suggests the affluent sugar-planter, is the merest dull eulogy. Another piece on the same gentleman, entitled *Truth's Champion*, is somewhat more to the purpose, and ends prettily in "Gloomy Darkness." Indeed, the preference for a melancholy conclusion is one of the few distinctive characteristics of the Scotch funeral elegy: the English elegies, like the elegiac eclogue, usually progress from mortuary lamentation to an exultant apotheosis; but, with the Scotch, the arrangement is less fixed; and the conclusion, perhaps because of the severity of Calvinism, perhaps because of the natal pessimism of the Scottish character, is quite as likely to conclude with dark or even sepulchral images as the joys of heavenly beatitude. The sorrow of *The Mournful Muse*[30] for Lord Basil Hamilton (1701) is expressed in references to his "pale Corps," and "hooting Owls and doleful Birds," and "Death's Insulting Rage": in fact, the elegist of the period, having described death as the universal tyrant, is perpetually astounded at his effrontery in visiting the clergy and the peerage. The *Elegie* on His Grace of Argyle (1703), although it starts bravely with a quotation from Horace, soon turns into a sort of Presbyterian *Essay on Man*:

> Man's Life's a flying Vapour which doth rise
> Like a small Spot 'twixt two Extremities;
> An empty shadow of a lying Dream,
> Where we Delusions for Delights esteem,
> Which in our best and prosperous state doth show,
> But Drops of Frailty plung'd in Seas of Woe. . . .

The lines on the "truly Pious George Earl of Sutherland" (1703) are in the conventional heroic couplets with the usual concluding epitaph; and such in general are the elegies by R. M. on the "Incomparable Thomas Fisher, Merchant in Edinburgh," with its mildly mortuary acrostic (1711), and the pieces on the Marquis of Tweddel (1713), the Earl of Cromarty (1714), the Earl of Farquhar (1715), Lord Strathnaver (1720), and Lord Panccutland (1729). The elegy on Farquhar has "Tears of Blood" and a few

---

[29] Signet Lib.

[30] This and the several following broadsides are to be found in the Signet Lib.

such touches; and the death of Commissioner Kelso (1716) was lamented with a *de casibus* of men killed by women, and proceeds to an almost comic application of these modern instances to the "Honoured Defunct." The lines on Sir Thomas Kirkpatrick (1720) show something of Neo-classical periphrasis in turning the grave into "dark Natures Bed"; and the elegy on the second Lord Belhaven by Mr. Pennecuik follows the pastoral in using the pathetic fallacy to express the hyperbole of grief:

> Nature turn'd gloomy fac'd, forbears to smile,
> All Cheeks are pale, and Sorrow sinks the Isle.

Somewhat later in the century, a softer, Sentimental note is apparent: an *Elegy* on the Duke of Argyle (1743)[31] urges Scotland to turn its "former Joys" to weeping and "thoughtful Sorrows"; and the author of the lines *To the Memory of Mr. David Drummond* (1741)[32] employs the heroic quatrain of Hammond, and seems to have discovered that there is a pleasure in a poignant grief:

> Forgive the Muse, that, with a heart sincere,
> With thee desires to drop a friendly tear;
> In grateful verse a common loss to mourn,
> And weep a while o'er Drummond's sacred urn.

The Scots Magazine, indeed, during this period reflects the lingering popularity of elegiacs. Among other pieces, it contains two laments on Lord Blantyre (1751),[33] one that starts with his funeral knell and proceeds with selected observations on "relentless Death," and the other at once ruder and more Sentimental:

> Drop, doleful pen, distill the swelling woe,
> And into melting elegiacs flow. . . .

A lighter touch, like that in the elegy on Queen Mary already noted, is usual in the poems on noble ladies. The *Elogie* on the Countess of Rothes (1700)[34] celebrates her as "the most Fragrant Flower of *Femal* Kynde," and the poem on Lady Ann Elcho (1700) is of similar tone. Janet Barclay (1700) is eulogized in

---

[31] Brit. Mus. broadside.
[32] *Scots Mag.*, III, 119.
[33] *Ibid.*, XIII, 281, 282.

[34] This and the following broadside are to be found in the Nat. Lib. Scot., XXIV.

Latin, and then for the vulgar reader in English, as "A Pastor's Daughter, and a Pastor's Wife."[35] Anne, Countess of Leven, (1702) receives the conventional couplets with an appended epitaph. The lines upon the Duchess of Athol (1707)[36] start with the usual comparison of death to a sergeant, which by then had probably lost all Shakespearean reference, and had become part of the regular elegiac stock in trade:

> Death is a Champion Bold, a Gyant fierce,
> A Serjeant Grim whose Countenance doth peirce
> The Stoutest Heart, where he doth point his Eye,
> Whom none dare Fight, and from him none can Flye. . . .

The Elegy[37] on the Marchioness of Montrose (1710) is the inevitable eulogy of a great lady and devoted wife; and that on the Countess Dowager of Southerland (1715)[38] is the usual feminine lament for the usual feminine virtues: one devoutly hopes that the dead ladies actually possessed at least half the excellencies enumerated in such catalogues. The Signet Library is especially fortunate in possessing a broadside by R. Douglass on the Duchess of Queensberry (1709) and also the original manuscript, apparently prepared for the printer, with an inked-in black border half an inch wide. The beginning is somewhat enigmatic in both syntax and punctuation; but there can be no doubt about the author's poetic fury:

> A moving Streak! A Princess Great this Day,
> Has fled from hence. (and can no longer stay)
> Upon the Summonds, of that ghostly Thing.
> Call'd awful Death! and Frightful Terrors King!
> This Rageing Gyant. Doth with cruel Face,
> Maw Down the Flower and chief of Human Race.

The latter part of the piece has a vivid passage on Death's "awfull Frown"; and, indeed, the author deserves credit; for it is not easy to restore to the legend of a well-worn coin the clarity and sharpness of the mint. For the most part, however, the elegies on noblewomen, written to gratify the taste of the survivors rather than to express any religious sentiment, present but little that is apposite to the present study. They are, however, not without importance

---

[35] This and the following broadside are to be found in the Signet Lib.
[36] Nat. Lib. Scot., XXII.
[37] Signet Lib.
[38] This and the several following broadsides are to be found in the Signet Lib.

in making a sort of neutral avenue by which an Episcopalian custom might enter the new Presbyterian Establishment, and in providing, one may suppose, a substantial subsidy to ensure continued production.

The elegies on royalty during this period have a peculiar significance. Like those on the nobility, they tend to be conventional enough: the broadside on the Electress Sophia, for example, and that on "Her most illustrious Majesty Ann." But there is a notable contrast between the elegies on James VII (1701) and those on King William a year later. The lamentations on King James are more numerous,[39] but exhibit Neo-classical restraint, and contain but few mortuary touches: their number suggests that, at the very beginning of the century, the funeral elegy in Scotland was still Episcopalian rather than Presbyterian; and their restraint is consonant with the cultural ideals of the Episcopalian nobility. There are but three elegies on King William: the one by Bishop Burnet,[40] though printed in Edinburgh, can hardly be said to reflect contemporary Scottish taste. The *Mournful Poem* on the late King seems to betray at once the Calvinistic and the bourgeois point of view in its exclamatory sorrow for "The Champion of our Isreal" and in a somewhat unmerited eulogy of King William's private virtues. *A Threnodie or the Lamentation of Scotland, England, France, Ireland . . . by J. P. Sc.* was published in 1702 at Edinburgh as a pamphlet, perhaps because of its length, or perhaps because of a prejudice against broadsides. Its mortuary details suggest a Calvinistic authorship that would agree with King William's own religious politics; and its combination of the pastoral pathetic fallacy with realistic details of rural nature, points forward to Thomson's *Seasons*. The following passage from *Britain's Lament* illustrates the piece in brief compass:

> Ah now for thee, what dismall howlings fill
> Our Alpish Mountains, and each Dale and Hill?
> Hear how the Rivers frame a doleful song,
> And murmur sadly as they glide along;
> Are not both *Forth* and *Thames* got hand in hand,
> And leave their Channels and their ousie Land?

[39] Signet Lib., and Nat. Lib. Scot., XXIV.

[40] This and the several following elegies are to be found in the Nat. Lib. Scot., XXIV.

> And see the flowers upon the humble bed
> As *Tulips, Dazies,* how they're withered
> The *Gilli-flower, Lillie* and *Marygold*
> Do shake as if they were distrest with cold. . . .

And so follow the Narcissus, Primrose, Rose, and Thistle, the "Groves and shady fens of Ireland," and other rural touches, occasionally reminiscent of Spenser's *Shepherd's Calendar,* occasionally of *The Faerie Queene.* Thus at the very beginning of the eighteenth century, the Scotch elegist perceived that realistic nature forms an admirable background for the stimulation of emotion, and supplies at the same time a grateful variety to moralizing and the horrors of the grave. An *Epitaph* on Sir Roger Hog (1700) and an *Elegy*[41] on the Countess of Leven (1702) are prologue to the omen; and bits of realistic nature-description are not uncommon in the Scotch elegies during the reigns of Anne and the Georges—an important fact in the literary background of Thomson's *Seasons* and Blair's *Grave.* The *Threnodie* on King William is a most significant transition-piece, showing the religious emotionalism of the Calvinist turning into the natural emotionalism of the Sentimental poet; and it is notable that no such development is apparent in the elegies of unquestionably Jacobite authorship.

After the Parliamentary Union with England in the reign of Queen Anne, Edinburgh was hardly more than a military and judicial capital; and the importance of the army and the law is signalized by a number of elegies devoted to members of these two professions. The *Elegy* on Sir David Hume of Crossrig,[42] "one of the Senators of the College of Justice" (1707) adequately typifies the former:

> True Grace and Virtue are such special things
> They Sweeten Gall, and blunt the pointed Stings
> Of Death and Hell, and other Plagues that rage
> 'Gainst sinful Man in this Corrupted Age.

Then follow the time-honored subjects of illness, the "Ghostly Serjant Death," Heaven, and a eulogy of the deceased. The reverse of broadsides is usually blank; but, in the present instance,

[41] Nat. Lib. Scot., XXIV.   [42] Nat. Lib. Scot., XXII.

the back was used to convey the news of a recent Anglo-French engagement off the Downs; and one judges, therefore, that the piece was written for public sale, rather than in the hope of lordly patronage. Generally similar in tone are the elegies on Sir William Anstruther (1711),[43] and on Sir James Stuart of Good-trees (1713).[44] An elegy on Lord Bowhill (1714)[45] exhorts the Muse: "Sob thou Dire Sighs, Pierce Adamantine Ears." Later, when the *Scots Magazine* was taking the place of broadsides for the memorializing of the dead, there appeared in its pages an elegy on Mr. Hugh Murray-Kynnynmound,[46] which manages to combine Neoclassical couplets with a tearful sentimentality. In general, however, the restraints of the law would seem happily to have carried over into the legal elegy.

The eulogizing of the military generally lapsed into purely biographical, versified obituaries itemizing intrepid and honorable deeds. *The Panegyrick Upon the Death of Lieut: Thomas Hadow,*[47] is of interest as being a Whig, and therefore Presbyterian, elegy as early as 1700; and the existence of such a piece makes one wonder whether the demand of the military for posthumous praises may not, as in the days of the Commonwealth, have forced the elegy upon the guardians of contemporary Calvinism. The piece on Captain Charles Dunbreck (1717) is notable only for its very mortuary border; that on Captain George Drummond, for its single phrase, "The Grave's devouring Hungar"; and the lines on Lochiel[48] "who lately shook this island with alarms" are chiefly given over to an apology for his Jacobite politics; and finally the author somewhat unconvincingly assures us that "good Lochiel is now a Whig in heaven." We piously hope that heaven took due cognizance of any death-bed apostasy that he may have committed.

The Scotch satiric elegy, unlike its English prototype, is not the political weapon of any one party or opinion. There had been a tradition of humorous elegies on the living that started at least as early as Sir Robert Sempill in the seventeenth century; and this

---

[43] Signet Lib.
[44] Nat. Lib. Scot., and Signet Lib.
[45] Signet Lib.
[46] *Scots Mag.*, IV, 63.
[47] Nat. Lib. Scot., XXII. The two following broadsides are in the Signet Library.

[48] *Scots Mag.*, X, 586. The military elegy continued into the second half of the century, *teste* the *Elegy On His Excellency James-Francis-Edward Keith*, Signet Lib.

strain of satire comes down not only into the poetry of Ramsay, Fergusson, and Burns but also into the broadside elegy. One of the earliest of these broadside satires is an *Elegy on Scotland* (1707)[49] against the unpopular Act of Union. There is a Latin elegy on the Duke of Hamilton and one in English directed against his murderer, Lord Mohun (1712); there is a diatribe against Louis XIV (1715); an *Elegy on Colonel James Gardiner* (1745) contains a bitter denunciation of the House of Stuart and their "anti-christian Mob"; and a frankly vituperative satire *On the unlamented Death of the Marquis de Guiscard*. One cannot, however, say that during this period either Whigs or Jacobites regularly used the broadside elegy as a political weapon or for ridicule; and, indeed, a number of the pieces are merely comic rather than satiric, like the *Elegie Upon Francis Marine, his Majesty's Trumpeter* (1721); and some, like Ramsay's serio-comic elegies,[50] are in Scotch dialect, and clearly imply that the broadside elegy finally seeped down into the lower classes, and there lay ready for the pen of Robert Burns.[51] The *Habbiack Elegy*,[52] indeed, suggests some of his satiric pieces; and the lines on Patie Birnie, "The Famous Fiddler," are almost in the style in which he celebrated his tavern cronies.

More important, however, in the general trend of eighteenth century poetry are the lamentations upon the clergy, most of the poems, like their subjects, painful and pious, sometimes, as in the *Elegie upon the Reverend Mr. John Anderson*, almost to the point of unconscious parody. Some are conventional enough;[53] but conventionality had entered like iron into the very soul of elegiac poetry, and so imbued it with inflexibility of sentiment and phrase that, like all much-repeated expressions, the words had lost their definite sense and become mere vague symbols of grief; and thus one bard is led to declare that he writes "While Sighs and Tears do drown his Warbling Eyes."[54] A few examples drawn from

---

[49] This and the several following elegies are to be found in the Signet Library.

[50] The one on Lucky Wood appeared on a broadside (Nat. Lib. Scot., VIII).

[51] For a sketch of the relation of Robert Burns to the elegiac tradition, see Appendix B.

[52] Copies of this and the following elegy are to be found in the Signet Lib.

[53] E.g., the elegies on Rule, Wilkie, Carstairs, and Delape (Signet Lib.); and perhaps one should add the pieces on Provost Peadie of Glasgow (Nat. Lib. Scot., XIV) and on Bishop Rattray (*Scots Mag.*, V, 364).

[54] *Elegie* on the Reverend George Meldrum (Nat. Lib. Scot., XXII).

the more mortuary pieces will serve to show how the elegiac manner of Puritanism waxed and flourished when once the Presbyterian hierarchy succumbed to the seduction of the Muse. The lines *On the Much Lamented Death of the Reverend Mr. Patrick Plenderleith, Minister of the Gospel at Sabine* (1715)[55] assure us that the subject made a good end, singing Hallelujahs on his death-bed. The *Elegy* on Stedman (1713) opens with the usual flat rhetoric of lamentation:

> Ah! Edinburgh, Lament in Floods of Tears,
> [F]or thy Great God is Angrey it appears.
> He dos not look upon you with a smile,
> His Frowns are heavy, which you seem to feel. . . .

And so this fertile vein is pursued to the limit of sterility. Ten years later, *Cries from the Desert, Bewailing the Loss of the Reverend, Pious, Painful Pastor, and Eminent Servant of Christ Mr. John Hepburn, Minister of the Gospel,* under the apt heading of a skull and cross bones, rejoiced in similar sentiments. But with the accession of the House of Hanover, Scotch Calvinism had fallen upon better and better days; and it could hardly survive its good fortune. In the very same year as the hyperbolic "bewailing" of Hepburn, *The Melancholy Muse* (1723) grieved over the Rev. Robert Calder with a sweet pensive lyricism that would seem to prepare the way for the "white melancholy" of Thomas Gray:

> Our Souls are seized with a Damp of Grief,
> Horrour hangs o'er the active Springs of Life.
> Since thou art gone, thou dear good natur'd Man,
> We sing thy Elegy like dying Swain;
> We hang the Head, and beat the labouring Breast,
> Farewel thou matchless Poet, matchless Priest.

The 1720's saw the development not only of a soft sensibility but also of Nature-description in the elegy, elements already noted in the *Threnodie* on King William. In 1721 was published at Glasgow a pamphlet elegy *To the Memory of the late Reverend Mr. Anderson,* which ends its conventional eulogy with the following couplets:

[55] Copies of this and the several following broadsides are to be found in the Signet Lib.

So in calm Ev'nings, the unclouded Skies,
Not less Illustrious, than when in his Rise,
The west'ring Sun into the Main Declines,
Bright and more bright; and as he sets, he Shines.

Indeed, passages like this in the broadside elegies of the period help
to explain the existence of similar material in Thomson's *Seasons*.
Let it also be remembered that Thomson's friend Riccaltoun could
apostrophize the "gloomy soul" with the most ominous complacence;[56] and the *Winter* of Riccaltoun was the chief influence on
Thomson's *Winter* in the *Seasons*. Indeed, in its earliest form,
Thomson's poem is very close to the elegiac tradition from which
it borrows its tone of pensive melancholy, its theme of *vanitas
vanitatis*, its use of the pathetic fallacy, and the climax in which
it likens winter to death followed by a sudden apotheosis in which
spring is taken as the symbol of immortality. Such themes in some
such arrangement persist in Romantic poetry; and Shelley's *Ode
to the West Wind* is composed of similar motifs, and follows a
similar plan. Thomson's own elegies on Newton and on Lord
Talbot are eulogistic rather than mortuary; for he did not linger
in the Calvinistic fold. The *Hymn* at the end of the *Seasons*
expresses his new Sentimental Deism; and his lines on Talbot
about "ye worst of Zealots" show his opinion of his former co-
religionists. This reaction against Calvinism that Thomson under-
went while at the University would seem to have been quite the
usual thing in his social class and generation; and the *Seasons*,
which is perhaps the fullest expression of this outlook on life, was
popular for a hundred years with the middle classes.[57] Indeed,
the funeral elegy vividly reflects the change; and a lament on the
Rev. Dr. Webster (1784)[58] passionately enjoins "every truly feeling heart" to come and "shed a mournful tear," very much in the
tone that sometimes appears in similar pieces by Burns.

If elegiac writing leads into the soft Sentimentalism of pensive
sorrow, it leads no less clearly into the hard Sentimentalism of the
horrific and the grandiose; and perhaps it is not by chance that the
best examples of this style are several pieces upon the Reverend
David Blair (1710), a redoubtable Whig who had been chaplain

---

[56] *Gent. Mag.*, X, 256.
[57] R. D. Havens, *The Influence of
Milton*, Cambridge (Mass.), 1922, 127.

[58] Signet Lib. Of similar tone is the
piece on Lord Elgin (1771).

to King William[59] and whose son was the celebrated author of
The Grave. From the mortuary strains that he inspired, one can
readily believe that, in the words of one eulogist, he was "a Son of
Thunder" and "A Wrestler for Zion in her Straits."[60] Another,
more Classical, admirer, who signs himself "A. B.," appended to
his *Elegy*[61] a Latin epitaph, and cheerfully looked forward to a
divine judgment because of the heavy mortality of eminent divines
"These three Years past."   Most notable, however, is the anonymous broadside entitled *Stanzas Sacred to the Spotless Memory of
the very Reverend Mr. David Blair*:[62]

> Forbear ye bold rapacious Worms forbear,
> Lest you the Relicts of a Saint prophane;
> Devour but slowly its uncommon Fare,
> For Saints and Kings die only now and then.
>   2 Riot on those who at their Souls Expence,
> Pamper those bodies that must pamper you;
> There be luxurious, but Crawl far hence;
> Sure some Respect to reverend Clay is due.
>   3 But ah how vain are all our Words and Tears!
> For on their prostrate Prey the Worms do fall. . . .

Stanza the sixth excuses grief as a "Weakness" but not a "Sin";
the piece ends in a dour eulogy and an epitaph; and the author
expresses his elegiac motto in the lines:

> Let no bright Thought in all my Stanzas shine,
> True grief appears the most indishabile.

Its vivid imagination, its high-keyed emotionality, its luxuriance in
the horrible and the disgusting, make the poem a link between
seventeenth century Puritanism and such Romantic pieces as *The
Monk* of Matthew Lewis, and at the same time make it an immediate precursor of *The Grave*.

The juvenilia of the younger Blair show a special inclination,
doubtless derived from his home surroundings, toward religious
and elegiac verse; and, as he never definitely broke with Calvinism
as did Thomson, his later masterpiece is more obviously in the

[59] Was he perchance the author of the
Threnodie on King William in spite of
the initials signed to that performance?

[60] *A Second Elegy on Mr. David Blair*,
Nat. Lib. Scot., XXII.
[61] Signet Lib.
[62] Signet Lib.

traditional strain. His youthful poem *Of the Glory of God and Heaven* has both Gothic and horrific details; the couplets on *The Destruction of the Canaanites* is as bloody as the elegies on Charles I; and, in his "juvenile performance" on "the Late Learned and Eminent Dr. William Law," Blair cannot "keep within its banks the swelling tide" of his woe. He "trembles at the greatness of his theme," and then proceeds to launch forth into a eulogy mixed with nature-description and lamentation. The picture of the widow's grief is especially affecting. But the *Grave*, which is the work of his maturity in the 1730's, quite eclipsed these earlier performances. The latter part shows it to have been intended as a generalized, though somewhat belated, elegy on his father; and, as such, it might well have been subject to the influence of the *Stanzas* already discussed. There may, to be sure, exist some influence of Milton, Shakespeare, and other writers that scholars have assigned as the basis of the poem;[63] but its most immediate and obvious antecedent is the broadside funeral elegy of contemporary Scotland. Indeed, so completely has the funeral elegy been overlooked in literary history and so early was it lost sight of, that in 1794 Anderson, that veteran biographer of literati, declared that he could find no analogies for this kind of writing in the Scotland of Blair's generation,[64] and all subsequent scholars have gone far afield in search of influences and analogues. The poem, indeed, belongs to the literary tradition of the middle classes; and the London publishers who rejected it because it would not be acceptable "to the fashionable and polite" were probably right in their reason, though very short-sighted in their rejection; for the publishers would seem to have had little realization of this great new public and of the new taste that it brought in, until the firm of Dodsley rose and flourished upon the new patronage. The popularity of the *Grave* runs parallel to that of Thomson's *Seasons*; and, like the *Seasons*, it rapidly ran through edition after edition down into the reign of Queen Victoria when the middle class seem to have finished passing through this plane of cultural development.

[63] See Dennis, *Age of Pope*, London, 1899, 84 and note; Havens, *op. cit.*, 384; Müller, *Robert Blair's "Grave" und die*

Grabes- und Nachtdichtung, Weimar, 1909.

[64] *Complete Edition of the Poets of Great Britain*, London, 1794, VIII, 856.

Upon analysis, the poem appears to be an *omnium gatherum* of the mortuary and didactic elements already usual in the elegiac composition of England and Scotland; but here, as in *Night Thoughts* and in Gray's *Elegy*, the gnomic elements are generally heightened with nature-description so that the moralizing and the scenic background usurp the chief interest in the place of the deceased. Like most didactic poems of the period, the *Grave*, without showing any very clearly marked logical progression, takes up in order the topics that its title suggests, and wanders essay-like about the mighty maze rather than attempts a well-ordered and exhaustive exposition. Like many funeral elegies, the poem plunges at once into the midst, and impresses upon the reader the horror of death, which rises to an immediate and vivid climax in the description of a Gothic ruin with tombs and moss and decay. The dramatic touch enters in with the school-boy hurrying through the graveyard at night and whistling to keep up his courage; and the "new made widow" weeping over a tombstone supplies something of the pensive, lyric note. Then the subject changes to that favorite Wordsworthian theme, rural Nature emotionalized in recollection; and the poet favors us with his fond memories of a woodland stroll with a friend now dead; and thus the grave is made to cast its shadow over rural scenery, very much as Wordsworth's regret for his lost youth and its angelic blisses dyed with a deeper tinge in his later years the vivid pictorial impressions of his adolescence. Next comes the telling contrast, dear to all moralists, between the darksome grave and the delights of Mammon; and somewhat inconsequentially there follows a description of the ostentatious funeral rites of the period. From funerals, we return to graves, and note how quickly tombstones decay—especially, one might add, monuments made of chalk-stone like those in southern England. This subject reminds the poet that death is the great leveller of all; and we are once more improving a familiar theme, and one that dominates the entire middle of the poem: the king, the fair lady, the strong man, the sage, the great soldier, the physician, the miser, all succumb; and the poet demonstrates *in extenso*, like any Puritan preacher, that Salvation resides in neither power, nor beauty, nor strength, nor wisdom, nor courage, nor knowledge, nor wealth. From here, we pass to a rather highly colored picture of the horror of death to the rich and the horror of eternal torment to the debauchee, and finally the horror of suicide, the "English sin." The poet implores Death to tell his secret; and this part of the poem ends with a general recapitulation of the entire subject of universal and inevitable death.

The last third of the *Grave* deals with Salvation, a sort of apotheosis-in-general which is particularized in the person of Blair's father whose godly virtues and pious death receive the usual elegiac eulogy. This section is introduced with the story of the State of Innocence and the Fall, taken from the "four-fold state of man," the staple theme of Presbyterian sermons of the period. There is an apostrophe to Sin and Death that perhaps owes something to Milton; and then, by the usual elegiac peripeteia, the subject of Salvation is introduced, with particular reference to the elder Blair. There is a passage on the Resurrection of the Body that at least has the virtue of avoiding the comic; there are a few lines of appropriate consolation to the sorrowing relict of the deceased; and the reception of the good man into eternal bliss completes the poem. Blair's *Grave* might be described as an extended elegy prefaced by a series of descriptive and moralistic introductions any one or two of which would have served the old-fashioned mortuary broadside. Most of the subjects thus improved by the poet had been common elegiac themes for several generations, the horror of death and of the tomb, death the inevitable leveller of all, rural nature as the background of death, and death as the gate to a moral retribution of rewards and punishments. The poem, moreover, has many of these themes in common also with *Night Thoughts* and with the *Elegy Written in a Country Church Yard.*

Not merely the general subject-matter but the details also of description and style are in the general tradition of the elegy. The *penchant* for the cosmic was apparent in Puritan mortuary poetry even before it appeared in *Paradise Lost*; and such lines as the following may go back to either source:

> Dark as was chaos ere the infant sun
> Was roll'd together, or had tried his beams
> Athwart the gloom profound.[65]

Mortuary passages abound, sometimes definitely associated with the churchyard, such as the description of the

[65] *The Grave*, line 15 *et seq.*

> . . . trusty yew,
> Cheerless unsocial plant; that loves to dwell
> 'Midst skulls and coffins, epitaphs and worms:
> Where light-heel'd ghosts and visionary shades . . . [66]

The vermicular motif, borrowed perhaps from the *Stanzas Sacred to the Spotless Memory* of the elder Blair, reappears in the description of the decay of beauty:

> Methinks I see thee with thy head low laid,
> Whilst surfeited upon thy damask cheek
> The high fed worm, in lazy volumes roll'd,
> Riots unscar'd.[67]

Disease also has its place in the poem, though less vividly described than in some seventeenth century pieces; for Neo-classicism had adorned the *Grave* with tags of generality and streamers of circumlocution; but the personifications are not the mere capitalization of lifeless abstractions:

> . . . Sicknesses
> Of every size and symptom, racking pains
> And bluest plagues, are thine.—See how the fiend
> Profusely scatters the contagion round!
> Whilst deep-mouth'd slaughter, bellowing at her heels,
> Wades in the blood new spilt.[68]

But the most piquant horror is supplied from Gothic sources; and an interior scene such as the following might well have served the needs of Mrs. Radcliffe or of the author of *Vathek*:

> The sickly taper,
> By glimm'ring through thy low-brow'd vaults,
> (Furr'd round with mouldy damps, and ropy slime)
> Lets fall a supernumerary horror. . . . [69]

The humidity which contributes so gruesomely to these lines is of course a touch of realism belonging to the English climate, in which even a new grave-stone will soon be "furr'd" with moss. Perhaps the finest Gothic touch, however, is the description of "yonder hallow'd fane," the details of which Blair seems to have

[66] *Ibid.*, line 22 *et seq.*
[67] *Ibid.*, line 245 *et seq.*
[68] *Ibid.*, line 627 *et seq.*
[69] *Ibid.*, line 18 *et seq.*

drawn rather indiscriminately from both abbeys and castles; for the early eighteenth century did not distinguish between types or periods of Mediæval architecture. The first line contributes meteorological heightening, a device borrowed perhaps from the mad scene in *Lear*, and in a later age freely used in the pictures of Turner:

> The wind is up: hark! how it howls! . . .
> Doors creak, and windows clap, and night's foul bird
> Rook'd in the spire screams loud: the gloomy ailes
> Black plaster'd, and hung round with shreds of 'scutcheons
> And tattered coats of arms, send back the sound
> Laden with heavy airs, from the low vaults,
> The mansions of the dead. . . . [70]

The passage continues with a plenitude of ghosts, with "riven trees," and "wild shrieks from hollow tombs." Truly, the *Grave*, far from being a unique depárture in the poetry of its age, is rather the summary and consummation of a century of elegiac tradition.

The generalizing of the elegy in the hands of Blair and his English contemporaries seems to have sapped the vitality from the parent stem; and the contemporary elegiac output in both the broadsides and the *Scots Magazine* reflects this decadence. Soft Sentimentalism did not care to have death too immediate and particular; and hard Sentimentalism craved a more theatrical theme than the denouement of life when all its fitful fever is laid to sleep. The mortuary verse published in early volumes of the *Scots Magazine* serves to illustrate the condition of elegiac poetry in Scotland during a decade or more before the publication of Gray's *Elegy*. Poetry was apparently only an incidental feature of the periodical: much of it was pirated from English magazines; and much more was merely conventional. There were no less than four Biblical paraphrases of a more or less mortuary cast, one of which makes a special bid for popularity by combining the "sons of Levi," the "Pierian wave," and the "sweet Benevolence" of Sentimentalism. Most significant are half a dozen pieces that, like the Biblical paraphrases, generalize upon the subject of death. The following lines *To Melancholy* (1739) might be allotted purely to the influence of Milton, were they not so clearly in the elegiac tradition:

[70] *Ibid.*, line 29 *et seq.*

Hail, Melancholy! gloomy pow'r,
Companion of my lonely hour,
  To sober thoughts confin'd;
Thou sweetly sad ideal guest,
In all thy soothing charms confest,
  Indulge my pensive mind.

Thro' yon dark grove of mournful yews,
With solitary steps, I muse,
  By thy direction led;
Here, cold to pleasure's airy forms,
Consociate with my sister worms,
  And mingle with the dead.

Hail, midnight horrors! awful gloom!
Ye silent regions of the tomb,
  My future peaceful bed;
Here shall my weary eye be clos'd,
And all my sorrows lie repos'd
  In death's eternal shade.

The piece ends in an elegiac apotheosis in which the soul, "sub-lim'd" by religion, aspires upward. *To Melancholy* would seem to constitute another link between the Calvinistic funeral elegy and the generalized graveyard poem. In some of these magazine pieces, Shakespeare is called into requisition, and in one Plato; but most of the images and ideas and sometimes even the plan are clearly derived from elegiac tradition; and, on the other hand, one is occasionally startled with a similarity to some well known Romantic poet. The following *Stanzas, written in Pancras church yard* (1743), for example, cannot but suggest Wordsworth's famous lines beginning "One impulse from the vernal wood":

From wanton scenes,—the shew of fools,
  Ye idle, here repair!
Where wisdom—yet untaught in schools,
  Embalms this calmer air! . . .
Here let me muse!—and wrapt in thought,
  The realms of death survey:
Till, by the view reflective, taught,
  I learn to live today.[71]

---

[71] *Scots Mag.*, VI, 6.

An ending on the vanity of life and the hope of Salvation gives the piece some Christian coloring, and associates its anti-intellectualism with the Calvinistic doctrine of salvation by Grace alone— as well as with the anti-intellectualism of Wordsworth.

The vogue of the funeral elegy came late to Scotland, and seems at first to have arisen among Episcopalians and Jacobites,[72] such as Ninian Paterson. Its period of evolution is, therefore, short; but this evolution illustrates in little the rise and development of the Calvinistic literary consciousness, which, when it once accepted the elegy as tolerable, soon learned to develop it as a stimulant, first of religious enthusiasm, later of personal grief, and later still of a rather indiscriminate emotionality. By degrees, the fear of God, and then even the friend whose loss occasioned the poem, grow less and less prominent: religion gives place to prudential moralizing or to Deistic Sentimentality; and even the sorrow of the mourners and the virtues of the deceased are overwhelmed, as in Blair's *Grave*, with the paraphernalia of emotionalized background. Some pieces on noblemen, soldiers, lawyers, and the like, because they were written as news-items or with a view to patronage, are mere summaries of events or mere panegyric; but those on the clergy show in its purest form the evolution of the Calvinistic mind. Indeed, as soon as Presbyterianism touched the elegy, the *genre* began to develop an emotionalism that brought with it a background of rural nature, of mouldering Gothic ruins, of midnight horrors, of guttering tapers and skeletons and skulls and full-gorged worms. All this was ready to the hand of Robert Blair who generalized the elegiac themes, and produced one of the mortuary classics of a mortuary age—a poem that, if it be not itself Romantic, renders that elusive adjective inapplicable to the Gothic Romance and to Coleridge's *Christabel*.

[72] Even the *débâcle* of '45 did not entirely silence the Jacobite elegists as the laments on Alexander Robertson of Strowan (*Scots Mag.*, XI, 244) and the Earl of Kilmarnock (G. S. Macquoid, *Jacobite Songs and Ballads*, London, n. d., 253), as well as the lines already mentioned on Lochiel, attest.

CHAPTER IX

THE FUNERAL ELEGY IN THE REIGN OF QUEEN ANNE

THE first decade and a half or the eighteenth century, which is roughly synchronous with the reign of Queen Anne, considered itself, not without a certain propriety, as the Augustan Age of English culture. In some sense, it was Augustan, not only because the Latin authors were widely read both in the original and in translation, but also because its ideal of restrained and balanced order is typically Roman. Society would seem to have taken the advice that Walsh gave to Pope, and determined to be, if not as magnificent as the court of Charles I, or as righteous as the Commonwealth, at least outwardly decent and formally correct. It was an age that followed neither the æsthetic ideal of superabundance nor the religious ideal of human need, but the comfortable, though rather uninspired, middle ground of sufficiency.[1] Restraint and order—though usually not logical order —are the practical essentials of every compromise; for compromise is like a bridge, static and rigid, and any instability of the supporting sides can easily destroy it. The Neo-classical compromise, therefore, held strictly to a prescribed decorum; and, since peace was the chief desire of the vast majority of persons,[2] it remained, and flourished; and, in the eyes of the common citizen, its decorum was consecrated as a law of nature: indeed, when writers of the age referred to "nature," they would sometimes seem to mean hardly more than its social or artistic conventions.[3] The government, the Church, and the nobles, were, on the whole, desirous of maintaining the *status quo*; for the continuity of their own enviable position depended largely upon it; and Queen Anne, unlike her successor, had tact enough to balance the Whigs and the Tories[4]

---

[1] See Chapter III. Sir Leslie Stephen finds the period to be characterized by a "hard worldly wisdom," which he attributes to the club-life of the age (*English Literature and Society in the Eighteenth Century*, New York, 1904, 79).

[2] E. Bernbaum, *English Poets of the Eighteenth Century*, New York, 1918, *Introduction*.

[3] E.g., Pope, *Essay on Criticism*, lines 139-140, and *Essay on Man*, line 13; see also references in J. E. Brown, *Critical Opinions of Samuel Johnson*, Princeton, N. J., 160 *et seq.*

[4] I. S. Leadam, *The History of England (1702-1760)*, London, 1909, 1-3, 34-35, 46, 123 *et seq.*, 160 *et seq.*, 178 *et seq.*, 211, and 218-222.

and so keep both fairly well content. The ministries were generally coalitions of varying tone; and her own High Church inclinations made it easier for her than for King William to command on occasion Tory support. This settled aspect of Church and State was buttressed by the constant fear of renewed religious wars "When men fell out, they knew not why"; and the truculence of the masses and their tumults at the time of the Sacheverell trial[5] impressed upon the minds of the thoughtful the necessity of some stable compromise.

Thus the Court, the Church, and the great houses, all supported the established order; and thus, in literature and the arts, the preponderating influence of their patronage was directed toward a Roman restraint of emotion and orderliness of detail. Roman literature, moreover, they knew and admired from the efficient interlinear translations and other devices then in vogue in the schools and universities;[6] and a number could actually read Latin with sufficient ease to enjoy it. In either case, they accepted it on the recommendation of the Renaissance and the Church; and found that it conformed most nearly to the aristocratic quiescence that Augustan sensibilities affected and admired. Emotionalism and irregularity, indeed, were discredited[7]: they were the paraphernalia of the dissenting commercial orders whose vagaries had wrought the shocking havoc of the Civil War, cut down the trees in ancestral parks, shot cannon-balls through ancestral mansions, and chopped out the colored windows and hacked the statuary in the churches. The hand of conservatism was turned against such doings; and institutionalized patronage,[8] therefore, favored an

[5] *Ibid.*, 168 *et seq.*; W. E. H. Lecky, *History of England in the Eighteenth Century*, New York,, 1892, I, 63 *et seq.*, 259, and 385. On the London mob in general, see Sir W. Besant, *London in the Eighteenth Century*, London, 1902, 475 *et seq.*

[6] See the present author, *The Theory of Translation in the Eighteenth Century*, *Neophilologus*, VI, 244-245.

[7] One must not, on the other hand, suppose that it was an intellectual age, comparable to the age of the humanists or even to the reign of Charles I: in science, it could hardly compare with the period of Boyle and of Newton's great discovery that preceded, or that of Hal-

ley and the Hunter brothers that followed; Bishop Berkeley, its one great philosopher, was ridiculed and neglected; and a similar fate befell Bentley and Theobald in literary scholarship. The age was one, not of learning, but of popularization; and the *Spectator* is perhaps the most characteristic single manifestation of its spirit and ideals.

[8] As yet patronage by the public at large had hardly come into existence. See Aldis, *Camb. Hist. of Eng. Lit.*, New York, 1907-1916, XI, 311 *et seq.*, and the present author, *Queen Anne's Act: a Note on English Copyright*, *Mod. Lang. Notes*, XXXVI, 146 *et seq.*, and the bibliographies appended to both.

opposition to melancholy and its psychological complement, "enthusiasm."[9] Although restrained emotion was allowed, lack of positive emotion was the more usual fact;[10] and herein lay an important distinction between truly Classical—that is, Hellenic—art, and the product of the pseudo-Latin "Classicism" of England.[11] Thus the æsthetic of Neo-classicism dominated all the arts: the square-cut gardens, French in the reign of Charles II, Dutch under William and Mary;[12] country mansions on Palladian models designed by Sir John Vanbrugh, with the stable balancing the kitchen in two projecting wings, showy and spacious, but cold in winter and inconvenient all the year around; the operas and oratorios of Handel in which the perfect symmetry of musical phrasing is maintained, no matter at what cost to the rhythm or meaning of the text; tragedies according to the "Aristotelian" unities of Castelvetro and on the model of Addison's *Cato* or later of Voltaire; and, so far as poetry was concerned, satire, epistle, epic, eclogue, georgic, and occasional pieces, all planned on Latin prototypes, and phrased with endless parallel structure in endless heroic couplets. All the arts were designed according to the æsthetic of imitation,[13] which is the outward and visible sign of reverence for authority, and of symmetry which is the outward semblance of orderliness and regular repose. Diction must be simple, and sentence-structure perspicuous—a sort of refined colloquial style on both prose and verse that may well owe something to the habit of conversation in the coffee-house. Alexander Pope was, indeed, the typical poet of the age; but he was also typical in that

---

[9] This largely explains the bitterness against the Quakers in the seventeenth century and against the Methodists in the eighteenth.

[10] That is, omitting the *sæva indignatio* of satire, which is negative and critical.

[11] The other two chief distinctions were the common weakness in fundamental unity in the Neo-classical work, for all its symmetry; and the imperfect cohesion of form and content, occasioned by the doctrine of formal imitation.

[12] James's translation of Le Blond in 1703 marks the beginning of the new Romantic gardening. See Myra Reynolds, *The Treatment of Nature in English Poetry*, Chicago, 1909, Chapter V. The formal style continued to dominate, however, for some years; and Addison and Pope did not actively champion the new taste until about the end of the reign of Queen Anne.

[13] Usually in the sense of copying masterpieces. See the present author, *Aristotelian* μίμησις *in Eighteenth Century England*, Publ. Mod. Lang. Assoc. Am., XXXVI, 372 *et seq.* Miss Reed (*Background of Gray's Elegy*, New York, 1924, 33) suggests that the prevalence of translation and imitation first arose as the only refuge of the Neo-classicist from divinity and morality.

he composed two elegiac pieces in a melancholy tone quite foreign to his other works.

Literary patronage, to be sure, was largely institutional; for the general public was ready for literature only in the homeopathic doses of *Spectator* leaflets. And yet there existed a social group rather less committed to Neo-classicism than the State and the Establishment: the Non-conformists, numerous in the larger centres of population, more or less organized and often wealthy, had been trained to tastes that craved quite a different literary pabulum;[14] and, as the old prejudice against the arts died out among them, there arose Isaac Watts, Mrs. Elizabeth Rowe, and others, who purveyed to this special class literature and even drama according to its desires.[15] Former chapters have noted the fundamental religious bias of this group toward Calvinism, and they have also noted a certain falling away from the strict spirit of the doctrine: the use of elegies at funerals, the introduction of original hymns, and most notably the rise of a new mental attitude in which the melancholy of life and death was cultivated for its own sake, and found to be agreeable. In short, the funeral elegy of the latter seventeenth century has chronicled the beginnings of Sentimentalism among the Calvinistic non-conformists. These beginnings were coincident with, and doubtless caused by, important changes, political, social, and intellectual: the practical removal of the disabilities laid upon dissent;[16] the wealth, slowly at first but constantly increasing, of the commercial classes,[17] with a consequent

[14] The social alignment of bourgeois-dissenter-Whig against Tory opponents continued even until the end of the century (E. Halévy, *A History of the English People in 1815*, New York, 1924, 372). The religious and melancholic tastes of the new classes of readers is discussed by Sir Leslie Stephen (*op. cit.*, 155-156) and by Miss Reed, (*op. cit.*, 111-112).

[15] A. Nicoll, *History of Early Eighteenth Century Drama*, Cambridge, 1925, 3 *et passim*.

[16] Lecky, *op. cit.*, I, 252 *et seq.*; Halévy, *op. cit.*, 352 *et seq.*; and H. S. Skeats, *History of the Free Churches of England*, London, 1868, 335 *et seq.* Dissent was declining both socially and intellectually; and the sects were more and

more subdividing into differing shades of opinion.

[17] The cause of this increase in wealth during the first half of the eighteenth century was chiefly the growth of foreign trade, as evidenced, for example, in the rise of Liverpool; during the second half of the century, the middle classes grew rich from the loot of India and the Industrial Revolution. J. B. Botsford, *English Society in the Eighteenth Century As Influenced from Oversea*, New York, 1924, 121-122 etc. A few of the great mercantile families were quickly absorbed in the old aristocracy, as for instance the Pitts; some achieved lesser honors, like Sir John Barnard, and the Barings who finally achieved the peerage in 1835 when the Whigs came into power; but,

improvement in living conditions;[18] and the discovery of scientific law[19] with the consequent Deistic trend in religion.[20] All three forces tended toward an easy optimism; for religious toleration gave freedom from clerical trammels; wealth, from pressing economic need; and the realization of scientific law dominating the universe, from the fear of an immediate and wrathful God. The new liberation at first affected only the wealthier and more intellectual dissenters, the *haute bourgeosie*;[21] but, as this upper stratum included in large measure the dissenting clergy, these bodies, and especially the Presbyterians,[22] were gradually brought over to the new point of view, which in its early stages may be described—if one may be allowed the appearance of a *contradictio in adjecto*— as an optimistic Calvinism.[23] Theologically, the new attitude approached, if not coincided with, Deism: God the Father became merely a distant and vaguely benevolent Creator; and a redeeming Savior, apparently inessential to such a scheme of things, sank more

during the eighteenth century, most even of the richest, like Lord Mayor Beckford, had to be content with merely municipal honors, and so remained in the bourgeois class, and started to develop, as in the France of the period, a nobility of finance. (Cf. Lecky, *op. cit.*, Chapter V.) Quite as important socially and politically as this increase in wealth was the improvement in banking and insurance that made it possible for a mercantile family to retain and pass on its accumulations. (See J. Ashton, *Social Life in the Reign of Queen Anne*, New York, 1925, 85 *et seq* and 102 *et seq.*)

[18] See Dorothy George, *London Life in the Eighteenth Century*, New York, 1925, 169 *et seq.*; and S. N. Patten, *The Development of English Thought*, New York, 1899, 193. The bills of mortality for London, moreover, show that human life was lengthening (Sir W. Besant, *London in the Eighteenth Century*, London, 1902, 381). The growing tendency of the rich Londoner, moreover, to remove for the week-ends, if not every night, to a suburban "hunting box," unquestionably helped to break up the solidarity of dissenting congregations, very much as the habit of Sunday motoring has tended in recent times to lessen church attendance. The rise of Bath and other spas and the increase of travel must also have had some effect. Just before

the rise of Methodism, dissent was certainly waning (Besant, *op. cit.*, 168, 361 etc. Cf. Lecky, *op. cit.*, III, 4).

[19] The discoveries of Newton served not only to put astronomy upon a surer foundation, but also popularized the science, and aroused the imagination by its cosmic immensity: indeed, Addison's Romantic theories in the *Spectator* papers on the *Pleasures of the Imagination* owe something of their inspiration to "those wild fields of æther, that reach in height as far as from Saturn to the fixed stars, and run abroad almost to infinitude."

[20] Patten, *op. cit.*, 183; and D. Bogue and J. Bennett, *History of the Dissenters*, London, 1808-1810, III, 217 *et seq.*

[21] See E. Halévy, *op. cit.*, 355. The cleavage increased in the latter part of the century.

[22] Even in Scotland, an analogous change took place; H. G. Graham (*The Social Life of Scotland in the Eighteenth Century*, London, 1906, 348 *et seq.*) goes so far as to say that between 1700 and 1800 the Church of Scotland, though under the same official creed, "followed two utterly different religions, and worshipped two opposite gods."

[23] Lecky (*op. cit.*, VI, 265) makes a similar comparison between Rousseau's characteristic doctrine and his Calvinistic origins.

and more into the background. Indeed, as early as 1718, a conference was held in London including the three chief dissenting bodies, Presbyterians, Independents, and Baptists, to counteract the growth among their members of Arianism;[24] and, in 1719, James Pierce was expelled from his Presbyterian pastorate for denying the equality of Christ with God the Father.[25] From the "modified Calvinism" of Watts and Doddridge,[26] Unitarianism was developing, despite conference and expulsion; and Protestantism was turning from a militant and ecstatic religion to a rationalistic and impersonal philosophy. For those affected by this change, religion lost its revivalistic force, and prayer its theological significance; and thus, for a class of persons whose emotions were strong, and yet whose position in society would not allow them to expend the emotional surplus in mob violence, and who had not been schooled in the decorum of restraint, the old outlet of religious enthusiasm was being closed by the increasing intellectualism of the chapel services.

The inception of this change seems somewhat to have antedated the return of the bourgeois class to general literary and artistic patronage;[27] and their outlook on life is reflected in the content, both the *ethos* and *pathos*, of their artistic performance: the *pathos*, or emotional side, was greatly augmented; the *ethos*, or intellectual and moral significance, suffered a strange distortion. God was not in his heaven; but all was right in the world. An expansive sense of the rightness of everything, especially human nature, seemed the natural attitude of life for a class of persons who were exchanging the battlefield of religious strife for the primrose paths of peace and plenty.[28] The old doctrine that man was born to sin, and could attain to Salvation only after a rigorous discipline enforced by the Grace of God, was discarded; the old Cavalier doctrine

[24] A. S. Tuberville, *English Men and Manners in the Eighteenth Century*, Oxford, 1926, 313 *et seq.*
[25] Stephen (*History of English Thought in the Eighteenth Century*, London, 1902, I, 428 *et seq.*) dates the rise of thoroughgoing Unitarianism from 1769.
[26] Halévy, *op. cit.*, 354 *et seq.*
[27] See J. W. Krutch, *Comedy and Conscience after the Restoration*, New York, 1924, 153 *et seq.* See also a review by the present author, *Mod. Lang Notes*, XLI, 332 *et seq.* The lower bourgeoisie read few books (Besant, *op. cit.*, 318, and 341); but they had news-sheets, pamphlets, broadsides, and the drama; and it is significant that broadsides and the drama first show Sentimentalism. On the drama, see A. Nicoll, *Restoration Drama*, Cambridge, 1923, 257 *et seq.*
[28] Cf. I. Babbitt, *Rousseau and Romanticism*, Boston, 1919, Chapters IV and V; and E. Bernbaum, *The Drama of Sensibility*, Boston, 1915, Chapter I, and 115 *et seq.*

that man was born a boor and must be educated by the Classics into social charm and usefulness, was, to this class of persons, new, difficult of execution, and not entirely to their tastes. They were indifferent to formal beauty and to logical symmetry.[29] The intensely social view of life expressed in Neo-classicism did not accord with the individualism fostered by the uncertainty and the keen competition of mercantile conditions.[30] They took life too seriously to enjoy Congreve's *Way of the World*, or even to appreciate to the full the gaiety of Prior or the dexterous felicity of *The Rape of the Lock*. They were especially anxious themselves to be taken seriously, and not as figures of fun, as in Restoration comedy; and this serious temper, derived partly from Calvinism, partly perhaps from the uncertainties of their occupation, made them express their surplus emotions in melancholy rather than exuberance, and, at a later date, gave it a practical turn in the direction of philanthropy.[31] Thus neither the old ideal of their own class, nor the ideal of the aristocracy, nor the compromise of Neo-classicism, entirely satisfied their new requirements; and, by degrees, during the latter seventeenth century, there had arisen a new ethics—or denial of ethics—in which human nature and "natural" human instincts were exalted and in which the old disciplines, religious and cultural, both in life and in art suffered discontinuance. The basis of the new philosophy was emotionalism, an easier, and more democratic ideal than the intellectual pursuit of the Renaissance: it was individualistic, for the cultivation of the emotions requires no social interplay of mind upon mind; it took life seriously, and so came to specialize in the pensive, the atrabilious, and even the horrific; it took itself and its own melancholy most seriously, and so achieved its neatest summary in the lyric cry of the *Weltschmerz*. Original Genius replaced Imitation as a guide to art and to life; and, according to this facile theory, the aspirations of the ages were declared to be within easy reach; and a royal road to all that men desire was advertised as opening out before the newly affluent

[29] Stephen (*English Thought*, I, 34) remarks on the characteristic "indifference to logical symmetry" of the English mind.

[30] One wonders whether the later interest in the exotic may not have developed largely from the foreign interests of the mercantile classes.

[31] See Sir Walter Besant, *London in the Eighteenth Century*, London, 1902, 154 *et seq.*; G. F. Richardson, *A Neglected Aspect of the English Romantic Revolt*, Univ. of Cal. Publ. Mod. Phil., Berkeley, Cal., 1915, III, 294 *et seq.*

importer of calicoes and the successful, retired dealer in mercery. Such a philosophy could not but allure converts from among the wealthy merchant class so recently recruited from humble origins;[32] and when, during the reign of Queen Anne, it seemed to find expression in the writings of an eminent personage who was at once a man of letters and a lord, it received the inestimable advantage of respectability, a quality peculiarly grateful to the middle class.[33]   Indeed, the philosophy of Shaftesbury,[34] although it in no sense started the wave of Sentimentalism[35] that swept Europe, must nevertheless have been important in crystallizing the doctrine[36] and in giving it the sanction of eminent authority.[37]

[32] At this period, most of the merchant-class were of humble origin, partly because, as already explained, the younger sons of the aristocracy no longer went into trade, and partly because business was only by degrees growing stable enough so that wealth could be hereditary in the mercantile families and culture implanted in the second or third generation.

[33] This increase in respectability doubtless led persons who had long held such sentiments to voice them the more readily; and Shaftesbury's very phrasing of them doubtless helped others too to put them into words.   The necessity of a moralistic pose to cover courtly license during the reign of William and Mary seems to have induced Sentimentalism among the upper classes to some extent. See A. Nicoll, *Restoration Drama*, 251 *et seq.*

[34] Philosophically, Shaftesbury may be described as a continuator of the Cambridge Platonists in their struggle against Hobbes: his identification of beauty and goodness, from which Sentimentalism can so easily develop, was "prevalent among the Renaissance Platonists" (W. A. R. Kerr, *Mod. Phil.*, V, 413, and C. G. Osgood, *Stud. in Phil.*, XIV, 168 *et seq.*); and, in order to sugarcoat his somewhat Stoical ethics, he glossed over its inherent rigor (Esther A. Tiffany, *Publ. Mod. Lang. Assoc. Am.*, XXXVIII, 642 *et seq.*) and so produced a philosophy that could easily be interpreted as Sentimental, whether it was intended to be so or not. Perhaps, moreover, it is not too fanciful to suppose that the Whig politics of his illustrious grandfather and of his own

political career gave him, in some sense, the same mental evolution as the dissenters who composed so important a section of that party.   At all events, he showed a Deistic trend that with them usually accompanied the development of emotional optimism. Cf. Stephen, *English Thought*, II, 19.

[35] Some critics would seem to date the beginnings of Sentimentalism during the early eighteenth century (e.g., T. O. Wedel, *Stud. in Phil.*, XXIII, 435-436), although Bruntière, significantly enough, is surprised that "so profound a transformation" could occur so "swiftly." The present author would date its social, and even its sporadic literary appearance as early as the reign of Charles II. (See A. Nicoll, *Restoration Drama*, 257 *et seq.*, and Alderman on the sermons of Whichcote, *Publ. Mod. Lang. Assoc. Am.*, XXXVIII, 183 *et seq.*, and the present author, *Mod. Lang. Rev.*, XXII, 15 *et seq.*)

[36] Shaftesbury, in spite of his fragmentary, somewhat incoherent, style, had clearly such a tendency (E. Bernbaum, *The Drama of Sensibility*, Boston, 1915, 114 *et seq.*); but its philosophic codification was developed by F. Hutcheson in his *Inquiry into the Original of Our Ideas of Beauty and Virtue* (1725), and taught from his chair of moral philosophy at Glasgow.

[37] The initiatory influence of Shaftesbury has been somewhat overstated; but, as an auxiliary force, it must have been considerable.   For English influences, see C. A. Moore (*Shaftesbury and the Ethical Poets in England, Publ. Mod. Lang. Assoc. Am.*, XXXI, 264 *et seq.*); for a

The Neo-classical compromise then, because it barred the emotionalism that the trading classes craved and that they could no longer express in their religion, was acceptable only to a limited degree among them; and, as the trading class grew in wealth and cultural ambitions, and increasingly patronized the arts, there developed a new and different sort of artistic performance to meet their increasing demand. In the person of Addison, the *Spectator*, for the most part, expresses pure Neo-classicism, restrained, decorous, Augustan, vaguely Christian and definitely religious, but disapproving of religious melancholy as "worn out among us" and as arising from "weakness of understanding": its philosophy, like Sentimentalism, is a complacent optimism; but it is not emotional.[38] Steele, on the other hand, rooted in the Calvinism of the Irish Church, finds in the contemplation of death "a sort of delight, which is alternately mixed with terror and sorrow." He lingers over a death-bed scene with exclamatory realism of detail, describing "those lips . . . so pale and livid" and moralizing, as in the veriest funeral elegy, upon the theme of *vanitas vanitatis*.[39] His attitude is similar to that of Watts who described the ideal dissenting sermon as "a Mixture of the Instructive and the Pathetick," and who exhorted the minister to dwell "on the most affecting parts largely" with "Pathetick Amplification."[40] Probably Steele and Watts could claim as many readers in the reign of Queen Anne as could Addison. Their public was of a lower social degree; but it was growing with the increase in wealth and education, and in a few years its opinions, by the sheer weight of its numbers, were to dominate English taste.

bibliography of German influence, see *ibid.*, 265 note 2; for French influence, see R. P. Legros (*Diderot et Shaftesbury, Mod. Lang. Rev.*, XIX, 188 *et seq.*); for Italian influence, see the presidential address of Prof. Croce before the Mod. Hum. Res. Assoc., 1923-1924. The present writer does not believe that a philosopher of the difficult style of Shaftesbury—or, indeed, any philosopher—could so quickly impress the mind of a continent, unless his ideas had previously been widely current at least among certain classes. Mankind are little swayed by abstract argument, and are little influenced by intellectual conviction: habit and convenience govern their actions; and the philosophy of the ordinary man is hardly more than a rationalization and justification of actions either habitual or determined upon for very practical reasons. Most of all is this practical, illogical temper characteristic of the average Englishman. See Stephen, *English Thought*, II, 381 *et seq.*

[38] N. B. Addison's approval of Dr. Sherlock's optimistic *Treatise on Death*. See the *Spectator*, Nos. 494, 497, and 513. On the position of Addison and Steele in the culture-history of the age, cf. W. Göricke, *Das Bildungsideal bei Addison und Steele*, Bonn, 1921.

[39] *Spectator*, No. 133. Cf. Miss Reed, *op. cit.*, 112 *et seq.*

[40] I. Watts, *Reliquiæ Juvenales*, London, 1734, 100 *et seq.*

This new emotionalism impressed itself not merely upon the themes and ethical substance, but on the very forms of the arts that the bourgeoisie patronized. The new æsthetic was dynamic, excitant, Dionysiac: it aimed to delight and arouse by the unexpected, rather than, as in Hellenic art, to quiet and satisfy by the inevitable. Reared on ship-board or in the shop or counting-house rather than at the public school and University,[41] the new class of readers cared little for imitation of Classical prototypes; but they did demand vivid, concrete material that would allow an outlet to their surplus emotions and lend amusement to their leisure hours. Thus arose the æsthetic of the tired business man. To accomplish these ends, they sought larger units and more fluid models[42] than the set forms of the Neo-classical "kinds," and a freer style than the nice confines of the heroic couplet. "Imitation," by degrees, began to mean the Realistic depiction of "Nature"—human nature, as they liked to think of it, and rural nature as they observed it on their Sunday visits to the country,[43] and finally as they knew it on vacation trips to the Lakes or even on their foreign travels;[44] and, in the third quarter of the century, all idea of imitation was abandoned[45] in favor of Original Genius, a conception entirely consonant with the new optimistic attitude toward

[41] Besant, op. cit., 236 et seq.

[42] The earlier tendencies were toward the imitation of Milton, Spenser, Shakespeare, and Pindar; later came a repudiation of models as such in favor of Original Genius, and Wordsworth even repudiated English poetic diction. These later poets, however, seldom lived up to the letter of such theories.

[43] This partly explains its initial pastoral unreality. The eighteenth-century Deistic idealization of Nature was incomprehensible to the real country-people, who saw rural life in the light of common day. The attitude of the Cumberland peasantry toward Wordsworth is significant; and Wordsworth is but the culmination, in both his descriptions and his pantheism, of Thomson and his school.

[44] The psychological Law of Limen operates on any art that depends on surprise and exaltation: the stimulant must be increased in order to sustain the effect. Thus when the novelty of the rural was exhausted, literature turned to the archaic and the exotic; when melancholy was exhausted, literature turned to the horrific and the Titanic. (Cf. D. Mornet, who has traced this evolution in the French literature of the period, Le Romanticisme en France au XVIIIe Siècle, Paris, 1912.) How far this turning to the exotic was occasioned by the actual voyages of Cook and others (See C. B. Tinker, Nature's Simple Plan, Princeton, N. J., 1922), and how far by the natural operation of psychological law, is hard to determine— just as it is hard to know how much the archaic movement was caused by the demands of psychological evolution and how much by such accidents as the opening of the British Museum and the publication of Mallet's History of Denmark in the mid-eighteenth century.

[45] See the present author, Aristotelian μίμησις in Eighteenth Century England, Publ. Mod. Lang. Assoc. Am., XXXVI, 372 et seq.

mankind. Thus were "imitation" and Aristotle discarded and models cast aside in favor of an artistic empiricism based on the titillation of the feelings. In drama, Sentimentalism broke down the "ancient" unities and rules, first in comedy, in the plays of Cibber and Steele, later in tragedy in the works of the London jeweller, George Lillo.[46] It substituted an appeal to the emotions for symmetry of form[47]: thus comedy was exaggerated into a sort of lachrymose farce, and tragedy into moralistic melodrama. Painting[48] and music[49] were slow to show the effect; but gardening gave early illustration of the new taste. Even in the seventeenth century, the wealthier merchants, relaxing somewhat their Calvinistic taboo against amusements, began to frequent the spas and pleasure gardens at Hampstead and Tunbridge; and later, by degrees, they ceased to live, as they had since time immemorial,[50] over their shops; deserted the "City," as did Pope's father; and converted their week-end "hunting boxes" into suburban residences.[51] Thus at an early period arose the new fashions in gardening;[52] for this class of patrons came in contact with this art before they began to collect pictures, or demand a music to their taste. In fact, the vogue of the Sentimental landscape spread so rapidly that the axes of Kent and "Capability" Brown, its two chief practitioners,

[46] This change is amply chronicled in the works already cited by Nicoll, Krutch, and Bernbaum.

[47] Neither the former nor the latter type of play truly accomplished katharsis, or saw life steadily and saw it whole. Both were class-expressions, with the limitations of class-psychology. Aristocratic Restoration drama had little of pathos; and bourgeois sentimental drama had little of ethos.

[48] Down to the mid-eighteenth century, painting was an aristocratic and largely an imported art. See Miss Reynolds, op. cit., Chapter VI.

[49] Puritanism had destroyed music as a national art; and, in the early eighteenth century, like painting, it was largely imported and aristocratic. It is significant, however, that even Handel set the pastoralism of Milton's "Let me wander not unseen" in a pensive, minor strain, with an almost dissonant close harmony between voice and accompaniment; and it is not insignificant that J-J. Rousseau should have initiated the musical change on the Continent with his Le Devin du Village.

[50] See S. O. Addy, The Evolution of the English House, London, 1910, Chapter VI; J. A. Gotch, The Growth of the English House, London, 1915; and the present author, Englische Studien, LX, 238 et seq.

[51] Besant, op. cit., 74 et passim and 412; and Tuberville, op. cit., 132. The rise of the suburbs comes largely in the second half of the century (Miss George, op. cit., 2-3, 77 et seq. and 329). On the interest of the London cit in pleasure-gardens in the seventeenth century, see W. Besant, London in the Time of the Stuarts, London, 1903, appendix VII. See also Robert Lloyd's The Cit's Country Box (1757) with its description of the garden ornamented with a "temple Gothic or Chinese."

[52] Miss Reynolds, op. cit., 252 and 255. It is significant that the Londoners Pope and Addison led the way.

shortly destroyed more ancient tree-lined vistas and straight-planted avenues than all their predecessors in the army of Cromwell. For the most part, these changes, ethical and æsthetic, made their first impress on the funeral elegy, the one literary expression that Puritanism regularly allowed. Indeed, as previous chapters have shown, the funeral elegy had developed overt Sentimentalism more than a decade before Cibber's *Love's Last Shift,*[53] and the new gardening can hardly be said to appear until Addison and Pope began to recommend it in the closing years of the reign of Queen Anne.[54] Thus elegiac literature, though of small literary value, is highly significant as a harbinger preceding still the progress of the Muses.

During the reign of Queen Anne, the funeral elegy shows but slight development: aristocratic eulogies and Calvinistic mortuary pieces continue to persist; but poems that show some sort of combination of these two types were increasing, and Sentimentalism also was growing, especially in connection with the charnel-house landscape. Among Anglicans at least, the elegy was no longer used as before in the funeral services, though it was still probably passed around on sheets gruesomely embellished with crude woodcuts: among the dissenters who still used the elegy at funerals, it was an edification to the mourners rather than an honor to the deceased, and was quite as likely to express a warning to the former as a eulogy of the latter. Time hardly varied nor custom changed the infinite monotony of its themes and style, its efflorescence of paper rhetoric and its tumid extension of sense into nonsense. The *Miscellanea Sacra* illustrates this persistent popularity of older as well as newer elegiac types. Intended apparently for a public at once indiscriminate and undiscriminating, the volume is well named a "miscellany"; it combines in one anthology *The Triumphs of Death* by "Mr. James Sherly"[55] and Prior's *Considerations* on *Psalm LXXXVIII;*[56] it combines Mrs. Wharton's

---

[53] There had been, to be sure, some earlier suggestions of the Sentimental in the plays of Crowne and others. See Nicoll, *Restoration Drama*, 257 *et seq.*

[54] Miss Reynolds in her *General Summary* (*op. cit.*, especially 330) puts the date of the rise of the new gardening even later. She takes Thomson's *Seasons* as beginning the movement in poetry; but she does not discuss the elegy. A comparison of her results with those of the present writer serves all the more to bring out the priority of the elegy in this development.

[55] *Miscellanea Sacra: Collected by Samuel Phillips,* third ed., London, 1707. The continued popularity of the Elizabethan literature of death is significant.

[56] *Ibid.,* I, 5. Under this influence, even Prior shows an inclination toward the ghastly.

"metaphysical" rendering of the *Lamentations of Jeremiah*[57] with a version of the "Eheu fugaces" of Horace;[58] it has poems in heroic couplets,[59] in octosyllabics,[60] and in long stanzas;[61] it has two excellent death-bed scenes[62] to make the mixture slab and good and a funeral elegy on an "eminent Divine" that lingers over "Wretched Mortality."[63] Last but not least, is *The Malcontent*,[64] a poem in neat heroic couplets that manages in one passage to combine the Neo-classical urge for peace and quiet with a mortuary landscape and a reminiscence of Hamlet's soliloquy, and to produce from the decoction a tasty *olla podrida* of Sentimentalism:

> My swelling Griefs intending to allay,
> 'Mongst winding Rocks I took my rugged way;
> In the Vast Cliffs a Natural Vault I found,
> Whose Entrance creeping Ivy hem'd around.
> Each object did with my sad Thoughts agree,
> And kindly seem'd to sympathize with me.
> With Joy, I rushed into the lonesome Nook,
> Then into these pathetick Numbers broke.
>
> Oh! when will *Nature* take the life she gave,
> And lodge me safe from Trouble in the *Grave?*
> Sleep there alone deserves the Name of *Rest*,
> No frightful Dreams the sleep of Death infest.

In both title and content, this strange compilation suggests that it was assembled for the purpose of appealing to the ordinary, bourgeois reader; and, as such, it is of interest as illustrating the unformed chaos of his literary preferences. The need of borrowing as far afield as Shirley, moreover, illustrates the paucity of poetic material suited to such tastes; and the editor, who was apparently as uncertain as his readers—perhaps even more so!—took refuge in a strange assemblage of poetic nondescripts. The number, however, of melancholy, or at least serious, pieces suggests that in one respect at least he had gauged his reader's demands; and so certain was he of this melancholy bias that he sometimes belied his title, and included lines, like those quoted from *The Malcontent*, that

---

[57] *Ibid.*, II, 73. See Chapter V for a fuller treatment of this poem.
[58] *Ibid.*, II, 24. See Horace, *Odes, Lib.*, II, xiv.
[59] E.g., *ibid.*, II, 15.
[60] *Ibid.*, II, 29 and 85.
[61] *Ibid.*, I, 18.
[62] *Ibid.*, II, 23 and 62-63.
[63] *Ibid.*, I, 18.
[64] *Ibid.*, II, 15. The title sounds Elizabethan, but the poem itself can hardly be so.

have no direct religious significance whatever. Thus one must infer either that the editor and his appreciative readers—who consumed at least three editions of the book—felt that sadness and religion were the same, or that they had made up their minds to enjoy the former under the cloak of the latter, and were already grown adepts in the mysteries of "sensibility."

Equally miscellaneous are the broadside elegies of the period, which show such variety as to suggest that their original *raison d'être* was no longer sufficient to commend them to popular attention. There is the veiled journalistic propaganda of the *Elegy On the much Lamented Death of Captain Thomas Green* (1705)[65] in answer to a sheaf of broadsides detailing his misdeeds as a pirate.[66] Another broadside takes the occasion of the death of Louis XIV to write political satire on his Huguenot policy.[67] There is an elegiac lampoon on Partridge, the almanack-maker (1708), who, under a picture of skeletons *à la* Doré, is dubbed "A Cobbler, Starmonger, *and* Quack."[68] As the middle classes grew less pious, they enlarged the scope of realism in their elegies; and Edward Milington, "the famous Auctioneer," is passed down to posterity with a vivid description of his professional practices.[69] The comedy of the piece is perhaps unintentional. Sir Roger L'Estrange (1704) is eulogized for refining the morals of the age[70]: the style of the elegy has a good measure of Neo-classical aptitude of phrase, and it combines Biblical and Latin allusion. The sentiments are intensely moral, and any lack of the mortuary in the lines is amply atoned for, as the accompanying illustration shows, by the lavish expenditure of black ink both on the border and in the four symbolic cuts. The dismal tone of the Commonwealth was by no means dead; and it lingered especially among the dissenting clergy, who, having once assumed the elegy, seem to have been loath to surrender it. Benjamin Keach (1704), a "Faithful and Laborious Minister" of Baptist persuasion, was elegized in the Puritan high style.[71] The author starts *in medias res*, with "Convulsions"

[65] Brit. Mus. broadside.
[66] See *Brit. Mus. Cat. sub.* Green, Thomas.
[67] *An Epitaph on the Death of the French King* (Nat. Lib. Scot., XXIV).
[68] Bagford Coll., III, No. 74.
[69] *Elegy Upon the Lamented Death of Edward Milington* (Brit. Mus. broadside).

[70] *An Elegy On the Much Lamented Death of Sir Roger L'Estrange* (Brit. Mus. broadside).
[71] *An Elegy On the much Lamented Death of that Faithful and Laborious Minister of the Gospel, Mr. Benjamin Keach* (Brit. Mus. broadside).

AN ELEGY

ON

The Much Lamented DEATH

OF

Sir Roger L Eftrange,

Who Departed this Life on *Monday* the 11*th*. day of *December* 1704. In the 88*th* Year of his Age.

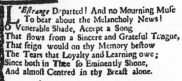

L'*Eftrange* Departed! And no Mourning Mufe
  To bear about the Melancholy News!
O Venerable Shade, Accept a Song
That flows from a Sincere and Grateful Tongue,
That feign would on thy Memory beftow
The Tears that Loyalty and Learning owe;
Since both in Thee fo Eminently Shone,
And almoft Centred in thy Breaft alone.

Ah! Who fhall now Thy bright Example give,
And Teach us how to Write and how to Live!
Who fhall Refine our Morals with our Tongue,
Or make our Language Beautiful and Strong!
None, none can tread the Paths which thou haft prefs'd,
L'*Eftrange*'s Worth fhould in his Words be drefs'd,
Thy Rifing Glories fhine above our Reach,
And Dare the Impotence of Human Speech.

Hail, Bright Unbodied Being, gone from hence
To be all Intellectual Eye and Senfe,
To Reign with Martyrs, and with Kings Dethron'd,
Rewarded for that Caufe the Juft have own'd.
Look down from thy Sublime Abode and fee
What Homage we would pay thy Loyalty,
What Obelisks we to thy Name would raife,
If Numbers were not wanting to thy Praife,
And 'twas in Nature's Power or in Arts,
To make our Tongues but equal to our Hearts.

But we to Verfe in vain muft have recourfe,
Where are there Words of a fufficient Force?.
Since thou the Genius of our Speech art fled,
Exprefiion needs muft Languish and be Dead.

Yet will the Mufe to thy Deferts be juft
And with her Tears bedew thy Learned Duft,
Though Faction Grins at thy lamented Fall,
And laughs to fee the Rife of *Dagon* and of *Baal*.
Adieu, thou bright Intelligence above
Thy Country's Pride, without thy Country's Love,
Alive diftinguifh'd for unfhaken Truth,
In *Old Age* Injur'd, and Traduc'd in *Touth*;
Juft to thy God, thy Neighbour, and thy Prince,
Thine *Actions* the Refult of *Thoughtful Senfe*;
All of a Piece fhould thy Bright Life be drawn,
The fame in its Declenfion as its Dawn.

What if thy Hoary Worth neglected lies,
And to thy Fame no Pyramids arife?
What if no Pomp attends thy Funeral Herfe,
And nothing decks thy Tomb but empty Verfe,
To Future Times thou muft Tranfmitted be,
Immortal by thy felf, though not by me.
In thy defence paft *Authors* fhall Unite,
Since thou haft more than done paft *Authors* Right;
Fam'd *Seneca* with *Cicero* fhall joyn,
Both *Heathens*, yet by thee made both Divine;
While by thy Means *Jofephus Englifh* Speaks,
And *Æfop* Edifies beyond the *Greeks*;
inftructs the Wicked, and Reforms the Loofe
With Morals of Importance and of Ufe,
Equal to theirs, thy deathlefs Works fhall be,
And thou fhalt live by them, and they by thee.

EPITAPH.

HEre lies an *Inftance* of one dead and gone.
  That Wrote, but never Scribled Pro and Con;
Who might be taken for a Bright Example
By Davenant, and the Mafter of the Temple;
Could thofe two Scribes Wealths Tempting Baits defie,
And live like him, that they like him might die.

London: Printed by *D. Edwards* in the Year 1704.

in his "tender Breast," experiences "dismal Fear" and "black Despair," and for a time is quite enamoured of capitalized passions in the abstract. The "sable Shades of Night" supply the setting; and he proceeds to lament the "Reverend Keach" both for himself and for the congregation. But even here, the tone is milder than of yore: there is no reference to disease, or putrifaction, or worms. Broadside elegies, in fact, were growing less significant and less numerous than in former decades. They were losing their place in the funeral services, even of the dissenters; and, as a mere mortuary compliment, they could more fittingly be published in a pamphlet or a volume of poems.

These elegies during the reign of Queen Anne published in books and pamphlets, unlike the legitimate poetry of the reign of Charles II, supply an abundance of mortuary detail. There are, to be sure, some purely Neo-classical pieces, like Edmund Smith's lines on John Phillips;[72] but the mournful had become an elegiac convention, almost as fixed and artificial as "nature" in the pastoral. As in the reign of William and Mary, poets of quite an opposite temper on occasion assume it: it had become a sort of Sunday-and-funeral manner, the recognized decorum of a decorous age. Even the sprightly Prior, when he versified a Psalm, was sicklied o'er with the pale cast of gloom. Robert Gould's *Mourning Swain: A Funeral Eclogue*[73] combines much of the pseudo-Classical with some mortuary touches such as, "Death grinn'd a horrid Smile"; and, in the *Oxford and Cambridge Miscellany,* Fenton included an elegy *On the Death of John Selden,*[74] that declared:

> . . . All others into crumbling Ashes fall,
> Ashes, the common Element of all,
> But Selden, like a Vatican on high,
> Dissolv'd into a deathless Library. . . .

Donne might have written in such a way. Even D'Urfey at last succumbed to the morose manner, and in his *Funeral Poem*[75] on

[72] E. Smith, *A Poem on the Death of John Philips,* London, n. d. (Nat. Lib. Scot., XVIII).

[73] R. Gould, *The Mourning Swain: A Funeral Eclogue to the Memory of James, Earl of Abington,* London, 1700.

[74] *Oxford and Cambridge Miscellany,* [ed. E. Fenton], London, [?1707], 236 *et seq.* Apparently a taste for the early seventeenth century style still existed in the reign of Queen Anne.

[75] T. D'Urfey, *The Poet's Vision,* in *Elegies, Poems and New Songs,* London, 1721.

Queen Anne reveled in "ominous Melancholy," purloining from the *Faerie Queene* the allegory of the seven deadly sins, and ingeniously combining these venial pilferings with his heritage from elegiac tradition. He does not lack in descriptions of hell and damnation that may or may not owe something to Milton, but that in literary excellence more nearly approach Blackmore.[76] Even a Classicist like Trapp[77] could bring himself to embellish the death of Julius Caesar with "shudderings" and "baleful Comets," and "Big, manly Bones dig'd from their open'd Graves," and other details suggestive of Shakespeare and of the funeral elegy rather than his Vergilian original. Sometimes the Classical, the Christian, and the Sentimental, are incongruously conglomerate.[78] But the single figure who more than any other represents mortuary poetry combined with Neo-classical details, and who made capital of its mournful felicities with at once the staidest propriety and the most enviable success was Edward Young, that perfect exemplar of respectable and egregious bereavement, who carried his bleeding heart into the home of every British tradesman, and fascinated him with versified melodrama under the guise of religion and morality. Young's *magnum opus* chronologically belongs to a later chapter of the present study, but his *Poem on the Last Day*, published oddly enough at Oxford, was a fitting prologue to his later achievement:

> Now Monuments prove faithful to their Trust,
> And render back their long committed Dust,
> Now Charnels Rattle; scatter'd Limbs, and all
> The various Bones obsequious to the Call,
> Self-moved advance; the Neck perhaps to meet
> The distant Head, the distant Legs the Feet;
> Dreadful to view! see through the Dusty Sky
> Fragments of bodies in confusion fly,
> To distant regions journeying, there to claim
> Deserted Members, and complete the Frame.[79]

Such a literal view of the Resurrection of the Body has a peculiarly unpleasant and incongruous effect upon modern sensibilities.

[76] E.g., an *Anonymous Journey to Hell*, London, 1700.

[77] *Oxford and Cambridge Miscellany*, ed. cit., 287 et seq. The volume also contains two mildly grievous Biblical paraphrases (*ibid.*, 147 and 290).

[78] E.g., *Threnodia Virginea: or, the Apotheosis. A Poem Occasion'd by the much Lamented Death of Mrs. Elizabeth Buckworth*, London, 1708.

[79] E. Young, *A Poem on the Last Day*, Oxford, 1713, 25.

The poem continues with the conventional idea of death the leveller, Pompey being paraded as the pious example; and then follows
a Gothic touch, and Westminster Abbey appears, the "Illustrious
Dome, Where soon or late fair *Albion's* Heroes come, . . . To
feed the worm, and moulder into Dust." Thus the poem combines Classical allusion with Neo-classical heroic couplet, and these
again with mortuary Puritanism and more than a suspicion of Sentimental luxuriance. Young can hardly be called the higher syn-
thesis of the culture-movements of his age, as were Goethe and
perhaps Spenser, but at least he achieved an undigested epitome of
its several elements; and undigested epitomes are the sign manual
of a transition period.

To call the age of Queen Anne a transition period is perhaps
too bold a paradox; but, in the broader sweep of culture-history,
it seems scarcely more than a momentary rest in the rapid evolution
from the intellectualistic and aristocratic world of the Renaissance
to the modern world of emotionalism and democracy; it is a truce
between contending forces, as was the Elizabethan age, and, like
every truce, a period of deep-laid preparation for ensuing conflict.
The upper classes, who chiefly enjoyed its benefits, most perfectly
reflect this compromise that gave them leisure to live, converse,
and write with ease; and the elegies of Lady Chudleigh, for the
most part, are formal lamentations, elegantly replete with the
euphemism of abstraction and periphrasis rather than downright
and vivid and concrete: the protected leisure class shielded themselves from reality, with its vital, though sometimes painful, experiences, and did not, like Keats, embrace a life of sensations—
or even a life of thoughts: Lady Chudleigh expressed grief with
a "Groan," a "Moan," and a "Flood of Tears,"[80] the merest convention and the vaguest generality; she described the mortuary
landscape in only the most colorless terms, a "Recess remote from
Human Kind," and "a close Asylum of Despair"; and finally she
ended the poem with the coldest of consolation. Sometimes, as
in her elegy on the Duke of Gloucester, she took refuge behind

[80] Lady Chudleigh, *Poems on Several Occasions*, London, 1703, 88, *On the Death of my Honored Mother Mrs. Lee: A Dialogue between Lucinda and Marissa*. These pedestrian couplets should have been actuated by some feeling. The elegy on "my dear daughter" is almost as chilly, *op. cit.*, 94 *et seq.* The exact dating of these pieces, as in the case of many other authors whose collected works have furnished examples for the present study, is most difficult.

pseudo-Pindaric laxity and the conventionalism of the pastoral.[81] In her essay *Of Death*, she suggests that this attitude arises at once from the *nil admirari* of the Classics and from a proper sense of Christian resignation;[82] and, in its passionless objectivity, her poetry is a good example of the Neo-classical compromise in religion and culture. Elegies written upon or addressed to royalty, even when composed by poets of the middle class, such as Dr. Gibbs' *Consolatory Poem Upon the Death of William Duke of Gloucester*,[83] were likely to be taken up with panegyric and apotheosis, largely to the exclusion of funereal detail. The good doctor, indeed, bids his reader, "Reflect not on the Dismal Scene of Woe"; and of like nature are three elegies by "Mrs. S. E." on Dryden and one on King William;[84] but the Renaissance tradition of the joy of life and its intellectual cultivation had permeated but little below the aristocratic classes; and, as these aristocratic classes began to compromise with their bourgeois rivals in the Neo-classical scheme of things, and as they later gave way to them, the ideals of the Renaissance and its view of life first suffered change, and then by degrees were generally submerged, to linger, if at all, in the attitude of modern science.

The voice of the old Puritanism, however, was still strong, though to be sure, it often quavered into Sentimental nasality. Something of its earlier austerity appears in the poetry of Isaac Watts; and something of the flaccid voluptuousness of its later days in the lines of his occasional imitator,[85] Mrs. Elizabeth Rowe. One of the earliest of Watts' elegies, and unquestionably the most significant, is the poem *To the Memory of Gunston* (1702): it contains almost every mortuary element, and many of them in a highly developed form; it was written by a noted Calvinist and non-conformist, and presented to a Lady Mayoress of London; and it unites the seventeenth century horror of death with a suggestion of the eighteenth century fondness for the pensive sadness

[81] *Ibid.*, 1.

[82] Lady Chudleigh, *Essays upon Several Subjects*, London, 1710, 45 *et seq.*

[83] [James?] Gibbs, *A Consolatory Poem Humbly Address'd to Her Royal Highness. Upon the Death of William Duke of Gloucester*, London, 1700.

[84] Mrs. S. E[gerton], *Poems on Several Occasions*, London, n. d., [?1705]. The name Egerton suggests a possible

connection with the noble houses of Ellesmere and Bridgewater. See also Bishop Burnet's broadside elegy on King William (*A Century of Broadside Elegies*, ed. the present author, London, 1928, No. 90).

[85] She accuses him of having inspired her, in a poem dedicated to him (*Miscellaneous Works*, London, 1739, I, 70-71).

of lingering memories.[86] A few passages will serve to illustrate
its value as a summary of mortuary realism in the poet's class
and age:

> . . . his sisters weep, and close his eyes,—
> And wait upon his hearse with never-ceasing cries:
> Lofty and slow it moves to meet the tomb,
> While weighty sorrow nods on ev'ry plume;
> A thousand groans his dear remains convey,
> To his cold lodging in a bed of clay,— . . .
> See the dull wheels roll on the sable road,
> But no dear son to attend the mournful load,
> And fondly kind, drop his young sorrows there,
> The father's urn bedewing with filial tear. . . .
> But night, eternal night, hangs black around
> The dismal chambers of the hollow ground,—
> And solid shades mingled round his bed
> Stand hideous; earthy fogs embrace his head,
> And noisome vapors glide along his face,
> Rising perpetual. Muse! forsake the place,
> Fly the raw damps of the unwholesome clay,
> Look to his airy spacious hall and say
> 'How has he chang'd it for a lonesome cave,
> Confin'd and crowded in a narrow grave!' . . .

The poet drops "the tribute of an hourly tear," and declares:

> Still [continually] I behold the melancholy scene,
> With many a pensive thought and many a sigh between.

Gunston's residence, already mentioned as an "airy, spacious hall,"
is later twice described as a "turret"—a Gothic touch implying
that, although the nobility of the age thought very little of their
hereditary castles, such places, in the imagination of the middle
classes, still symbolized the boast of luxury and pomp of power;
and one wonders how much such an association had to do with the
Gothic revival later in the century. The elegy continues with
appropriate sentiments on the vanity of human wishes; there is
much of the pathetic fallacy and some description of the moon
and moonlight scenery—a motif that is generally considered rare
in Queen Anne literature.[87] But Watts is not sufficiently Senti-

---

[86] On memory as a poetic subject, see
the present author, *William Mason*, New
York, 1924, 160 *et seq.*

[87] See Miss Reynolds, *op. cit.*, 20 *et
seq.*

mental to sport uninterruptedly with Amaryllis in the gloaming; and in the midst of his nocturnal reverie, he reminds the reader once more of the horror of death:

> But not one ray can reach the darksome grave
> Or pierce the solid gloom that fills the cave
> Where Gunston dwells in death.

The last line is particularly notable as expressing once more the curiously un-Christian concept of Puritanism that the vital essence inhered in the body rather than the soul.[88] Watts' later elegies show more restraint; and they suggest that the Neo-classical example of his literary contemporaries was not without its influence. His *Elegy on Sophronia* (1711) has two lines descriptive of the author's lamentation and a bit of Realistic description of the dead lady's face splotched with the marks of small-pox; and eleven years later, in composing· an *Elegiac Ode* on Sir Thomas Abney, who had also been a Lord Mayor of London, he contented himself with remarking upon the "general groan." Many of his non-elegiac pieces contain pertinent passages. His poem on *The Day of Judgment* refers to "the living worm" that is "gnawing within" the "guilty wretches"; and his ballad-stanzas on *Death and Eternity*, which are an early work published in the *Horæ Lyricæ* (1706), a volume of hymns intended specially for use in dissenting churches, contain a number of mortuary passages:

> The tyrant [Death], how he triumphs here!
> His trophies spread around!
> And heaps of dust and bones appear
> Through all the hollow ground.
>
> These sculls, what ghastly figures now!
> How loathsome to the eyes!
> These are the heads we lately knew,
> So beauteous and so wise.

This graveyard touch may have been inspired by the well-known scene in *Hamlet,* but is quite as likely to have grown out of the

---

[88] This probably arose partly from their belief in the resurrection of the body as declared in the early creeds and partly from the theological dilemma occasioned by their belief in a Judgment Day at the end of the world rather than immediately, and their concomitant denial of Purgatory. Thus since their religion, as popularly understood at least, provided no place for the soul to go to after death, they were rather obliged to centre their elegiac attention on the body.

actual   condition of many country burying grounds, with their
bones and skulls strewing the mounded earth; and, even in London, Bunhill Fields was no better.[89] The latter stanzas are given
over to moralizing that reminds one at once of the epitaphs on old
New England tombstones and of the last lines of Gray's *Elegy*:

> Some hearty friend shall drop his tear
> On our dry bones, and say,
> "These once were strong as mine appear,
> And mine must be as they."

Among the lesser poetic lights of the Puritan tradition, the
most luminous is the moist star of Mrs. Elizabeth Rowe. In her
Thoughts on Death, published in 1696 at the age of twenty-two,[90]
she reflected with becoming propriety on her lengthening years,
and imaginatively anticipated her final decease:

> 'Tis not the painful agonies of Death,
> Nor all the *gloomy horrors* of the Grave;
> Were that the most, unmov'd I'd yield my breath
> And with a smile the King of Terrors brave.

She proceeds to explain that Judgment Day and Hell are the chief
occasion for her anxiety; and, although she occasionally allows
herself the luxury of a pastoral, a large number of her later pieces
are either inspired by the *Bible* or at least are tagged to Biblical
texts as if they were so inspired. Her poem *Despair*,[91] apparently
written rather late in life, would seem to illustrate the length of
her progress along the road of "sensibility":

> Oh! lead me to some solitary gloom,
> Where no enliv'ning beams, nor chearful echoes come,
> But silent all, and dusky let it be,
> Remote, and unfrequented but by me;
> Mysterious, close, and sullen as that grief,
> Which leads me to its covert for relief.
> Far from the busy world's detested noise,

[89] See C. J. Abbey and J. H. Overton,
*The English Church in the Eighteenth
Century*, London, 1906, 426 *et seq.*;
Wordsworth's essay *Upon Epitaphs*; Bish-
op Berkeley, *Guardian*, No. XXXIX; and
C. Box, *Elegies and Epitaphs*, Gloucester,
1892, 110-111.

[90] [Mrs. Elizabeth Rowe], *Poems on
Several Occasions. By Philomela*, London, 1696, 28.
[91] Mrs. Elizabeth Rowe, *Miscellaneous
Works*, London, 1739, I, 71-72.

> Its wretched pleasures, and distracted joys. . . .
> Far from the studious follies of the great. . . .

This interest in solitary retirement is an odd parody of the Neo-classical urge for retirement as expressed in Pomfret's *Choice*: Pomfret wishes quiet for study; Mrs. Rowe wishes solitude for an emotional debauch of self-pity. The similarity is accidental rather than essential. In this happy locality, she wishes to play her lyre, not to the songs of happy birds:

> Only the pensive songstress of the grove,
> Let her, by mine, her mournful notes improve;[92]
> While drooping winds among the branches sigh,
> And sluggish waters heavily roll by.
> Here to my fatal sorrows let me give
> The short remaining hours I have to live,
> Then with a sullen deep-fetched groan expire,
> And to the grave's dark solitude retire.

The piece is analogous to the self-dedicated Puritan elegies occasionally found in the pocket of the pious and reverend Mr. So-and-so at the time of his decease; and the poem represents the Sentimentalizing of a peculiarly Puritan literary type.

No picture of the Calvinistic Muse of the period can afford to omit the name, notorious in the annals of literature, of Sir Richard Blackmore, physician in ordinary to King William, and poet in extraordinary to the Non-conformist conscience. His *Creation* is a revisal of the subject-matter of *Paradise Lost* to meet the taste of the humblest London tradesman; and, for that purpose, it borrowed the most infelicitous conventions of the mortuary style. His minor poems contain an occasional passage about the "cold Grave" and its "endless Torments and Despair," and the inevitable "King of Terrors";[93] but it seems hardly necessary to linger over a figure who is so thoroughly qualified for admission to the same poets' corner in paradise as Bævius and Mævius; nor does it seem necessary to quote from the anonymous *True State of Mortality*[94] with its "*dolorous Cries*" and "Icy Hand of *Death*," or from the

---

[92] Shelley and Keats, a hundred years later, were more modest in comparing their poetry with the birds; but then the ornithological had since come into fashion.

[93] Sir Richard Blackmore, *Collection of Poems*, London, 1718, 346 *et seq.*

[94] *The True State of Mortality*, London, 1709. The poem is based on *Job*, V, vii.

anonymous *Funeral Poem to the Memory of Sir John Cook*,[95] whose subject was a Londoner and, quite naturally, a Whig partisan of King William. One need give no more than passing mention to an elegy by "J. S." on one Nathanael Taylor, clergyman,[96] who is celebrated in the earlier style of the mid-seventeenth century, with much Calvinism and no clear indications of the Sentimental. Indeed, social, and especially intellectual, evolution moves slowly, and leaves many fossils and petrified fragments strewn along its path; and the change from a genuine religious motive, the fear of death and damnation, to a spurious religiosity is both subtle and gradual in operation; but it would seem to have left many traces upon elegiac literature of the late seventeenth and early eighteenth centuries—traces that cannot always be interpreted or dated with exactitude, but which, when surveyed at large, indicate clearly the general tendencies of literary and social growth.

The change that came over English literature during the eighteenth century, because it affected the mood, affected also the subject-matter of poetry. Melancholy had at first been cultivated as a by-product of religion, and later for its own sweet sake. When it thus became the main object of composition, poets very naturally developed those stylistic devices by which it could most readily be superinduced. Generalization and abstraction are the *modus operandi* of the intellect, and are the hall-mark of the Neo-classical school of restraint; but the individual, the concrete, and the vivid, are the natural language of the emotions, which are more closely connected with the senses and depend on them for stimulus. Thus the new urge expressed itself in a larger quantity of description;[97] and, indeed, the foregoing chapters have chronicled the development of the mortuary landscape. In order, however, to illustrate the growth of interest in Nature as a corollary[98] of intensified emotionalism, a brief review of the ground already covered may not be amiss before taking up mortuary description in the reign of Queen Anne. The Elizabethans not uncommonly heightened sadness by the use of an appropriate Realistic setting, as in the

[95] *Funeral Poem to the Memory of Sir John Cook*, London, 1710.

[96] J. S[hute], *A Poem to the memory of Mr. Nathanael Taylor, Late Minister of the Gospel*, London, 1702. The omission of the title "Reverend," as well as

the nature of the poem, suggests that "Mr. Taylor" was a dissenter.

[97] Cf. Mornet (*op. cit.*, 120 *et seq.*), who traces a parallel, though somewhat later, development in France.

[98] The present author takes the Natur-

prodigies at the death of Julius Caesar, in the storm-scene in *Lear*,
and in such a lyric as Beaumont's lines *On the Tombs in Westminster Abbey*.[99] One of the earliest funeral elegies, Jonson's
lament *On the Lady Jane Pawlet*, has its "fatal" yew; and the
species of tree selected—a species long characteristic of English
graveyards—suggests that even the great Elizabethan Classicist
derived this touch from realistic observation rather than from
Greek or Latin literature. The mortuary landscape, though largely
of English inception and predominantly native throughout, shortly
received accretions from Classical sources: the pathetic fallacy
descended in pastoral tradition from Theocritus,[100] intermingled
with it in the work of "the matchless Orinda," whose *Reverie* is
embellished with "a brook that sobbed aloud and ran away"; and
sometimes the pastoral and the mortuary were combined as in the
elegy *On the Memory of Mr. Caleb Skinner and Mr. Hezekiah
Middleton* (1688). As the seventeenth century progressed, and
melancholy was found to be agreeable, the poetry that expressed
it was naturally assimilated to the sweet pathos of Ovid and to
the other Latin elegists: Roman custom supplied the cypress tree,[101]
which took its place with the yew in the poetic graveyard; Roman
literature supplied such passages as the description in Catullus of
verdant Tempe, with its arching laurels and cypresses,[102] and
Ovid's setting for the story of the unhappy Actæon:

> Iussa viri faciunt intermettuntque laborem.
> Vallis erat piceis et acuta densa cupressu,
> Nomine Gargaphie succinctæ sacra Dianæ,
> Cuius in extremo est antrum nemorale recessu,
> Arte laboratum nulla: simulaverat artem
> Ingenio natura suo; nam pumice vivo

alistic aspect of the movement as subordinate, partly because its early development seems to have been incidental to
the development of melancholy, partly
because lyric poetry is more deeply concerned with the emotions than with
ideas, partly because Nature was clearly
falsified ("idealized") for the sake of
emotional stimulus (Mornet, *op. cit.*,
Chapter III), and partly because the
movement in its last stages, in Baudelaire, le Parnasse, Whistler, and the
æsthetes, repudiated Nature.

[99] Cf. H. G. De Maar, *A History of
Modern English Romanticism*, Oxford,
1924, I, 202 *et seq.*
[100] See Marion K. Bragg, *The Formal
Eclogue, Univ. of Maine Studies*, Orono,
Maine, 1926, 7 *et passim*.
[101] The Romans planted cypresses about
their tombs; and, to the Latin mind, the
cypress had a mournful and unpleasant
connotation, *e.g.*, the uses in Vergil,
Æneid, Lib. II, 714, and III, 680.
[102] Catullus, LXIV, 285 *et seq.*

Et levibus tofis nativum duxerat arcum.
Fons sonat a dextra tenui pelucidus unda,
Margine gramineo patulos incinctus hiatus.[103]

Propertius, moreover, now and again gives snatches of description of Roman tombs covered with laurel and ivy, horticultural details such as English poets occasionally employ.[104] The Sabine farm of Horace may have assisted; and the Bible certainly supplied inspiration.

For the most part, however, the concrete material of these descriptions is taken from actual English scenes; for the Elizabethans drew mainly from the life around them; and, after 1650, the funeral elegy emanated chiefly from the middle classes who were not for the most part trained in the Classics, and who were out of sympathy with the Court and its literary fashions. Donne's sunset followed by a star that "Twinkles and curls" is not Latin, nor is his *Charnel House*; and even Cowley's "Bow'r for sorrow made," is graced with a "black Yew" and a "mourning Willow[105] rather than by cypress, laurel, or ivy. Quarles supplies but little natural scenery; and the Puritans also, perhaps because they were so much under his influence, at first have little of it. That little, however, like their other mortuary touches, is clearly the outgrowth of immediate Realism introduced as a fitting background to morality and moralizing. During the Commonwealth period, rural scenery forms merely an occasional bit of setting, like the landscape backgrounds occasionally found in Renaissance religious painting: the "rugged hills and darksome groves of Caledonia," for example, are the merest incident to the elegy on General Deane. Sometimes, however, such passages show a daring cosmic hyperbole, as in Daniel Evance's lines on the Earl of Essex (1646) and in one of the pieces on Rainsborowe (1648) with its "mutinie and discord" of the stars.[106] Burrill's *Elegie* on Barnardiston has a charnel-house description that may owe some-

---

[103] Ovid, *Metamorphoses*, Lib. III, 155 *et seq.*
[104] Miss M. P. Aiken kindly supplies me with the following examples from Propertius: Lib. II, xiii, 32-34; Lib. II, xxviii, 36-39; Lib. III, xvi, 23-24; Lib. IV, vii, 79-80; and there are references to forests and caves, though in no way funereal, in Lib. III, iii, 13-14, and Lib.

III, xiii, 32 *et seq.* One is surprised that the hyacinth, which appears in Greek mythology, in Vergil, and in Milton's *Lycidas* (line 106), should apparently never have taken any really firm hold on English elegiac tradition.
[105] See Appendix A.
[106] Cf. *Troilus and Cressida*, I, iii, 94 *et seq.*

thing to Vergil and Spenser, but seems mainly to reflect contemporary conditions. In the courtly poetry of the reign of Charles II, there is but little nature-description, and that little is not emotionally excitant; but in the funeral elegies of the dissenters, the nature-touches, though generally brief, are often striking because of their gruesome realism or their almost Miltonic magnitude: not content with the usual "Vale of Tears," the broadside elegist of Janeway bewails him with an "Abyss of Sorrow" and a "Lamentable Storm of Sighs and Groans," sweeping across a land parched and adamantine as an alkali plain. Flatman, likewise, developed this descriptive manner, borrowing from the Bible and from Christian tradition for his *Dooms-Day Thought*. Arwaker's Pindaric elegy on Charles II is a curious combination of the Classical and the mortuary; and in its imagery combines "the *Mournful* Cypress and *Unlucky* Yew" to make a scene of "dismal" and *"darkest"* "Solitude."[107] Puritan elegies of the middle and latter seventeenth century are rich in "crawling Worms" and "the horror of eternal night"; but these are occasional touches with but slightly developed natural setting, until religion gave way to Sentimentalism as the motive for this type of versifying. In New England, where the old Calvinism disintegrated but slowly, only a few fragments of nature-description appear; but, in Old England, as early as the accession of William and Mary, both Sentimentalism and the concomitant emotionalism of Nature are clearly evident. Fleming has his "Tapers" in the *"dismal* Night"; Browne describes the nocturnal more at length, and finds his "dark Alcove" —doubtless a cavern or perhaps a "grot" in the manner of Pope— entirely to his liking, and describes it as "sweet"; Hopkins delights in "gloomy cypress Trees" and "solid Gloom," with ghosts, tombs, groans, "putrid Rust," and other accessories. In Scotland, the emotionalizing of Nature appears about 1700 when the Presbyterians started to write elegies, and is rather highly developed in a Whig *Threnodie* on King William, written perhaps under the inspiration of Spenser. In the elegies of Jacobites and Non-jurors,

---

[107] This poem also seems to show the influence of Spenser. The "Spenserian revival" would seem to have been (like the "Miltonic revival") rather less a revival than some scholars have supposed. Spenser apparently remained in vogue among the same class that read and wrote funeral elegies; and, when this class arose to renewed literary patronage, it brought popularity to Spenser along with its other literary preferences.

English or Scotch, mortuary descriptions are seldom to be found; and the motif appears but rarely among the "mob of gentlemen that wrote with ease": one can hardly escape the conclusion that this type of poetry was the peculiar development of the Calvinistic bourgeoisie, and was cultivated by them as a regular adjunct of the funeral elegy long before it appeared in those poems by Lady Winchelsea, Parnell, William Pattison, and others that are generally credited with having initiated the "new attitude toward nature."[108]

The Augustan period also supplies a number of excellent examples of the Sentimentalizing of Nature in funereal verse. Arwaker, who has already been mentioned as combining mortuary description with the Pindaric elegy, brought into being in a later period a similar hybrid in his pensive pastoral, *The Birth-Night*.[109] It starts with darkness and the sleep of beast and insect:

> Man's all-compos'd, his Passions all serene;
> No troubled Thought disturbs his setled Mien;
> His careless Limbs in peaceful Rapture spread,
> Like Death his Sleep, and like the Grave his Bed.

These proper sentiments are thrown against the background of the rising moon:

> While prostrate Vales with dusky Gloom are fill'd,
> She forms with softest Shade and smoothest Light
> The pleasing Landskip of the lovely Night.

To Arwaker, night is not terrible—at all events, it is not repulsive. It is beautiful, perhaps because it has a certain awe, for such a poet is not above the titillating relish of a "new shiver." He finds pleasure in the "awful Hush" and the "solemn Grandeur" of the night—not the religious horror of the Puritan, or the somewhat patronizing and chilly generality of the Neo-classicist, but the joy of one who finds lyric sympathy in rural scenes because they supply an emotional craving within himself. Some of the happiest examples of the emotional use of Nature have already been quoted:

---

[108] Cf. H. A. Beers, *A History of English Romanticism in the Eighteenth Century*, New York, 1916, 102 *et seq.*; and Myra Reynolds, *op. cit.*, 58 *et seq.*

[109] E. Arwaker, *The Birth-Night*, London, 1705. Most of the poem is conventional enough, but it seems to have some Spenserian touches.

the "Malcontent," who rushed "With Joy . . . into the lonesome Nook," and found delight in "vast Cliffs" and "creeping Ivy"; Young who employed a Gothic touch of Westminster Abbey; Watts who supplied Lord Mayor Gunston with a castellated "hall"; and Mrs. Elizabeth Rowe who took pleasure in "solitary gloom" with "drooping winds," "sluggish waters," and a "pensive song-stress of the grove." Of greatest interest, however, is the elegy on Queen Anne by Lewis Theobald, who, though a Classical scholar of no mean acquirements, commingled with references to Pan and Urania a death-bed scene in the best Puritan style, enriched with "strong Convulsions" and "Shrieks and Lamentations," and added a fine mortuary landscape with an unblushingly Sentimental *finale*:

> Snatch me, ye Pow'rs to some unhallow'd Grove;
> The seat of Sorrow and unprosp'rous Love;
> Where Solitude in sullen Pomp presides;
> Where none resort, but whom Despair misguides;[110]
> Where *Pan* ne'er Revell'd, nor the *Nymphs* e'er play'd;
> Where no Enquiring Rays the Gloom invade;
> Nor Gaiety presumes t'infect the Rev'rend Shade.
> Where Russet Leaves still blast, as they renew:
> And low'ring Clouds descend in constant Dew.
> Where Birds, and whisp'ring Zephyrs are unknown;
> But Paddocks croak, and Winds ungentle Groan,
> There on th'Unwholesome Grass my Limbs I'll spread,
> And on a Riv'let's Bank support my Head.
> To ev'ry murm'ring Wave in Tears complain,
> And to the Hollow Blasts sigh out my Pain;
> And if my Anguish can still higher grow,
> Let Horror and the Place th'Encrease bestow;
> From Horror and the Place, I'll cherish rising Woe.[111]

Theobald, in short, is admittedly using the landscape as a lugubrious aphrodisiac, very much as Sir William Chambers in a later generation turned gardening to a similar purpose in his Chinese paradise.[112]

The mortuary landscape generally concerned itself with one of

---

[110] Cf. *Faerie Queene*, Book I, IX, 21 *et seq.* The use of "still" and "Paddock" also suggest Elizabethan influence.

[111] Lewis Theobald, *The Mausoleum*, London, 1714.

[112] For a brief discussion of Chambers' theories in relation to contemporary gardening and to the development of Romanticism, see the present author, *William Mason*, 241 *et seq.*

three subjects: hell and Judgment, with details borrowed chiefly from Christian tradition; the churchyard and charnel, chiefly based on realistic fact with an occasional Gothic touch; and the sadly pensive forest scene with a grot and a purling stream and perhaps an awful jagged cavern, drawn partly from the Classics, partly from common English scenery, and partly from the Bible. The authors of the Puritan broadsides commonly note the source of their Biblical allusions; but sometimes these reminiscences are vague and hard to trace, the thunder storm, the angry sea, the fallen column, the crashing oak or cedar, the valley of bones or skulls. Sometimes, they appear in direct description; sometimes, in metaphor or simile; sometimes, in combination with native realism, as when the body of William Bates is described as "This thatched Cottage, this poor House of Clay."[113] Hell and Judgment are the themes most characteristically Puritan, the least subject to sentimentalizing, and the least important as an early influence on the new movement; the charnel-house and the ancient ruin enter into graveyard poetry and finally into the Gothic romance; and the pensive landscape, popularized by the growth of Deism and its exaltation of Nature initiates that long line of pantheistic poets from Thomson to Wordsworth.[114] All three types, with infinite variations, continued to appear throughout the century; for, just as some of the aristocrats, like Chesterfield, hardly entered into the Neo-classical compromise, and barely gave lip-service to religion and morality, so, in like fashion, many of the bourgeois class refused to accept the restraint of Neo-classical art and culture; and these latter, as they rose into social prominence and expressed themselves more and more in the fine arts, by degrees, building upon the art-traditions that they knew and approved, developed new arts and a new æsthetic theory that would give outlet to an emotionalism no longer countenanced by their religion, and that would reflect dignity upon themselves. As these *nouveaux riches* multiplied, more slowly in the earlier part of the century from wealth accumulated in foreign trade, more rapidly in the later decades from the spoils of India and the exploitation of the proletariat in the Industrial Revolution, the ideals for which they stood became the predominant ideals of literature and art; the half-educated nobility

[113] Brit. Mus. broadside.   Nelson in the library of the University
[114] See a dissertation in MS. by N. E.   of Minnesota.

found them pleasant; and an emotional dilettante like Walpole paved the way for such an aristocrat of Sentiment as Byron. Even in the reign of William and Mary, the new emotionalism had begun to spread; the dissenter and the tradesman were long its chief fountain-head; but, during the reigns of the Georges, it ceased to be a class-movement, and extended over England, and indeed all over Europe, changing the literature, the culture, and the ideals of the age, and making art no longer the hand-maid of courtly patronage, but the expression of the taste, such as it was, of an increasingly numerous public.

CHAPTER X

THE FUNERAL ELEGY IN THE REIGN OF
GEORGE I

THE year 1714 witnessed in England the second dynastic crisis within a generation; and, for the second time, the crisis was resolved in favor of the Whigs and their nonconformist allies. Queen Anne might flatter herself that she ruled by Divine Right; but there could be no doubt that the sovereignty of George I was purely the creature of Parliament and of the Whig party. Parliament and the Cabinet System constituted the machinery of politico-social compromise; and thus, in an age when absolutism was being established in almost every state in Europe, and when the yeomanry, the bulwark of British liberty in times past, were declining in strength and numbers, yet the king was becoming a political nonentity, and had even ceased to preside at the meetings of his own cabinet. During this age, the arrangement of government by compromise between various classes and conflicting interests achieved practical fixity. The prime advantage of such a system is flexibility, the power of rapid adjustment to meet fresh conditions; and, indeed, the social compromise, as it appears in the reign of George I, shows a coloring quite different from that of the Restoration or even the "Bloodless Revolution" of 1688: the commercial and industrial classes had "acquired a new preponderance in politics, and theological influence had at least proportionately declined."[1] That the influence of the Anglican clergy should decline was a natural result of the dominance of the Whigs who looked with a jealous eye upon their political power. The declining influence of non-conformity seems to have arisen from a number of causes,[2] the chief of which was probably its internal disintegration under the influence of Deism. The non-

---

[1] W. E. H. Lecky, *A History of England in the Eighteenth Century*, New York, 1892, II, 227.

[2] Lecky, *op. cit.*, I, 253 *et seq.*; D. Bogue and J. Bennett, *History of the Dissenters*, London, 1808-1810, 320 *et seq.*, 382 *et seq.* The causes of the decline of dissent caused some pamphlet discussion. S. Gough, a young dissenting minister, assigned the disintegration of the dissenting bodies as the cause (*Inquiry into the Causes of the Decay of the Dissenting Interest*, 1730); and N. Neal declared Arianism the cause (*A Free and Serious Remonstrance*, 1746).

conformist classes, however, though they lost influence religiously, gained it from economic considerations; for, during the eighteenth century, wealth poured in from foreign trade and later from the labor-saving devices of the Industrial Revolution. This new wealth was by no means evenly divided; and, indeed, a great number of artisans, whose place was being taken by machinery, were reduced to misery by the change,[3] while a few enjoyed a perilous and usually short-lived ascent into the capitalist class. During the reign of William and Mary, the existence of a national debt had become a permanent fact of British politics—a debt which was constantly increasing during the eighteenth century and especially during the Seven Years War; and it was to this new capitalistic class that the government was obliged to turn again and again for immediate financial succour. The reign of George I was, significantly enough, ushered in by the building of a new Exchange on the Strand; and the years that followed were largely dominated by the policies of Sir Robert Walpole, who, though a country squire by ancestry, was by political policy first of all a practical economist, and who made finance the centre of his Parliamentary career. Thus the accident of the dynastic crisis and the increase in their wealth, restored in some measure to the middle classes their former influence in the state.

Of more direct import, however, to the present study was the social and cultural status of the bourgeoisie. In the period of Elizabeth, as has already been noted,[4] the great merchants were largely recruited from the county families, and in consequence carried into trade aristocratic ideals of art and culture, and contributed to the homogeneity of that heroic age. The seventeenth century saw the trading classes recruited more and more from the lower orders; and, in the eighteenth century, the rise of individuals from these lower orders, due to the opportunities of trade and to the spread of popular education especially in London,[5] made them

[3] Lecky, op. cit., II, 82; Besant, London in the Eighteenth Century, London, 1902, 37, 46, 51, et passim; Dorothy George, London Life in the Eighteenth Century, New York, 1925, 169 et passim; A. S. Tuberville, English Men and Manners in the Eighteenth Century, Oxford, 1926, 160 et passim; and H. G. Graham, Social Life of Scotland in the

Eighteenth Century, London, 1906, 146 et seq.

[4] See Chapter V.

[5] Lecky says that "In the fifteen years ending in 1712 as many as 117 schools were set up in London and Westminster, and nearly 5,000 children were taught in them" (op. cit., III, 33). Some of these schools doubtless did not survive; but

an ever increasing influence in the cultural life of the nation, although still subsidiary to the nobility. The improvement in insurance growing out of Lloyd's coffee-house, the greater safety of finance since the foundation of the Bank of England, and the popular experience gained from the South Sea Bubble, all helped to stabilize commercial wealth, though much was still to be desired in this regard; and as yet, though there was but little special legislation to protect the merchant as the corn laws protected the aristocracy of the soil, yet in spite of danger from losses, several great mercantile houses were actually founded, in which commercial wealth, like landed property, was passed on to the second and third generations; and these, being relieved from the drudgery of gaining a livelihood, might spend their energies in pursuing the cultural amenities of life. During the eighteenth century, such families commonly took on in succeeding generations, as did the Pitts for example, the culture and the point of view of the nobility; but many of those who inherited more moderate fortunes were raised by the increase of education and the greater abundance of the necessities of life, more or less permanently into the class of artistic patrons; and thus a great new body of the half-educated, whose culture had usually been acquired too sporadically or too late in life to be quite their own and who carried with them tastes and points of view that belonged to the antecedents from which they had lately sprung—such a body of new patrons, but partly schooled in the time-honored traditions and decorums, began to exercise an influence upon literature and the arts. All this, moreover, was coincident with the reigns of two German monarchs who cared nothing for English literature, and whose ministers, fearing religious and political controversy, chose to direct Parliamentary legislation, not by pamphlets and appeals, but by the more efficient road of direct and open corruption, so that the literary patronage of Church and State that had largely supplied with daily bread the Augustan authors of the reign of Anne, was rather suddenly removed at the very moment that a new and wider patronage with quite different literary tastes was beginning to appear. The measured intellectualism of the Renaissance thus gave way before the democratization of society.

even so London was better than the rural
districts. Cf. Besant, *op. cit.,* 154.

These new recruits to the class of the comfortably situated were at first inclined to spend their surplus incomes in the substantial pleasures of dress and of the table; and the age was one of heavy eating and hard drinking.[6] For the country squire, who led a life of strenuous animalism, this was well enough; but, for the city dweller, nobleman, fine lady, or rich merchant, lack of exercise brought the spleen and the vapours: indeed, Gay, whose own corpulence suggests that he might well speak from experience, imputed the illnesses of the age to a superabundance of the fruits of good living without any concomitant physical exertion;[7] and, in 1757, "Estimate" Brown blamed the apparent decadence of England on the excessive growth of the commercial classes and their propensity for the sedentary life.[8] The prevalent melancholy of the period was ascribed by a French traveller to excess in drinking;[9] for the substitution among the rich of port for French clarets after the Methuen Treaty in 1703, and the orgy of gin-drinking among the poor, especially in the second quarter of the century, certainly affected the physique and doubtless also the morale of the generation. Perhaps it is not quite a coincidence that the death of Parnell, one of the early poets of the Graveyard School, seems to have been hastened by his intemperance;[10] and intemperance is certainly more nearly related to the mercurial emotional experiences of Sentimentalism than to the ordered middle way of *nil admirari*. Thus all classes were susceptible to the facile view of life expressed in the new emotionalism; and what had been yesterday the brand of the *nouveaux riches* became the accepted vogue of Society tomorrow.

Most important, however, in determining this cultural bias was not the intemperate manner of life nor yet the fads and fancies of the leisure class but the fixed habits of mind ingrained in childhood; and, as most of these new patrons of learning and letters, like the actual poets themselves, as Schöffler[11] has pointed out, arose from the fertile soil of Calvinism, they had come to idealize emo-

[6] John Ashton, *Social Life in the Reign of Queen Anne*, New York, 1925, 141 et seq.

[7] *Trivia*, I, 70 et seq., 105 et seq. See also Tuberville, op. cit., 117.

[8] Cf. Lecky, op. cit., II, 85 et seq.

[9] Tuberville, op. cit., 88, 104, 228. Between 1688 and 1750, the distilling of spirits in England is said to have increased twentyfold. See also Dorothy George, op. cit., 27.

[10] See T. Seccombe, *Camb. Hist. Eng. Lit.*, IX, Chap. VI, 186 et seq.

[11] H. Schöffler, *Protestantismus und Literatur*, Leipzig, 1922.

tional exaltation, so that, even when their Calvinism faded out to a Deistic haziness, the old attitude toward the excellence of emotionalism remained, and emotionalism, without religious or other adequate motive can only be termed Sentimental. But Sentimentalism was no longer the special prerogative of the dissenting tradesmen. George I, though generally a niggardly patron of letters, is said to have given Steele a "handsome present" for the *Conscious Lovers*;[12] living conditions of the nobility were almost as favorable to it as among the rich bourgeoisie; the teachings of Lord Shaftesbury seemed to lend it aristocratic countenance; and the leisure classes, demanding constant variety to escape *ennui*, found a new pleasure in the cultivation of the lachrymose.[13] Indeed, "between 1709 and 1719, each of the writers whose best work may be described as neo-classic and optimistic, paid his court in one fashion or another to Melancholy";[14] and a recent critic of the drama declares that the triumph of Sentimentalism by 1725 was practically complete.[15]

Toward the end of this period, philosophical controversy lent its aid in spreading the new doctrines. Hutcheson systematized the scattered *dicta* of Shaftesbury's ethical theory into as coherent an arrangement as an anti-intellectualistic philosophy would allow, and set it forth with the stamp of academic authority from his chair in the University of Glasgow.[16] The vogue of such teachings, moreover, was considerably, though quite unintentionally, increased by Bernard Mandeville, whose *Fable of the Bees* appeared in a series of continually augmented editions during the 1720's and '30's. The comfortable compromise of Neo-classicism had apparently solved the age-long problem of simultaneously serving God and Mammon, by accommodating the pleasures of this world as expressed in the traditions of the Renaissance with the duties required by the next as expressed in the ideals of the Reformation; and Mandeville, in search of clever paradox, satirized with an almost vitriolic sting the inevitable discrepancies between

[12] J. W. Krutch, *Comedy and Conscience after the Restoration*, New York, 1924, 225.

[13] J. W. Courthope, *History of English Poetry*, London, 1895-1905, V, 360 *et seq.*

[14] Amy L. Reed, *The Background of Gray's Elegy*, New York, 1924, 111-112.

[15] Krutch, *op. cit.*, 221. For culture in general this date is somewhat too early.

[16] See his *Inquiry into the Original of Our Ideas of Beauty and Virtue* (1725). He was Professor of Moral Philosophy 1729-1746.

abstract ethics and actual life. Like Hobbes, that master-bogey of
seventeenth century thought, Mandeville believed, or affected to
believe, that man was incurably depraved; and, by a strange twist
of *non-sequitur*, he derived from this fact all the major advan-
tages of human society, giving voice to his paradox in the famous
summary: "Private vices, public benefits." In the average man,
schooled in the "common sense" of Neo-classicism as in the Book
of Common Prayer, such a philosophy could only produce repul-
sion; and when, furthermore, Mandeville added to this paradox
the conclusion that mankind should therefore let evil be their good,
he aroused against him all the ghostly powers and the argumenta-
tive acumen of the clergy, who justly looked upon themselves as
the official guardians of morality. Of the two assertions on which
his philosophy was built, the first has always been a commonplace
of Christian theology: the opposition of true righteousness to the
world, the flesh, and the devil. In combating his opinions, however, a number of writers, led by their zeal, attempted to prove
rather more than their case required, and so fell into the opposite,
and equally un-Christian, assertion of man's innate goodness, the
basic assumption of Sentimental philosophy.[17] Thus the cynicism
of Mandeville, by outraging the "common sense" of the man in
the street and by assailing a fundamental doctrine of Christian
morality, called public attention to the inherent weakness of the
Neo-classical scheme of things, and at the same time accelerated
the rising popularity of a soft and optimistic Sentimentalism; and
thus the Anglican clergy, in the face of a common adversary were
obliged to tolerate and countenance, even though they might not
accept, the Sentimental doctrines that seemed so cogent in combating the intellectual position of this new and dangerous enemy.[18]

Indeed, a combination of great social influences was effecting a
wide and lasting vogue of sentimentality. The religious changes
in dissent incident upon the rise of Deism, and the growing afflu-
ence of the bourgeoisie and their more comfortable way of life

---

[17] See Sir Leslie Stephen, *History of English Thought*, London, 1902, II, 33 et seq.; *The Fable of the Bees*, ed. F. B. Kaye, Oxford, 1924, I, cxx et seq.; and F. B. Kaye, *The Influence of Bernard Mandeville*, Stud. in Phil., XIX, 83 et seq. The chief influence on philosophy was perhaps toward utilitarianism; but the average man seems to have followed the easier Sentimental reaction.

[18] Fielding's *Tom Jones* also might be taken as a criticism of, if not an attack upon, the Neo-classical *status quo*, and this may well explain why the author's reputation was pursued with such bitter rancor.

had given the old Calvinism a more optimistic and easier tone. Meanwhile, they were rising in economic importance and political, if not social, influence; for the financial classes cannot be ignored by a state that needs to borrow and borrow again to maintain its domestic policies and fight its foreign wars. This same attitude of mind, moreover, appeared among the Anglican aristocracy, who shared somewhat the conditions of life of the wealthy bourgeoisie, and whose growing dilettantism obliged them to seek farther and farther afield for novelty and diversion. The Anglican Church, meanwhile, was falling from its position of political hegemony; the Whigs, fearing its influence among the lower classes, preferred to the Bench only such lukewarm prelates as it might hope to control; and, in fact, with the advent of Deism and infidelity on the one hand and the cynical antinomianism of Mandeville on the other, clerical controversialists were quite taken up with other subjects of attack. Thus the old enemy of the dissenting interest was weak; the compromise of Neo-classicism was on the defensive; and the facile charms of "sensibility" were free to operate upon the public at large. The religion of the British merchant had become a dissent, not of the intellect, but of the feelings; and with his gradual economic, political, and social triumph, triumphed also his opinions, his psychology, and his attitude of mind.

During the reign of George I, the number of broadside elegies shows a considerable decrease from the output of earlier periods. And even of the elegies printed in volumes, there are perhaps fewer on particular individuals than of yore. This loss, however, is amply recompensed by the great quantity of generalized elegiac, or at least melancholic, poetry that appears for the most part in the works of very minor literary aspirants. All these pieces, as one might expect in an age of rapid cultural transition, show a great variety of form, authorship, point of view, and literary relationship. The elegy, indeed, had been long in the germination; but at last it had sprung up to flourish in every soil. Some authors continued the tradition of Herrick, and wrote of death with a Classical *nonchalance*, such as Prior showed in the epitaph on his own tombstone; and Parnell, though his Muse was usually more solemn sad, could for a moment echo this almost merry note in his *Elegy to an old Beauty*. In general, however, the elegies have at least something of the mortuary note of Puritanism. Even John Gay, whose surname had a certain cognomenal felicity, in his *Contemplation on Night* refers to its "gloomy reign." His *Thought on Eternity* illustrates Christian and Neo-classical orthodoxy; and his *Panthea* combines the bucolic tradition of the Classics with the mortuary tradition of the Puritans, applying to the rural subject-matter of the former something of the melancholy tone and descriptive realism of the latter:

> Oh! lead me to some melancholy cave,
> To lull my sorrows in a living grave;
> From the dark rock where dashing waters fall,
> And creeping ivy hangs the craggy wall,
> Where I may waste in tears my hours away,
> And never know the seasons of the day.

Thus the piece belongs to the same tragical-comical-pastoral type as the elegy already discussed *On the Memory of Mr. Caleb Skinner and Mr. Hezekiah Middleton* (1688), as Pottenger's *Pastoral Reflections on Death* (1691), as the *Funeral Eclogue* on Queen Mary (1695), and as Robert Gould's *Mourning Swain* (1700). The combining of the elegiac and the pastoral goes back to Alexandrian literature; but the deepening of its sadness with mortuary details is the peculiar contribution of this generation of poets. Such pieces are a direct anticipation of Thomson's *Seasons*, and especially of *Winter*, which in its initial form was intended to be a melancholy, if not actually a mortuary, eclogue.[19] Even Pope, whose background was neither Whig nor Calvinistic, and whose poetical essays and satires do not ally him with the sombre style, lapsed into it on occasion when he bewailed the "unfortunate lady" with a "beck'ning ghost" and "moonlight shades," and a "mournful bier"; and his pat couplets take on a demure and dying fall with still remembered rhymes on "Tomb" and "woe" and "mourn'd." His *Eloisa*, moreover, has its picture of "Black Melancholy" seated

> . . . o'er twilight groves and dusky caves,
> Long-sounding aisles, and intermingled graves. . . .

And Eloisa herself is a perfect little Sentimentalist, a type of which the early eighteenth century doubtless supplied a plenitude of models

---

[19] Of course there were also bucolic poems that were not mortuary, and that may well have influenced Thomson, such as Pope's *Seasons* and the more vividly descriptive *Seasons* by Hinchcliffe (*Poems*, London, 1718, 37 *et seq.*

both for the poetry and the "she-tragedies" of the period. On the other hand, he could translate *Adrianis Morientis ad Animam* with Neo-classical nicety and restraint: death has no horrors, but is rather a soft sleep; and then heaven at once opens to the poet's eyes. Indeed, the undigested eclecticism of the *Essay on Man* is a true index of Pope's versatility of thought, which allowed him to state precisely and pithily any and every point of view with a fine disregard for consistency.

More especially among the lesser poets, however, the mortuary tradition grew in magnitude, if not in grace. Hinchcliffe's *Elegy* assumes quite the tone and point of view of *Night Thoughts*, and, like Young's masterpiece, is addressed to an erring Lothario who is properly admonished on an appropriate occasion:

> See, wretched Youth, where thy fond Mother lies
> Panting, and chill! behold her dying Eyes;
> Restless they roll, and search the chearful Light
> In vain, the Shades of Death have veil'd their Sight;
> And those bright Orbs must set in endless Night.
> Triumphant Death drives swiftly thro' her Veins;
> And binds the Purple Streams in frigid Chains. . . .

Her death is described, and following that, her apotheosis. D'Urfey, who already in the reign of Queen Anne had started to reset his sails to catch the new breeze of popularity, continued to spice his elegies with mortuary detail. Lord Leicester's demise is celebrated with "Storms of Sorrow, Tears, and Sighs and Groans," and is significantly entitled a *Funeral Poem*. The *Elegy* on Lord Leigh starts with a complimentary apostrophe to Stoneleigh House as a "stately Pile"; and the Earl of Portland's *Elegy* is embellished with a reverential comment on Westminster Abbey as "stately" and ancient.[20] The piece is headed with a skull and cross bones, as if it were a broadside—indeed, it may first have been published in that form. Whether or not it ever was so published, the appearance of such pictures in a dignified volume of poems is important as a concrete representation of broadside influence, a precursor of similar pictorial influence upon the title-page of the first edition of Gray's *Elegy*. In even sadder strains, Christopher Pitt bewailed the Earl of Stanhope. His *Poem* starts with a "Riot

[20] T. D'Urfey, *Elegies, Poems, and New Songs*, London, 1721, 307, 313, *et seq.*

of Destruction" and "Tyrant Death," continues with "th'Angelick Choirs . . . Wrapt in a Cloud of Grief," and refers modestly to the "mournful Transports" of Pitt's "Muse." One passage, on Lady Stanhope, is worth quotation:

> Behold the Partner of his Cares and Life,
> Bright in her Tears, and beautiful in Grief,
> Shall then in vain those Streams of Sorrow flow,
> Drest up in all the Elegance of Woe?
> And shall the kind officious Muse forbear
> To answer Sigh for Sigh, and tell out Tear for Tear? [21]

Britannia also mourns; and her "rising Groans load ev'ry Wind." Then follows the eulogy and the apotheosis. [22] So widespread was the mortuary vogue in the reign of George I that the passages just quoted are actually more mortuary than the *Divine Poem* on the death of the non-conformist minister, Richard Claridge (1723), who was sung in folio broadside with "briny Tears" prefixed to an itemized summation of his thirteen cardinal virtues. [23] Melancholy, indeed, had spread her vast prerogative as far as Jove's, and no longer counted among her votaries merely the men of traffic in the mart and the conscientious followers of dissent. A Mr. Wilkinson, a clergyman—at least his style suggests as much—made tearfulness his *forte*. His elegy *On the Much Lamented Death of Samuel Edwin Esq.* starts with "Inexorable Death! triumphant Fiend!" He fittingly describes his own verses as "this Flood of Tears," and asks for power to mourn for Edwin as David did for Saul: his prayer was not granted. His *Elegy* on Archbishop Daws is even more lachrymose; for he threatens to "dissolve into one watry Eye," quite in the manner of a seventeenth century metaphysical. [24] Not only soft, but also hard Sentimentalism has its votaries. A long poem *On the Death of Sir Herbert Powell, Baronet,* is made up of this sterner stuff; and, in spite of the Latin quotation at the top, it revels in "gloomy Horror." [25] Indeed, the reign of George I saw the cultivation of almost every species of the elegiac kind, in the hands of bourgeois and aristocrat alike.

[21] [C.] Pitt, *Poem on the Death of the late Earl of Stanhope*, London, 1721.

[22] See also C. Pitt, *Poems and Translations*, London, 1727, 57-58, *On the Death of a Young Gentleman.* This piece is the typical Anglican moralistic panegyric.

[23] Brit. Mus. broadside.

[24] [John Wilkinson], *Poems on Several Occasions*, London, 1725, 5 and 28. See also note 36.

[25] *Miscellaneous Poems* published by D. Lewis, London, 1726, 276 *et seq.*

A survey of the poems on the death of so characteristic a Neo-classical figure as Addison will perhaps best serve to give further illustration to this point. Mary Masters did an octosyllabic eulogy in no particular style.[26] Cobden wrote the conventional panegyric biography in the aristocratic tradition of the reign of Charles II;[27] and Arbuckle added to this strain a *basso profundo* of "fantastick Shades" and "solemn Pomp of Elegiac Woe."[28] But the chiefest of these pieces is clearly that by Tickell, addressed, probably for pecuniary reasons, to the Earl of Warwick. Dr. Johnson called it "sublime and elegant"; and, in our own day, it has been held up as a perfect summary of elegiac Romanticism.[29] It starts with the time-honored declaration that true grief cannot express itself in good poetry: thereupon the author, booted and spurred, mounts his Pegasus for a prolonged excursion. One hopes, for the sincerity of the elegists, that bad poetry may be taken as a proof of the genuineness of their sentiments; but perhaps it is unsafe to credit the converse of a mighty truth. At all events, Tickell proceeds to adorn Addison's funeral in the contemporary Westminster-Abbey style, and to detail to us *seriatim* his own sorrowful impressions:

> Can I forget the dismal night that gave
> My soul's best part forever to the grave!
> How silent did his old companions tread,
> By midnight lamps, the mansions of the dead,
> Thro' breathing statues, then unheeded things,
> Thro' rows of warriors, and thro' walks of kings!
> What awe did the slow solemn knell inspire;
> The pealing organ and the pausing choir;
> The duties by the lawn-rob'd prelate pay'd;
> And the last words that dust to dust convey'd!
> While speechless o'er thy closing grave we bend,
> Accept these tears, thou dear departed friend. . . .[30]

During the reign of William and Mary, such satires as still took the funeral elegy for their form were no longer directed in any

[26] Mary Masters, *Verses to the Memory of Mr. Addison* (*Poems*, London, 1733).

[27] Edward Cobden, *A Poem on the Death of the Right Honourable Joseph Addison*, London, 1720. (Worcester Coll. Lib.)

[28] James Arbuckle, *An Epistle to the Rt. Hon. Thomas Earl of Hadington On the Death of Addison*, London, 1719.

[29] E. Legouis and L. Cazamian, *Histoire de la Littérature Anglaise*, Paris, 1924, 721.

[30] *Works of the Most Celebrated Minor Poets*, London, 1749, 237.

special way against dissent.[31] In the reigns of Anne and George I, satiric elegies are even fewer, and generally of slight historic importance. There is something of elegiac parody in *The Way to Heaven in a String, Or Mr. Addison's Argument Burlesqu'd* (1700); and *The Guardian* (1713), though it ridiculed the outworn conventions of the all-too-common pastoral elegy, had nothing to say against the mortuary *genre*.[32] *The Dirge*, moreover, in Gay's *Shepherd's Week*, likewise makes merry at the expense of the bucolic tradition. In the same strain are Allan Ramsay's Scotch elegies on Maggy Johnson, John Cowper, Lucky Wood;[33] Swift's *Pastoral Dialogue* and the lines attributed to him on the notorious Lady Hilaretta are, again, merely attacks on pastoralism; and of a similar theme is Smedley's poem *On the Death of Ranter*, a favorite hound.[34] It starts with the pastoral-pathetic fallacy, and then proceeds in mock-serious apostrophe:

> Mourn! all ye Fields . . .
> No more you'll hear the Dog's delicious Cry!

Whereas the satiric elegy of the seventeenth century, especially in the days of the Commonwealth and Charles II, was largely directed against the "enthusiastic" excesses of the Puritans of the middle class; in the eighteenth century, it was directed against pastoral conventionalism and lack of emotion. This change reflects a difference in literary vogue and, deeper still, a new attitude in men of letters like Swift and Gay toward the taste of the average Englishman.

Not a few elegies like Tickell's piece upon Addison are cast in a mould not strictly elegiac, but in the more generalized form of the poetic essay. One feels that, as in *Night Thoughts*, the particular death is but an excuse for improving an auspicious occasion. Two poems by William Broome illustrate perhaps as vividly as any the close relationship between the elegy proper and the mortu-

[31] The Tories seem to have made some slight effort to revive the elegy as a vehicle for satire in *The Funeral Ticket of Mr. Hypocrite Low-church*, with its super-mortuary heading (1711), a broadside in the Lambeth Palace Library; and clerical satire appears also in *An Elegy on Moderation*, on the Sacheverell trial (Lambeth Palace Lib.).

[32] *The Guardian*, No. XXX.

[33] Ramsay's serious elegies he regularly marked "Elegiac," and wrote in Neoclassical style in English dialect; like Burns, he seems to have felt that Scotch was unsuited to his most serious performance.

[34] J. Smedley, *Poems on Several Occasions*, London, 1721, 165.

ary, meditative lyric. *Melancholy, An Ode*,[35] which was "Occasion'd by the Death of a beloved Daughter" (1723),[36] in spite of this sad event, takes quite a generalized point of view, and even assimilates to the funeral elegy with its graveyard attributes, so impersonal an influence as Milton's *Il Penseroso*:

> Adieu vain Mirth, and noisy Joys!
> Ye gay Desires, deluding Toys!
> Thou thoughtful Melancholy deign
> To hide me in thy pensive train!
>
> If by the Fall of murmuring Floods,
> Where awful Shades embrown the Woods,
> Or if where Winds in Caverns groan,
> Thou wand'rest silent and alone;
>
> Come, blissful Mourner, wisely sad,
> In Sorrow's Garb, in Sable clad,
> Henceforth, thou Care, my Hours employ!
> Sorrow, be thou henceforth my Joy!
>
> By Tombs where sullen Spirits stalk,
> Familiar with the Dead I walk;
> While to my Sighs and Groans by turns,
> From Graves the midnight Echo mourns.
>
> Open thy marble Jaws, O Tomb,
> Thou Earth conceal me in thy Womb!
> And you, ye Worms, this Frame confound
> Ye brother Reptiles of the Ground.

Broome's *Poem on Death* (?1727), on the other hand, though general in subject, follows rather closely the plan and style of the funeral elegy:

> . . . See! in the horrors of yon house of woes,
> Troops of all maladies the fiend enclose!
> High on a trophy rais'd of human bones,
> Swords, spears, and arrows, and sepulchral stones,

---

[35] William Broome, *Poems*, London, 1750.

[36] John Wilkinson (mentioned above) seems to have plagiarized rather extensively from this poem in his *Ode to Melancholy* (*Poems*, London, 1725, 31). The death of Broome's daughter in 1723 would seem to settle the authorship as Broome's. See *D. N. B.* Havens (*Influence of Milton on English Poetry*, Cambridge, Mass., 1922, 669) notes the Miltonic influence, and this piece in turn may have influenced Gray.

In horrid state she reigns! attendant ills
Besiege her throne, and when she frowns she kills.
Thro' the thick gloom the torch red-gleaming burns,
O'er shrouds, and sable palls, and mould'ring urns;
While flowing stoles, black plumes, and scutcheons spread
An idle pomp around the silent dead. . . .[37]

It concludes with the common theme of death, the leveller of beggars and of kings, and in lieu of the usual apotheosis, touches briefly on the Redemption.

Indeed, this period is most notable for elegies, not even occasioned by individuals, but in a general way on the subject of death. Of these, some are of a more religious turn; and some, more purely moralistic, and for the most part Sentimental. Poetical meditations on religion have always been a staple of English literary diet; and even Gay, in his *Contemplation on Night*, fell in for a time with this generalized melancholy style. More often, however, the myrmidons of the Neo-classic Muse, when they wrote upon life, death, and immortality, developed their subject rather in the coldly moralistic vein of Pope's *Essay on Man*; and the melancholic Uvedale, in addressing his *Death-Bed Display'd* to the Bishop of Dromore, says that he expects his poem to find a "cold Reception" among "the witty and fashionable Scoffers of these Times, who laugh at RELIGION, and the Terrors of ETERNAL Torments."[38] The piece was founded on Jeremy Taylor, and is ushered in with a quotation from Vaughan's *Man in Darkness*: a double proof of the continuity of the mortuary tradition from the early seventeenth century. The versifying of David's lament over Jonathan, moreover, was not at an end;[39] Henry Baker was still lauding death as the cure of human ills and "the Road to everlasting Life";[40] and death, hell, and Judgment took up the mind of Simon Brown. He contributed *A Thought of Death and Eternity*,[41] some rousing stanzas on *Death and its Consequences*,[42] and hymns on eternal damnation and kindred topics: there were doubtless still dissenting congregations that sang them

[37] William Broome, *Poet. Works*, ed. Cooke, London, 1796, 44.

[38] Uvedale, *The Death-Bed Display'd*, Westminster, 1727.

[39] See a piece of that title by E. Taswell, *Miscellanea Sacra*, London, 1718, 14.

[40] Henry Baker, *Original Poems*, London, 1725, 72-73.

[41] Simon Browne, *Hymns and Spiritual Songs*, London, 1720, 144.

[42] *Ibid.*, 58.

with gusto. His piece called *The Sad Death of Rich Sinners*, written in ballad stanzas, is just such a thing as would have been hawked about the streets on broadsides a generation before[43]: indeed, much of the material that of yore would have found publication only in the humble broadside was now given the dignity of appearing bound between boards:

> Even kings like other men must die,
>   And turn to common earth;
> And level'd in the grave must lie,
>   With those of meaner birth.
>
> Then the cold pavement of the tomb,
>   Will be their softest bed;
> And dismal shade and frightful gloom,
>   Their brightest scene succeed.
>
> Death on their guilty souls shall prey,
>   The worms their flesh devour;
> Their strength and substance waste away,
>   And own their conqueror's power.

The piece achieves the usual happy ending, with the resurrection of "the saints"; and its plan, as well as its stylistic detail, shows plain traces of elegiac influence: after all, what is more natural than that the hymnology of dissent should be initially based upon the only other type of poetry that dissent had previously allowed, the funeral elegy? This mortuary-religious style, however, was no longer confined to dissent: the confusion between self-terror and righteousness invaded even the episcopal Bench; and the *Preparations for Death*[44] of Bishop Ken, though mainly optimistic and consolatory, pictures the last day with the eternal trumpet sounding "through the hollow Graves," very much as the Archangel trumpet in *Paradise Lost* sounded "through the vault of heaven" while "the faithful armies sung Hosannah to the Highest." Then follows a section on hell, with the usual "endless Flames," "Brimstone Lake," "Gnashing Teeth," and "Fiends who in tort'ring

[43] *Ibid.*, 156. Was not the revival by Romanticism of stanza-forms to some extent an outgrowth of their use in the sung broadside-ballads, still dear to the middle classes even in the eighteenth century?

[44] *Works of the Rt. Rev. Thomas Ken D.D., Bishop of Bath and Wells*, London, 1721, IV, 50 *et seq.* The bishop's death in 1711 gives this piece an earlier date.

Pleasure take." His passage on the grave demands quotation as illustrating how emotional such poetry can be without actually becoming Sentimental:

> Oft of my Grave I take Reviews,
> On what Death is, I daily muse;
> 'Tis Separation to endure
> Betwixt my Soul and Flesh impure;
> Flesh falls to Dust, when in its urn,
> Soul will to God, her Source, return. . . .
> Flesh, when 'tis buried in the Grave,
> Will nothing want, will nothing crave;
> It as insensible will be,
> As 'twas before its vital Tie;
> While Worms devour its very Heart
> 'Twill not Disturbance feel, nor Smart.

And even later in his treatment of death as a "Crown'd King,"[45] Ken stresses the consolations of immortality; for a poem a hundred and fifty pages in length, the piece has rather little of the mortuary. Truly the mortuary-melancholy style had become ubiquitous when even the Anglican prelacy deigned to employ it.

Of a less clearly religious cast, and yet not didactic like the School of Pope, is a group of mortuary versifiers who cultivated their poetic fury mainly for its own sweet sake. John Hughes, the Spenserian, associates "Religion" and "Woe," and proceeds to give his chief attention to the latter, enjoys ruins "awful in Decay," and revels in death by earthquake and tidal wave.[46] Mallett's *Funeral Hymn*, likewise, joins in the cult of "awful terrors," but draws its effects rather from a description of the nocturnal funerals of the day:

> Lo! as the surplic'd train draw near
> To this last mansion of mankind,
> The slow sad bell, the sable bier,
> In holy musings wrap the mind!
> And while their beam
> With trembling stream
> Attending tapers faintly dart,
> Each mould'ring bone,
> Each sculptur'd stone
> Strikes mute instruction to the heart.[47]

---

[45] *Ibid.*, 105-106.

[46] J. Hughes, *The Ecstasy, An Ode*, London, 1720. Hughes came from a background of dissent.

[47] Miss Reed (*op. cit.*, 172) seems to find influence of *Il Penseroso* in the piece; but Havens does not list the *Hymn*.

Stafford introduces a mausoleum, and admonishes the reader that rich and poor "Alike must moulder in the Domes of Death"; he then proceeds to improve the occasion as follows:

> To some Church-Yard resort,
> Where the grim Tyrant keeps his Court,
> Where his immence Plantations spread,
> There learn the End of Man,
> Learn, that thy Life is but a Span,
> Which will e'er long contract, and sink thee to the Death.

Then follows a passage that brings to mind Gray's lines on "The boast of heraldry, the pomp of power." We are invited to survey "yonder Monument, a king's tomb":

> His Pedigree no more he now does trace,
> Nor boasts the Grandeur of his Ancient Race,
> No more the Rabble to his Lordship bow,
> And bare six Foot of Earth is all his portion now.

And the same fate is described for the "fam'd Philosopher," the "Ideot," and "the Wretch afflicted, destitute and poor."[48]

The pieces just under consideration are of particular import as showing how the interest in Gothic architecture developed in poetry from a somewhat Sentimental attachment to "awful" ruins as an element of mortuary setting, and from the descriptions of funeral services in churches and of burial vaults in churchyards. This Gothic element had come down through the Puritan elegy: it had appeared in the Commonwealth period in Burrell's House of Death and in the *Elegiack Memoriall* to General Deane; it had appeared in the Caroline period in wood-cuts of castles and towers at the top of broadsides; somewhat later, Watts had endowed Gunston with an "airy spacious hall," twice designated as a "turret." Young had brought Westminster Abbey into his *Poem on the Last Day* (1713); and the 1720's supply several apt examples, a full generation before Horace Walpole started to Gothicize his villa at Strawberry Hill. The most notable of these examples, however, is yet to be discussed, *Westminster-Abbey*,[49] a long poem attributed to John Dart, headed with a picture of appropriate ruins in

[48] Stafford, *Poems on Several Occasions*, London, 1721, 53.

[49] [? John Dart], *Westminster-Abbey: A Poem*, London, 1721.

the best style of eighteenth century garden architecture. The poet invokes his Muse to lead him "through the Dwellings of the Dead,"

> Where *Loves* no more but marble Angels moan,
> And little Cherubs seem to sob in stone.

The images are so vivid as even to suggest Keats' "carven angels ever eager-eyed"; and again and again these poets call to mind Milton and Thomas Gray:

> In holy Contemplation wrap'd profound,
> Indulg'd by the loud-pealing Organ's Sound:
> With Eye erect the figur'd Roof behold,
> Rich with Intaglio, and bestreaked with Gold;
> With the gay-pictur'd Windows richly dight. . . .

But in a few pages, the poet's emotions rise to a higher flight; and a lyric outburst ensues that seems hardly to belong to the year of Grace, 1721:

> With wild surprise I cast my Eyes around,
> And press with trembling feet the holy Ground;
> A sacred, solemn Fire inflames my Soul,
> My Breast a thousand crouding Thoughts controul.

There follows moralizing on the "strange Vicissitude of Things" and on "Death's unbounded sway"; and then comes a sketch of the history of England occasionally suggestive of Gray's famous ode. Again the "Gothick Tow'rs" of the Abbey supply an architectural touch; and the *macabre* is not lacking in the description of Alexander's "moist Carkass" that "nests a hateful Brood, The hissing Serpent, and the panting Toad." Later are depicted the death and funeral of a rich, vain man, and then the obsequies of a deserving Christian, and then comes an *andante* passage on the grave:

> There Songs no more can tender Passions move,
> Raise warm Desire, or fan up glowing Love.
> The soft Spinett no more shall Mirth inspire,
> Nor Notes float dying on the trembling Wire;
> Nor warbling Musick leave the pleasing Tongue,
> But solemn Chaunting, and the Ev'ning Song:
> No Wax-lights there in polish'd Glass aspire,

But weak dim Tapers sleep along the Quire.
The twinkling Lamps in distant Isles depend,
And massy Pillars deeper Shadows send. . . .

The very end suggests that the piece was, in part at least, intended
as an elegy on the English poets; and the lines are well worth
quoting for their similarity to Gray's *Elegy*:

Poets themselves like common Mortals die,
Such are the Laws of hard Necessity;
Not the sweet Musick of the pleasing Tongue,
The heav'nly numbers nor harmonious Song,
Can plead suspension to the fleeting Breath,
Or charm th'inexorable Ears of Death,
Who interrupts him even while he Sings,
And with rude fingers breaks the sounding Strings.

Very much in this same Gothic tradition is Parnell's melancholy
Muse.[50] The poet came of Puritan stock; and, at the Restoration,
his father had left the ancestral home in Cheshire for Ireland,
where fear of the Roman Catholic masses made the government
countenance and even favor Protestant extremes. Parnell himself
was a fine specimen of religious melancholy; but the personal influence of Pope and Swift, who were his literary mentors, turned
most of his writing toward a didactic style that sits but in uneasy
fashion upon his Pegasus. His *Hymn to Contentment* is a Deistic
contemplation of God-in-Nature: like Wordsworth, he enjoys the
therapeutic repose of a "Mossy Seat" in "Hours of Sweet Retreat,"
and mistakes a salutary rest-cure for "The Joys which from Religion flow." More important for the present study is his famous
Night-Piece on Death, sometimes compared favorably even to
Gray's *Elegy*, and praised by the reviewer[51] and by such contrasting critics as Dr. Johnson and David Hume.[52] The piece seems
to have been inspired by the death of Parnell's wife in 1711,[53]
though no mention of the event appears in the lines themselves—
an impersonality that may be imputed either to the author's Neo-
classical advisers or to the growing generality of the elegiac form.
In either case, the poem may be termed a generalized elegy; for

[50] On his melancholy, see Miss Reed, *op. cit.*, 119 *et seq.*
[51] *Critical Review*, XXX, 44 *et seq.*

[52] H. G. De Maar, *History of Modern English Romanticism*, Oxford, 1924, I, 186.
[53] Miss Reed, *op. cit.*, 123.

the chief themes and the arrangement of these themes are clearly borrowed from elegiac tradition. It has the mortuary landscape, midnight out of doors, and the sepulchral church or abbey. Ghosts rise; Death is personified as a king; and, toward the end, in place of the apotheosis, is a generalized statement of salvation as in Bishop Ken's *Preparations for Death* and Broome's *Poem on Death*. It combines the mortuary with a touch of the Gothic and perhaps something of the Miltonic,[54] and delighted the taste of at least two generations of readers. Its historical significance has usually been defined as inceptive: Miss Reynolds seems to find Parnell one of the very first eighteenth century poets to appreciate the "charm of the external world";[55] and Clark declares that he "restored melancholy to literature."[56] A survey of the history of the funeral elegy renders the first of these statements dubious, and the second more than improbable. Parnell's historic importance is to be found rather in his helping to popularize a theme and a point of view that previously had been more or less confined to a large but subordinate class of readers.

Closely intertwined with the Gothic strand in the development of the funeral elegy, was the related influence of Spenser. It appeared in various forms during the century following the outbreak of the Civil War, when he is generally supposed to have had few admirers. Literary fashions, to be sure, had left him far behind; and one can hardly imagine Lord Rochester's indulging in any great delight over the *Faerie Queene*, if for no other reason, because of its Puritan associations. In 1679, an edition of Spenser was actually put on the market and presumably sold; his influence on the funeral elegy suggests that his vogue, like that of Quarles, lingered among the middle classes; and a dissenter, John Hughes, brought out the only edition printed in the first half of the eighteenth century.[57] His influence cannot always be noted with certainty; but emotionalized personifications in the style of the morality plays seem to have been a common characteristic of

---

[54] The present writer is inclined to agree with De Maar (*op. cit.*, I, 183) in finding Miltonic influence in the piece, though Havens omits it.

[55] Myra Reynolds, *The Treatment of Nature in English Poetry*, Chicago, 1909, 70.

[56] H. H. Clark, *A Study of Melancholy in Edward Young*, Mod. Lang. *Notes*, XXXIX, 130.

[57] Hughes was educated at the same academy as Watts. His edition first appeared in 1715.

bourgeois taste; and the usual opinion that Spenser's influence declined to a vanishing point about the mid-seventeenth century, can hardly be upheld. His tradition descended to the two Fletchers; and his moralistic concreteness is apparent in the poetry of Quarles. Partly through these media, and partly directly, he seems to have lived on: as noted in an earlier chapter, his direct influence seems to appear in an *Elegie* on Colonal Rainsborowe (1648) and in Burrell's "House of Death" (1653), with its details of the charnel in imitation of the House of Pride. Arwaker's *Vision* (1685) has touches of Spenserian allegory; for it was the moral allegory of the *Faerie Queene* that the age most approved. Hopkins' *Victory of Death* (1698) again has reminiscences of the House of Pride. Arwaker, once more in the *Birth Night* (1705) drew refreshment from the pure wells of the elder poet; and Theobald's *Mausoleum* (1714) actually attempted Elizabethan diction, and seems to owe something to the Cave of Despair.[58] Surely it is not quite insignificant that Theobald, who was so important in the new vogue and restoration of Shakespeare, should also have been concerned in Spenserian imitation and in writing graveyard poetry. Meanwhile, in Scotland, the Whig eulogist of King William would seem to have drawn touches of nature-description not only from the *Faerie Queene* but from the *Shepherd's Calendar*; and one suspects that Pope, and, in their earlier imitative efforts, Shenstone and Thomson, ridiculed the Spenserian style not only because it seemed antiquated and out of fashion but also because they associated it with dissenters and tradesmen. Truly, the "Spenserian revival," usually taken as beginning with Shenstone, or at least no earlier than Croxall, cannot strictly be considered a "revival" any more than the contemporaneous rise in popularity of Milton. Indeed, bits of the moral allegory of Spenser, along with the cosmic style that one associates with Milton, had appeared again and again in the mortuary elegy ever since the Puritans first took over the form in the mid-seventeenth century; and it is significant that the non-Puritan works of both poets, the *Amoretti* and *L'Allegro*, for example, had no popular vogue during the seventeenth century, though shorter and more easily understood than the *Faerie Queene* and *Paradise Lost*.[59] The middle classes did not desire literature

---

[58] The present writer has noted no certain borrowings outside the first book of the *Faerie Queene*.

[59] The narrative-element of the poems and their inherent greatness, may, to be sure, in part explain this vogue; but the

as such; but, as Bunyan well knew, they wished to find accepted moral precepts expressed either in the vivid cosmic imagery of the Bible or in the traditional garb of chivalric allegory. The emergence into new popularity, therefore, of these two authors early in the Georgian period constitutes another proof that the literary revolution of the eighteenth century was essentially, in its beginnings at least, the expression of the economic and social progress of the trading class. As they rose, they carried with them their artistic and literary tastes, an idealization of nature,[60] a love of the concrete, the cosmic, the gruesome, and the Gothic, a fondness for Shakespeare, Spenser, and Milton, as they understood these authors, and above all an intense emotionalism, which they cherished as a thing good in its very self.

Puritans cared little for poetic excellence as such; and Spenser's shorter and simpler narratives in the *Shepherd's Calendar* were little read.

[60] See Chapter IX.

CHAPTPER XI

THE FUNERAL ELEGY IN THE REIGN OF
GEORGE II

THE title of the present chapter is perhaps misleading; for the survey contemplated in this study properly embraces only that part of the reign that precedes and includes the publication of Gray's *Elegy*; but it is not easy to find an apt designation for this quarter-century. The year 1727, indeed, is a rather unsatisfactory date of demarcation; for the coming to the throne of George II is perhaps the first accession in English history that marked no change in either domestic or foreign policy: Walpole continued to head the Treasury Bench; and, though his exclusive temper and notorious corruption drove from him every colleague possessed of either independence or political scruples, his regime continued through the new reign, supported in the royal household by the influence of the Queen, in the nation at large by the rich merchant class, and in Parliament by open and unblushing bribery. A country squire himself, Walpole won over even his obstinate colleagues of the soil by a system of peace, plenty, and practical politics, based on the somewhat mundane assumption that every man has his price: it was the perfect illustration to the country at large of the ironic philosophy of Mandeville! Thus a new dynasty, who in the eyes of legitimists were no better than usurpers, and who were all too obviously foreigners, without the least desire of improving themselves by adopting English speech and ways—such a dynasty, within a single generation, found its way so completely into the hearts and purses of the people that the Stuart invasion of '45 provoked hardly more than an antiquarian curiosity even in the minds of the northern squires through whose lands Prince Charlie led his diminishing army of Highlanders. Indeed, George III, who presumed upon this loyalty to reëstablish a personal rule not unlike that of the House of Stuart, could divide but could not overcome the Whigs, so powerful had become their position in English politics; and it was not until Fox led his party to its Waterloo by espousing the cause of the French Revolution that the Whigs lost their hold, even temporarily, upon the popular mind. The reign of George II can be treated then as a mere continuation of his father's; and the slightness of difference occasioned by the change of rulers indicates the growing strength of the Cabinet System, the decline of royal power, and the beginning of a more modern epoch in British politics.

The literature of melancholy continued the evolution already marked out in the two preceding chapters. The funeral elegy was more and more merging into the graveyard poem of general scope; and, as the dissenters laid aside the remnants of their anti-artistic dogmas, and as melancholy more and more grew to be the prevailing mode in fashionable circles, the new emotionalism waxed and flourished among all classes of readers. With the rise of Wesleyanism, it began to permeate even the laboring classes,[1] whose primitive culture had scarcely been touched since first in the Middle Ages they had assimilated Christianity to their half-barbarous superstitions. The Renaissance, which was chiefly a movement among the aristocracy, and the Reformation, which was chiefly a revolt of the middle classes, had hardly affected them. For the most part, they had continued to till the soil with the same crude implements and the same wasteful system of cultivation, holding their lands in communal villages under a local overlord or squire, as one finds in small communities of half-civilized people the world over. There had been minor upheavals, peasants' revolts, and class-bitterness at times; but, not until the Industrial Revolution in manufacturing, commerce, and transportation, tore the old communities asunder, and introduced a competing individualism, did the condition of the lower classes suffer any effectual change. The spiritual side of this change was the Methodist Movement, which substituted individualized Salvation for the old institutionalized religion of the Roman and Anglican Communions: the Methodists, like the Franciscans of an earlier day, went forth to save the souls of the socially oppressed; and, taking up the "enthusiastic" individualism but lately abandoned by the Quakers, they made the ecstatic conversion of the individual the paramount fact of life. The poetic expression of this con-

---

[1] W. E. H. Lecky, *History of England in the Eighteenth Century*, New York, 1892, III, 80 *et passim*. Lecky significantly attributes the success of Methodism to its investing the prosaic life of the poor "with a halo of romance" (*ibid.*, 100).

version was in the hymns of Charles Wesley. Salvation by the
power of the Church had, in Calvinistic theology, given way to
Salvation by the Grace of God, and in Wesleyan teaching, to Salvation by emotional uplift. Emotional uplift was the immediate
purpose and effect of the sermons of John Wesley and of Whitefield; the joys of a regenerate life form the subject of Charles
Wesley's hymns;[2] and, even when the poet perchance takes death
as his subject, it is to write a *Triumph*.[3] One must remember that
the Wesleys lived and died Anglican clergymen, professing the
Arminian theology of Laud and the High Church proclivities of
the Tory Party.[4] They belong, therefore, as did the lower class
to whom they appealed, in the tradition of the Cavalier elegists
who stressed the Resurrection and not the Puritan writers who
made so much of bodily decay. The Reformation affected the aristocracy in the reign of Henry VIII; the bourgeoisie, in the seventeenth century; and, a hundred years later in the Methodist Movement, the lowest strata of society experienced it in their own particular way.

The literary reactions of this great spiritual change were not
slow to appear; for the Methodists had little of the Puritans'
prejudice against the arts; and the elegy, a form of literature apt
to reflect religious transformations, gives happy illustration at an
early stage of the Methodist attitude toward death. The verses
*To the Memory of Mrs. Mary Whitelamb, Daughter of the Late
Rev. Mr. Wesley, Rector of Epworth and Wroot* (1736),[5] like
the Laudian poetry of the School of Donne, present death as a
happy release and Salvation almost as a certainty:

[2] Lecky (*op. cit.*, III, 120) associates
graveyard poetry with Methodism; but
conversion rather than death is the theme
of the official poetry of Methodism; and
certainly the point of view of that body
was generally optimistic, especially as
compared with that of the Calvinists.

[3] *The Sunday Service of the Methodists*, London, 1788, 423.

[4] Methodism was based on the very
theories that brought Charles I to the
block: Arminian theology with its hopeful outlook, an ecclesiastical discipline as
severe as Archbishop Laud's, and politically the doctrine of Divine Right, for
Wesley was a thorough-going Tory. This

similarity is to be explained by the fact
that the classes below the bourgeoisie in
the seventeenth century shared the point
of view of the lords of the manor rather
than that of the tradesmen of the towns;
and any successful appeal to them in the
eighteenth century must, therefore, be
based on this attitude. The power of
the Queen Anne clergy, as well as of the
Wesleys, was based on their sympathy
with the point of view of the masses.

[5] See *Gent. Mag.*, VI, 740. Cf. *Verses
on the Death of Mr. Matthew Wesley*,
Gent. Mag., VII, 374-375. It ends with
an unblushing comparison of the deceased
to Christ.

> If blissful spirits condescend to know
> And hover round what once they lov'd below,
> *Maria*! gentlest excellence; attend
> To one who glories to have call'd thee friend!
> Remote in merit, though allied in blood,
> Tho' worthless I, and thou divinely good.

There follows a eulogy of "the godlike virtues of the friend and saint." Such a piece never sprang from the doctrines of Original Sin and Salvation by Grace alone. The elegies also of Samuel Wesley happily illustrate the background and state of mind from which Methodism was derived: the "Triumph" of Mr. Morgan[6] is quite taken for granted; there is not an implication that Dr. South[7] was subject even to the uncertainties of Judgment; and Mrs. Morice,[8] as befitted a bishop's daughter, received an unquestioned apotheosis. This attitude, derived apparently from their father, is to be found in the poetry of both the organizer and the hymnologist of Methodism. The *Funeral Hymns* of John and Charles Wesley, some of them written on the deaths of particular individuals, are given over almost entirely to the "lovely Appearance of Death"[9] and, as in the Caroline poets, to its happy release from the whips and scorn of time. The elegies proper that Methodism produced, if not so very numerous, at least ran to unusual length; but their unvaried theme is the ecstasy of heaven. Charles Wesley celebrates Robert Jones as immediately "received among the Blest"; and, in the same poem, he significantly pays tribute to St. Charles, King and Martyr, and prays that he also may "for the *Church of England* die."[10] The Methodists, instead of reserving the apotheosis for the climax of the elegy commonly state it boldly at the start. Charles Wesley's *Elegy* on Whitefield (1771),[11] for instance, begins by taking it quite for granted:

> And is my WHITEFIELD entered into rest,
> With sudden death, with sudden glory blest?

[6] Samuel Wesley, *Poems on Several Occasions*, Cambridge, 1743, 85 *et seq.* Apparently there were still some that misliked the elegy, for Wesley takes it for granted that "Critick Wits" will not approve his verses.

[7] *Ibid.*, 162 *et seq.*

[8] *Ibid.*, 191 *et seq.* See also 207 and 297.

[9] [John and Charles Wesley], *Funeral Hymns*, third edition, London, 1753.

[10] [C. Wesley], *An Elegy on the Death of Robert Jones Esq.*, second ed., Bristol, n. d.

[11] Charles Wesley, *Elegy on the Late Reverend George Whitefield*, Bristol, 1771.

The question is merely rhetorical, and serves to show that the writer had no doubt as to the fact. This fundamental tone of Methodism did not change; and when, in 1788, Creighton[12] bewailed the death of Charles Wesley himself, in the very first stanza he aptly calls his poem a "Song of Triumph." As early as the 1740's, devotional poetry shows an increasing tendency toward the optimistic,[13] greater than it had displayed, except for some pieces by Non-Jurors, since the Civil War; but the lower classes had neither the time nor the money to be patrons of the arts; for the wealth of foreign trade and the Industrial Revolution, which brought riches to the bourgeoisie, left the proletariat if anything worse off than before; and thus these momentous changes within this great mass of the population, changes both economic and spiritual, were largely inarticulate, and made but little impress upon the literature of the day.

The determinant cultural forces of the eighteenth century, therefore, continued to be the Neo-classical aristocracy and the Sentimental bourgeoisie; and the chief immediate effect of the proletarian changes was merely to weaken the former by lessening the power and cohesion of the Established Church. The struggle of these determinant forces operated as in the reign of George I, more and more in favor of the Whigs and their commercial allies. Methodism, however, even if it did not become a paramount power in literature, at least had a very real indirect influence in the person of James Hervey,[14] an influence that may not have been optimistic,[15] but at least produced an intensified emotionalism. Hervey's *Meditations among the Tombs* (1745) are a kind of generalized elegy in prose, occasioned by the death of Miss R. T., somewhat as Parnell's *Night-Piece* was immediately occasioned by the death of the poet's wife. Hervey meditates upon the tomb of a young man—a youth doubtless to fortune and to fame unknown—and his melodramatic fancy at once supplies the suggestion that the youth died in the midst of his nuptial celebrations, a gratuitous assumption, but one that appealed to the emotionalistic sensibilities of the writer; and, in the best exclamatory style of Shaftesbury,

---

[12] James Creighton, *Elegiac Stanzas occasioned by the Death of the Rev. Charles Wesley*, London, 1788.
[13] E.g., *God is Love* (*Gent. Mag.*,

XIX, 467).
[14] Lecky, *op. cit.*, III, 39.
[15] Hervey's chronic invalidism doubtless accounts for this prevalent mood.

he gloats over this crude contrast between love and death; and, like a true elegist, in the midst of his lamentations he reads a righteous moral:

Dreadful vicissitude! to have the *bridal* festivity turned into the *funeral* solemnity! Deplorable misfortune! to be shipwrecked in the very happiness!—What a memorable proof is here of the frailty of man, in his best estate! Look, O! look on this monument, ye *gay* and *careless*! Attend to this date and boast no more of tomorrow.

Who can tell but the *bride-maids*, girded with gladness, had prepared the marriage-bed? . . . Death, relentless death, is making him another kind of bed in the dust of the earth. . . .[16]

The Ephuistic style of balance and alliteration continues with the "gloomy hearse" and the "icy arms of death"; but the mortuary Sentimentalism of Hervey needs no further illustration. Such a tone was by no means new in elegiac writing; but Hervey is notable as an especially flagrant practitioner and one who gloried in his deeds. With gusto, he quoted the lines from Book VIII of *Night Thoughts* in which Young recommends "gloomy paths to joy";[17] and, at the very beginning, he apologizes for his own *Meditations* as *"serious* and *mournfully pleasant."* His popularity is an index of the spirit of the age: his masterpiece passed through no less than seventeen editions before the end of the century, unhappily eclipsing Law's *Serious Call*;[18] it was turned into blank verse by Newcomb, and favorably reviewed;[19] it was imitated in prose "By a Lady";[20] and for a long time after its publication, the *Gentleman's Magazine* was still printing congratulatory poems upon its composition. The death of the author in 1758 called forth at least one elegy by an "apprentice to a Jersey-comber in the town of Northampton," which is significant as suggesting the social longitude of Hervey's vogue and the appeal of his Sentimentalism:

. . . O thou, to whom all sacred themes belong,
Pour forth the sweetly-melancholy song!
"Alas! grim death hath shot the fatal dart,

---

[16] J. Hervey, *Works*, Edinburgh, 1792, I, 14 *et seq.* Such writings were not uncommon at the time. See Burnham's *Pious Memorials* and Pearsall's *Contemplations.*

[17] *Ibid.,* VI, 39.

[18] Sir Leslie Stephen, *English Literature and Society*, New York, 1904, 154, and *History of English Thought in the Eighteenth Century*, London, 1902, II, 438.

[19] *Monthly Rev.,* XVI, 289-298.

[20] *Gent. Mag.,* XX, 409.

"Which long seem'd pointed at his languid heart,
"Th'infuriate tyrant, crown'd with funeral gloom,
"In triumph drags him to the hollow tomb:
"Who now so well can paint the blooming flow'r,
"Or preach from *Sepulchres* at midnight hour?"

The Methodists might have little of the mortuary elegy; but, among the older bodies of dissent, it was by no means a matter of the past. With every note in the elegiac compass, Watts was tunefully bewailed. Softly sweet in pensive measures, one poet soothes his sad and travailing emotions:

> Upon a mossy Grave I sat reclin'd
> In pensive Mood, on solemn Subjects bent,
> The gloomy Scenes held my Attention fix'd
> (The grisly Tyrant and the gaping Tomb)
> Nor gave me leave to gaze,—but weep, weep o'er
> A Prophet dead![21]

Thomas Gibbons, in an earlier vein, gave a fine picture of "Hell's unbottom'd Gulph":

> That wasteful World of Vengeance, where no Glimpse
> Of Light appears, but from the horrid Gleams[22]
> Of ever-burning Sulphur, where the Worm
> Of Conscience—gnaws in agonizing Pains,
> And wild Despair inflames the tort'ring Rage. . . .[23]

And in *The Triumphs of Bigotry* "By a Lady" the eulogy of the deceased is curiously commingled with satire of the Rev. Thomas Bradbury.[24] Gibbons was a dissenting minister of some poetic virtuosity: not only could he, as in the elegy just quoted,

> With yon infernal horrors dwell,
> And plunge your boasted bliss to hell. . . .[25]

but he could also combine the "warbling Lyre" with the most proper Neo-classical "Transports" and the most sweetly copious

---

[21] *Poem Sacred to the Memory of the Reverend and Learned Isaac Watts, D.D.,* London [?1748].

[22] Gibbons would seem to have been reading Milton's description of hell.

[23] T. Gibbons, *An Elegiac Poem to the Memory of the Rev. Isaac Watts, D.D.,* London, 1749.

[24] *Monthly Rev.*, II, 6 *et seq.*

[25] *Ibid.*, III, 337. See also III, 333-335.

"Floods of Sorrow" and "Lengths of Groan."[26] Indeed, the demarcation in style between Anglican elegies and those of the Calvinistic non-conformists grew less and less distinct, as the old sharpness of theological difference faded into the' past. Among the minor figures it is difficult to tell which are to be accounted dissenters: the lives of some seem lost in obscurity; and some are like Sayer Rudd, who started as a Baptist minister, was accused of Unitarianism, and finally ended his days in an Anglican living. He wrote several elegies, most notably one on Thomas Hollis,[27] which in its latter lines illustrates the persistence of the mortuary style:

> But tho', to death resign'd, this lifeless clay,
> Resolves to dust for kindred worms a prey.

Even more in the seventeenth century dissenting style is a broadside *Elegy Sacred to the Memory of Mr. Samuel Stockwell* (1750).[28] It begins:

> Stockwell is dead, no more you hear him groan,
> With Grinding Pains of *Gravel* or of *Stone*;
> No more in *Pulpit* hear his warbling Tongue. . . .

And later, we are told that his soul "long'd to be Strip'd of Clay." The *Elegy* by M. C. on William Bentley,[29] the non-conformist divine (1751), shows perhaps some influence of Methodism, although the Methodists and the dissenters were not on very good terms: the apotheosis is announced as early as the third line, where we are told "Brave Bentley's Landed in the Realms of light"— very much as the safe arrival of a cargo might be posted at Lloyd's. Probably non-conformist also is the elegy that watered the "cold grave" of John Thompson (1753) with much weeping and lamentation.[30] John Hughes, editor of Spenser and school-fellow of Isaac Watts, would seem, though a dissenter at least in origin, to have been on good terms with the Establishment.[31] His *Monu-*

[26] *The Mourner's Complaint Considered*, London, 1746. It is at times difficult to separate the elder and the younger Thomas Gibbons, for both wrote elegies.
[27] Sayer Rudd, *A Poem on the Death of the late Thomas Hollis, Esq.*, London, 1731.

[28] Brit. Mus. broadside.
[29] Brit. Mus. broadside.
[30] *Roxburghe Ballads*, ed. Chappell, London, 1871, *Publ. Ball. Soc.*, III, No. 561.
[31] John Hughes, *Letters*, London, 1773, III, xcvi.

mental Ode to Mrs. Elizabeth Hughes (d. 1714), lingers over the decay of tombstones and of mausoleums, and gives honorable mention to the Egyptian pyramids:

> Whate'er their vast and gloomy Vaults contain,
> No Names distinct of their great Dead remain,
> Beneath the Mass confus'd, in heaps thy Monarchs lie,
> Unknown, and blended in Mortality.[32]

The comparative restraint of the piece and its use of the odic form show that Hughes was not maintaining the non-conformist style in all its pristine purity; and the *Verses* (?1735) to his memory "By a Lady" are entirely Neo-classical eulogy.[33] Indeed, not merely were poets of all sorts and denominations taking over the literary manner of dissent, but some of the dissenters themselves abandoned it; and, perhaps because they were anxious to distinguish themselves from the "enthusiastic" Methodists, tended more and more to cultivate an unwonted restraint.

By all odds, however, the most interesting figure among the non-conformist elegiac poets of this generation is the elusive personality of Thomas Gutteridge. His biography is yet to be written; and even the dates of his birth and death are unknown; but his period of productivity roughly coincides with the reign of George II. Most of his earlier works seem to have perished; but, from footnote references in his six signed broadsides in the British Museum, we know that in his younger days, he wrote a poem under the inspiration of Locke called *A Man of Wit*, and elegies on the dissenting ministers, Daniel Wilcox (d. 1733) and Robert Bragge (d. 1738) and on a certain Smith. The address of his house in Shoreditch is known to us; and he seems to have eked out an uncertain living, partly from his broadsides, which he sold at his own house, and partly from teaching a new method of shorthand that he had invented. His only surviving works would seem to be some crudely written and wretchedly printed broadsides on the deaths of six Presbyterian and Independent clergymen.[34] The manner

---

[32] John Hughes, *Poems on Several Occasions*, London, 1735, I, 98 *et seq*. Not very accurate Egyptology, one fears.

[33] *Ibid.*, I, lxv.

[34] The broadsides in the British Museum by Gutteridge are on John Newman (1741), James Wood (1742), John Hubbard (1743), Mordecai Andrews (1750), William Bentley (1751), and Thomas Hall (1762). A short life of Newman is to be found in *D. N. B.*; and the others are briefly discussed by W. Wilson (*History of Dissenting Churches*, London, 1808-1814).

of their printing suggests the utter decadence of elegiac broadside
typography; and the manner of their poetic style suggests that dissent in London, its greatest centre, was taking on a new emotional
restraint. The mortuary note had entered general literature, and
no longer was specially prized as the hall-mark of non-conformity.
Dissent, moreover, had become respectable; and this new respectability was signalized by new efforts at decorum.[35] The old pictures, to be sure, sometimes remain, as in the elegy on Newman
which is prefaced with a skeleton, two skulls and cross bones, and
a female figure with hour glass and scythe and the cheerful motto,
"Eternity hath no End." Sometimes the old gruesome touch remains, as in the piece on Stockwell already mentioned. Sometimes,
Gutteridge indulges in a truly seventeenth century conceit:

> Refresh'd in Prayer, his Soul did sweetly sail,
> Under the Spirit's Breath's—with a full Gail;
> In the Red Sea of the Redeemers Blood,
> Where all the Childrens Sins sink in the purple Flood.[36]

Sometimes, moreover, he finds "Pleasure" in death, and even goes
so far as to impute this feeling to the nearest and dearest of the
departed:

> That Man of God, he's dead, whose dying Moan
> Would melt a Heart, to hear him sigh or moan.
> O! his dear Spouse can say her Heart did melt,
> And by a Sympathy his Sorrows felt.
> These pierc'd her Ears and Heart, and both gave Grief,
> But here's the Pleasure, here the Grand Relief—
> His Soul in Sea of Gospel sweetly sails,
> And tho' his Flesh was weak—His Spirit had strong Gales.[37]

On the whole, however, the mortuary passages in Gutteridge are
few; and, usually, the sickish sweetness of his verse is relieved only
by faulty meter and strangely entangled syntax. The broadside

---

[35] It is sometimes hard to tell how far
this change is the influence of Methodism and how far the reaction from it.
The new optimism seems Methodistic;
but probably it is merely Sentimentalism
independently developed.

[36] An Elegy in Memory of the Reverend Mr. John Newman (Brit. Mus.
broadside). Like the Methodists, he takes
Salvation for granted at once.

[37] An Elegy Sacred to the Memory of
the Reverend Mr. William Bentley (Brit.
Mus. broadside).

elegy had ceased to be an incident to religion; and Sentimentalism expressed itself more aptly in more general literary forms.

Indeed, of miscellaneous elegists, and miscellaneous elegies, and miscellaneous poems that approximate or borrow from the elegiac form, the reign of George II is full to abundance. A rapid glance at some such pieces is enough, for the mere purpose of illustrating the prevalence of elegiac themes. Publication was still the road to preferment in the Church, and sometimes in the State; and such ardent youths as had not the patience for scholarship, and who thought their Original Genius too great for translation, composed poems on the occasion of something or other, and sometimes on no occasion at all. As the pastoral elegy declined,[38] the generalized poetry of Nature, melancholy, and death, arose from elegiac sources in its stead. James Ralph, the hack-writer who is remembered for his early intimacy with Benjamin Franklin, wrote a poem called *Night* with a "ruin'd castle" and "the horrid call of death."[39] Thomas Fitzgerald did an elegy *Upon the Death of the Countess of Orrery*,[40] indulging quite frankly in the "Luxury of Grief," and shedding "copious" tears over her "sad Urn." The mortuary style even found its way into the poetic works of Robert Tatersal, the poetical brick-layer: his *Elegy* on Mrs. Jane He—ly, for the most part Neo-classical enough, ends with the couplet:

> My last Farewell, I take, and kiss thy Tomb,
> I follow shortly to the silent Gloom.

His poem *To Death* (1733)[41] refers to the fell sergeant as the "Dread King of Terrors," to man as "vile Dust," and to "this rotten Flesh, which Worms devour." Sometimes, his imagery is almost Mediæval in its *macabre* Realism:

> . . . unexpectedly grim Death appears,
> And strait away the hardy Miscreant tears;
> Dragging the Wretch reluctant to his Grave. . . .

Mary Masters, whose elegy on Addison has already been discussed,

[38] Marion K. Bragg, *The Formal Eclogue, Univ. of Maine Studies*, Orono, 1926, Chap. V.

[39] J. Ralph, *Night, A Poem*, London, 1728.

[40] T. Fitzgerald, *Poems on Several Occasions*, London, 1733, 77.

[41] R. Tatersal, *Bricklayer's Miscellany*, London, 1734, 16.

was nightly troubled with "Sad mournful Visions of a dying
Friend." Her thoughts naturally turned to "the darksome Grave,"
and she pondered upon "the pale Corpse . . . a thoughtless Lump
. . . Disfigured and unlovely to the Eyes." [42]   And Mrs. Dixon
indulged in extended *Reflections on the Sight of a Tomb*:

> In this dark Gloom by the pale Taper's Light
> How my Soul shudders at th'amazing Sight!
> Solemn Tranquility; most awful State!
> Tremendous Ruin! wretched Mortal's Fate!
> Ye silent Horrors!—Where's the *Grandeur* now
> With which you made your En'trance here below?
> When *Dust* on *Dust* and *Earth* on *Earth* is thrown,
> The pomp retreats, and we are left alone;
> That undisturb'd th'insatiate *Worm* may feed,
> Seize the cold Prey, and wanton o're the Dead. . . . [43]

After having adorned "the squalid Heaps" with every possible
moral, the poetess concludes, elegy-wise, with a few brief remarks
on immortality, very much as a Sentimental comedy, having pleased
the rakes for four acts with a tale of bawdry, suddenly in the fifth
brings in an unprepared-for happy ending that is all regeneration
and joy.   Indeed, failure and success, pleasure and pain, are often
presented to us in the literature of this age quite without motive
or moral reason. [44]   Thomas Cooke was the author of several elegies, [45] in which he moralizes in Sentimental style over "the darksome Tomb," and indulges in nature-description *à la* Thomson.
Thomas Newcomb [46] did at least four poems on the commonplace
subject of Westminster Abbey, and gave one of them a fresh
piquancy by advertising it as "Wrote in Westminster-Abbey, at a
funeral."   At least once, he rings a change upon the old themes:

> Those piles aloft that raise their head,
> And the great king, or warrior shew;

---

[42] Mary Masters, *Poems on Several Occasions*, London, 1733, 173 *et seq.*

[43] Mrs. Dixon, *Poems on Several Occasions*, Canterbury, 1740, 55.

[44] The causes for this immoralism, reflected also in the philosophy of Mandeville, are doubtless to be found in the
conditions of the age: it was a century
of political and mercantile adventures in
India as well as at home, when great
stakes were lost or won apparently by
chance on a single throw rather than by
following fixed principles over a long
period of years. The tremendous vogue
of gambling seems to be part of this
same psychology.

[45] T. Cooke, *Original Poems with Imitations and Translations*, London, 1742.
At least one of these elegies was written
as early as 1725.

[46] T. Newcomb, *Miscellaneous Collection of Original Poems*, London, 1740,
194 *et passim.*

> Shine they to please the mighty dead,
> Or the vile worm that crawls below? [47]

William Tans'ur's *Poetical Meditations* on Death, and Judgment, Heaven and Hell,[48] may be taken as typical of many long versified cogitations on religious subjects. Its final climax, the apotheosis of "The righteous Man," is thoroughly elegiac; and it freely uses elegiac themes along the way: it is introduced, like a broadside, with an illustration showing a graveyard and an allegorical representation of death; the letter-press has something of worms and of "Sculls and Bones"; death is the universal democracy where kings and peasants are the same; the mortuary landscape, the pains of death, and the horrors of hell, all have their place. One might almost say that such poetry could not have been written had not the Puritan funeral elegy prepared the way. Occasionally as in Hammond,[49] the Classical influence still prevails; sometimes, as in Dr. Winstanley,[50] the delicacy of Prior. Ashley Cowper's elegy on his only son has almost an Elizabethan touch in its sharp rhythm and in some of its details:

> Dig a *Grave*, and dig it *deep*
> Where my *Child* and *I* may *sleep*
> Near some haggard, blasted *Oak*,
> Where the Midnight Ravens *Croak*;
> Or some nodding frightful Cliff;
> Whence the *Wretched* find *Relief*. . . . [51]

John Whaley of Kings College, Cambridge, has the usual *Night Thought* with much reflection on death and the usual sort of elegy *On the Death of a Young Bride*.[52] Truly the reign of George II showed no poverty of mortuary verse and no poverty of melancholic themes.

A few poets of somewhat greater note, should perhaps be separated from the general herd. Aaron Hill has been ranked with Watts and Young as an expression of middle-class melancholy;[53]

---

[47] *Ibid.*, 219.

[48] William Tans'ur, *Poetical Meditations on the Four Last Things*, London, 1740.

[49] James Hammond, *Love Elegies*, London, 1743.

[50] John Winstanley, *Poems Written Occasionally*, Dublin, 1742.

[51] [Ashley Cowper] *The Norfolk Poetical Miscellany*, London, 1744, II, 98. See also his essay *On Fortitude in Death*.

[52] John Whaley, *A Collection of Original Poems and Translations*, London, 1745, 307.

[53] Amy Louise Reed, *The Background of Gray's Elegy*, New York, 1924, 100.

but his connection with Lord Paget[54] hardly associates him with the middle classes; and his elegiac verse is more likely to be in the tone of Catullus,[55] or of the pastoral,[56] or of Prior.[57] He has, however, a cosmic treatment of *The Judgement-Day*,[58] a rendering of David's lament,[59] and at least one couplet of morbid mawkishness:

> Welcome, ah! welcome, *life's* last friend, *decay!*
> Faint on, tir'd *soul* and lapse, *unmourn'd* away.[60]

The growing strength of the Miltonic movement is signalized by West's *Monody on Queen Caroline*,[61] with its obvious borrowings from *Lycidas*. Collins embroidered *Cymbeline*[62] with a "wailing ghost," a "wither'd witch," "goblins," and a storm—a combination of elements that belongs to the Puritan funeral elegy rather than to the Elizabethan dirge. His *Ode on the Death of Colonel Ross* is too aerial to be mortuary, in spite of its fine personification of "deep Despair"; and his *Ode* beginning, "How sleep the brave," is a fine example of the generalized military panegyric but is in no sense a mortuary elegy. Rather more in the mortuary tradition is Christopher Smart, whose lines *On the Sudden Death of a Clergyman*,[63] portray the "wretched corse, untenanted and cold" and "Th'enthusiastic"[64] flight of wild despair. Shenstone attempts various elegiac styles, and once mentions the "yew's funereal green";[65] but he seldom runs to the lower notes of the gamut, preferring higher and brighter tones. Indeed, the mid-eighteenth century shows an avid reaching out toward every possible variation of the well known themes and styles; and the elegiac was widely cultivated by the more notable as well as the lesser poets.

A survey of the periodicals gives this fact even further proof. The periodicals had become the vehicle for occasional and casual

[54] See Dorothy Brewster, *Aaron Hill*, New York, 1913.

[55] A. Hill, *Poems*, London, 1753, III, 153.

[56] *Ibid.*, III, 313, and IV, 296.

[57] *Ibid.*, III, 158.

[58] *Ibid.*, IV, 263.

[59] *Ibid.*, III, 326. The versified paraphrase of the Bible was not discontinued: e.g., H. Travers' paraphrase of Esdras II, vi, 38 (*Miscellaneous Poems*, London, 1731), and the paraphrases of Job in

Translations and Poems, Edinburgh, 1731.

[60] A. Hill, *Poems, ed. cit.*, III, 87 *et seq.*

[61] *Collection of Poems*, ed. Dodsley, London, 1748, II, 277.

[62] The *Dirge in Cymbeline*.

[63] *The Student*, II (1751), 393.

[64] Is not the gradual rise of this word to a favorable meaning closely associated with the rise of those classes that had so long been accused of "enthusiasm"?

[65] See *Elegy IV*.

verse, gradually taking the place of broadsides and pamphlets; and the quantity of elegiac material in the *Gentleman's Magazine* during this period received some notice at the beginning of the present study—a surprising quantity in view of the fact that the publication of verse was only incidental to the main purpose of the magazine. The printing, or reprinting, of short poems, however, soon became a regular department—a department, in fact, that doubled in size during the early 1740's. In spite of this increase, the amount of elegiac material shows a slight decline: the mortuary style was being absorbed into other forms. The *Gentleman's Magazine*, during its first twenty years in the 1730's and '40's, printed a wide variety of elegiac types and styles under a number of contrasting literary influences; but practically all of these pieces are easily traceable to the common types discussed in the foregoing chapters, or at least are hybrids of two or more of them. The pastoral elegy finds a place, though less often than one might expect,[66] and sometimes written in a mortuary tone.[67] The Biblical paraphrase[68] and the Shakespearean reminiscence[69] are still supplying elements of gloom. The lighter tone of Prior is used for women and children,[70] sometimes with a suggestion of Wordsworth's *We Are Seven*. Some of the formal eulogies show the cold formality of second-rate Neo-classicism, sometimes combined, as of yore, with Classical reference.[71] These formal eulogies, as always, make up a large proportion of the number: some are on noblemen, such as the Dukes of Chandos[72] and Argyle;[73] there are several eulogies, elegies, and odes on Queen Caroline;[74] there is a military eulogy of Captain C——[75] that reminds one a little of Collins; the cloth is occasionally celebrated.[76] The law-

[66] *Gent. Mag.*, II, 971, *To the Memory of Mrs. ——*; *ibid.*, XIII, 266, *Cosmelia*; *ibid.*, XVI, 609, *Robin*.

[67] *Ibid.*, XI, 380-381, *Alcæus*.

[68] *Ibid.*, XI, 384 and XIII, 437, paraphrases of *Job*.

[69] *Ibid.*, XXI, 566. See also Stevenson's *On Seeing a Scull* (*ibid.*, XIX, 375).

[70] *Ibid.*, I, 261, *An Elegiac Poem by Mr. H.*; *ibid.*, VI, 417, *On the Death of Mrs. Sa— E——rds*; XIV, 500, *On the Death of Miss ——*.

[71] *Ibid.*, II, 1025, *On the Death of Mr. Wilks*.

[72] *Ibid.*, XIV, 446.

[73] *Ibid.*, XIII, 550. See also the curious piece "By a person of distinction" *To the Earl of M——t*, chiefly eulogy of the son, from whom patronage was doubtless expected!

[74] *Ibid.*, VII, 693, 759, 762; VIII, 102, 214. The second of these pieces is a regular Pindaric ode.

[75] *Ibid.*, XVIII, 325.

[76] *Ibid.*, IX, 41, J. W.'s elegy on the Rev. Mr. Blackmore; *ibid.*, XIII, 546, *On the Death of the Rev. Mr. Grove*.

lords were not forgotten;[77] and the scholar and the physician received a tribute.[78] Oddly enough, however, perhaps the most exalted eulogy is a piece *On the Death of Richard Savage*,[79] who certainly, dead or alive, could hardly have been looked to as a possible patron! These Classical and Neo-classical elegies are commonly elaborated not only with scraps of mythology and fragments from the pastoral tradition, but also with the pathetic fallacy[80] and personification[81] and much moralizing.[82] Indeed, the persistence of this literary type for generation after generation, first on broadsides and then in the magazines, is one of the most unfortunate consequences of the literary system of aristocratic patronage.

Elegies of quite a different type also survived; and the pieces that developed from the middle class tradition are often quite as unfortunate, though in a different way. These also use moralizing, but of a gloomier cast, and often turn the pathetic fallacy toward their melancholy bent; but emotional Realism is the hallmark of their style. The old mortuary themes, though sometimes softened and generalized, and sickly sad rather than disgusting, still remain: the death-bed "With all the softest elegance of grief,"[83] the sorrows of the survivors and the corpse "benumb'd in the cold arms of death,"[84] the funeral,[85] and the "noisome grave."[86] Traces of the old Calvinism still appear in several elegies on Watts[87] and in one on "the Rev. Mr. Hughes, late of Hellidon . . . in Northamptonshire," who was able more proficiently

> To rouse the indolent, the stubborn fright
> With the sad horrors of eternal night.[88]

Some of the pieces on Watts, however, and especially one on Miss Ll——d,[89] announce with shocking certainty the Salvation of the

---

[77] *Ibid.*, V, 101, *Elegy to the Memory of William Jessor*; *ibid.*, XX, 278, *On the Death of the Hon. Sir Thomas Abney.*

[78] *Ibid.*, XV, 104; V, 103. The lines on Lloyd have a comic touch.

[79] *Ibid.*, XIII, 439.

[80] Apparently this figure was considered especially appropriate to the noble fair. See *ibid.*, IV, 286; VII, 762; XI, 326-327; XX, 87.

[81] *Ibid.*, XI, 550; XIII, 268.

[82] *Ibid.*, XIV, 502; XVI, 376; XX, 566.

[83] *Ibid.*, VIII, 317, Trapp's lines *To the Queen on the Death of Prince George of Denmark.*

[84] *Ibid.*, VI, 221, *To the Lady W——e.*

[85] *Ibid.*, VI, 158, *On the Death of Mrs. Birch.* The elegy is of special interest as showing the influences of Milton and the elegy and as pointing forward to Gray.

[86] *Ibid.*, XI, 156, *On the Death of a Beloved Child.*

[87] *Ibid.*, XIX, 39 *et seq.*; 134 *et seq.*

[88] *Ibid.*, V, 496.

[89] *Ibid.*, V, 103-104.

deceased; and a piece on W——m M——n combines this optimism with a considerable degree of religious doubt.[90] The old spirit, although somewhat softened, is perhaps most fully exemplified in the stanzas *On the Death of a Delectable Child four Years old*:

> Hath Death, with awful Terrors clad,
>   Been watching at the door;
> And ravish'd hence a pleasant babe,
>   Whose charms delight no more?
>
> How shall we bear the smarting stroke,
>   This chastisement from God;
> How well improve the providence,
>   And profit by the rod?
>
> Lord, 'tis thine hand, thy sov'reign pow'r,
>   Form'd the dear living bust;
> And 'tis the same almighty word
>   Commands its frame to dust.
>
> Far heavier strokes our sins deserve,
>   If thou should'st be severe;
> With patience therefore all resign'd,
>   Thy just rebuke we'll bear.[91]

A number of the pieces, especially those on Mrs. Rowe[92] and other ladies, display a more or less overt Sentimentalism. They are "pensive" rather than mortuary, but sometimes borrow the mechanism of emotionality from Puritan sources; and, indeed, it is not to be forgotten that Mrs. Rowe was herself a sort of Calvinist, a Sentimental Calvinist, if one may be permitted a contradiction in terms.

But toward the latter part of this period, the elegiac style was beginning to pall: as early as 1743, the *Gentleman's* quoted from Blair's *Grave*[93] only passages of moralizing, an indication that the London publishers who had rejected it were perhaps right in declaring that mortuary verse had no appeal, or perhaps no longer an appeal, "to the fashionable and polite." The *Monthly Review*

[90] *Ibid.*, IV, 267.
[91] *Ibid.*, IX, 379. Cf. the poems on children by Watts and by Prior. A comparison of the Neo-classical and the Calvinistic views of child-life would make an interesting study.

[92] Mrs. Rowe seems to have been the centre of quite a poetic school. *Ibid.*, VII, 183, 247; IX, 152, 262; XII, 540. See also V, 155; X, 518; XI, 438, 548.
[93] *Ibid.*, XIII, 323.

in 1751 passed over *The Triumphant Christian,* an elegy on Joseph Weatherill of Southwark, because it "needed no comment."[94] Elegies were largely the product of the provinces, of women-writers, and of the poorer classes. There are pieces from Lincolnshire,[95] Yorkshire,[96] Shropshire,[97] from Wales,[98] from Ireland,[99] and even from New England[100] and Virginia.[101] Some of the pieces are barely literate; many are on women; and many are signed, if not by women's actual names, at least by feminine pseudonyms, such as "Carolina," and "Melissa," and "Ophelia." Not all these pieces are quite contemptible. Witness the following couplet, which gives a new turn to the old idea that the poet immortalizes his subject:

> The Fame my Muse would *give* do thou *bestow,*
> And o'er *thy* Marble, let my Laurels grow.[102]

The elegy seems to have been the first poetic exercise in the literary gradus of the half-educated; and those social groups, the women, the middle classes, and the provincials, who were desirous of proving their culture to the polite world, in an age when culture still meant the appreciation, if not the actual composition of poetry, embraced any convenient occasion to take a trial flight. The elegy was short and not too exalted; its subject-matter was universal and appropriate; and its tone consonant with the state of mind of persons whose life was hard and whose religion was, or had been, Calvinistic. If the mortuary style had depended merely on the fickle love of change among the aristocracy, it would soon have passed away; but, as education slowly worked downward in society during the eighteenth century, the elegiac stage of culture received a constant stream of postulants, put its stamp upon them, and sometimes passed them on to other cultural planes. Gray's *Elegy* was widely read and praised, not only because of the undoubted genius of the author, but also because of the universality of its subject and the popularity of its literary type.

---

[94] *Mon. Rev.,* V, 464.

[95] *Gent. Mag.,* XVI, 158, perhaps an epitaph rather than an elegy.

[96] *Ibid.,* XXI, 36, 181, 276. Are all these by the same "Ophelia"?

[97] *Ibid.,* XIII, 157.

[98] *Ibid.,* V, 381; XIX, 470; *Mon. Rev.,* I, 461.

[99] *Gent. Mag.,* VI, 616 and 680.

[100] *Ibid.,* V, 549. The piece contains a good orthodox picture of hell.

[101] *Ibid.,* XX, 231. Doleful, but a telling contrast to the preceding contribution.

[102] *Ibid.,* VIII, 482, *Verses to the Memory of the Most accomplish'd and lamented Mrs. Rebekah Booth,* by Moses Browne.

Indeed, especially in the provinces, the elegy in most of its traditional forms, lingered at least sporadically throughout the eighteenth and far down into the nineteenth century. It is not the purpose of the present study to trace its evolution beyond the publication of Gray's masterpiece; but a general indication of its persistence at least among the rank and file of versifiers, is perhaps allowable. Gray's own fame and the superiority of his performance attracted a host of imitators, as the pages of Northup's *Bibliography* attest, until finally it fell upon the evil days of parody:

> Consign'd to mingle with his parent earth,
>   His name in distant lands will ne'er be known;
> Dull apathy presided at his birth,
>   And ignorance mark'd the infant for her own.[103]

The Newgate lamentation, popular since the days of Elizabeth, continued even into the nineteenth century with such pieces as the *Lamentations of John Thomson & David Dobie* (1830),[104] notorious murderers. The clerical broadside was not dead, even as late as 1793, when there appeared an evangelical *Elegy on the Rev. John Berridge* of Bedfordshire;[105] and a more Neo-classical lament on the Rev. Richard Brome came out in the *Suffolk Garland*.[106] Doggerel eulogies of all descriptions appear on early nineteenth century broadsides.[107] The mortuary was still extant: an *Elegy* on George Canning touches on the "varied torments" of his death, praises his accomplishments, introduces a mortuary landscape, and at the end gives him the conventional apotheosis;[108] and, in 1881, the death of Lord Beaconsfield was solemnized with a black-bordered broadside and an anonymous acrostic printed in Liverpool.[109] In the remoter parts of New England also, the elegy lingered, sometimes on broadsides[110] and occasionally even to-day in the rural

---

[103] *Verses Written after the Funeral of Billy Twigger, Suffolk Garland*, Ipswich, 1818, 300 *et seq*. The subject seems to have been an idiot boy.

[104] Brit. Mus. broadside, probably printed in Edinburgh.

[105] Brit. Mus. broadside.

[106] *Suffolk Garland*, ed. cit., 311 *et seq*.

[107] E.g., Mrs. Anna Colburn, *Lines* on the death of Mrs. Bowker (Harvard Lib. broadside) (1811).

[108] *Elegy on the Death of the Right Honorable George Canning*, London, 1827.

[109] Brit. Mus. broadside.

[110] See two broadsides in Harvard Lib.: R. Cook, *Expostulating with the Messenger on the Pale Horse, while reflecting upon the Death of Mary Leach, who died at Raymond* [Maine] *Jan. 5, 1827*; and *Lines Composed on the death of Mrs. Jessy Benson, of Bar Harbor, Maine* (1870). *The Poets of Maine*, compiled

newspapers. Literary forms once established among the lower classes die very hard. But the contribution of the elegy to general literature was made in the eighteenth century when it placed the stamp of its manner and plan upon the poetry of melancholy and upon the prose of the Gothic romance and remotely even on such tales of Poe's *Usher* and the *Red Death*.

As early as the 1730's and '40's, the vogue of the elegiac Muse was beginning to decline; and the fact is evident in the increasing use of the form for satire and parody. There are more or less gamesome elegies on dogs[111] and birds[112] and even on a "favorite

by George Bancroft Griffith and published at Portland, 1888, contains few poems that can be classified as funeral elegies unless we so account: *On the Death of George III*, by Stephen Sewall (1734-1804); an extract from a *Eulogy on George Washington* delivered 1800 by Jonathan Ellis (1672-1811?); *On the Death of Edward Payson, D.D.*, by Nathaniel Parker Willis (1806-1867); *Death of Napoleon*, by Isaac McLellan, Jr., (1806-   ); a fragment of *A Mournful Song*, 1804, by Nathaniel Hawthorne; *Kittie's Grave*, by Jacob Wardell Browne, 1822-   ); *Requiem in Memory of Major General Hiram G. Berry*, by Z. Pope Vose (1835-   ); *The Graveyard at Sippican*, by Edward Noyes Pomeroy (1836-   ); *Loved and Lost*, by Henry Bernard Carpenter, (c. 1840-   ); and *McClellan*, by John Dix Williams, (1843-   ). This astonishing state anthology, however, was itself the occasion of one mock elegy published in the *Boston Journal* (presumably during or soon after 1888) entitled a *Lament for a Maine Poet. By the Rest of Them*:

Ye pines of the mountain, ye elms of the vale,
Ye maples of hillside and plain, . . .
And so forth and so on—come help us bewail
The death of a poet of Maine!

He was one of four hundred and thirty and odd—
We are most of us poets, in Maine;
And the world stands amazed, as the fact gets abroad,
To think how her citizens ever can plod
At ditching and tilling her obstinate sod. . . .

We shall try to deplore you, disciple of song,
We shall name you with sorrowful soul—
But we hope you'll not think we are doing you wrong
If we don't sit in sackcloth and coalashes long—

For you see for yourself, we're so mighty a throng
(We mentioned above, we are four hundred strong)
That you leave but a very small hole!

To your shadowy manes libations we'll pour,
In our future collections of verse. . . .
But alas we regret, we sincerely deplore
The sorrowful fact that we can't miss you more—
Feel bad that we can't feel worse!

Farewell! We are sorry you died in your bloom,
Yet we mourn not as wholly bereft;
We'll toast you in cider, and carve on your tomb
"E Pluribus Unum" . . .

'Tis the accurate caper to sit here in gloom . . .
Our heads like a fountain, our eyes like a flume—
But still there are lots of us left!

[111] *Gent. Mag.*, XXI, 422, *An Elegiac Ode to Cato* (a dog).
[112] *Ibid.*, XI, 45, *On the Death of a Robin*; and E. Tankerville, *An Elegiack Poem on the Death of a Lady's Sparrow*, Dublin, 1731.

Cow"[113] and a walking stick![114] The reaction against the pastoral elegy[115] continued to produce parodies;[116] and mock pastorals were still to be found; but satire was turning more and more against the funereal type, and even the hallowed lines of Young's *Night Thoughts* were not spared.[117] The pastoral form was apparently considered as especially appropriate to the praise of shameless women;[118] and the funeral elegy had quite as bad a fate in the obscene verses of James Eyre Weekes,[119] a self-styled disciple of Prior and of Swift. He even supplied an elegiac prologue and epilogue to his ribald tale *The Mistake*; the parody cannot be misdoubted:

> Think *mortal* man upon thy *end*,
> Still to thy *final* hour attend,
> Hear then a true, but serious story,
> And take it as—*memento mori*.[120]

Personal satire abounds: ridicule of "old Gripus," a miser;[121] a bitter excoriation of Mathias Merrideth, Governor of St. Giles Workhouse,[122] possibly by an inmate; a clever piece on Captain Weekley, "the late eminent tabacconist";[123] an obscene satire of the broadside funeral elegy aimed at Captain Molineux "who was supposed to have been most barb'rously strangled by an inhuman Strumpet, with his own Two-leg'd wig";[124] and a bit of Neo-classical vituperation *On the Death of Mr. Dennis* (1734).[125] But one must not take these satires as too great an indication of contempt for the elegiac *genre*: Dr. Winstanley, who wrote the lines on Molineux, and also a self-elegy in imitation of Dean Swift, could besides compose an elegy on Queen Caroline, in which he described her "lovely Limbs" as "stretch'd pale in Death":

[113] *Gent. Mag.*, III, 604, *Letter from a Young Person to an old one on the death of his favorite Cow.*

[114] *Ibid.*, IX, 42, *In Memory of Dapple.*

[115] Trapp, *Lectures on Poetry*, tr. Clarke, London, 1742, 172 *et seq.*

[116] E.g., *Gent. Mag.*, III, 542, XX, 36.

[117] *Ibid.*, XVII, 444, *New Night Thoughts* (by Whitehead?). See also Thomas, *Le Poète Edward Young*, Paris, 1901, 493 *et seq.*

[118] *Edrisa*, London, 1743; *Elegy on the Death of Lady Hilaretta*, London, [?1730] (by Swift?). See also the ob-

jection to such pieces, *Gent. Mag.*, V, 327.

[119] J. E. Weekes, *Poems on Several Occasions*, Corke, 1743, 46. The number of Irish elegies during this period is notable. See also *Gent. Mag.*, X, 30.

[120] Weekes, *op. cit.*, 145 *et seq.*

[121] *The Student*, Oxford, 1750, I, 197.

[122] Brit. Mus. broadside.

[123] *Gent. Mag.*, VIII, 99-100.

[124] John Winstanley, *Poems Written Occasionally*, Dublin, 1742.

[125] *Gent. Mag.*, IV, 42.

> Lost to Despair, in wild Laments we moan,
> And distant Regions echo Groan for Groan.[126]

But a form as emotional and as conventionalized as the funeral elegy could not stand the sharp scrutiny of satiric parody; and the decade of the '40's, which saw the publication of Blair's *Grave* and Young's *Night Thoughts* and the composition of Gray's *Elegy*, seems also to have witnessed the first indications of the declining vogue of the mortuary style. Indeed, the very existence of two or three masterpieces gave a sort of summation to the *genre*; and lesser poets must beware unless they would merely imitate.

If the social and historical importance of the funeral elegy lies in the great number of pieces mediocre or worse, its artistic value lies chiefly in a few poems of considerable, if not permanent, merit that were the direct outgrowth of the form: Parnell's *Night-Piece*, Blair's *Grave*, Young's *Night Thoughts*, and Gray's famous *Elegy*. The two former have already been discussed; but it remains to indicate, at least rapidly, the debt of the latter poems to the elegiac tradition, a debt which, though natural and obvious, could hardly be defined before the history of that tradition had been explored; and any reader who has followed the preceding pages must see that these poems are notable, not as new departures, but as the consummation of a common type.

Edward Young was not without experience in the mortuary style. As early as the reign of Queen Anne, he had written in appropriate fashion upon the Last Day; and he had attempted ever since at once to follow the wits and to cultivate an improving gloom. He had done a *Paraphrase on Job*, which won faint praise from Johnson;[127] but *Night Thoughts* is his undoubted masterpiece, the epic of the middle class mind,[128] an anthology of melancholy,[129] and above all an epitome *in extenso* of elegiac themes. A complete analysis of the poem would take many pages more than the plan of the present study will allow; but a brief survey

[126] Winstanley, *Poems, ed. cit.,* 4. Certainly, the good doctor showed a wide virtuosity in elegiac styles.

[127] J. E. Brown, *Critical Opinions of Samuel Johnson*, Princeton, N. J., 1926, 550-551.

[128] Sir Leslie Stephen, *English Literature and Society in the Eighteenth Century*, New York, 1904, 154-155. Evi-

dently some readers felt him superior, because more religious and moral than Pope (*Gent. Mag.*, XIV, 329).

[129] See H. H. Clark, *A Study in Melancholy in Edward Young, Mod. Lang. Notes*, XXXIX, 129 *et seq.*; and Amy L. Reed, *The Background of Gray's Elegy*, New York, 1924, 192 *et seq.*

of the piece in the light of the history of the funeral elegy can not be omitted. The elegiac influence upon Young's work has largely been ignored,[130] although his poem is a clear example of the generalized didactic lamentation, and was supposed to celebrate the deaths of several members of his own family. For the most part, it is made up, like many elegies, of sombre moralizing and horrific description; and the circumambient atmosphere of gloom, as in the Puritan elegists who accentuated the anguish of the mourners, is largely personal to the author: he is more sorry for his own sorrows than for any ill that may betide either the deceased or the dissolute youth to whom he addresses his moral apothegms. A short survey of the first book and parts of the second and fifth will serve to show in brief the elegiac nature of Young's work. The poem begins with a verbose parody of Hamlet's famous lines on sleep: for over a century elegists had been despoiling *Hamlet* of precious fragments, very much as Turkish plunderers used the temples of ancient Greece. Night is to be his theme—not the "Dear Night" of Vaughan a hundred years before, nor the "verdorous glooms" of Keats almost a century later, but a pasticcio of trite moralizing and stage-horrors. The emotionalism of Vaughan is delicate and wistful and takes its guidance from his reason; that of Young is unripe and crude, unrestrained and even forced. In Keats, the crude emotionalism of Young has submitted to artistic refinement; it is much the same mood but expressed by a finer poet in a later age when the technique of lyric ecstasy had been developed and subtilized far beyond the rude machinery of the funeral elegy. The Graveyard School of poetry may be taken as an early step in this technical evolution: Gray supplied a Classic compression; and Young's *Night Thoughts* something of the sound and sweep of the grandiose, modelled on Milton's mighty line.

Night and the sadness and horror of night are then to be the theme of Young's poem; and he proceeds to borrow metaphors from the elegiac tradition to accentuate the sadness of the dark. He refers to the "Knell" of his own "departed Hours," much as the elegist might introduce the subject of his complaint—but Young centres his sadness upon himself. He borrows the verbiage of the

[130] Miss Reed, *op. cit.,* 195; and W. Thomas, *op. cit.,* 363 *et seq.*

elegy to call himself a "frail Child of Dust" and a "Worm"; and one feels that the impersonality of the Elizabethans and the Neo-classicists has given place to a new egoistic world, a world that had been anticipated by the self-elegies of the Puritan divines and by the constant emphasis in their elegies upon the sorrows of mourners rather than the tribulations of the deceased. Next follows a sort of middle-class essay on man, in which the poet compares the world to a "melancholy Vault" and a "Vale funereal" with "sad *Cypress* gloom," fragments taken, it would seem, from the mortuary landscape; and Father Time appears with his "enormous Scythe," for all the world like the picture at the top of a broadside. Finally, Young introduces death as the "Insatiate Archer," and comes to the point of bewailing the three supposed deaths in his family that he took as the occasion of his poem. *Night Thoughts* is full of such borrowings as these from elegiac tradition; and, indeed, Young had no other poetic tradition in English on which to build; and one cannot write a masterpiece of melancholy without calling up the images that have at once a melancholy and a poetic connotation. There follows a rhapsody of lamentation with special attention to Young's own misfortunes; and then is introduced the straw-stuffed figure of the wicked Lorenzo who expiates his former misdemeanors by listening with an infinite patience to an infinity of good advice. The Vale of Tears and the Day of Judgment figure prominently in these parleyings; and so the author draws the first night to a close, comparing himself first to a lark, and then to his master, Milton.

Night the Second, on Time death and Friendship is replete, like most of the following books, with admonitions to Lorenzo. Heaven and hell, the death-bed, sin and repentance, the relapse into sin again, and forever and forever death in every variation and form, supply the subject of the verse; and fragments of the mortuary landscape or cosmic figures in apocalyptic style give it vividness and horror. In the fifth *Night,* after defending the composition of poetry, as so many elegists had done, Young proceeds to favor his hearer, who listens perforce in silence like a congregation in church, with a brief discussion of his own poetic labors:

> Think'st thou, Lorenzo! to find pastimes here?
> No guilty passion blown into a flame,
> No foible flatter'd, dignity disgrac'd,

No fairy field of fiction all on flow'r,
No rainbow colours, here, or silken tale,
But solemn counsels, images of awe,
Truths, which eternity lets fall on man
With double weight, thro' these revolving spheres,
This death-deep silence, and incumbent shade:
Thoughts, such as shall revist your last hour;
Visit uncall'd, and live when life expires;
And thy dark pencil, Midnight! darker still
In melancholy dipt, embrowns the whole.

Young then, like all Puritans since the time of Elizabeth, disowns the æsthetics of delight, and gives notice that he will ride forth on his Pegasus only on errands of approved knight-errantry. Nevertheless, in this same dour severity, he takes his pleasure: he hails "auspicious Midnight" as "Delightful gloom," and says that the man is "blest" who "Is led by choice to take his fav'rite walk Beneath Death's gloomy, silent cypress shades." Did Young write of night chiefly because it was "auspicious" of his soul's future or because it was "Delightful" to his present experience? Herein lies the difference between Calvinist and Sentimentalist. Young is a fine example of the transition, a transition that was already far advanced toward the new ideal, without as yet quite surrendering the forms and protestations of the old. The poet next meanders through a burying-ground with appropriate reflections, and justifies the churchyard frontispiece with which he ushered in the first edition of *Night II*. And so the poem goes on and on, until the reader is improved past all patience; and at last all is very fittingly concluded with the end of the world and "universal Midnight." Parnell gave English poetry the generalized funeral elegy in little; Blair wrote it *in extenso*; and Young inflated it to pseudo-cosmic proportions and justified the ways of God to men for the benefit of the veriest vulgar.

Thomas Gray was peculiarly well qualified to accomplish the summation of the elegiac *genre*. He was himself sprung in part from the middle classes, had known something of "chill penury," and might well have seemed "a youth to fortune and to fame unknown." He had a natural aptitude for the "tender & elegiac,"[131] and even composed a sardonic self-obituary.[132] Beside

---

[131] T. Gray, *Letters*, ed. Tovey, London, 1909-1912, I, 172.   [132] *Ibid.*, I, 196-197.

this, he had the education and travel of the upper classes, and so was admirably fitted to interpret the melancholy of the bourgeoisie to their social betters—so successfully, indeed, that even the great *"Ursa Major"* could not but praise the event. Gray's fastidious taste had been cultivated by a wide reading and considerable study of the Greek classics; and he knew the value and the technique of restrained compression. Young's masterpiece he considered over long, and charged it with "redundancy of thought";[133] and his own poem presents not only a condensation of elegiac elements but also a fine selection of details borrowed from the allied school of Thomsonian nature-realism and from the Classics. Indeed, he borrowed far afield;[134] and, during the years he took in writing the *Elegy,* he assimilated to its form elements that had hardly been combined before; and yet, in fundamentals of structure and in numerous details, it is based upon the tradition that is the subject of the present study.

In the larger aspects of plan and point of view, the poem, like Blair's *Grave,* is essentially a funeral elegy with interpolations apropos. Like the *Grave,* it has a long, generalized introduction that prepares the reader for the elegiac mood. It follows this with a lament for a melancholy youth; and finally ends, like most of the broadside elegies since the days of the Commonwealth, with an epitaph. Whether this melancholy youth was the author, or West,[135] or some imaginary person, is rather secondary to the present study; but, if Gray had himself in mind, then the poem is to be classed with the self-elegies of the non-conformist divines, and is even more fully in the Puritan tradition. The similarity of the piece to the broadside elegy seems to have occurred to the person, whoever it was, who designed the title-page; for two black bars of mortuary symbols were gratuitously introduced, of almost precisely the same design, indeed, as appears in the border of a broadside elegy on Queen Mary.[136] One of these bars reappears at the top of the first page of verse, for all the world like the heading of a broadside.

Detailed similarities to the *Elegy* are legion in the poetry of the

[133] N. Nicholls, *Reminiscences.* See Gray, *Letters, ed. cit.,* II, 276 *et seq.*
[134] Miss Reed, *op. cit.,* 226 *et seq.*
[135] *Ibid.,* 246; and O. Shepard, *A Youth to Fortune and to Fame Unknown, Mod. Phil.,* XX, 347 *et seq.*
[136] See the illustration, much reduced in size, opposite p. 196.

A N

E L E G Y

WROTE IN A

Country Church Yard.

by Mr Grey.

L O N D O N:

Printed for R. DODSLEY in *Pall-mall*;

And ſold by M. COOPER in *Pater-noſter-Row*. 1751.

[Price Six-pence.]

previous hundred years, and the present study has noted a considerable number especially in funereal and meditative verse. Many of these poems, Gray doubtless never read; and few of them could have been actual influences; but they serve to show that he was working in a continuous and well recognized vein; and the public acclaimed the result not so much on account of its novelty as because of its perfect adaptation to a previously developed taste. The poem opens with a darkening landscape and the "knell" of departing day, as so many elegies begin with a touch of rural scenery and the death-knell of the deceased; but the *Seasons* had recalled to English poetry a Realism of wider scope than before; and Gray develops his mortuary countryside with delicate, life-like details, the "lowing herd," the "beetle's droning flight," and the distant tinkling of sheep-bells. Thus gradually the world is left to darkness and to the author, whose own melancholy is by no means forgotten, though more subtly expressed than Young's. The Gothic touch of an "ivy-mantled tower" calls the poet's attention to the scene before him—the mounded graves and the yew: indeed, the frontispiece of the second part of Young's *Night Thoughts* would have made a perfect illustration for this part of the *Elegy*. The poet then proceeds to contemplate the brevity, and perhaps something of the vanity, of life. Like Thomson and Somerville, he pictures rural scenery, narrowing their broader canvasses to the space of a vignette; and, like the elegists, he sings the emptiness of worldly rank, "The boast of heraldry, the pomp of power," the complaint of the middle classes who had tasted and then lost the sweet prerogatives of rule, and who, like true Calvinists, called such things empty and pointed to the "fell Sergeant," the summoner of beggars and of kings. One wonders whether the line about flattery, soothing the "Dull cold ear of death," may not be a reference to the courtly eulogies of Neo-classicism: but perhaps Gray had merely funerals orations or epitaphs in mind. At all events, the grandiose figures about the "storied urn" and the "rod of empire" are quite in the elegiac style; and the moralizing of poverty and death that follows is not far removed from the lamentable strain. Gray would seem to have had some taste for mortuary poetry, or at least would seem to have preferred the "uncouth rhymes" of the rustic tombstone to panegyrics that "heap the shrine of luxury and pride"; and truly it is impossible to sup-

pose him quite ignorant of the elegiac tradition that ran back a
hundred years or more behind him.   Gray's idealization of the
"cool sequestered vale of life" seems to be a borrowing from the
Neo-classical mean; but the melancholy youth who forms the subject of the latter stanzas is certainly far removed from the ideal
of Pomfret's *Choice* and of Sir Roger de Coverley.   He would
seem to be the Original Genius of Gray's imagination, perhaps a
glorified picture of West, perhaps what Gray desired that he himself might be: he wanders through natural scenes, coloring them
with his own pensive emotions; he wastes away and dies; his
funeral exequies are pictured for us in one vivid line; and then
comes the restrained, sweet sadness of the *Epitaph*.   The Puritans
had known religious melancholy; and their successors had cultivated a Sentimental gloom.   Both moods had been voiced in the
funeral elegy, and been generalized at length in the poems of
Blair and of Young; but here the poet is more sophisticated, the
mood more complex, and the voicing of it more restrained, more
compact, more perfect.   Indeed, Gray's *Elegy* not only points back-
ward toward the pious sentiments and the vivid horrors of the
funereal tradition, but also forward; and, in the personality of
the wayward "youth" and in its exquisite propriety of diction and
phrase, it anticipates the reminiscent pensiveness of Wordsworth
and of Keats.

If beauty may be defined as perfect adequacy of expression, then
the funeral elegy can hardly be termed beautiful; and, in sooth,
one wonders what definition of beauty it would entirely fulfill.
The history of the *genre* up to the mid-eighteenth century was
governed chiefly by two changes: a rise in social status with the
rising middle class, and a change in purpose and message from the
religious to the æsthetic.   The Puritans had used it as an auxiliary
to Salvation; their wealthy descendants of the eighteenth century
found in it their first crude feeling of the joys of art and beauty;
and, as this feeling was refined, the poets refined the elegiac form,
enlarged it and combined it more and more widely with other
themes and *genres*, and made the expression of its melancholy
more and more adequate and perfect.   During the reign of George
II, a few of the old pious lamentations still remain; more numerous are the mediocre pieces composed by a mob of persons who
were not gentlemen but who hoped to prove their gentility by

writing with fluency and ease.   Magazine verse and even books
appeared from the pens of ambitious blue-stockings like Mrs. Rowe,
of provincial aspirants to fame, and of the sons of petty tradesmen,
even like Thomas Gray; and some of these, again like Thomas
Gray, had a catholicity of knowledge and an elegance of taste that
purged the old form of absurdities, combined it with bits of foreign
themes, and gave the whole a new pith and marrow of compression.
The funeral elegy had turned from a religious to an æsthetic
medium; and, as it changed, it entered, with its middle class patrons,
once more into the general current of literature and cultural life,
and so gradually was changed into a thing of permanent beauty.
As a literary form, it lost identity and perished in the process: at
first it was generalized and didacticized in the poetry of the Graveyard School; and later it merged yet more into a thousand Protean
shapes of evanescent sadness.   Its influence cannot easily be extri-
cated from the multiform types and tendencies of this latter day;
but at least it may be said that the funeral elegy supplied what
neither the Classics nor the Renaissance could give, a diction and
metaphor of the emotions, a whole technique of ecstasy and lamentation fit for this later age of great ideals and great disillusionment.

CHAPTER XII

THE FUNERAL ELEGY AND THE RISE OF ENGLISH ROMANTICISM

IN the seventeenth century, the central fact of life to the average serious-minded citizen was Original Sin; in the nineteenth, Original Genius—literary genius, artistic genius, the military and political genius perhaps, but especially the genius of modern big business. This idealization of the merchant and manufacturer reveals him as the predominant caste of our capitalistic age; just as the special reverence for the pious and painful preacher three hundred years ago betokened a society, or at least a social group, still dominated by institutionalized religion. Even as late as the reign of Charles II, the church—some sort of church, used for various purposes human and divine—was the pivotal centre of most men's lives; and the change to modern commercialism is momentous, perhaps ominous.[1] The 1660's saw the bourgeoisie at the lowest point to which they have ever fallen since the Mediæval towns first wrested charters from their reluctant suzerains; and the 1860's saw this class at perhaps its highest point, the nobility having succumbed at the time of the Reform Bills, and the proletariat hardly touched as yet with the doctrines of Socialism. So swift and grave an alteration in the balance of social power could not but affect art, literature, thought, and all that makes up the culture of nation and continent. The latter stages of this change, the Industrial Revolution in manufacturing, transportation, and agriculture, the spread of individualism in ethics and political theory, the new lyricism in the fine arts, all these have been much written upon; and a multitude of facts sorted, weighed, and fitted together; but perhaps the most significant period in this evolution is its initial stage, when the chief events were not merely the rise in wealth and power of a given class, its conquest of new markets abroad, and the conquest by its patronage of the arts and sciences, one by one, at home, but more especially the esoteric psychological changes within its own groping consciousness, the shifting of its

---

[1] Certainly ominous to such historians as credit the fall of the Roman Republic and the decadence of Roman life to the growing power of the equestrian class.

main interest from a rather dubious Salvation to a very certain and tangible prosperity, the gradual atrophy of its religious ideals under the combined influence of science and wealth, and its turning to the fine arts as an outlet for such inner cravings as could not prudently be expressed in the business world. These subtle changes in mind and attitude, the bourgeois literature of the seventeenth and early eighteenth century records; and the lingering religious prejudices of the group allowed them to express these changes in no body of documents more fully or more continuously than in the mournful strains of the funeral elegy.

The funeral elegy, indeed, is a happy index of social change, not merely because it furnishes numerous examples in unbroken development, but also because there is a parallel stream of elegiac poetry belonging to the aristocracy that can be compared in both matter and manner with contemporaneous bourgeois compositions; and, indeed, not many single types of poetry have appealed simultaneously for a considerable period to two social classes of readers in two disparate forms. Even in its origins, the funeral elegy shows this duplex tendency: its sporadic beginnings appear among the aristocratic authors of the School of Donne, such figures as Vaughan, Cleveland, King, Cowley, and especially Quarles; and, at about the same time, there are London broadsides intended for the consumption of the less pious cits in which the death, usually of a notorious criminal, but occasionally of an ordinary respectable townsman, is lamented, or at least detailed for public contemplation. During the Civil War in the 1640's, the broadside was largely the creature of Cavalier propaganda; and the deaths of various military heroes, and especially the execution of Charles I, were chronicled at length in its elegiac verse; and thus the elegy became a definite organ for the arousing of sympathy *ad hoc*. The Puritans had not been slow to follow Cavalier example, though their first use of the form was to lend magnificence rather than to stir the softer emotions, and their divines seem at first to have looked askance upon the custom.

The decade of Puritan triumph in the 1650's saw a decline in broadside literature, and, perhaps for that reason, the acceptance of the funeral elegy by the Independent clergy, who developed in such pieces an emotionalism particularly gruesome. The Puritan, steeped in the uncertain and immoralistic world of the Renaissance, looked on the life hereafter with as many misgivings, though of a different kind, as the modern agnostic; and he consequently reasoned from what he knew, and centred his elegiac attention on illness and death and worms and charnel-house decay: his was a realistic, factitive mind, suspicious of the doubtful and the abstract; and the mental habits of his commercial pursuits can be somewhat traced in his literary preferences; for, though he seek artistic relaxation in long-passed ages or in distant climes, he demands a certain solid appeal to the sense; and the development of concrete description for its own sake would seem to have arisen *pari passu* with his growing control of literary patronage. At all events, vivid description, for little apparent purpose beside its emotional reflex, developed early in the elegy. At the same time appear touches reminiscent of Shakespeare, Spenser, and Milton, the first two of whom had long been dear to the ordinary Englishman, and the last two of whom were directly connected with the Puritan cause: such literary traditions, together with the English Bible, were those most obvious in the newly developing form. The emotionalism of the Puritan's religious life, the only life he knew outside the work-a-day world, found a large place in these elegies. His ecstatic melancholy, moreover, is personal and immediate: the sorrow of the mourners is described at length, and especially the sorrow, nay, horror, of the elegist. These pieces have a subjective lyricism foreign to the dramatic spirit of the great age of Elizabeth, when most writers concealed, rather than revealed, themselves in their art. The broadside elegies are individualistic, like the outlook of the bourgeoisie who, as the Mediæval guilds decayed, lived more and more in conditions of fierce business competition. The intellectual ties, moreover, and the cultural amenities that bind man and man together were not highly developed in a world that drew but little of its education from books or from the decorum of the University or the Court. The predominant facts in the life of the Puritan tradesman were his education and business, which made him an individualist, and his religion, which gave him a sort of katharsis by appealing to the sombre emotions. Is it by mere chance that these are the characteristics of the "lyric cry" of Burns, Byron, Shelley, and so many other poets of the age that witnessed the economic triumph of commercialism in the Industrial Revolution, and that ushered in its political and social triumph in the 1830's? The literary expression of these characteristic themes is at first imperfect and crude; but, as the class to whom they chiefly appealed rose in the social scale, and as they were expressed with increasing adequacy by poets of greater and greater genius, the technique of their phraseology was gradually accomplished; and upon the ruins of the literature of aristocratic decorums arose a new literature of vivid, realistic description, of individualism, and of those special emotions that form the characteristic virtue of the individual.

At the Restoration in 1660, the Cavaliers returned to power; and, fortunately or otherwise, they had learned something and forgotten much. Religion, they had largely forgotten, though they supported the Established Church for political motives; and they had learned in their travels a somewhat un-British levity that was not without license; and England, wearied of Puritan restraints, was willing for the nonce to make merry too. The restored Stuart Court hardly revived the elegiac style of the 1640's with its vivid mysticism and beatific exaltation; they took rather as their poetical platform a somewhat cynical pleasure, called it virtue, and declared all melancholy vice. Thus, following doubtless the old Latin adage, *de mortuis nil nisi bonum,* they made eulogy, deserved or undeserved, their elegiac theme, and with all its variations in every major key, developed it in the trite conventions of the pastoral, in formless "Pindaric" strophes, and sometimes, perchance, in humbler broadside couplets. Generality and complimentary abstraction were their stock in trade, not the common parlance of the work-a-day world; and thus "noble language" was confounded with "the language of the nobility."[2] They were more interested in forms and style than were the Puritans; and, as their lives were largely taken up with matters of etiquette, they thought more of elegant propriety and less of fact. Theirs is the psychology of a ruling caste sheltered from reality, not the hard realism of the sharp-eyed man of barter and exchange. Like the Mediæval romancers, they saw life through a mirror that made up for imperfection of image by the brilliance of its light. The Puritans, now fallen from their high estate, clung more and more closely to the consolations of the elegy. They had hoped for a

[2] This phrase is taken from Professor Babbitt.

greater share in both Church and State than the policy of Clarendon had allowed; and, silenced from the open voicing of their
sorrows, they expressed them in bewailing reverend colleagues and
departed saints. Thus melancholy, to which their natural bias was
inclined, grew upon them; they developed the means of its literary
expression, found in it a balm of Gilead, and cultivated it as a
good and godly sign that Salvation still awaited the remnant of
the Elect. In New England, meanwhile, the elegy, having been
planted during the Commonwealth, took root and flourished, especially among the Congregational clergy of Boston and the envi-
rons: the Levite tribe of Mather both approved and practiced the
custom; in time, it spread throughout New England, going as far
afield as Pennsylvania; and, in time, it was applied not merely to
the priestly caste, but also to merchants and civil officers, as they
grew in wealth and godliness. In Scotland also, during the reign
of Charles II, the elegy had a sporadic beginning at the hands of
Episcopalians such as Ninian Paterson, later to be taken over by
the Presbyterians and given a more mortuary bent. In England
itself, during this period, it spread to the Presbyterians and Baptists; and thus, for more than a generation, from the middle of
the century to about 1685, the funeral elegy was the peculiar
literary attribute of the Calvinistic dissenters in England and
America; and, somewhat later, in Scotland also, it became the
poetic organ of Calvinism.

The reign of James II is indirectly one of the most momentous
in social history; for it cemented in some sort of agreement the
Protestant dissenters of the towns and the Anglican bulk of the
population: after the dissenters had refused to support the King
against the Bishops in the Tower, the official guardians of the
Church could hardly look upon them with such bitterness as before;
and the accession of William and Mary, with the primacy of
Archbishop Tillotson, gave a new strength to that tolerant and
inclusive, though somewhat vaguely defined, attitude within the
Anglican Communion that goes by the name of the Broad Church
Party. This policy of conciliation not only won over to conformity a number of dissenters both laymen and clergy, but also
gave a new dignity to those that remained outside the pale of the
Establishment—gave a higher standing to their opinions, to their
moral views, and to their cultural and literary ideals. King Wil-

liam moreover, as a professing Dutch Calvinist, could see no valid reason why the state religion of Holland should be under a ban in his British dominions. Thus the mortuary note of the funeral elegy began to be heard even in poetry intended for courtly consumption; and the political compromise of the reign, entering culture, began to affect literature also. The Bill of Rights, moreover, sanctified by the philosophy of Locke, confirmed the limited monarchy of Charles II; and, because their wealth was necessary in the conduct of William's Continental wars, the rich merchants began to wield, in small measure, the power of a capitalistic class. They took the opportunity, furthermore, to consolidate their economic position by the reform of the currency and the foundation of the Bank of England: in time, the income from commerce was to become as stable and as sure as that of landed property; and the princes and petty governors of commerce were to become the patrons of the arts. The elegy, however, reflects not merely this great social change, the first steps in the recovery of the merchant class, but also a significant change in the very psychology of this rising social group. The Establishment had grown more tolerant; and they also had softened. More and more, they were tasting of the fruits of good living; and, although they did not go to the University or take the grand tour to Italy, the growing scope of business gave to some of them an increasing breadth and urbanity; they must think in terms of America and the Orient; sometimes their insularity was even subjected to actual travel in foreign parts: and Calvinism in all its rigor can hardly withstand such various translation. Moreover, the scientific life of the age, which the mercantile classes for practical reasons could not entirely ignore, demanded some revision of the old religious concepts; and it became more and more difficult to believe in the doctrines of Predestination and Election, and more and more difficult to maintain that melancholy demeanor and emotionalized self-debasement that were the outward signs of godliness within. Thus there germinated an intellectual revolt that took effect in the Arianism of the early eighteenth century; and, at an even earlier date, was evident an emotional revolt, sometimes in a growing optimism as in the Quakers and later the Methodist movement, sometimes in a sedulous cultivation in life and in the arts of the old melancholic emotionalism.

This last endeavor gave rise to the Sentimental; for an emotion cannot be artificially developed for its own sake and still be quite genuine psychologically. In the old days, merriment and cheer had, in the nature of things, seemed wicked to a social group that found themselves under the ban of Church and State; and, moreover, the example of the suffering Israelites, on whom the Puritans modelled their theocracy and social system, held up before these inveterate readers of the Bible an example of stern and stiff-necked resistance to the blandishments of Mammon, and a melancholy fortitude that foresaw the worst and yet expected worse than it foresaw. So a tumultuous and exalted depression became their psychological ideal, the symbol and expression of their ultimate Salvation. This symbol suffered the fate so common to religious symbols, of being sought for and treasured as an end in itself, especially by the brethren of weaker vision, without regard for the causes whence it sprang or the original inner meaning that it had possessed. So much was this mood looked upon as conducive to Salvation that many believers clung to it as the very essence of religion, and, even after abandoning the dogma of Puritanism and the regular acts of worship, they still found comfort, if not pleasure, in an occasional lapse into its somewhat specious consolations. And when a noble lord, the pupil and scion of the mighty Locke, assured them, with due condescension, of the identity of such pleasure with virtue, the stamp of high authority and irrefragable truth was set upon their most cherished doctrine. To trace the evolution of class-psychology is the most hazardous enterprise; but the persistence of melancholy, often Sentimental, in the mind of the average Englishman down almost to our own day, unless one accounts for it purely on the basis of climate or what not, would seem largely to originate in the deeply ingrained religious mood of the sixteenth and seventeenth centuries.

Even as early as the reign of Charles II, the funeral elegy began to mark the new tendency toward the Sentimental. The elegists seem at first to find a soft consolation and then a positive delight in its pathetic exuberance; and, as Sentimentalism advanced, they turned the elegy into an expression and outlet of their surplus feelings and sometimes into a convenient means for awakening these delectable sensations. The funeral elegy was the one form of literature that preëminently had about it the odor of sanctity and could claim the traditional approval of even the most severe: what could be a more appropriate vehicle for those exalted feelings that in a growing number of individuals was all that remained of the Protestantism of the Protestant religion and the dissidence of dissent? The poetry of the early eighteenth century shows the mortuary style spreading, with the rise of the trading class, to other localities and other social groups. Pope and Gay assume it at will; but especially in those strata that were just aspiring to education and culture, women and provincials as well as tradesmen, the type achieved a vogue. The Cowleian Pindaric was a thing of the past; and the elegiac eclogue gave place to a gloomier strain. The mortuary tone, moreover, spread to new poetic types that had had no part or lot with Puritanism; it was no longer confined to the bewailing of an individual, and became on occasion pensively descriptive or generally meditative in character. The *Night-Piece* of Parnell and Gray's *Elegy* are summaries of elegiac themes, with the sorrow of a particular death implicit rather than evident in the lines. The mortuary landscape developed into Thomson's *Winter*; and the gnomic motif, into Young's *Night Thoughts*. Meanwhile, into the elegy itself, foreign elements more and more found their way. Young had assimilated it to the parallel Puritan style of Milton; and Gray borrowed from nature-poetry and from the Classics. So mortuary melancholy and its elegiac technique passed into the general stream of poetry, and, in so passing, produced the Graveyard School. The mood of lyric—or should one say, melodramatic?—gloom so deeply interpenetrated the mind of the reading public that it continued to demand its expression in the horrors of the Gothic romance, and in the poetic anguish of the *maladie de siècle*. It is not the purpose of the present study to suggest that Shelley or Byron wrote with the immediate purpose of pleasing tradesmen patrons: by their generation, this point of view had so entered into the taste of the great general public,[3] which had taken the place of noble patronage as the arbiter of poetic fame, that whoever would write found such material at his very hand, and such feelings within himself. And especially the poets of social revolution had reason to see the world gloomily in the dark days following the French Revolution.[4]

[3] The objection to the themes and ideals of Wordsworth was not their novelty—for his ideas are commonplaces of eighteenth century thought—but their newly acquired association with revolution on the Continent.

[4] Romanticism in France and Germany was definitely associated with revolution.

The immediate effect of this rise of the middle classes during the reign of William and Mary was a sort of working compromise between them and the aristocracy, who had previously been the recognized guardians of national culture; and thus arose a new national ideal, combining the moral propriety of the Puritans and the courtly elegance of the Cavaliers—an ideal that found its ripest manifestation a few years later in the literature, and especially the periodical essay, of the reign of Queen Anne.[5] Politically, this reign was less an advance than a reaction: the Queen herself was a believer in Divine Right; the Church was still for the most part militantly Tory; and thus the balance of the aristocracy against the growing wealth of commerce was for a time maintained, and the period of compromise sufficiently prolonged so that it appeared to be the final epiphany of social progress. Every age tends to look upon itself, with some complacency, as the ultimate peak in the development of the human species; and so perfect and reposeful seemed the balance between conflicting forces for almost a generation that one need not be surprised that the *status quo* assumed in the minds of men a fetish-like ideal, a thing that should not and indeed could not be changed. The poetry of Neo-classicism reflects this static finality; and indeed, it carried the ideal of its own particular decorum to the summation of refinement: its literature is nothing if not elegant; and it improved every polite occasion with appropriate moral maxims. Into this stately ideal, however, the emotions, which are the very well-spring of movement and of change, could hardly enter: tumultuous exhilaration cannot coëxist with a nice balance of contending forces; and the emotionalism of the bourgeoisie, which went deeper than their religion or their morality, could not become a party to the adjustment of Neo-classicism. The self-contained Augustan might sneer with Pope or fulminate with Swift, but he could hardly weep with Cowper or rhapsodize with Blake. Like a true son of Locke, he saw the intellect as dominating the human mind, and tried, with some success, to make his vision real. Thus the characteristic expressions of Neo-classicism are didactic or satiric pieces, not elegies, or lyrics, or laments; for it is hard to maintain a nice decorum in

---

[5] It is significant of the power of the matter-of-fact middle classes that this is the first age in which the national literature is characteristically a literature of prose. The rise of scientific thought also had something to do in bringing this about.

the face of death.   Pope's *tour de force* on the "unfortunate lady"
is hardly to be included within the bounds of Neo-classicism; and
the Neo-classical Pindarics and pastorals of the reign of Charles II
and the broadside eulogies on departed generals and statesmen can
hardly be said to touch upon the real subject of the elegy at all.
They treat of death by ignoring it, and neither inspire terror like
the Puritans, nor offer consolation like the Anglican poets of the
School of Donne.   The elegy, then, entered but superficially into
the Neo-classical compromise; and, although a number of pieces
were written that show an intermixture of the Classical and the
mortuary, one feels that it is a mechanical mixture rather than a
chemical combination of constituents.   Melancholy was the key-
note of the Puritan funeral elegy; and melancholy, at least in any
advanced form, could not compound with Neo-classicism.

Perhaps nothing more vividly illustrates the social history of the
funeral elegy than its satiric use.   During the early seventeenth
century when elegies were rare and were largely the possession of
the broadside balladists and the privileged classes, satire of the
genre is not common; but perhaps the most notable example is the
volume of Puritan rejoicing over the murder of Buckingham in
1628.   During the Civil Wars, though serious elegies were much
written by both sides, satiric parodies were few in number; for
neither party would hold up to scorn the funeral literature with
which it bewailed its own heroic dead, and as yet the Cavalier and
Puritan styles were hardly differentiated.   After the execution of
King Charles and the failure of the literary effort to enlist sympathy for his cause, the Cavaliers, either by choice, or perforce on
account of the censorship, abandoned the elegy to their opponents,
and proceeded to make game of the mortuary style that was particularly affected by the Puritan divines.   Ridicule was the key-
note of the Restoration; and the Cavaliers, no longer hampered
by an opposing government, besmirched the funeral elegy with
obscene parody, and composed their own elegiac pieces in utterly
distinct Pindaric or pastoral styles.   The Puritans had started
during the 1640's to give these pieces a liturgic use in their funeral
ceremonies, and continued so to use them down into the eighteenth
century; but the Cavaliers, after the Restoration, largely gave up
the custom and, in response to Puritan attacks upon the Prayer
Book, took particular delight in heaping Hudibrastic ridicule upon

this sacred literature of dissent. The Puritans occasionally attempted to reply in kind; but the censorship was against them; satire was not their *forte*; and indeed their appeals for sympathy and crabbed vituperations are hardly the progeny of the satiric Muse. The political, economic, and social compromise of the reign of William and Mary, by giving Calvinism a fresh repute and by reviving the funeral elegy among the higher classes, silenced the satire directed against it. The reigns of Queen Anne and George I saw quite a new development. Emotionalism had become the accepted convention of elegiac meditation; and the colder, pastoral tradition, with its fixed conventionality became the object of ridicule. ' Thus was signalized the victory of the Puritan type of the *genre*, when even the elegant and polite preferred the funeral elegy to the Classical tradition of their own social class. The form had reached the highest point in the turn of Fortune's fickle wheel. Pale grief and pleasing pain now began to pass into other poetic forms; and the lyric cry of the coming age was developing its infinite variety of technique. Even in the reign of George II, the funeral elegy was still the property of the intellectually and socially *nouveau*. In the allied poetry of the Graveyard School, it made its contribution to the main stream of letters; and, even in the '40's, at the time of its summation by Young and Gray, it was once more becoming the butt of ridicule, not on a religious or political account, but because men always find something amusing in the fashions of yester year.

The reign of Queen Anne was but a pause in the kaleidoscope of social change; and the accession of George I saw those social elements that formed the groundwork of the Whig Party acquire a yet augmented power, not as organized ecclesiastical dissent, for non-conformity was declining, but as a plutocracy whose money made Parliament its creature and sustained a foreign king—some called him a usurper—upon the English throne. These forward-looking merchants, like true Englishmen, employed rather than destroyed the old institutions and the old nobility—even in the days of their triumph in the 1830's, when they finally wrested an acknowledgment of their superiority from the other social orders; but, none the less, beneath these ancient forms, they were a constantly growing power throughout the eighteenth century; and it is significant that the attempt of George III to hold the balance between the opposing factions and to support the declining power of the nobility and Crown as Queen Anne had done, was as conspicuous a failure as in the reign of Queen Anne it had been a notable success: the Industrial Revolution had intervened; and the aristocracy of commerce and manufacturing were not to be gainsaid; and indeed, had it not been for the blighting fear that the French Revolution put upon men's minds, the younger Pitt would have brought about a Parliamentary reform in favor of the commercial interests as early as the 1780's, fifty years before such reform was actually accomplished.   Not only did this great social change threaten Neo-classicism from without, but an inward decay also sapped its strength.   Based as it was, so largely upon the intellect, it was peculiarly susceptible to intellectual attack; and the rival philosophy of Shaftesbury and Hutcheson, together with the satiric flings of Mandeville, could not but shake the confidence of the strongest.   The compromise, like most practical things, would not bear close logical inspection; and thus it was assailed in the very precinct of its power, and found wanting.

Long after its vital essence had gone, Neo-classicism lingered, very much as the old institutions continued under the long ministry of Walpole; for there was at the moment nothing to replace them.[6] No one wished to repeat the experiment of the Commonwealth; and the bourgeoisie were only beginning to emerge into economic stability.   Of culture and the arts, they had as yet but little of their own: a reverence for and some reading of Shakespeare, Spenser, and Milton, they had never quite lost; and these three they raised to a new preëminence; Gothic castles, they had long respected as the attributes to awe and government; and, ignorant of the inconvenience and ennui of the life within, they had admired from without the towers and battlements; and, as an external feature of the landscape and as a symbol of their own social advance, they revived Gothic in *papier mâché* as a sort of garden ornament. Nature, they had known and loved, as the city-dweller loves it who sees it pastoral-wise, on holidays; and, in the poetry of Nature and in their own "natural" gardens, they recaptured something of this holiday delight, a pleasure lost upon the true countryman, who

---

[6] Moreover, it was, of course, good policy to make the coming of the new dynasty as little as possible a break in the political continuity of the national life.

thought Wordsworth strange and could not understand his poetry. But most of all, and most closely associated with the yearning of those who had been long in cities pent, was the lure of emotionalism itself, the same lure that had made possible the yellow journalism of the Elizabethan broadside, a search for the *piquant* and *frappant* as described by Schiller, the valuing of a thrill simply and solely for itself. The days of tedious triviality in the shop or factory required a sharp reaction. The excitant powers of simple English scenery having been exhausted, the law of stimulation demanded more and more powerful agents: in the funeral elegy, the *macabre* lay at hand; all history was ransacked, not for its deeper meaning, but for stories and moving tales; and, as the merchants voyaged more and more to the ends of the earth, the vogue of the exotic grew: *Vathek* was written and Landor's *Gebir* and the Indian romance of Moore and Byron's tales of the Levant. By degrees also a suitable technique was discovered, or rediscovered, from past ages. New forms of literature were invented and Elizabethan and even Mediæval forms revived, though generations of endeavor were needed to bridge the gulf between the crude emotionalism of a Puritan minister bewailing a deceased colleague and the lofty beauty of Shelley's *Adonais*: many lessons of culture had to be learned and much of Classical restraint.[7]

The exact relation of the present investigation to "Romanticism" depends somewhat upon one's definition of that elusive epithet. An exhaustive study of these definitions can hardly be attempted here;[8] but perhaps a brief survey is justified of some of the more widely held opinions, and some effort may properly be made to show the bearing upon them of the evolution outlined in the present study. Of these definitions, some are made merely from the point of view of literature and perhaps a few of the other arts; some are generally cultural, and regard Romanticism as an attitude of mind expressing itself more or less in all phases of society. Most of the literary, or æsthetic, definitions seem to be reducible to one of three points of view: the definition of Romanticism in terms of the

---

[7] In the opinion of the present author, this advance in technical subtilty of emotional expression is perhaps the most important aspect of eighteenth century literature.

[8] See for example the definitions discussed by A. O. Lovejoy (*On the Discrimination of Romanticism, Pub. Mod. Lang. Assoc.*, XXXIX, 229 *et seq.*) and P. Kaufman (*Defining Romanticism: A Survey and a Program, Mod. Lang. Notes*, XL, 193 *et seq.*).

archaic, or of the Realistic, or of the imaginative. The material presented in the present study would seem to oblige the sponsors of any one of these three definitions to look upon Romanticism, at least in its earlier stages, as the artistic development of the rising bourgeoisie. The archaic movement first expressed itself in the "revival" of Milton, Spenser, and Shakespeare; and the history of the funeral elegy shows that the tradition of all three of these authors had deeply permeated the middle class consciousness; and their apparently sudden increase in vogue during the second quarter of the eighteenth century synchronizes with the rising prestige of this class under the ministry of Walpole, and with their consequently increasing wealth, education, and literary patronage. An appreciation for Gothic architecture, moreover, and of the grandeur of the Mediæval past seems to have lingered, as did a fondness for the old romances, in the bourgeois mind, and was revived with the revival of their own position in society. The second definition of Romanticism, a vivid Realism, especially as applied to natural scenery, is anticipated in the mortuary landscape and in the piling up of concrete details descriptive of illness and death and decay; but, in this regard, Flaubert and Zola could hardly be more unrelenting and intense than the Puritan clerics of the seventeenth century. Thirdly, imagination has been taken as a criterion of the Romantic; and surely in these broadside elegies, there is imagination, though harsh in subject and crude in expression: the wild hyperboles of grief, the cosmic magnitude, and straining of pathetic fallacy are surely the stuff of the imagination, or the tales of Welsh folklore possess no such quality. Even allowing for crudity and convention, their imagery is not fancy, and is not to be confused for a moment with the charming pleasantry of Pope's mock-epic. Any one of these three definitions, therefore, seems to lead one to the conclusion that the Romantic movement was the literary development of the tradesman class.

Some scholars, however, find Romanticism not so much a literary as a generally cultural phenomenon; and these usually define it either as Individualism, expressing itself in the arts with a new subjectivity, or as the urge for democracy, or thirdly as Sentimentalism, the cultivation of emotion as a good in itself. Individualism is the very essence of the dissidence of dissent; and the funeral elegy reflects it in a constant emphasis on the sorrow of the elegist and his fellow-mourners, and in the lachrymose egoism of Edward Young. The cry for democracy was the slogan of the emerging middle classes[9] in their struggle to power; and it shows itself indirectly in the funeral elegy by a constant harping upon the theme of death the equalizer of beggars and of kings, death, which ushers in the righteous doom of God, very much as the armies of Cromwell had prepared the way for the work of the regicide judges. Sentimentalism developed in the funeral elegy as it developed in the middle classes, in the reign of Charles II, and grew apace during the generations that followed, as the main by-product of disintegrating Calvinism and the main element of the middle class mental life that could not enter into the sublimation of Neo-classicism. Indeed, whichever of these cultural definitions one accepts, it seems hard to avoid the association of Romanticism with the bourgeoisie.

Perhaps, in the welter of opinions and definitions, the present writer may claim as good a right as any to express his own views of the essence of Romanticism, although the acceptance of this view is not essential to agreement with the main thesis of the present study. All of the six definitions of Romanticism just reviewed are, at least sometimes, to be found as characteristics of that body of literary documents and artistic monuments that the world, by common consent, calls Romantic; but the limitation of this adjective to literature, or even to the arts in general, seems rather unfortunate if the present study is right in associating Romanticism with the contemporary economic, social, and political trend. Even aside from this consideration, moreover, the first three definitions seem unsatisfactory; the limitation of Romanticism to the archaic would leave out practically all the most significant poetry of Wordsworth and of Byron, the "natural" gardening of Kent and Brown, and the music of Schubert, Schumann, and Chopin, who invented new musical forms rather than revived old ones;[10] and such a definition runs counter to the whole idea of Original Genius,

[9] Of course many of them did not really mean a full democracy; and the French Revolution impressed upon them all the more the fact that, though they might use the lower classes on occasion against the nobility, the "swinish multitude" were hardly to be included within the pale of the new privileges.

[10] Many of the texts to which Romantic music was set were, to be sure, old; but the technique as music, so far as it was not a consistent building upon the tradition of the day, was a new invention rather than a revival of Greek, Mediæval or Renaissance prototypes.

which constitutes the very basis of Romantic æsthetics. The archaic, however—and one might add, the exotic—are an important incident in Romantic development; and the essence, whatever it be, of Romanticism must explain the rise of these related aspects. The definition of Romanticism in terms of the Realistic, and especially the closer observation of external nature, leaves out the more intellectual side of such a poet as Shelley and seems to include such writers as Thackeray and Fielding, the ballads of Prior and the *Trivia* of Gay—not to mention Dante and Homer. Are all these Romantic? Let us at least try to keep Romanticism as the description of a quality rather than an indiscriminate term of eulogy or contempt. If accurate Realism be the ultimate criterion of the Romantic then the Naturalists of the School of Zola are its most perfect examples: are they not rather the expression of its disillusion and decadence? One of the most widely held definitions of Romanticism, especially among those who look upon it as the summa of artistic achievement, is that which equates it with the imagination, in the exalted Coleridgean sense. The framers of this criterion would make all great poetry Romantic, and would contend that the rest of literature is the mere outgrowth of convention or of "fancy." Such a definition would be consoling if it were sound. But did we not a moment ago find much plain, literal Realism in the poetry of the Romantic Muse; and is it not also full of conventions of idea and of technique? Even more serious, can one deny that Defoe and Swift, not to mention Bishop Berkeley and Hume and Gibbon, had imagination? Most serious of all, does not Pope in the *Arbuthnot* show a high degree of imagination? If imagination be the vivid invention of objects to the very life and of beings in the very flesh and blood, if Chaucer's pilgrims be the children of the imagination, are not also Pope's swift vignettes, not only of Addison and Lord Hervey, but, even more vivid, of the moon-struck law-clerk, who "pens a stanza when he should engross," of the recalcitrant son who scribbles the walls of his prison with verses in charcoal, of the starveling poet who

> . . . high in Drury Lane,
> Lull'd by soft zephyrs through the broken pane,
> Rhymes ere he wakes and prints before term ends,
> Oblig'd by hunger and "request of friends."

Is one's definition of Romanticism to include the masterpiece of Alexander Pope?

The cultural definitions of Romanticism are more satisfactory because of their broader scope. Individualism as a Romantic criterion, however, presents serious difficulties: in what sense is the *Eve of St. Agnes* more subjective than Prior's ballads? Is Scott a subjective individualist? On the other hand, is not intellectual individualism a common characteristic of Renaissance humanism? Was it not even the ideal of Dr. Johnson's famous dictum: "I dogmatize and am contradicted; and in this I take my delight"?[11] The definition of Romanticism as democracy will hardly allow it to apply to literature at all, or at least not to literary form and technique. Such a definition flies in the very face of common use. As the earlier pages of the present study have perhaps suggested, the present writer believes that the crux and basis of Romanticism lies in emotionalism cultivated as an end in itself. Although this is not a characteristic of the greatest art, it has developed from time to time in the literary history of the world, expressing itself in an outburst of lyric fervor. According to this view, Romanticism is the more or less adequate artistic expression of the Sentimental state of mind: at its best, it can be appealing and even exquisite; but it cannot be sublime; for its meaning is not deep, and it concentrates its chief effects upon the feelings rather than upon the mind as a whole. At its worst, it can most properly be described, in both meanings, as merely sensational. To the present writer, it seems that all the poets called Romantic regularly cultivate some note or group of notes in the gamut of heightened emotionalism, from the intense sensibility of Wordsworth to the grandiose world-weariness of Byron. Falsity, conventionalism, and dullness are to be found in Neo-classical authors, but not a glorification of "enthusiasm." This definition, at any rate, will not include them; and it does seem to define the essence of Romanticism in the major arts of the epoch. The history of Romantic gardening from the reign of Queen Anne to Sir William Chambers is the story of increasing emotionalism.[12] The history of Romantic music from Beethoven and Weber to Wagner and Liszt is the story of the sacrifice of the

---

[11] See P. H. Houston, *Doctor Johnson,* Cambridge [Mass.], 1923.

[12] See the survey on eighteenth century gardening in relation to æsthetic theory by the present author, *William Mason,* New York, 1924, 211 *et seq.*

old symmetry of form for the new emotional appeal. Architecture forsook the reposeful lines of the perpendicular and horizontal for the dynamic slants and the ornamental variety of Gothic. Painting grew colorful and even lurid in the canvasses of Turner; and in drama, comedy was sacrificed to the emotional heightening of farce, and tragedy to melodrama. In poetry the psychological Law of Limen drove the poets farther and farther afield for stimulating subjects for their verse, from natural Realism to the archaic and the exotic, and so to the horrific and at last to the anti-natural.[13] Politically, this emotionalism expressed itself in a desire for greater scope and freedom,[14] for the emotions can hardly brook constraint; and socially it was allied to a subjective individualism, for one's moods and emotions are personal things, difficult to express or to share with one's neighbors. The middle classes exalted the emotions because this was the peculiar capability with which they were endowed; and, as they rose in social eminence, they made "sensibility" the ideal of the age. The funeral elegy seems originally to have been cultivated by the middle classes as an auxiliary to their pietistic melancholy; and then, as their piety chilled and declined, it became the channel for their reflexes of unrestrained emotion. As religious bans were more and more removed, and as the middle classes became patrons of the other arts, by sheer weight of numbers they made their preferences the current vogue. The bourgeoisie were the great dynamic power of the age; they expressed their rich emotional life in the rise of Romantic art; and the funeral elegy furnishes a key to their life and to this art in the first crude, germinating stage.[15]

---

[13] Cf. the present author, *The Summa of Romanticism, The Colonnade,* (1922), XIV, 257 *et seq.*

[14] Some Romanticists gained this scope by seeking solitude; Napoleon, who was Romantic at least in his literary taste, bent society to his will.

[15] This discussion is the merest survey, and so is open to the dangers of generality and abstraction: the danger of generality is the exception; the danger of abstract terms is vagueness and difference of definition and of connotation in the use of different persons.

APPENDICES

APPENDIX A

NOTES ON THE SYMBOLIC USE OF THE WILLOW

ALTHOUGH the present study is in no wise designed to cover the wide and interesting field of broadside iconography, the introduction of some miscellaneous observations on the symbolic use of the willow in the seventeenth and early eighteenth centuries may not be amiss. The weeping willow, such as one might expect to find rather common in broadside woodcuts, never appears in the seventeenth century; and even the straight-branched variety, such as one sees along the banks of sluggish streams in France and southern England, is hardly to be found. Willows do not appear in the woodcuts that regularly serve as headings in the Pepysian, Roxburghe, and Bagford collections;[1] and the present writer has not observed any upon seventeenth century English tombstones. The willow, indeed, was not traditionally the symbol of death, but of distressed lovers. Howell's *Devices* (1581) refers to "The Willow branch most fit for wofull wights";[2] Spenser speaks of it as "worne of forlorne paramours";[3] and a broadside entitled *The Willow Green. or, The Distressed lovers Complaint*[4] leaves no doubt as to its significance. Of Shakespeare's dozen or more references to the willow listed in Schmidt's *Lexicon*, including the famous *Willow Song* in *Othello*, every one, with the possible exception of Ophelia's drowning from a willow-branch, uses the tree as a symbol for unrequited, or at least unhappy love; and, this being the case, one wonders whether Shakespeare did not intend it symbolically to represent Ophelia's madness and death as caused by love of Hamlet, rather than, as other characters in the play declare, by the shock of her father's murder. This use of the willow for unrequited love continued more or less throughout the seventeenth century; and as late as 1665, Matthew Stevenson in his *Willow Garland*[5] associates the tree with a lady forsaken by her lover. A more general association, however, with

---

[1] There are a few trees portrayed, but they seem to be of indeterminate species.
[2] Thomas Howell, *Devices*, Oxford, 1906, 36 (ed. princ. 1581).

[3] *Faerie Queene*, I, i, ix.
[4] Roxburghe Collection, III, No. 132.
[5] M. Stevenson, *Poems*, London, 1665, 144.

grief was also beginning to appear. In the *Tears of Amynta,* Dryden makes the willow typify sadness; and, when "J. H. Esq." sang his lament for the death of Charles II "Beneath a doting Willows Shade,"[6] his poem is not a song of unrequited or unhappy love in the sense that the *Willow Song* in *Othello* could be so termed: unhappy love has been extended to embrace the loss by death of a friend or protector.

This new use begins to appear about the middle of the seventeenth century; and the willow, by an extension of meaning, is applied to any pensive melancholy. Possibly the predominance of Puritanism, with its prejudice against the amorous passions and its bias toward religious melancholy, had something to do with the change. In any case, it was now associated with "the *Mournful Cypress,*"[7] which had figured as a funereal symbol since Roman times, and the *"Unlucky* Yew,"[8] an auxiliary symbol of like intent borrowed from actual British churchyards. Thus all three trees might be used for elegiac purposes. "The matchless Orinda" indulges in her *Reverie* under a willow;[9] and Cowley, in atrabilious mood, refers to "the mourning Willow's careful gray."[10] This very natural broadening of application was doubtless assisted by the Biblical passage in which the willows of Babylon were associated with the sorrowings of the exiled Children of Israel; and, in a broadside pastoral elegy entitled *Great Britain's Lamentation: Or, the Funeral Obsequies Of that Most Incomparable Protestant Princess Mary of Ever Blessed Memory, Queen of England* (1695),[11] the "beauteous Virgins" are urged to hang their shepherd's reeds on the "sad Willows" with an obvious reference to the Jews by the waters of the Euphrates. Such a document, of apparently Puritan antecedents, supports the theory that Puritanism had something to do with extending the symbolic meaning of the willow tree.

During the eighteenth century, the willow as an expression of love in distress would seem to disappear. In *Winter,* Pope, adapt-

[6] J. H., *A Pindarick Ode on the Death of His Late Sacred Majesty King Charles II of Blessed Memory.* The piece was probably published in London; and the colophon dates it as 1685.

[7] *A Cordial Elegy* (on the Duke of Gloucester), and *Some Tears Dropt on the Herse of the Duke of Gloucester* (1660). Copies are to be found in the Thomason Collection in the British Museum.

[8] E. Arwaker, *The Vision* (on the death of Charles II), London, 1685.

[9] *Caroline Poets,* ed. Saintsbury, Oxford, 1905-1921, I, 556.

[10] See *The Complaint,* discussed in Chapter II.

[11] British Museum broadside.

ing the scenery of the Eurotas to that of the Thames,[12] substituted English willows for the laurels of the original, and doubtless intended a mournful connotation; but Neo-classicism was not favorable toward symbolism and allegory, and the symbolic use of willows is not common until the rise of Romanticism, which took a different view of symbolic art and looked with an approving eye on all forms of melancholy. Perhaps, moreover, the introduction of the weeping willow from China, probably coincident with the Chinese craze in porcelain and in gardening,[13] gave the symbol a new vogue. Certain it is, however, that by the end of the eighteenth century willows,[14] and especially weeping willows, are a regular part of the apparatus of melancholy in poetry, in mortuary pictures, and, in America, even on gravestones. The willow adorns several frontispieces in Cooke's edition of *British Poets*, published during the 1790's; and there is at least one elegiac broadside,[15] undated but apparently belonging to the late eighteenth century, that is headed by a picture of a Gothic ruin, a swan, a pensive figure leaning on a burial urn, and a willow tree.

[12] See Myra Reynolds, *The Treatment of Nature in English Poetry*, Chicago, 1909, 81.

[13] The weeping willow (*salix babylonica*) is a native of China, and perhaps also of Babylonia, though the reference in Psalm cxxxvii probably alludes to the poplar. The weeping willow was first introduced into England during the eighteenth century, perhaps by Pope but more probably by a Mr. Vernon, a Turkey merchant, in 1730. It was used in the Levant, France, and Germany for burial grounds, where it displaced the cypress during the eighteenth century. In England, it became an important adjunct of Romantic gardening, as the illustrations in Loudon attest (J. C. Loudon, *Arboretum et Fructicum Britannicum*, London, 1838, *s. v.*)

[14] Even as late as 1764, the picture that introduces Shenstone's *Elegies* (*Works*, I, 13) though it shows several sorts of trees surrounding a mortuary urn, has no weeping willow.

[15] *An Elegy on the Death of the Pious and Charitable James Thompson Esq. of Mansfield*. The piece was printed in London, but would seem to have survived only in a single copy preserved in the Signet Library, Edinburgh.

APPENDIX B

NOTES ON THE FUNERAL ELEGY AND THE
POETRY OF BURNS

THE influence of elegiac melancholy and of elegiac literary conventions upon the poets of the Romantic Movement was wide and deep; but perhaps no writer of the period shows more obvious and direct indebtedness to the funeral elegy than does Robert Burns—not so much an indebtedness to specific pieces that can be demonstrated in parallel passages, as a general borrowing of arrangement and details that were common stock in trade. As a number of examples in the Signet Library attest, broadside elegies were not extinct even in Burns' own generation; but he was deeply interested in, and often borrowed from, earlier Scottish literature; and some of his elegiac borrowings suggest that he was acquainted with Scottish broadsides of the sort at least as far back as the 1720's when they were sometimes written upon ordinary folk in the native dialect. Such comic and satiric pieces as the *Habbiack Elegy* (1724) and the lines on Patie Birnie "the Famous Fiddler" (1721) might well have survived in popular tradition down to his own day; and some of the numerous mementos on clerics, moreover, the *Elegie* on Anderson for instance, are extreme enough to suggest such parodies as *Holy Willie's Prayer*, which might almost be a self-elegy, and the *Epitaph*, which appropriately follows it in some editions.

Like many of the eighteenth century elegists, Burns was inclined to neglect the occasional aspect of the form; for he seldom troubled to wait for the death of his subject to vent his feelings and opinions: he is usually inspired to elegiac composition by a tavern quarrel or an act of kindness; and, in this way, the subject of the piece had the advantage of seeing his necrology in advance. Perhaps nothing shows more certainly Burns' wide acquaintance with Scotch elegiac literature than the variety of types and styles that he adapted to his purposes. Indeed, he fittingly celebrated almost every profession and walk of life with epitaphs and elegies, in English dialect, in Scotch dialect, in styles serious, comic, and satiric. He wrote on soldiers like Captain Roddick and Captain Lascelles, on

John Wilson, the parish schoolmaster,[1] on James Humphrey, a mason,[2] on "Tam the Chapman," on Tam Samson, the sporting seedsman, and on "John Dove, Inkeeper": these were his tavern-cronies or his local rivals. He wrote on his "Ever Honoured Father"; he penned lampoons on dignitaries of the church, eulogies on men of rank, and dainty-wrought verses on ladies of quality. His elegiac poems span the abyss between the scurrility of Rabelais and the society verse of Prior.

Burns' eulogies of his social betters, like nearly all the broadside elegies on this type, are regularly in English rather than in Scotch. Some are epitaphs in a single quatrain, like the pieces on Robert Aiken and Gavin Hamilton; and sometimes these epitaphs are appended to a preceding elegy, an arrangement very usual on broadsides, especially of Puritan authorship. Burns' most usual stanza is the quatrain; and sometimes, as in the *Elegy* on Sir James Hunter Blair, he seems to be following the versification of Gray. Sometimes, as in the lines on Miss Burnet, he uses the couplet, the commonest verse-form of the broadside elegy. The *Elegy* on Blair employs just such touches of scenic background as one finds in elegies even as far back as the seventeenth century: the "darkening air," the "rocky cave," "shooting meteors," and a "raving storm"; and the Shakespearean sonnet on the death of Robert Riddell reminds one of William Fowlers' similar use of the Spenserian sonnet two hundred years before. The *Elegy*, already mentioned, on Miss Burnet of Monboddo starts, like so many funeral elegies on great ladies, in the tone of Prior; then it changes to the note of Pope's *Seasons*, with a "flowry shore" and a "woodland choir"; and later still it grows more realistic with "mossy streams, with sedge and rushes stor'd," and even has something of the awful in its "rugged cliffs o'erhanging dreary glens." The following stanza, however, seems best to illustrate its obvious debt to the elegiac tradition:

> Princes, whose cumb'rous pride was all their worth,
>   Shall venal lays their pompous exit hail,
> And thou, sweet Excellence! forsake our earth,
>   And not a Muse with honest grief bewail?

Indeed, no themes are commoner, especially among the seventeenth

---

[1] See *Death and Dr. Hornbook.*   [2] See the *Epitaph on a Noisy Polemic.*

century Puritans, than to bewail the venality of the elegiac Muse and to express horrified surprise that no poet has yet celebrated the virtues of the deceased; and the foregoing quotation combines both themes, varying them ever so slightly to fit them together. The next stanza is compact of vague panegyric; and the last is on the grief of the parents—a conclusion on a minor note that suggests that the poet's mind was stored with Scotch rather than purely English archetypes. The *Monody on a Lady Famed for Her Caprice*, with its appended epitaph, is an interesting example of Burns's effort to write the satiric elegy in English dialect;[3] but, even here, he borrows from traditional themes in the description of her funeral and the references to monumental and poetic memorials.

Also satiric, but with more spice and interest, are several of his pieces in Scotch dialect. There are the lampooning epitaph on William Hood, the ruling elder, and the similar piece, already mentioned, on Holy Willie, and a mortuary epigram on James Smith that cuts two ways at once. Like certain Puritan divines, Burns celebrated his own death in an elegy,[4] not to mention two epitaphs; but, like Dean Swift, he gave his lines an ironic touch. Indeed, he seems hardly to have taken funereal poetry, at least that that was written in Scotch dialect, over seriously: perhaps it was associated too closely with the conventional gloom of the Presbyterian hierarchy whom he so detested; perhaps, like the pastoral tradition, it was worn out past all reviving. Even in these serio-comic pieces, however, he borrows, not merely the conventions, like the appending of an epitaph, and the themes, but occasionally the very phrases and images common to the elegiac tradition. The *Epitaph* on John Dove has a reference to *Memento mori*, the inevitable motto of mortuary iconography; in the *Epitaph* on Rankine, death is mentioned as "that gruesome carl"; in *The Song of Death*, it is apostrophized as "Thou grim King of Terrors; thou Life's gloomy foe!"; and again, in the *Elegy* on Captain Henderson, it is called upon by name as "thou tyrant fell and bloody." The same poem refers to "sculptur'd tombs" and an "eldritch tower" quite in the mortuary-Gothic manner. Elegy,

---

[3] Cf. the *Epitaph on Humphrey Squire,* also a satric necrology in English.

[4] See the *Elegy on the Death of Robert Ruisseaux.*

epitaph, self-elegy, general mortuary poem, and elegiac dialogue[5]: Burns has them all, and takes on occasion their plan, their themes, and their very phrases.

The few scattered notes brought together in the present appendix can hardly pretend to be an adequate treatment of the poet's debt to the elegiac tradition; but it serves to illustrate how this tradition, even in its more obvious and less gracious forms, persisted, and so is woven, like a warp, into the fabric of Romanticism. Sometimes it appears rather clearly as in Burns; but more often it is implicit and covered over with foreign philosophies and attitudes of mind.

[5] Cf. *Death and Dr. Wilson* to the popular broadside dialogue, *Death and the Lady*, attributed to Flatman.

INDEX

INDEX

Elegies are indexed under the names of the author and of the person elegized rather than under the titles. Discussions of abstractions, such as *bourgeoisie*, *melancholy*, and *Neo-classicism*, are regularly listed. In the notes to each chapter, there is at least one full bibliographical reference, usually the first, to each book cited in the chapter. Broadsides are referred to the library in which a copy is to be found or to the volume in which the piece is reprinted.

A. R.: 110, 214.
Abbey, C. J.: 68n, 253n.
Abney, Sir T.: 252, 300n.
Act of Settlement: 180n.
Act of Uniformity: 122n.
Act of Union: 222.
Addison, Joseph: 18, 42, 65, 66, 67, 119, 166, 183, 185, 234n, 235, 236, 237n, 241, 243n, 244, 273-274, 295, 312.
Addy, S. O.: 243n.
Æsthetics: 242 *et seq.*, 309, etc.
Aiken, Mary P.: 192n, 257n.
Aiken, Robert: 339.
Ailmer, Dr.: 73.
Albemarle, Duchess Dowager of: 102.
Albemarle, Earl of: *See* Monck, General.
Alciati: 48, 72n.
Alden, John: 168.
Alderman, W. E.: 64n, 150n, 240n.
Aldis, H. G.: 234n.
Allen, Henry: 53n.
Allyne, Robert: 9n.
Amadis of Gaul: 61.
Anderson, John: 215n, 222, 223.
Andrews, Rev. Mordecai: 293n.
Anglican Communion: 26, 35, 62 *et seq.*, 70n, 72, 96, 98, 102, 104, 105, 107, 115 *et passim*, 127, 132n, 135-136, 143, 148, 155, 178, 188, 197 *et passim*, 244, 263-265, 269, 286 *et passim*, 317 *et seq.*; the Low Church, 122n, 135-136, 140, 151n, 192; Scotch Episcopalianism, 108 *et passim*, 207 *et passim*; Irish, 241.
Annandale, Lord: 210.
Anne, Princess: 134n.
Anne, Queen, (consort of James I): 30.
Anne, Queen: 65, 104, 106, 117n, 172, 233-234, etc.
Anstruther, Sir William: 221.
Anti-intellectualism: 232, 267.
Anti-naturalism: 255-256n, 331.
Arbuckle, James: 273.

Archaic: 327 *et seq.*, etc. *See also* Gothic, Spenser, Shakespeare, etc.
Arden of Feversham: 94.
Argall, Richard (pseud.?): 9n.
Argyle, Duke of: 216, 217, 299.
Arianism: 119, 138, 238, 319. *See also* Unitarianism.
Aristotle: 65, 235, 238, 242n, 243.
Arminianism: 52, 63, 287. *See* Anglican Communion.
Armstrong, Sir Thomas: 138, 211.
Arnold, Matthew: 75n, 151.
Arnold, Samuel: 165.
"Art for art's sake": 93-94.
Arwaker, E.: 147, 194n, 195, 258, 259, 283, 336n.
Ashe, S.: 82.
Ashton, John: 106n, 107n, 237n, 266n.
Athol, Duchess of: 218.
Atkins, F.: 57n.
Atwell, Hugh: 50.
Angus, Lord: 214.
Augustan: 233, 249, 259, 265, 322.
Ayres, P.: 192.

B., A.: 225.
Babbitt, Irving: 4n, 14n, 19n, 65n, 111n, 185n, 238n, 317n.
Bacon, Lord: 183.
Bagford broadside ballads: 47, etc.
Bailey, J. C.: 5n.
Baker, Henry: 276.
Baker, Nathanael: 172.
Balcares, Earl of: 41.
Bale, Bishop: 93.
Ballads, popular: 24, 96. *See also* broadsides.
Bampfield, Francis: 143, 146.
Bank of England: 319.
Banks, John: 51.
Baptists: 111, 116, 117n, 143 *et passim*, 246. *See* Calvinism and Non-conformists.

Barber, Mrs. Jane: 203.
Barclay, Janet: 217.
Baring family: 236n.
Barnard, Sir John: 236n.
Barnardiston, Sir N.: 79 *et passim*, 114.
Barnstorff, J.: 4n, 17.
Baron, Robert: 43, 46.
Barrowe (nonconformist): 111.
Bates, Dr. William: 190, 261.
Bath: 237n.
Baudelaire, Charles: 147, 256n.
Baxter, R.: 138n, 143.
Beaconsfield, Lord: 303.
Beaumont, F.: 26, 61, 256.
Beaumont, Dr. J.: 44, 46, 194.
Beckford, William: 229, 237n, 326.
Bedloe, Captain: 149.
Beeching, Canon H. C.: 6.
Beethoven, L. van: 330.
Beers, Henry A.: 4n, 11n, 14, 76n, 259n.
Belcher, Governor: 171.
Belhaven, Lord: 217.
Bell, Robert: 175.
Bell, William: 136n.
Benlowes, Edward: 43, 46.
Bennett, J.: 152, 237n, 263n.
Benson, Jessy: 303n.
Benson, R. H.: 122n.
Bentley, R.: 234n.
Bentley, Rev. William: 292, 293n, 294n.
Beowulf. 24.
Berkeley, Bishop: 234n, 253n.
Bernbaum, E.: 20n, 153n, 205n, 233n, 238n, 240n, 243n.
Berridge, John: 303.
Berry, General H. G.: 304n.
Besant, Sir W.: 97n, 107n, 122n, 234n, 237n, 238n, 239n, 242n, 243n, 265n.
Bible: 18, 24, 34, 35, 47, 72 *et passim*, 93, 94, 96, 98, 114, 129, 131, 140, 157, 163, 183, 187n, 194, 201, 202, 230, 245, 246, 247, 253, 257, 261, 298n, 299, 306, 316, 320. *See also* David's Lament.
Bill of Rights: 180, 319.
Billingsby, John: 67.
Birch, T.: 107, 152.
Birnie, Patie: 222, 338.
Blackmore, Sir R.: 186, 248, 254-255.
Blackmore, Rev. Mr.: 299n.
Blair, Rev. David: 224-225, 229.
Blair, Sir J. H.: 339.
Blair, Robert: 4, 5, 14 *et passim*, 38, 76, 111, 170, 198, 220, 225 *et seq.*, 301, 306, 310, 312.
Blake, Admiral Robert: 89.
Blake, William: 4, 86, 322.

Blantyre, Lord: 217.
Blood, Colonel: 128.
"Bloodless Revolution": 180, 263.
Bogue, D.: 152, 237, 263n.
Bold, H.: 134n.
Bolingbroke, Lord: 183n, 184.
Bolton, S.: 79.
Bonner, Bishop: 27n.
Book of Common Prayer: 94 *et passim*, 111, 118, 185, 268, 323.
Boston, T.: 67.
Boswell, J.: 110.
Botsford, J. B.: 236n.
Botticelli, Sandro: 35n.
Bounty Act: 181n.
Bourgeoisie: 62, 121 *et seq.*, 151, 178 *et seq.*, 189, 219, 236 *et seq.*, 261-262, 264 *et seq.*, 266 *et seq.*, 285 *et passim*, 296 *et passim*, 300 *et seq.*, 314 *et seq.*, 327 *et passim*, 331.
Bowes, Robert: 208n, 209.
Bowhill, Lord: 221.
Boyd, Z.: 77.
Boyle, Robert: 103n, 183, 188, 200, 234.
Box, C.: 6, 253n.
Bradbury, Thomas: 291.
Bradshaw, John: 58.
Bradstreet, Anne: 158-159.
Bradstreet, Mary: 156n.
Bragg, M. K.: 7n, 8n, 71n, 192n, 256n, 295n.
Bragge, Rev. Robert: 293.
Breda, Declaration of: 122n, 178.
Bredvold, L. I.: 28n.
Bret, A.: 132n.
Brewster, D.: 298n.
Bright, Dr. T.: 15n, 26.
Brisco, Joseph: 158.
Bristow, James: 128, 135.
Broadsides: 47 *et seq.*, 156 *et seq.*, 187 *et passim*, 207 *et seq.*, 246-247, 292 *et seq.*, 310, 315 *et passim*; iconography of: 47-48, 101n, 102n, 157, 208, 335.
Broadwell, Mrs. Mary: 156n.
Brome, Alexander: 44, 46.
Brome, Rev. Richard: 303.
Bronson, W. C.: 65n.
Brooke, Lord: 54.
Broome, William: 274-275, 282.
Brown, Carleton: 24n.
Brown, J. E.: 233n, 306n.
Brown, John, "Estimate": 266.
Brown, Lancelot, "Capability": 243, 328.
Brown, Simon: 276.
Browne, Edward: 43.
Browne, J. W.: 304n.
Browne, M.: 190, 203, 258.

Browne, Sir Thomas: 24.
Browne, William: 45.
Brunetière, Ferdinand: 240n.
Buccleuch, Lord: 110n.
Buckingham, Duke of: 27, 51n, 83, 128.
Buckminster, Rev. Joseph: 174.
Buckworth, Mrs. Elizabeth: 248n.
Bunyan, John: 87, 119n, 124n, 153, 284.
Burke, Ædanus: 175.
Burke, Edmund: 123n, 182, 184.
Burnet, Bishop Gilbert: 133, 202.
Burnet, Miss, of Monboddo: 339.
Burnham (religious writer): 290n.
Burns, Robert: 31, 222, 224, 316, 338 et seq.
Burrell, C.: 80-81, 194n, 257, 279, 283.
Burrell, Timothy: 80n, 103.
Burroughs, J.: 86.
Burt, J.: 117n, 168.
Burton, R.: 16, 17, 26, 66.
Butler, Samuel: 66, 129, 234.
Byll, Thomas: 49.
Byles, Rev. Mr.: 171.
Byron, Lord: 134, 262, 316, 326, 328, 330.

C., M.: 292.
Cabinet System: 263, 286.
Calamy, Edmund: 115n, 143, 144.
Calder, Rev. Robert: 223.
Calvinism: 21 et seq., 52, 63 et seq., 92, 108 et passim, 119, 147, 152-153, 155, 180, 208 et passim, 223 et passim, 232, 236 et passim, 254 et passim, 267 et passim, 292 et passim, 309, 328.
Cambridge, Duke of: 133n.
Camden, W.: 95.
Campbell, T.: 198.
Canning, George: 303.
Care, Henry: 193.
Carew, Thomas: 35.
Carpenter, F. I.: 29n.
Carpenter, H. B.: 304n.
Carter, Admiral: 187.
Carter, J.: 112.
Capel, Lord: 54.
Capel, Charles: 129n.
Capen, Joseph: 160n, 162.
Capitalism: 264, 319. See Bourgeoisie.
Carlton, Mary: 134.
Caroline, Queen: 171n, 299.
Carstairs (elegy on): 222n.
Cartwright, T.: 62.
Castelvetro: 235.
Catholicism: See Anglican Communion and Roman Catholicism.
Catullus: 25, 31, 192, 256, 298.

Cazamian, L.: 21, 180n, 273n.
Chadderton, Dr.: 38, 200.
Chambers, E. K.: 33n.
Chambers, Sir William: 260, 330.
Chandos, Duke of: 299.
Charles I: 28, 38, 39, 40, 45, 52, 55-56, 59, 62, 79, 94, 101, 195, 203, 209, 226, 233, 288, 315.
Charles II: 40, 42, 56, 65, 101, 102, 107, 108, 113n, 119n, 122 et passim, 147, 181, 195, 206, 211, 336.
Charlie, Prince: 285.
Charnock, Stephen: 147.
Chatham, Earl of: 182, 184n.
Chaucer, G.: 24, 29n, 61, 80.
Cheek, Sir J.: 24.
Cheever, Rev. Mr.: 165.
Chesterfield, Lord: 65, 261.
Chettle, Henry: 9n.
Chevallier, Dr.: 106.
Chichester, Sir Arthur: 43, 100.
China: 24, 337 etc.
Christ's Hospital: 105.
Chudleigh, John: 35.
Chudleigh, Lady: 249.
Church of England: See Anglican Communion.
Cibber, C.: 22, 153, 243, 244.
Clarendon, Earl of: 152, 178.
Claridge, R.: 272.
Clark, H. H.: 4n, 10, 19, 282, 306n.
Clark, Rev. Mr.: 164-165.
Clark, Robert: 136n.
Clarke, Samuel: 67, 78n, 88n, 112n, 114n, 210.
Classics (Greek and Roman): 6 et seq., 13, 16n, 18, 25, 31 et passim, 56, 57n, 65, 81, 94 et seq., 104, 118, 125, 133, 140, 148, 185 et seq., 192-193, 201-202, 209 et passim, 225, 233 et seq., 239, 242 et seq., 256-257, 260, 269 et passim, 297, 310, 313, 321 et passim, 328n. See also Neo-classicism, Pindarics, Sapphics, Pastoral, etc.
Cleveland, John: 35, 38, 39, 42, 45, 55, 57, 100, 134, 200, 213, 315.
Clough, B. C.: 6n.
Cobden, Edward: 273.
Coburne, Samuel: 209.
Cockayne, George: 116, 190.
Cockburn, Major: 213.
Coleman, Priscilla: 174.
Coleridge, S. T.: 232.
Colles, H.: 132.
Collier, Jeremy: 186, 198.
Collins, N.: 117, 163.

Collins, W.: 8n, 13, 16, 65, 204, 298, 299.
Common Prayer, Book of: *See* Book of Common Prayer.
"Common sense": 185.
Congregationalism: *See* Independents and Non-conformists.
Congreve, William: 194, 195, 239.
Corn Laws: 265.
Cook, Colonel Edward: 134.
Cook, Sir John: 255n.
Cook, R.: 303n.
Cook, Samuel: 113.
Cook, Thomas: 296.
Corbet, Bishop: 200n.
Cordier, L.: 153n.
Cosmic: 228, 284, 309. *See* Milton.
Cotton, Rev. Mr.: 111.
Cotton, Charles: 187.
Cotton, John: 168.
Cotton, Seaborn: 166.
Courtesy books: 185.
Courthope, W. J.: 12, 21, 116n, 186n, 187n, 197, 267n.
Coventry, Thomas: 53n.
Cowley, A.: 32, 35, 40-42, 45, 46, 76, 81, 91, 124, 126, 148, 257, 315, 336.
Cowper, Ashley: 297.
Cowper, William: 4, 170, 322.
Crabbe, George: 4.
Craig, Alexander: 209n.
Crashaw, Richard: 35, 40, 63, 69, 125, 200n.
Crawford, Lord: 214, 215.
Crawshaw, W. H.: 70n.
Crécy, Battle of: 121.
Creech, T.: 192n.
Creighton, James: 289.
Croce, B.: 241n.
Cromarty, Countess of: 109.
Cromarty, Earl of: 216.
Cromwell, Oliver: 32n, 44, 59, 78, 89, 94, 112, 125, 136, 244, 328.
Cross, T. P.: 70n.
Cross, W. L.: 5n.
Crouch, J.: 133, 134n.
Crowne, John: 244.
Croxall, S.: 283.
Cunliffe, J. W.: 51n.
Cunningham, F.: 98.
Cunningham, James: 211.
Cutts, Baron: 196.
Cutts, Lady: 193.

D., F.: 161.
Dallaway, J.: 98n.
Dalziel, General: 213.

Dance of Death: 51.
Danforth, Samuel: 117n, 168.
Dargan, E. P.: 4n.
Dart, John: 279.
Dartmouth, Lord: 192n.
D'Avenant, W.: 58, 135.
David's lament over Saul and Jonathan: 24, 44, 95, 129, 143, 194-195, 276, 298.
Davis, Rose M.: 189n.
Davison (poet): 26.
Davyes, T.: 89.
Daws, Archbishop: 272.
Deane, General: 48, 88, 113, 257.
Decorum: 143, 157, 185, 233, 241, 247, 294, 316. *See* Neo-classicism.
Defoe, D.: 116, 128, 180n.
Deism: 119, 183-184, 198, 224, 232, 237, 242n, 261, 263, 267 *et passim*, 281.
Delape (elegy on): 222n.
De Maar, H.: 10, 11n, 15, 19, 256n, 282n.
Denham, Sir J.: 32, 124, 202.
Dennis, John: 195, 305.
Dennis, J. (*Age of Pope*): 226n.
Dethick, Sir William: 98.
Desportes, P.: 25.
Devonshire, Countess of: 103n.
Dey, Robert: 127.
Dide, A.: 153n.
Diderot, Denis: 4n, 241n.
Digby, Lady V.: 31.
Diodati, Charles: 70.
Divine Right of Kings: 179, 181, 263, 287n, 322 etc.
Dixon (*Romantic Revival*): 14n.
Dixon, Mrs.: 296.
Dobie, David: 303.
Dobrée, B.: 151n.
Doddridge, P.: 67, 116, 238.
Dodsley, Robert: 226.
Donaldson, J.: 214n.
Donne, John: 9, 16n, 26, 32, 38n, 39, 56, 57, 71, 99, 119, 125, 130, 133 *et passim*, 163, 166, 188, 200, 201, 202, 247, 257; School of, 28, 35 *et seq.*, 45, 46, 59, 71 *et passim*, 90, 124 *et passim*, 187, 199, 204, 206, 287, 315, 323.
Dorchester, Lord: 133.
Doré, Gustave: 246.
Dorislaus, Dr.: 58.
Dorset, Lord: 188.
Doughty, O.: 12-13.
Douglas, Elizabeth: 209.
Dove, John: 340.
Dowden, Edward: 14n.

Dowglass, R.: 218.
Draper, J. W.: 13n, 19n, 20n, 23n, 48n, 57n, 64n, 76n, 77n, 83n, 119n, 134n, 151n, 186n, 190, 198, 208n, 213n, 234n, 235n, 238n, 242n, 243n, 250n, 251n, 260n, 330n, 331n.
Drayton, M.: 29, 100.
Dromore, Bishop of: 276.
Drummond, David: 217.
Drummond, Captain George: 221.
Drummond of Hawthornden: 213.
Drury, Mrs. Elizabeth: 34.
Dryden, John: 54, 88, 106, 124 et seq., 147, 188, 194, 195, 250, 336.
Du Bartas, G.: 159.
Duck, Stephen: 189.
Dudley, Thomas: 158.
Dunbreck, Captain Charles: 221.
Dunstan, St.: 24.
Durel, J.: 107n.
D'Urfey, Thomas: 9n, 188, 193, 247, 271.
Du Val, C.: 129.

Edson, Ruth: 172n.
Education: 66, 121-122, 185-186, 234, 242, 261, 264-265.
Edwards, J.: 172 et passim.
Edwin, Samuel: 272.
Egerton, Mrs. S.: 250.
Elcho, Lady Ann: 217.
Elderton, William: 47.
Elegy: See Funeral elegy.
Elesius Calentius: 25n.
Elizabeth, Queen: 27n, 61, 63, 83, 107, 121, 159, etc.
Ellis, C.: 88n.
Ellis, Jonathan: 304n.
Elogy: 86n etc. See Funeral elegy.
Emblem-books: 72n.
Emotionalism: See Sentimentalism and Enthusiasm.
England, Church of: See Anglican Communion.
Enthusiasm: 5, 64, 124n, 136, 152 et seq., 234, 238, 286, 293, 298n, 330. See also Sentimentalism and Romanticism.
Epicedium: 99-100, 132, etc.
Essex, Earl of (Capel): 138, 211.
Essex, Earl of (Devereux): 6, 86, 114, 257.
Ethos: 296.
Euphuism: 290.
Evance, D.: 86, 114n, 257.
Evans, Charles: 117n, 158n.
Evelyn, J.: 66, 103.

Exequy: 99-100.
Exotic in literature: 239n, 329 et seq.

F., Sir F.: 148.
F., J.: 193n.
F., S.: 9n.
Fairfax, Lord: 86.
Farquhar, Lord: 216.
Fawne, Luke: 87.
Fenton, E.: 247.
Fenwick, Sir John: 197.
Fergusson, Robert: 222.
Festus: 95n.
Fiction: 326. See Richardson, Fielding, Gothic novel, etc.
Fielding, H.: 268.
Finch, Anne: See Winchelsea, Lady.
Finch, Lord: 198.
Finch, M. B.: 4n, 153n.
Firth, C. H.: 122n, 178n et passim.
Fisher, Payne: 9n, 27, 44, 113.
Fisher, Thomas: 216.
Fitzgerald, Thomas: 295.
Flatman, R.: 130.
Flatman, Thomas: 129 et seq., 137, 147, 195, 200, 258.
Flaubert, Gustave: 327.
Fleming, Robert: 24n, 189, 194, 258.
Fletcher, Giles: 30, 283.
Fletcher, John: 17n, 18, 26.
Fletcher, Phineas: 26, 30, 35n, 70, 72, 283.
Forbes, Bishop: 209, 210n.
Ford, Sir R.: 142.
Ford, W. C.: 156n, 161n.
Foster, J. R.: 5n.
Foster, John: 160.
Fowler, Rev. Mr.: 138n.
Fowler, J.: 192n.
Fowler, W.: 208-209.
Franciscans: 286.
Franklin, B.: 173, 175, 295.
Franklin, J.: 173.
Frascatoria: 125.
Frederick, Prince of Wales: 107.
Freeman, Ralph: 51.
French Revolution: 285, 325, 328n.
Freneau, Philip: 174.
Frevile, Sir George: 53n.
Fuller, T.: 136.
Funeral elegy: numerous, 3, 295 et seq.; in periodical literature, 3, 217 et seq., 298 et seq.; generally neglected, 5; definitions of, 6, 28; recipe for, 173; vogue explained, 12-23; in early seventeenth-century poets, 27-45, 71-82; on animals, 31; in broadsides, 46-59,

84-90, 131 et seq., 156 et seq., 189 et seq., 208 et seq., 246 et seq., 269 et seq., 293 et seq.; use at Anglican funerals, 96-104; at dissenting funerals, 107 et seq., 129; in Scotland, 27, 108-111, 207 et seq., 257; in New England, 117, 156 et seq., 302-304n; aristocratic types, 123-128, 187, 257, 317; the satiric elegy, 136, 197, 273-274, 305, 323, 340; Puritanism and, 71 et seq., 129, 139 et seq., 159 et seq., 189 et seq., 250 et seq., 291, 315, 336; Sentimentalism and, 153, 176, 203, 224, 232, 259, 278, 320 et seq., 325, 328; Neo-classicism and, 192 et seq., 215 et seq., 244, 249, 318 et seq.; Non-Jurors and, 197; Thomson and 224; Nature-description and, 255, 261; versification of, 157 et passim; the generalized elegy, 223 et seq., 274 et seq., 281, 306 et seq.; the Gothic tradition and, 279; the Spenserian tradition and, 282 etc.; Methodism and, 287 et seq.; on women, 133-134, 217 et seq., 287 et passim, 302; on Charles II, 147, 195; on Queen Mary, 195; on the elder Blair, 224; on Addison, 273; Romanticism and, 4, 326 et seq.

Gabry, Jane: 134.
Gardening: 12, 20, 235, 243, 260, 330.
Gardiner, Colonel J.: 116, 222.
Gardyne, Alexander: 209n.
Garnier, R.: 25.
Gauden, Bishop: 135, 136n.
Gay, John: 13, 105, 186, 266, 269-270, 274, 276, 321.
Geneva: 153.
Gentleman's Magazine: 3, 299, etc.
George I: 267 etc.
George II: 105 etc.
George, Captain: 103n, 187.
George, Dorothy: 237n, 243n, 264n, 266n.
Gerrish, Mary: 167.
Gesner, S.: 153n.
Gibbon, Edward: 183n.
Gibbons, Thomas: 291, 292n.
Gibbs, James?: 250n.
Gill, John: 95-96, 104.
Gillies, J.: 107n.
Gittos, George: 139.
Gwinn, Madam: 134.
Gloucester, Duke of: 101, 132, 249, 336n.
Godfrey, Sir E.: 115.
Godwin, William: 183.
Goethe, J. W. von: 5, 249.

Goldsmith, Oliver: 4, 7, 8n, 10, 105, 151n.
Good, J. W.: 14-15.
Goodall, Charles: 203.
Goode, C. T.: 70.
Göricke, W.: 241n.
Gosford, Mr.: 213.
Gosse, Sir E.: 4n, 10.
Gotch, J. A.: 243n.
Gothic architecture: 12, 93, 149, 166, 203, 226 et passim, 243n, 249, 251, 260, 261, 273, 279-282, 284, 311, 325, 327, 331, 340.
Gothic novel: 5, 61, 66, 89, 304.
Gouge, Thomas: 116.
Gough, S.: 263n.
Gould, Robert: 9n, 188, 247, 270.
Grafton, Duke of: 193.
Graham, H. G.: 64n, 109n, 153n, 209n, 237n, 264.
Grand Tour: 319.
Gray, Anne: 77, 88, 133n.
Gray, Thomas: 4, 6, 13 et passim, 34, 41n, 48, 65, 128, 174, 198, 227, 228, 230, 253, 271, 275n, 279 et passim, 285, 300n, 302, 306, 309 et seq., 324.
Greek: See Classics.
Green, Mrs. J. R.: 121n.
Green, M.: 68.
Green, S. A.: 117n, 160n et passim.
Green, Thomas: 246.
Greene's Funerals: 25n.
Grey, Edward: 100.
Griffith, G. B.: 304n.
Grosart, Dr. A. B.: 17n.
Guarini: 30.
Guiscard, Marquis de: 222.
Gunning, Henry: 106n.
Gunston, Lord Mayor: 250 et passim.
Gustavus Adolphus: 39.
Gutteridge, Thomas: 293-294.
Gwatkin, H. M.: 180n.

H., J.: 148, 336.
Habbiack Elegy: 222.
Habington, William: 200n.
Hadow, Thomas: 221.
Hagthorpe, J.: 32.
Hale, Sir M.: 103n.
Halévy, E.: 236n et passim.
Hall, Rev. Thomas: 293n.
Hamilton, Lord Basil: 216.
Hamilton, Duke of: 222.
Hamilton, Gavin: 339.
Hammond, James: 6, 69, 77, 217, 297.
Hampden, John: 84, 113.
Hanbury, B.: 111n.

Handel, G. F.: 14, 235, 243n.
Hanford, J. H.: 70n.
Hannay, Patrick: 30.
Harman, Captain W.: 134.
Harman, Captain T.: 134n.
Harrington, Lord: 34.
Harris, W.: 67.
Harrison, George: 89.
Hart, Charles: 103n.
Hastings, Lord: 88, 124, 125n.
Hastings, Dr. Thomas: 170, 171.
Havens, R. D.: 15, 43n, 224n, 226n,
    275n, 278n, 282n.
Hawthorne, N.: 304n.
Hay, Lady Anne: 35.
Hearne, T.: 24n, 95.
Heath, James: 136.
Heath, Robert: 39n.
He—ly, Mrs. Jane: 295.
Henchman, Bishop: 135.
Henderson, T. F.: 213.
Henrietta Anne, Princess: 134n.
Henry VIII: 121.
Henry, Prince: 27, 29, 34, 56, 99n.
Hepburn, John: 223.
Heralds' College: 97-98, 104.
Herbert, Lord: 42-43.
Herbert, George: 35, 45, 63, 69, 200.
Herbert, Thomas: 53n.
Hern, N.: 142.
Heroic couplet: 201, 245, 249, etc. See
    Versification.
Herrick, R.: 25, 31, 63, 128, 269.
Hervey, James: 15, 289-290.
Hervey, William: 40-41.
Hewitt, John: 57n.
Hey, Sir W.: 110.
Heywood, T.: 27n, 30.
Hibben, G. H.: 183n.
Hildeburn, C. R.: 156n.
Hill, Aaron: 297-298.
Hinchcliffe, W.: 270n, 271.
Hobbes, Thomas: 268.
Hog, Sir R.: 220.
Holland, Samuel: 77, 88, 133.
Hollis, Thomas: 292.
Holmes, T. D.: 213.
Homer: 24, 93.
Hood, William: 340.
Hooker, R.: 66, 98.
Hooker, Thomas: 157.
Hopkins, J.: 193, 194, 258, 283.
Hopkins, P. T.: 64n, 106n, 107n.
Horace: 18, 31, 32, 95n, 186, 201, 245,
    257.
Houston, P. H.: 330n.
Howell, James: 43.

Howell, Thomas: 335.
Hubbard, Rev. John: 293n.
Huguenots: 181, 246.
Hughes, Mrs. Elizabeth: 293.
Hughes, Helen S.: 20n, 153n.
Hughes, John: 278, 282, 292, 293n.
Hughes, Rev. Mr., of Hellidon: 300.
Hugo, Herman: 72n.
Hull, Thomas: 52n.
Hume, David: 183n, 281.
Hume, Sir D.: 220.
Hunnewell, J. F.: 156n et passim.
Hunt, T. W.: 6, 29n.
Hunter, John: 234n.
Hurd, Richard: 42.
Hurne, Elizabeth: 134.
Hutchinson, Elizabeth: 167.
Hutchinson, F. E.: 35n, 38n, 72n, 76n.
Hutcheson, F.: 146, 140n, 267, 325.
Huxley, Thomas: 183.

Imagination: 327 et seq.
Imitation: 239, 242.
Independents: 111 et seq., 143 et passim,
    155, 186n, 315. See Non-conformists
    and Calvinism.
India: 236n.
Individualism: 327, 330, etc.
Industrial Revolution: 236n, 261, 264,
    286, 289, 314, 316, 325.
Innocent XI, Pope: 211.
Irby, Sir Antony: 30.
Ireland: 281, 305n. See also Anglican
    Communion.
Ireton, H.: 113.

J., T.: 134.
Jackson, F. J. F.: 64n.
Jacobites: 197, 222, 232, 258-259.
James I (James VI of Scotland): 51, 56,
    62, 121, 208.
James II (James VII of Scotland): 101n,
    102, 138, 179 et seq., 197 et passim,
    219, 318.
James, R.: 69, 72n, 77, 78, 115.
Janeway, James: 145, 258.
Jefferson, Thomas: 176.
Jeffreys, Judge: 180.
Jenkins, William: 138.
Jesse, Henry: 143, 146.
Jessor, William: 300n.
Jodelle, E.: 25.
Johnson, Dr. S.: 94, 110, 126, 205, 273,
    281, 306, 310, 330.
Johnny Campbell: 24.
Jones, Andrew: 141.
Jones, Robert: 288.

Jones, Sir William: 142.
Jonson, Ben: 27, 38, 39, 71, 98, 198, 200 *et passim*, 256; School of, 28, 30 *et seq.*, 45, 87.
Jordanes: 24.
Juvenal: 186.

K., P.: 149-150.
Kaufman, P.: 326n.
Kaye, F. B.: 268n.
Keach, B.: 116, 117n, 246, 247.
Keats, John: 249, 254n, 280, 307, 312, 330.
Keith, J. F. E.: 221n.
Kelso, Commissioner: 217.
Ken, Bishop: 277-278, 282.
Kent, W.: 22, 243, 328.
Kerr, W. A. R.: 240n.
Killigrew, Anne: 126.
Killigrew, Thomas: 135n.
Kilmarnock, Earl of: 232n.
King, Edward: 38-39, 52.
King, Bishop Henry: 35, 42, 45, 46, 99, 315.
Kingscourt, Katharine: 129.
Kinnoul, Lord: 210n.
Kirkpatrick, Sir T.: 217.
Kirkton: 67.
Kitel, Mahitebell: 173.
Kittredge, 'G. L.: 126n.
Klaeber, F.: 24n.
Korff, H. A.: 12.
Krutch, J. W.: 20n, 151n, 238n, 243n, 267n.

Lake, Dr. John: 192n.
Lamentation of a Sinner: 96, 200.
Landor, W. S.: 326.
Lascelles, Captain: 338.
Laud, Archbishop William: 34, 38, 55, 63, 287.
Lauder, G.: 9n, 110n, 210.
Laurens, Colonel: 175.
Law of Limen: 242.
Law, William: 183n, 198, 226, 290.
Lawes, William: 39n.
Lawrence, James: 175.
Lawton, I.: 126.
Leach, Mary: 303n.
Leadham, I. S.: 233n.
Le Blond (on gardens): 235n.
Lecky, W. E. H.: 11, 20, 119n, 123n, 178n, 234n, 236n, 237n, 263n, 264n, 266n, 286n, 287n, 289.
Lee, Anne: *See* Wharton.
Lee, Mrs. Hannah: 156n.
Lee, Mrs.: 249n.

Lee, Sir S.: 25n.
Legouis, E.: 21, 180n, 273.
Leigh, W.: 79.
Leonard, T.: 117n, 168.
L'Estrange, Sir R.: 246n.
Leven, Lady: 218, 220.
Lewis, Matthew: 225.
Lewis, William: 82.
Library of the Society of Antiquaries: 49.
Lightfoot, Thomas: 156.
Lillo, George: 243.
Lingard, Dean: 136.
Lisle, Sir George: 54n.
Litzt, F.: 330.
Liverpool: 236n.
Lloyd's: 265.
Lloyd, Mary: 5, 26n.
Lloyd, Robert: 243n.
Llwelyn, M.: 101, 132n.
Lochiel, The: 221.
Locke, John: 65, 182 *et seq.*, 193, 198, 293, 320.
Lodge, R.: 122n, 178n *et passim*.
Lorraine, Duke of: 103n.
Loudon, J. C.: 337n.
Louis XIV: 222.
Lounsbury, T. R.: 186n.
Love, C.: 56-57.
Loveday, Samuel: 143, 144.
Lovejoy, A. O.: 19n, 185n, 326n.
Lovelace, R.: 31 *et passim*, 187.
Lowe, Edward: 57.
Lucas, Sir Charles: 54.
Luckyn, Lady: 74.
Lucretius: 18, 131, 201, 202.
Luttrell Collection: 41n, 52n, etc.
Luttrell, Colonel John: 84, 86, 113, 208n.
Luttrell, Narcissus: 137, 138, etc.
Lykewake Dirge: 96, 193, 200.
Lyly, John: 61, 185.

M., R.: 216.
M., T.: *See* Fisher, P.
Machiavelli, N.: 185.
Macquoid, G. S.: 232n.
Macquoid, P.: 97n.
Macrobius: 95.
Maidment, J.: 109n, 210n, 212n.
Mallet, P. H.: 242n.
Mallett, D.: 9n, 18n, 278.
Malory, Sir Thomas: 29n, 194n.
Mandeville, B.: 267-268, 285, 296n, 325
Marine, Francis: 222.
Marini, G.: 30, 33.
Marriot, T.: 80n, 115.
Marsh, J.: 117, 166.

Martial: 18, 201.
"Martin Mar-prelate": 62.
Marvell, Andrew: 62, 69, 78.
Mary II: 48, 101n, 102, 195-196, 205, 211n, 214, 217, 336. See also William and Mary.
Massinger, P.: 18, 66.
Masson, P. M.: 4n, 21, 153n.
Masters, Mary: 273, 295, 296n.
Mather family: 318.
Mather, Cotton: 117, 159, 160, 163 et seq.
Mather, Increase: 158n.
Mather, Richard: 112, 158n.
Mathieson, W. L.: 67n, 209n.
McIntyre, Clara: 66n.
McKenzie, Sir G.: 48, 110, 208, 214.
McKillop, A. D.: 4n.
McLellan, Isaac: 304n.
Mead, Rev. M.: 101n, 190-191, 203.
Mediæval: 24, 28 et passim, 35n, 46, 49-51, 61, 64, 80, 93, 96 et passim, 104, 108, 118, 121, 295, 317.
Melancholy: 15 et seq., 65 et seq., 90, 116, 143 et seq., 149, 203, 215, 230-231, 241, 248, 255-257, 267 et passim, 281, 295, 304, 316 et passim.
Meldrum, Rev. George: 222n.
Melvil, Captain George: 214.
Mercer, William: 84, 86, 113.
Merchant Taylors' School: 122.
Merrideth, Matthew: 305.
Merry, Thomas: 137.
Mervyn, Sir H.: 114.
Methodism: 11, 65, 107n, 156, 183n, 184n, 235n, 237n, 286 et seq., 292, 294n, 319.
Methuen Treaty: 266.
Micklethwaite, Dr. J.: 135.
Middle classes: See Bourgeoisie.
Middleton, H.: 116n, 203, 270.
Milington, Edward: 246.
Milne, Umphrey: 211, 214.
Milton, J.: 7, 14 et seq., 55, 56, 61, 62, 69-71, 76, 86, 94, 111, 158, 201, 202, 226, 228, 231, 242n, 243n, 248, 257n, 275n, 280 et passim, 291n, 298, 300n, 307, 308, 316, 321, 325, 327; School of: 87. See also Cosmic.
Mirror for Magistrates, The: 51.
Mitchell, Jonathan: 157n, 160, 161.
Mohun, Lord: 222.
Molineux, Captain: 305.
Monck, General: 129, 134, 137.
Montagu, Charles, Lord Halifax: 181.
Montagu, Elizabeth: 199n.
Montagu, Duchess of: 211.

Monmouth, Duke of: 179, 211.
Monteith, George: 212n.
Montrose, Lady: 218.
Montrose, Marquis of: 110, 128.
Moray, John: 53, 100.
Morgan, M.: 188.
Morgan (elegized by Wesley): 288.
Morice, Mrs: 288.
Morwent. Charles: 125.
Mornet, D.: 242n, 255n, 256n.
Moore, C. A.: 66n, 240n.
Moore, Sir Jonas: 132.
Moore, T.: 326.
More, Hannah: 183n.
More, Sir Thomas: 24.
Morton, N.: 157n, 160n, 161n.
Motteux, P. A.: 195.
Murford, N.: 69, 77.
Müller, K.: 4n, 17, 18, 201n, 226n.
Murray-Kynnynmound: 221.
Murray, Mungo: 210.
Music: 243 etc. See Æsthetics.

Napoleon: 331.
Nash, Josephus: 170-171.
Nashe, Thomas: 26.
Nason, A. H.: 97n, 99n.
"Nature": 89, 148 et passim, 183, 191, 196-197, 203-204, 219-220, 226 et seq., 233, 239, 242n, 247, 255 et seq., 261, 295, 310, 325-326.
Neal, N.: 263.
Neilson, W. A.: 152n.
Neo-classicism: 11, 13, 20, 72, 94, 134, 157 et passim, 169 et seq., 178 et seq., 199n, 202 et seq., 215, 219, 229, 233 et seq., 269, 291, 311, 322, 323, 324-325, 337. See also Classicism (Greek and Roman).
Nesbitt, John: 189.
Nethercot, A. H.: 35n, 72n, 76n, 124n.
Netherlands: 178.
Newcomb, Thomas: 296.
New England: 90, 111, 117-118, 155 et seq., 253, 258, 303, 318.
Newgate: 303.
Newman, Rev. John: 293, 294.
Newton, Sir I.: 183, 224, 234n, 237.
Nicholls, N.: 310n.
Nicoll, A.: 20n, 151n, 153n, 236n, 238n.
Nisbet, Sir John: 213.
Nitze, W. A.: 4n.
Non-conformists: 21, 96n, 108 et seq., 123 et passim, 132n, 138 et seq., 178 et seq., 207 et seq., 236 et passim, 263, 294, 310, 327. See also Arians, Baptists, Presbyterians, Quakers, etc.

Non-jurors: 21, 197-200, 258-259, 289.
Norcot, John: 143, 146, 154.
Norfolk, Duke of: 133.
Norris, John: 17, 198.
Northampton, Lord: 124.
Norton, J.: 117, 159.
Nottingham, Lord: 198.

Oakes, Urian: 117, 159, 160.
Ode: See Pindarics.
Oldham, J.: 125, 129, 194.
Oldmixon, John: 197.
Oldsworth, Dr.: 100, 101n.
On the Death of a Favorite Cow: 3.
"Ophelia": 302.
Optimism: 237, 241, 267, 277, 289.
Orient: 319. See also China.
Original Genius: 66n, 74n, 239, 242, 295, 312, 314, 328.
"Orinda": See Philips, Mrs. K.
Ormond, Duke of: 193, 203.
Orrery, Earl of: 132.
Orrery, Lady: 295.
Osgood, C. G.: 240n.
Ossory, Earl of: 129, 134.
O'Sullivan, M. I.: 26n.
Otis, W. B.: 160n.
Overbury, Sir T.: 27, 50.
Overton, J. H.: 68, 253n.
Ovid: 25, 192, 256.
Owen, John: 143, 144.

P., S.: 110n.
P., J.: 219.
Padelford, F. M.: 29n.
Page, Sir George: 95.
Paget, Lord: 298.
Paine, Thomas: 175.
Painting: 243, 331, etc. See Æsthetics.
Palladio: 235.
Palmer, Edward: 128.
Palmer, Rebecca: 146, 147, 154.
Pamphlets, for publication of elegies: 133, 138, 247, etc.
Panccutland, Lord: 216.
Pantheism: 183n. See also Deism.
Park, Henry: 196.
Parker, Martin: 53, 58.
Parnell, Thomas: 4, 8, 10, 14, 15, 18n, 19, 259, 266, 269, 281-282, 289, 306, 321.
Partridge, John: 212, 246.
Pastoral: 7 et seq., 71, 192-193, 196, 204, 205, 219, 247, 250, 259, 270-271, 274, 298 et passim, 305, 321, 323. See Classicism, Vergil, Theocritus, etc.
Paterson, Ninian: 9, 111, 212-213, 318.

Patronage: 27n, 234 et seq., 264 et seq.
Patten, S. N.: 122n, 182n, 187n, 237n.
Pattison, William: 259.
Pawlet, Lady Jane: 31.
Payson, Edward: 304n.
Peacham, Henry: 99n.
Peadie, Provost: 222n.
Pearl, The: 24.
Pearsall, Rev. Mr.: 290n.
Pecke, Thomas: 57n.
Peers, E. A.: 4n, 153n.
Pembroke, Lord: 132.
Penn, William: 143n.
Pennecuik, Mr.: 217.
Pentland Rising: 179.
Pepys, Samuel: 103.
Pepysian broadside ballads: 47, 49.
Percy, Bishop T.: 24n.
Periodical literature: 3, 217 et passim, 290, 291, 298 et seq.
Perkins, Joseph: 198.
Perth, Lord: 210.
Petrowe (elegist): 51.
Petrarch: 30.
Phellipps, W. F. M.: 5n.
Phelps, W. L.: 14.
Philips, Katherine "the matchless Orinda": 32, 41, 203, 256n, 336.
Phillip, John: 49.
Phillips, John: 247.
Phillips, Samuel: 140, 244n.
Philosophy as a social force: 241n.
Pierce, James: 238.
Pilkington, Sir John: 190.
Pindar: 242n. See Pindarics.
Pindar, Sir Paul: 56.
Pindarics: 124 et passim, 147 et passim, 193, 200, 201, 205, 250, 258, 259, 293, 299n, 317, 321, 323.
Pitt family: 236n, 265.
Pitt, Christopher: 271-272.
Pitt, George: 88.
Pitt, William (the Elder): See Chatham.
Pitt, William (the Younger): 184n.
Platonists, Cambridge: 240n.
Pledger, Elias: 147.
Plenderleith, Patrick: 223.
Poe, E. A.: 304.
Pomeroy, E. N.: 304n.
Pomfret, John: 32, 205-206, 254, 312.
Pool, Madam: 188.
Pope, Alexander: 10, 14, 17, 18n, 72, 76, 87, 105, 166, 186n, 196, 216, 233, 235, 239, 243n, 244, 258, 270, 271, 276, 278, 281, 283, 321 et passim.
Popham, Edward: 114.
Popish Plot: 179.

Porter, Dr.: 35.
Potenger, John: 192, 193, 270.
Pound, Louise: 96n.
Powell, Sir H.: 272.
Praz, M.: 33n.
Presbyterianism: 108 et seq., 143 et passim, 189, 207 et seq., 237n, 238, 318, 340. See also Non-conformists and Calvinism.
Price, M. L.: 4n.
Price, L.: 87, 91.
Prior, M.: 129, 134, 186, 239, 244, 247, 297, 298, 299, 301n, 305, 330, 339.
Proletariat: 286, 289, etc.
Propertius: 25.
Prose: 322n.
Protestantism: 181, 238, etc. See also Calvinism, Non-conformity, Puritanism, etc.
Prynne, W.: 112.
Pseudo-Hadrian: 7.
Publius Faustus: 5n.
Puritans: 26, 29, 38n, 39 et passim, 47, 51 et passim, 62 et seq., 91, 108 et seq., 122 et passim, 131-132, 138 et seq., 152-154, 155 et seq., 185, 191, 250 et passim, 281, 312-313, 315 et passim, 336. See also Non-conformists.
Puttenham, G.: 99-100.
Pym, John: 84, 113.

Quakers: 124n, 138, 143n, 153, 155, 174, 198, 235n, 286, 319.
Quarles, F.: 18, 26, 35n, 48, 58, 69, 71-77, 79, 81, 87, 91, 127, 133, 140, 160, 202, 257, 282, 283, 315.
Queensbury, Duchess of: 218.

Radcliffe, Mrs. A.: 229.
Rainborowe, Colonel: 87, 257, 283.
Ralph, James: 295.
Ramsay, Allan: 213, 215, 222, 274.
Ramsay, Sir Andrew: 213.
Ramsay, Mary P.: 28n.
Rapin, R.: 192.
Rattray, Bishop: 222n.
Rawlet, John: 140, 192.
Realism: 13, 91, 133, 219-220, 242, 252, 255 et seq., 295, 300, 310, 311, 327, 329, 331.
Reath, Lord: 214.
Reed, A. L.: 4n, 10, 11n, 15, 18, 26n, 65n, 184n, 201-202, 235n, 236n, 241n, 267n, 278n, 297n, 306n, 310n.
Reed, George: 189n.
Reed, Joseph: 175.

Reform Bills: 122, 314.
Reiner, John: 162.
Renaissance: 24 et passim, 64, 118, 121-122, 185, 192, 234, 239, 249, 250, 265, 267, 286, 313, 315, 328, 330.
Reynolds, J.: 184, 193.
Reynolds, Myra: 10, 19n, 199n, 243n, 244n, 251n, 259n, 282, 337.
Rhodes, M.: 50.
Rhys, E.: 41n.
Riccaltoun, Robert: 224.
Rich, Lady: 32.
Richards, N.: 56.
Richardson, G. F.: 20n, 239n.
Richardson, Samuel: 82.
Richmond, Duke of: 133n.
Richter, Helene: 11n.
Rig Vida: 24, 94.
Robertson, A.: 109, 232n.
Robertson, J. G.: 20n, 187n.
Robertson, Thomas: 213.
Robinson, Ralph: 79.
Rochester, Earl of: 102n, 128n, 129, 133, 202, 282.
Rodney, Sir Edward: 53n, 57n, 100.
Rollins, H. E.: 49n, 52n, 53n et passim, 87n.
Roman Catholicism: 24, 94 et passim, 102, 132n, 148n, 155, 179, 183n, 187n, 211, 286.
Romanticism: 4, 11-13, 20, 21, 23, 153n, 170, 177, 232, 273, 326 et seq.
Roscommon, Lord: 128, 129n.
Rose, Aquila: 156n.
Rose, Joseph: 156n.
Ross, Bishop of: 212.
Ross, General: 175.
Rothes, Lady: 217.
Rousseau, J. J.: 21, 153n, 237n, 243.
Rowe, Mrs. Elizabeth: 199n, 236, 250, 253 et seq., 260, 301, 313.
Roxburghe broadside ballads: 47 et passim.
Royal Exchange: 121, 264.
Royal Society: 183.
Rudd, Sayer: 292.
Rule (elegy on): 222n.
Rupert, Prince: 134.
Russell, Lord: 138.
Russel, Noadiah: 168n.
Rutherford, Lord: 134.
Rutledge, Edward: 175.

S., T.: 102, 106, 210.
Sabin, J.: 156n.
Sacheverell, Dr. H.: 234, 274n.
Sadler, Thomas: 136.

Saint Poole, Sir G.: 30.
Saintsbury, George: 5n, 19.
Salisbury, Lord: 133n.
Sancroft, Archbishop William: 198.
Sanderson, Bishop: 135.
Sandwich, Lord: 134.
Sapphics: 142.
Sappho: 177.
Sanders, Chief Justice: 135.
Savage, Richard: 300.
Scheills, Alexander: 216.
Schelling, F. E.: 28n, 97n.
Schiller, J. C. F.: 13, 326.
Schubert, F.: 328.
Schöffler, H.: 21, 266.
Schumann, R.: 328.
Science: 184 et seq. See Royal Society.
Scotland: 27, 108 et seq., 128, 153, 207
    et seq., 237n, 257, etc. See also Pres-
    byterianism, Anglican Communion, etc.
Scott, H.: 212n.
Scott, Sir W.: 128, 330.
Scroggs, Sir William: 135.
Seaman, Lazarus: 143n.
Seccombe, Thomas: 15n, 266n.
Sedgwick, O.: 114n.
Selden, J.: 247.
Sempill, Sir Robert: 221.
Seneca: 18, 201.
Sentimentalism: 17, 19 et seq., 42, 47,
    68, 72, 88, 146, 149, 151 et seq., 165,
    166, 172, 176, 189, 191, 203 et seq.,
    217, 220, 221, 224, 230, 232, 238n,
    240, 243, 245, 246, 248 et passim,
    259 et seq., 266 et seq., 290, 309, 312,
    320, 328 et seq.
Seton, Sir John: 208n, 209.
Settle, E.: 142.
Sewall, Hannah: 167.
Sewall, Rebekah: 167.
Sewall, Stephen: 304n
Shaftesbury, Lord (the Elder): 137, 138,
    139, 151n.
Shaftesbury, Lord (the Younger): 19, 22,
    146, 150, 182n, 240, 241n, 325.
Shakespeare, William: 17, 25, 26, 33, 43,
    47, 61, 66, 74n, 80, 93, 94, 97, 98,
    130n, 142, 160, 162, 167, 171, 218,
    226, 230, 242n, 245, 248, 252, 256,
    283, 284, 307, 316, 325, 327, 335,
    336.
Sharp, Archbishop: 211.
Sheffield, J.: 82.
Sheldon, Sir J.: 142-143.
Shelley, P. B.: 86, 164, 224, 254n, 316,
    326.
Shenstone, W.: 6, 283, 298, 337.

Shepard, O.: 310n.
Shepard, Thomas: 160.
Sherard, Abigail: 54.
Sherburn, G. W.: 14n, 15n.
Sherlock, Dr.: 241n.
"She-tragedies": 271.
Shirley, J.: 32n, 99n, 244, 245.
Shovel, Sir C.: 105n.
Shute, Josias: 44n, 84.
Shute, J.: 255.
Sidney, Algernon: 138.
Sidney, Sir P.: 25, 97, 98, 159, 185.
Simpkins, J. E.: 109.
Sinclare, John: 189.
Skeats, H. S.: 186n.
Skelton, John: 24.
Skinner, Caleb: 116n, 203n, 256, 270.
Slater, S.: 89.
Smart, Christopher: 298n.
Smedley, J.: 274.
Smith, Edmund: 247.
Smith, G. G.: 100n.
Smith, James: 340.
Smith, Rev. Mr.: 293.
Smollett, T.: 5n.
Social Contract: 182.
Socialism: 314.
Socianism: See Arianism.
Socio-psychology: 296, 317.
Solitude, Romantic: 111, 258.
Somers, John, Baron: 181.
Somerville, W.: 311.
Sonds, George: 115.
Song of Roland: 93.
Sonnet: 208-209.
Sophia, Electress: 219.
South, Dr.: 288.
South Sea Bubble: 265.
Southwell, Robert: 26, 200n.
Southerland, Lady: 218.
Spasmodist School: 4.
Spenser, E.: 25, 56, 66, 72, 84, 87, 148,
    169, 185, 194, 201, 208, 209, 220,
    242n, 248, 249, 258, 259n, 260n, 278,
    282-284, 316, 325, 327, 335; School
    of, 28 et seq., 45, 46.
Spingarn, J. E.: 201, 204n.
Spinola, Benedict: 50.
Sprague, Sir Edward: 101.
Squire, Humphrey: 340.
St. Albans, Earl of: 132.
St. John, Buckingham: 174.
Stainton, M.: 51.
Stafford, Dr. Thomas: 197.
Stafford (elegist): 279.
Stafford, Lord: 137.
Stanhope, Lord: 271.

Stanhope, Lady: 39.
Stanhope, Sir Edward: 50.
Stanley, T.: 30, 101.
State of Innocence: 67, 228.
State of Nature: See Nature.
Stationers' Register: 49.
Stedman (elegy on): 223.
Steele, Sir Richard: 22, 106, 196, 241, 243, 267.
Stephen, Sir Leslie: 19n, 152n, 183n, 233n, 236n, 238n, 239, 240n, 241n, 268n, 290n, 306n.
Stepney, G.: 195.
Stevenson, M.: 126-127, 335.
Stockwell, Samuel: 292.
Stoddard, Solomon: 171.
Stoll, E. E.: 26n.
Strafford, Earl of: 53.
Strange, N.: 136.
Strathnaver, Lord: 216.
Strawberry Hill: 279.
Stuart, Sir James: 221.
Suckling, Sir J.: 31, 36.
Suetonius: 95n.
Sutcliffe, M.: 66.
Sutherland, Lord: 216.
Swift, J.: 7, 14, 274, 281, 305, 322, 340.

T., J.: 43.
Talbot, J.: 196n.
Talbot, Lord: 224.
Tankerville, E.: 304n.
Tans'ur, William: 297.
Taswell, E.: 276.
Tate, F.: 98.
Tate, N.: 193.
Tatersal, Robert: 295.
Taylor, Jeremy: 276.
Taylor, John, "the Water-Poet": 9, 53, 100.
Taylor, N.: 255.
Temperley, H. W. V.: 180n.
Temple, Sir William: 204n.
Tenor, O.: 118.
Texte, J.: 4n, 5n.
Thacher, Peter: 168.
Theocritus: 7, 8n, 192n.
Theobald, L.: 234n, 260, 283.
Threnodia: 73, 132.
Threnodie on King William: 219-220 et passim, 258.
Thomas, W.: 4n, 10, 17n, 19, 305n.
Thomason Collection: 54n et passim.
Thompson, B.: 117, 167.
Thompson, Edward: 166.
Thompson, James: 337n.
Thompson, John: 292.

Thompson, John (murderer): 303.
Thomson, James: 76, 81, 86, 219-220, 224 et passim, 261, 270, 283, 296, 310, 311, 321.
Thynne, James: 199.
Thynne, T.: 103n, 138n, 139.
Tibullus: 6, 25.
Tickell, T.: 18n, 273-274.
Tieghem, M. van: 10, 21.
Tiffany, Esther A.: 240n.
Tileson, Thomas: 160.
Tillotson, Archbishop John: 107, 318.
Tinker, C. B.: 242.
Titanic: 242n.
Tiveot, Lord: 133n, 134.
Tolerance in religion: 179, 184 et seq., 237.
Toland, J.: 17.
Tolmash, General: 103, 211.
Tolman, A. H.: 29n.
Tourneur, C.: 27n.
Tomkins, Nathaniel: 54n.
Tory: 137 et passim.
Translation: 234-235. See also David's lament, etc.
Trapp, J.: 248, 305n.
Travers, H.: 298.
Trent, W. P.: 156n.
Trentals: 97.
Tresnes, Duc de: 105.
Trumbell, John: 174.
Tuberville, A. S.: 65n, 238n, 243n, 264n, 266n.
Turell, Jane: 168n.
Turner, J. M. W.: 93, 230, 331.
Turner, Sir William: 197, 204.
Tweddel, Marquis of: 216.
Twisden, Sir William: 199.
Twiss, Dr.: 78, 85.
Tyrconnel, Lord: 110n.

Unitarianism: 155, 238.
Utilitarianism: 268n.
Uvedale (elegist): 276.

Vanbrugh, Sir John: 196, 235.
Vaughan, Henry: 16n, 35, 36-38, 45, 46, 69, 200, 276, 307, 315.
Venning, Ralph: 143, 145.
Vergil: 7, 8n, 18, 93, 186, 201, 248, 256n, 257n, 258.
Vernon, John: 144.
Vernon (merchant): 337n.
Versification: 200-201, 245, 277n, 307.
Victoria, Queen: 226.
Villiers, Lord: 54, 78.
Viner, Robert: 142.

Vines, R.: 79, 114.
Voltaire: 235.
Vose, Z. P.: 304n.

W., N.: 192n.
Wadsworth, Thomas: 143, 147.
Wagner, R.: 330.
Waldron, F. G.: 99n.
Walbeoffe, Charles: 37.
Waller, E.: 32, 42, 44, 46, 102, 103n, 124, 188, 202.
Walpole, Horace: 12, 61, 65, 105, 128, 261, 279.
Walpole, Sir Robert: 264, 285, 325, 327.
Walsh, William: 9n, 196, 233.
Walton, I.: 35n.
Ward, Ned: 105.
Warner, John: 58, 86.
Warton, J.: 14n.
Warton, T.: 13.
Warwick, Earl of: 273.
Washington, George: 175, 304n.
Waterton, Justice: 83.
Watson, George: 51.
Watsonne, Christopher: 49.
Watts, Isaac: 68, 92, 116, 118, 119, 186, 236, 238, 241, 250 et seq., 260, 279, 282n, 291, 292, 297, 300, 301n.
Weatherill, Joseph: 302.
Weber, K. M. von: 330.
Webster, J.: 18, 27n.
Webster, Rev. Dr.: 224.
Wedel, T. O.: 240n.
Weekley, Captain: 305.
Weekes, James E.: 305.
Wegelin, O.: 156n, 160n.
Weld, E.: 161.
Wells, John: 147.
Welsh folklore: 327.
Weltschmerz: 151, 239.
Wemyss, Lord: 210.
Wendell, B.: 170.
Wesley, C.: 107n, 170, 287 et seq.
Wesley, J.: 107n, 183n, 184n, 287 et seq.
Wesley, Matthew: 287n.
Wesley, Samuel: 287-288.
Wesleyanism: See Methodism.
West, N.: 140.
West, R.: 298, 310, 312.
Whaley, John: 297.
Wharton, Mrs. Anne: 102n, 140, 244.
Whichcote, Rev. Mr.: 240.
Whig: 137 et passim.
Whistler, J. McN.: 256n.
Whitaker, J.: 82, 90, 139.
Whitefield, George: 287 et seq.

Whitehall, John: 147, 195.
Whitelamb, Mary: 287.
Whitmore, W.: 102.
Wigglesworth, Michael: 158.
Wilcox, Rev. Daniel: 293.
Wilde, Dr. R.: 57n, 129n, 137, 139.
Wilkie (elegy on): 222n.
Wilkinson, Mrs. E.: 88n.
Wilkinson, John: 272, 275n.
William III: 110n, 196, 219, 223, 225, 234, 250.
William and Mary, reign of: 148, 180 et seq., 187 et passim, 202 et passim.
Williams, J. D.: 304n.
Williams, Robert: 198n.
Williams, Sir Roger: 49n.
Williamson: G.: 45n.
Willis, Dr.: 133n, 140, 192n.
Willis, N. P.: 304n.
Willow tree: 335 et seq.
Wilson, Dr.: 74, 341n.
Wilson, John: 117, 158, 160, 161, 164, 293, 339.
Wilson, T.: 78.
Winchelsea, Lady: 10, 22, 66, 198-200, 259.
Windsore, R.: 77.
Winstanley, Dr. John: 171n, 297, 305, 306n.
Winstanley, Lilian: 29n.
Winthrop, Governor John: 160.
Wiseman, Sir Richard: 53.
Wiswell, Ichabod: 165.
Witham, R. A.: 96n.
Wither, George: 72.
Wollstonecraft, Mary: 75.
Women: 302 etc.
Wood, Rev. James: 239n.
Wood, Lucky: 222n.
Wood, P. S.: 153n.
Wordsworth, William: 7n, 38, 227, 231, 242n, 261, 281, 299, 312, 326, 328, 330.
Wortley, Sir F.: 39n.
Wright, Sir H.: 127.
Wright, Joseph: 129n.
Wyan, R.: 53.
Wyndham, Sir E.: 132n.

Young, Edward: 4, 5, 7, 14, 15, 17, 19, 48, 76, 107, 140, 170, 227, 228, 248-249, 260, 271, 274, 279, 290, 297, 306 et seq., 311, 312, 321, 324, 328.

Zola, E.: 327.